ANOTHER KIND OF EVIDENCE

CIPS Series on The Boundaries of Psychoanalysis
Series Editor: Meg Beaudoin, PhD, FIPA

CIPS

CONFEDERATION OF INDEPENDENT PSYCHOANALYTIC SOCIETIES

www.cipsusa.org

The Confederation of Independent Psychoanalytic Societies (CIPS) is the national professional association for the independent component societies of the International Psychoanalytical Association (IPA) in the USA. CIPS also hosts the Direct Member Society for psychoanalysts belonging to other IPA societies. Our members represent a wide spectrum of psycho-analytic perspectives as well as a diversity of academic backgrounds. The CIPS Book Series, The Boundaries of Psychoanalysis, represents the intellectual activity of our community. The volumes explore the internal and external boundaries of psychoanalysis, examining the interrelationships between various psychoanalytic theoretical and clinical perspectives as well as between psychoanalysis and other disciplines.

Published and distributed by Karnac Books

When Theories Touch: A Historical and Theoretical Integration of Psychoanalytic Thought by Steven J. Ellman

A New Freudian Synthesis: Clinical Process in the Next Generation edited by Andrew B. Druck, Carolyn Ellman, Norbert Freedman and Aaron Thaler

ANOTHER KIND OF EVIDENCE
Studies on Internalization, Annihilation Anxiety, and Progressive Symbolization in the Psychoanalytic Process

Norbert Freedman, Marvin Hurvich, and Rhonda Ward

with

Jesse D. Geller and Joan Hoffenberg

KARNAC

First published in 2011 by
Karnac Books Ltd
118 Finchley Road
London NW3 5HT

Copyright © 2011 by editors for the edited collection, and to the individual authors for their contributions

The rights of the contributors to be identified as the authors of this work have been asserted in accordance with §§ 77 and 78 of the Copyright Design and Patents Act 1988.

All rights reserved. No part of this publication may be reproduced, stored in a retrieval system, or transmitted, in any form or by any means, electronic, mechanical, photocopying, recording, or otherwise, without the prior written permission of the publisher.

British Library Cataloguing in Publication Data

A C.I.P. for this book is available from the British Library

ISBN-13: 978-1-85575-852-0

Typeset by Vikatan Publishing Solutions (P) Ltd., Chennai, India

www.karnacbooks.com

CONTENTS

ACKNOWLEDGEMENTS ... ix

SERIES EDITOR'S PREFACE ... xiii

ABOUT THE MAIN AUTHORS ... xvii

ABOUT THE CONTRIBUTING AUTHORS ... xix

PREAMBLE ... xxiii
Norbert Freedman

PART I: HOW THERAPY LIVES ON

FOREWORD
Joan Hoffenberg and Norbert Freedman ... 3

CHAPTER ONE
The effectiveness of psychoanalytic psychotherapy: the role of treatment, duration, frequency of sessions, and the therapeutic relationship ... 5
Norbert Freedman, Joan Hoffenberg, Neal Vorus, and Allan Frosch

CHAPTER TWO
Patients' representations of the therapeutic dialogue:
a pathway towards the evaluation of psychotherapy
process and outcome — 17
*Jesse D. Geller, Donna S. Bender, Norbert Freedman,
Joan Hoffenberg, Denise Kagan, Carrie Schaffer,
and Neal Vorus*

CHAPTER THREE
The RTD Coding System and its clinical application:
a new approach to studying patients' representations
of the Therapeutic Dialogue — 29
*Jesse D. Geller, Donna S. Bender, Norbert Freedman,
Joan Hoffenberg, Denise Kagan, Carrie Schaffer, and
Neal Vorus*

CHAPTER FOUR
Representations of the therapeutic dialogue and the
post-termination phase of psychotherapy — 55
Jesse D. Geller and Norbert Freedman

CHAPTER FIVE
Reminiscing and recollecting — 67
Jamieson Webster and Norbert Freedman

COMMENTARY
How therapy lives on — 83
Norbert Freedman and Joan Hoffenberg

PART II: THREE PATHWAYS TOWARDS THE MODIFICATION OF ANNIHILATION ANXIETY

FOREWORD
Marvin Hurvich and Norbert Freedman — 89

CHAPTER SIX
The *Propositional Method* for the study
of psychoanalytic concepts — 91
Marvin Hurvich and Norbert Freedman

CHAPTER SEVEN
Meet Mohamed and the method implemented 105
Marvin Hurvich and Norbert Freedman

CHAPTER EIGHT
Annihilation Anxiety and its transformation during early
transference engagement: sessions 3 and 4 119
Norbert Freedman, Marvin Hurvich, and Alexandra Petrou

CHAPTER NINE
Termination crisis and a panic attack: sessions 41 and 42 139
Norbert Freedman, Marvin Hurvich, and Alexandra Petrou

CHAPTER TEN
Transformations in long-term psychoanalytic
psychotherapy: the case of Ms K 159
Rhonda Ward, Norbert Freedman, and Marvin Hurvich

CHAPTER ELEVEN
Severely traumatized patients' attempts at reorganizing
their relations to others in psychotherapy: an
enunciation analysis 167
Sverre Varvin and Bent Rosenbaum

COMMENTARY
Three pathways towards the modification
of Annihilation Anxiety 183
Marvin Hurvich and Norbert Freedman

PART III: A SPECIMEN OF WORKING THROUGH

CHAPTER TWELVE
A very broad concept seen through a very narrow lens 191
Norbert Freedman and Rhonda Ward

CHAPTER THIRTEEN
Method and findings: the case of Ms Y:
the patient and her analyst within the context
of a recorded psychoanalysis 203
Norbert Freedman, Richard Lasky, and Rhonda Ward

CHAPTER FOURTEEN
The induction of transference regression during the symbolizing phase: sessions 232 to 243   223
Norbert Freedman and Rhonda Ward

CHAPTER FIFTEEN
The emergence of *nodal moments* during the desymbolizing phase: sessions 245 to 249   245
Norbert Freedman and Rhonda Ward

CHAPTER SIXTEEN
The enactive phase: sessions 252 to 255   267
Norbert Freedman and Rhonda Ward

CHAPTER SEVENTEEN
The cycle and the spiral during the re-symbolizing phase: the erotic transference, the extraordinary countertransference, and the preservation of the analytic process: session 257   283
Norbert Freedman and Rhonda Ward

CHAPTER EIGHTEEN
Nodal moments and the essence of *Progressive Symbolization*   297
Norbert Freedman and Rhonda Ward

POSTSCRIPT
Towards a psychoanalytic definition of symbolization and desymbolization   309
Norbert Freedman, Rhonda Ward, and Jamieson Webster

REFERENCES   323

INDEX   341

ACKNOWLEDGEMENTS

From the beginning the Institute for Psychoanalytic Training and Research (IPTAR) conceived of itself as a society committed to research in psychoanalysis. As a psychoanalytic society, we are dedicated to conducting research, to the *teaching* of research, and to the communication of research discoveries to the community at large, that is, to making psychoanalytic inquiry a part of the consciousness of the next generation of psychoanalysts. This volume, and its title, *Another Kind of Evidence*, celebrate our history, and the work of our members and partners in this pursuit.

* * *

For the authors of this volume I would like to acknowledge:

The founders of IPTAR, particularly Daisy Franco, who in 1960 formed the first IPTAR Research Committee, which directed its efforts towards learning and exploring the then new discoveries about dreaming, the separation-individuation process, and gender identity. These achievements were recorded over the decades in *IPTAR Reports*.

The 1989 IPA Rome Congress, which made IPTAR, after years of exile, a member of the international psychoanalytic community, and the then president and president-elect, Robert Wallerstein and Joseph Sandler, who at that time designated us as *"the new voice from North America"*. This was the impetus for the establishment of the Confederation of Independent Psychoanalytic Societies (CIPS).

The Confederation of Independent Psychoanalytic Societies (CIPS), its board of directors, and Margaret Beaudoin, series editor. We especially want to mention Frederic Perlman, past president of CIPS, who had the vision and wisdom to create and make the present innovative book series an actuality. With the creation of this book series, CIPS has given "the new voice from North America" an ongoing presence.

The IPTAR Clinical Center (ICC), its founders—Richard Lasky, Audrey Siegel, and Allan Frosh—who not only provided an innovative clinical psychoanalytic service to the community and secured financial backing, but also laid the foundation for developing an empirical database, an invaluable resource for the studies on treatment effectiveness and the process of internalization, as will be reported in this volume.

Wilma Bucci, who, as the originator and shaper of the concept and measurement of the *Referential Process*, has given our field an empirically derived measure of the symbolizing process during the analytic hour as a method to evaluate the course of analytic treatment. Her innovative work and her collaborative support in our study of recorded psychoanalysis has been a source of invaluable insight and yielded a deeper understanding of our observations. And Bernard Maskit, who through his statistical and mathematical sophistication, has lent substance to the application of the measure of the *Referential Process* to our database.

Sverre Varvin, from Oslo, Norway, who, as the psychoanalytic therapist of *Mohamed*, the subject of our studies on Annihilation Anxiety, made the transcripts of audio recorded sessions available for our joint empirical studies. Thanks to both Bent Rosenbaum and Sverre Varvin who helped us shape a psychoanalytic group linking New York and Scandinavia, SCAN-NY, which has become an ongoing working collaboration spanning the Atlantic Ocean.

We are also grateful to Stanley Grand, Mark Grunes, Richard Lasky and Tracey Vorus, who joined us in the early formulation of the *Propositional Method*.

Profound gratitude is expressed to Alexandra Petrou who has been responsible for so many aspects of the preparation of this manuscript, from editing to formatting, evaluating, and scoring. Furthermore, we have been fortunate to have the graduate students in IPTAR's Pre-Psychoanalytic Training Program participate in this project in the scoring of transcripts, statistical evaluation, and summarizing of data. A special appreciation is expressed to Adam Joncich, Ceylan Demir, Kate Eaton, Laima Sappington, and Smigda Rathor.

Finally, the most significant personal appreciation is addressed to Richard Lasky, the co-founder of our studies of recorded psychoanalysis, who made it possible to obtain the requisite recorded clinical data. He and I jointly developed the original methodology for defining analytic hours as either *A* (integrative) or *Z* (non-integrative) and established the reliability and validity of these designations in relation to the process of symbolization. Our joint work has already appeared in three journals and here in Chapter Thirteen it is given a detailed presentation. The imprint of Richard Lasky's creative line of thought may be found throughout this volume.

Norbert Freedman

SERIES EDITOR'S PREFACE

We are particularly pleased to have *Another Kind of Evidence* as the third volume in the CIPS Book Series, *The Boundaries of Psychoanalysis*. With this volume we find ourselves on the boundary between psychoanalysis and science. Norbert Freedman and his colleagues have committed themselves to the application of the scientific method to the study of clinical psychoanalysis in order to establish the legitimacy of our field of study. Their approach however is one that does not presume the illegitimacy of the field, by eliminating essential aspects of it in order to study it scientifically. Rather, this is a commitment to research without reduction, an attempt to find and apply methodologies that give rise to evidence for psychoanalytic concepts and clinical phenomena, evidence which is not purely conceptual, purely clinical, or purely behavioural, i.e. another kind of evidence.

Freedman et al. recognize the methodological challenges inherent in psychoanalytic therapy outcome research, wherein the problems that initiate treatment are not easily operationalized and the conduct of the treatment itself is based on the individual patient's needs rather than upon standardized procedures. In this work, these recognitions result in the development and the use of new "investigatory tools" which aim at capturing the essential nature of the psychoanalytic process.

The volume begins with a review of a study (Freedman, Hoffenberg, and others) on the effectiveness of psychotherapy that is based on the patient's own experience of treatment. This investigation and its results lead to the question, what was it in treatment that accounted for the differences in its perceived effectiveness?, which results in the study of the effectiveness of therapy post termination. To answer such questions, the authors (in particular Geller) have developed powerful investigatory tools, the Schedule of Therapy Remembered (STR) via which the data is collected, and the Representation of the Therapeutic Dialogue (RTD), a multidimensional classificatory system that aims to capture the essence of the psychoanalytic therapy process.

The application of these methodologies to the clinical data itself results in the development of an enriched account of the concept of internalization. This leads the authors to direct themselves to the development of a method that would enable the confirmation or disconfirmation of psychoanalytic concepts. The result of these efforts is the Propositional Method (Hurvich and Freedman), a method that takes into account the particularity of psychoanalytic concepts, specifically their elasticity and context dependency. By means of this method, concepts are defined through clinical propositions that rely both on clinical observations and generalizations. This is fundamentally a phenomenological method that aims at discovering the essence of a concept, its invariant nature, which the authors call "coreness", along with its variations, which the authors refer to as "modifiers".

The reader is treated to an application of this method to the correspondingly enriched study of the concept of "trauma" in general and the concept of "annihilation anxiety" (Hurvich) in particular. In the course of the empirical analysis of recorded psychotherapy, three paths that lead to the moderation of annihilation anxiety are delineated. Along each of these pathways it becomes clear that it is symbolization that is necessary to the modification of annihilation anxiety.

The culmination of this extraordinary work is the examination of the concept of working through as fundamental to therapeutic change, and the rediscovery of the concept of "progressive symbolization" as the basic organizing concept of working through. The idea of progressive symbolization, a dialectical process of symbolization, desymbolization, and reintegration, is a remarkably rich concept in and of itself. But what is even more remarkable in this work, is that the concept of this process of progressive symbolization as therapeutic action bedrock is arrived at vis a vis the exceptionally detailed study of an audio recorded four times weekly psychoanalysis (Freedman and Ward). This process research is a multiperspective examination that makes use of each of the methodologies previously specified. As is the case with the empirical studies of therapy remembered and annihilation anxiety, the examination of working through is a paradigmatic example of the way in which work at the interface of research and clinical psychoanalysis should be conducted and the riches that result from such efforts.

Meg Beaudoin, PhD, FIPA
Series Editor

ABOUT THE MAIN AUTHORS

Norbert Freedman, PhD, FIPA, is training and supervising analyst, as well as former president and former dean of training at the Institute for Psychoanalytic Training and Research (IPTAR). He is adjunct clinical professor and supervising analyst at the New York University Post-doctoral Program in Psychotherapy and Psychoanalysis, professor emeritus of psychiatry and former director of clinical psychology, SUNY Downstate Medical Center. He is the author of numerous publications on the clinical and empirical study of symbolization and transformations in the psychoanalytic process.

Jesse D. Geller, PhD, is a clinical professor of psychology at Columbia University Teachers College, and associate clinical professor at Yale University School of Medicine. He is a fellow of the Division of Psychotherapy of the American Psychological Association, a member of the Society for Psychotherapy Research, and an honorary member of the Institute for Psychoanalytic Training and Research (IPTAR). He is the author of more than 70 clinical, theoretical, and empirical publications about psychotherapy, and has produced two films to educate prospective patients about how to use psychotherapy for personal benefit. He currently maintains a private practice in New Haven, Connecticut.

Joan Hoffenberg, PhD, FIPA, is training and supervising analyst and current president of the Institute for Psychoanalytic Training and Research (IPTAR) and past director of the IPTAR Clinical Center (ICC). She has taught at several psychoanalytic institutes in New York. She is co-editor of the book *Terrorism in the Psychoanalytic Space*. Her research interests include the effectiveness of psychotherapy, and the distinction between grief and depression. She is in private practice in Brooklyn and Manhattan.

Marvin Hurvich, PhD, DP, ABPP, FIPA, is a training and supervising analyst at the Institute for Psychoanalytic Training and Research (IPTAR), the New York Freudian Society, and the New York University Post-doctoral Program in Psychotherapy and Psychoanalysis. He is professor of psychology at Long Island University, Brooklyn Center. He is co-author with L. Bellak and H. Gediman of *Ego Functions in Schizophrenics, Neurotics and Normals* and his current writings are on theoretical, clinical, and empirical aspects of annihilation anxieties.

Rhonda Ward, LCSW, FIPA, is associate adjunct professor at New York University School of Social Work. She is a member at the Institute for Psychoanalytic Training and Research (IPTAR), as well as the New York Freudian Society, where she is currently chair of progression. She is faculty member and research associate at the IPTAR Program of Research in Psychoanalysis, and is faculty member of IPTAR's Respecialization Program She is the co-author of *The Upward Slope: a Study of Psychoanalytic Transformations*, and is in private practice in New York City.

ABOUT THE CONTRIBUTING AUTHORS

Donna Bender, PhD, FIPA, is currently an associate professor at the University of Arizona and was previously a faculty member and research scientist at the New York State Psychiatric Institute/Columbia University. She is on the faculty of the Arizona Center for Psychoanalytic Studies and president-elect of the Southwest Psychoanalytic Society. She has published on treatment in a number of journals and books, and is co-editor of the *Textbook of Personality Disorders and the Essentials of Personality Disorders*. She is in private practice in Tucson, Arizona.

Allan Frosch, PhD, FIPA, is training and supervising analyst, faculty member, twice past president, and former dean of training at the Institute for Psychoanalytic Training and Research (IPTAR). He also served as co-director of the IPTAR Clinical Center (ICC). He has published a number of articles on psychoanalysis, and is currently editing a book, *Absolute Truth and Unbearable Psychic Pain: Psychoanalytic Perspectives on Concrete Experience*. His article entitled "The effect of frequency and duration on psychoanalytic outcome: a moment in time" appeared in *Psychoanalytic Review*, February 2011.

Denise Kagan, PhD, is staff psychologist and assistant professor of psychiatry and behavioral sciences at Baylor College of Medicine. She was a post-doctoral fellow at the Austen Riggs Center where she completed an advanced fellowship in clinical psychology. She is currently involved in the DSM-V field trials that will be testing the proposed new criteria for assessing both major depression and borderline personality disorder. Her research interests include psychoanalytically-oriented psychotherapy treatment and research, particularly with "treatment resistant" patients.

Richard Lasky, PhD, DP, FIPA, is an adjunct clinical professor of psychology and supervising analyst at the New York University Post-doctoral Program in Psychotherapy and Psychoanalysis, and past president of the Psychoanalytic Society of the New York University Post-doctoral Program in Psychotherapy and Psychoanalysis. He is associate dean of training, faculty member, and training and supervising analyst at the Institute for Psychoanalytic Training and Research (IPTAR). He is a research associate and supervisor of adult psychotherapy at the Doctoral Program in Clinical Psychology at the City University of New York, and supervisor of adult psychotherapy at the Doctoral Program in Clinical and School Psychology at Pace University.

Alexandra Petrou, MA, is an advanced PhD candidate in clinical psychology at the New School for Social Research. She is an adjunct faculty member of psychology at Medgar Evers College, City University of New York. She is a psychoanalytic candidate at the Institute for Psychoanalytic Training and Research (IPTAR).

Bent Rosenbaum, MDSc, is an associate clinical research professor at Copenhagen University, Faculty of Health Sciences. He is a training analyst at the Danish Psychoanalytic Society and president of the Danish Psychoanalytic Society 2004–2011. He was president of the Danish Psychiatric Society from 1998 to 2000 and vice-president from 1996 to 1998. He was director of the Department of Psychotherapy at the Psychiatric University Hospital, Aarhus, from 1988 to 1999. His special areas of research interest include psychoanalytic psychotherapy for persons with psychosis and psychoanalysis of personality disorders, general and developmental psychopathology, and communication and semiotics.

ABOUT THE CONTRIBUTING AUTHORS

Carrie Schaffer, PhD, is clinical assistant professor of psychiatric medicine at the School of Medicine at the University of Virginia. She serves as clinical supervisor and director of group therapy and outreach for the Charlottesville League of Therapists. Her research focus has been on attachment and affect regulation and on the processes of internalization. She is also a painter and collage artist, and teaches in the Department of Workforce Services at the Piedmont Virginia Community College in Charlottesville. She is in private practice in Charlottesville, Virginia, providing individual and group psychotherapy, and consultation to organizations with an emphasis on mental health services.

Sverre Varvin, MD, Dr Philos, is training and supervising analyst at the Norwegian Psychoanalytic Society and a senior researcher at the Norwegian Centre for the Studies of Violence and Traumatic Stress, affiliated to the University of Oslo. He is a past recipient of the Mary S. Sigourney Award Trust recognizing his involvement in work with human rights. His research interests include the treatment of traumatized patients and symbolization. He is the author of *Die gegenwärtige Vergangenheit, Extreme Traumatisierung und Psychotherapie, Mental Survival Strategies after Extreme Traumatization, Violence or Dialogue?, Psychoanalytic Insights on Terror and Terrorism,* and *The Influence of Extreme Traumatization on Body, Mind and Social Relations.*

Neal Vorus, PhD, FIPA, is an adjunct clinical professor at the New York University Post-doctoral Program in Psychotherapy and Psychoanalysis, and an adjunct faculty member in the Forensic Psychology Graduate Program at John Jay College. He is on the faculty of the Adult Psychoanalytic Training Program, and chair of the Faculty and Curriculum Committee at the Institute for Psychoanalytic Training and Research (IPTAR). He is a supervisor in the Clinical Psychology Doctoral Program at the City University of New York. He is in private practice in Manhattan.

Jamieson Webster, PhD, is an assistant adjunct professor of psychology at the New School and a post-doctoral fellow and psychoanalytic candidate at the New York Psychoanalytic Institute. She writes on the relationship between psychoanalysis and philosophy, as well as on clinical work, with a focus on symbolization and the work of Jacques Lacan. She is the author of numerous articles published in the *Journal of the American Psychoanalytic Association, Cardozo Law Review, The Symptom, Bedeutung, Contemporary Psychology,* and others. She is in private practice in New York.

PREAMBLE

Norbert Freedman

In our current professional climate, with calls for "evidence-based treatment", and in light of the prestige accorded to this emblem, we can ask: for what purpose do we seek evidence? For our students? For the public at large? For an inner sense of feeling supported by science? A provocative line of thought was offered by Beenen (2004), who in his essay on conceptual psychoanalytic research, noted that each discipline goes through recurrent activities of reproducing itself. Most disciplines are concerned with cumulative knowledge, aimed towards self-affirmation and self-definition, that is, establishing a sense of legitimacy.

The three parts of this volume are directed towards the goal of affirming a public and private sense of the legitimacy of psychoanalysis, thereby shaping professional identity. In each contribution we adhere to the precepts of "scientific inquiry", with a commitment to affirming or disconfirming clinical propositions, utilizing consensually agreed upon methods of observation, and arriving at inferences that are persuasive and have the potential to move the field forward. Beyond this, each part of this book describes distinct methodologies that generate evidence pertaining to public health policy, the persuasiveness and integrity of our psychoanalytic concepts, and phenomena encountered in daily clinical practice.

In Part I, How Therapy Lives On, we report on the effectiveness of analytic therapy both during treatment and after termination. The primary methodology here is the Representation of the Therapeutic Dialogue (RTD). In Part II, Three Pathways towards the Modification of Annihilation Anxiety, we direct attention to a derivative of the trauma concept, namely Annihilation Anxiety, and introduce the *Propositional Method* for the evaluation of psychoanalytic concepts. In Part III, A Specimen of Working Through, we enter into the details of the psychoanalytic hour through the realm of process research. This too calls for a method of its own, the method of Sequential Specification. Now for the details.

* * *

Psychoanalysis, as a process that aims to effect an alteration of mind, derives its legitimacy by documenting "lives in progress" (White, 1952). Such evaluations of the consequences of treatment are usually subsumed under the heading of "outcome research". In studying effectiveness, we enter into the realm of public health policy, for it touches upon the mental health of the community at large. In this part of the volume, we address two questions: does psychoanalytic psychotherapy make a difference during treatment?, and further, how does therapy live on in the mind of the patient after termination?

In Chapter One, *The effectiveness of psychoanalytic psychotherapy: the role of treatment, duration, frequency of sessions, and the therapeutic relationship*, we affirm the foundational assumptions of the analytic frame through well-trod quantitative methods of evaluation. Our conclusions, which had been arrived at some ten years ago, were reaffirmed from other quarters (Shedler, 2009), through a comprehensive meta-analysis of many studies based on a wide range of treatment modalities.

Now when we evaluate effectiveness the issue of time also looms as an important consideration. What matters is not only the impact of therapy while it is ongoing, but its consequences beyond, that is, after termination. Only then can we conclude that psychotherapy affects "lives in progress" (White, 1952).

A procedure that captures patients' experiences after termination was developed: the Schedule of Therapy Remembered (STR). Through a semi-structured interview, we were able to glean answers to such questions as: how does the patient think about his treatment?, how does he remember the therapist?, what dreams, images, feelings about crucial events linger on?, what are the ongoing memories?, what were the good and the difficult moments?, how is this related to early origins? In short, we sought to capture a detailed snapshot of therapy remembered after termination, and the concept and the method of the RTD were the result (Chapters Two and Three).

Through this method, we were able to define the properties of a post-termination phase, and with this step we were in a position to revisit a long-standing theoretical psychoanalytic issue: how to understand internalization. In Chapter Four, *Representations of the therapeutic dialogue and the post-termination phase of psychotherapy*, Geller re-examines and reformulates the concept of the internalization of the psychoanalytic experience, this time within the frame of the RTD methodology.

* * *

The language of psychoanalytic concepts is the language of psychoanalysis. The affirmation of concepts is crucial to our profession, to colleagues in adjacent disciplines, and to the next generation of analysts. This identity shaping role has its historical roots. There are certain core assumptions that have been with us from the very beginning. Despite the fact that Freud's original concepts have been worked and reworked over the decades, we believe it is incumbent upon us to relate current understandings to their historical origins.

The task of selecting relevant evidence in support of psychoanalytic concepts was shaped by Waelder's (1962) seminal contribution "Psychoanalysis, Scientific Method, and Philosophy". He noted that Freudian psychoanalytic theory is derived from five sources: direct observations, clinical generalizations, clinical interpretations, clinical theory, and metapsychology—all of which were influenced by Freud's personal philosophy. As psychoanalytic researchers, we suggest that it is the spheres of clinical observations and clinical generalizations that provide the most relevant focus for the assessment of psychoanalytic concepts. We embrace Waelder's line of thought in the development of our *Propositional Method* for the evaluation of psychoanalytic concepts. In our method, we seek to identify the core of the concept, its dimensions, and modifiers. This is the path we choose to confirm or disconfirm any major psychoanalytic concept (Chapter Six).

We applied the *Propositional Method* to the study of trauma. Trauma has been a pivotal organizing concept, both in the history of psychoanalytic thought and in the understanding of pathogenesis. In Part II, our focus will be on a particular manifestation of trauma, namely Annihilation Anxiety, a threat to the survival of ego or self. This concept has been developed in the writings of Hurvich (2003). It is a clinically grounded concept, which has its historical roots in Freud's trauma theory (1916, 1920, 1926a) and has found clinical affirmation through decades of analytic writings. Moreover, Annihilation Anxiety is a notion that can be spelled out through empirically grounded clinical process analysis.

In *Three pathways towards the modification of Annihilation Anxiety*, we extend the *Propositional Method* to the study of patients suffering from severe adult onset trauma and trauma of early developmental origin. Annihilation Anxiety as a signifier of trauma is a mental quality that persists throughout life, yet we ask: can it be modified and/or can it even be transformed in the course of analytic treatment? We advanced the propositions that the core of Annihilation Anxiety persists throughout treatment, that it may undergo modification, and that the modification may arise within two contexts: Desymbolization and Symbolization. These propositions were successively confirmed, first through detailed clinical description, then through quantitative scoring of audio recorded transcripts of sessions, and were finally buttressed by the method of Visual Analysis of graphic representations.

In Chapters Eight, Nine, and Ten, three pathways towards modifying Annihilation Anxiety will be delineated. The first was found in a phase of early transference engagement and the second, a year and a half later, during a phase of transference regression. Both instances were drawn from a recorded psychotherapy of a patient who had survived severe torture. The third pathway was observed in the long-term treatment of a patient suffering from severe developmental trauma. There we also noted the persistent presence of Annihilation Anxiety, and how later these signals of dread became embedded within a new context of meaning making—they had now become symbolized.

* * *

Now, as psychoanalytic researchers, we want to go inside the analytic hour. The evidence from psychoanalytic research must speak, perhaps most importantly so, to issues of clinical practice. Questions relevant for process research are: what is the character of the hour?, how does change occur from session to session?, how is the patient's experience registered in the analyst's consciousness?, and how do we define transference and countertransference? Process research requires methodologies of its own. Here, the investigative enterprise adds to the validity of our daily clinical work.

In his 2001 essay, "The Enduring Scientific Contributions of Sigmund Freud", published in relation to the Freud Exhibition at the Library of Congress, Gedo stated:

> In my judgment Freud's most lasting and valuable scientific contribution was not conceptual; hence it tends to be overlooked by non-specialist historians. This achievement was the development of a novel observational method through which it became possible for the first time to gain reliable data about man's inner life. From about 1890, when he began to practice the "talking cure" invented by Breuer, it took Freud roughly twenty years to standardize a "psychoanalytic method" that permitted independent observers to collect such data. It is these unprecedented observations about mental functions and the control of human behavior that have defined the boundaries of psychoanalysis as a scientific domain (pp. 106–107).

Only in recent decades has the use of audio recordings, supplemented by computer generated analysis of text, been introduced to obtain a reliable and credible view of the events within the analytic session. To be sure, there are many obstacles related to the use of recordings: the disruption of the privacy of the clinical encounter, the request for the signing of informed consent, and in spite of disguise, the impact for the patient of finding aspects of sessions in print. In undertaking the study of a recorded psychoanalysis, the substance of Part III, A Specimen of Working Through, these obstacles were carefully considered. We concluded, as have many others, that "good enough" psychoanalysis can co-occur within such a research oriented treatment frame.

Process research entails the tracking of mental events, session by session, in order to delineate aspects of change over time. Bucci (2005), in a comprehensive review of process research, notes that there have been three waves of such undertaking, three generations of process research. The first generation was concerned with the development of reliable instruments, such as the Core Conflictual Relationship Themes (CCRT), and the Patient Experience of the Relationship to the Therapist (PERT). Each coding schema was based on a particular vision of the psychoanalytic process. Then there was a second generation, such as the CAMP model initiated by Wallerstein, involving collaborative efforts by several analytic research centres, where researchers, each with their own methodology and coding schema, joined and applied their procedures to a common database. Finally, Bucci notes a third generation of process research that broadens the scope and builds a connection between coding schemas and crucial events in the clinical situation. Within the IPTAR Program of Research in Psychoanalysis, we seek to build on this third generation by blending methods of process research with psychoanalytic conceptual research.

In our approach, the Method of Sequential Specification, we, too, use audio recordings and consensually agreed upon coding schemas. But additionally, we look at each event—a moment, a phase within a session, an entire session, or even a specimen comprising a block of hours—and describe and evaluate such from three perspectives: that of the patient, the analyst, and the clinical observer, who interprets and integrates the events within the perspective of major psychoanalytic concepts. This is a *Rashomon approach*, where multiple vantage points may yield a new synthesis (Chapter Thirteen).

Through this approach, we offer a portrait of *working through*, derived from the study of a specimen, covering 25 analytic sessions of a recorded psychoanalysis. In successive chapters, we will depict phases within the specimen that highlight the manifestations of *transference regression, enactments, erotic transference*, and the *extraordinary countertransference*. In each phase we discovered what we have termed *nodal moments*, the markers of symbolic transformation (Chapters Fourteen–Seventeen). Through this tracking study, we arrive at an organizing concept for working through: *Progressive Symbolization*.

This volume concludes with a comprehensive statement of what we consider to be the essence of *Progressive Symbolization* (Chapter Eighteen).

PART I

HOW THERAPY LIVES ON

FOREWORD

Joan Hoffenberg and Norbert Freedman

In the preamble, we stated that psychoanalytic research aims at the legitimization of our discipline not only for our patients, but for us as analysts, for analytic training, and for the community at large. There is general agreement that the goal of any psychoanalytic treatment is the patient's satisfaction or the perceived effectiveness of that treatment; thus, psychoanalytic research must be concerned with assessing satisfaction and effectiveness.

While there has been cumulative evidence in a number of studies in the last ten years that psychoanalytically informed treatment is efficacious with consistently larger effect sizes in comparison to non-psychodynamic treatments—particularly when post-termination time increases—these results are based largely on efficacy studies that do not consider patients' experience of the treatment received, are symptom driven, and are of time-limited exposure. It is for these reasons that we begin the section of *How therapy lives on* with a restatement of the major findings of our 1999 study, an anchoring point for a line of inquiry into the consequences of a psychoanalytic experience.

* * *

The demonstration of effectiveness in our 1999 study represents a baseline for us and our study of the therapy experience. In fact, how therapy alters people's lives must be the baseline for all effectiveness studies. By establishing the effectiveness of psychoanalytic psychotherapy, we can move on to the study of the post-termination phase.

In this section we extend our study of the therapy experience through the reconstruction of therapy after termination. This allows the focus to be on the impact of treatment in the post-termination phase. We then turn to the internalization of the analytic dialogue and, finally, offer a critical review on the meaning of therapeutic reconstruction, even among apparent failure cases.

CHAPTER ONE

The effectiveness of psychoanalytic psychotherapy: the role of treatment, duration, frequency of sessions, and the therapeutic relationship[1]

Norbert Freedman, Joan Hoffenberg, Neal Vorus, and Allan Frosch

The above title of the 1999 study names the implicit ingredients of both psychoanalysis and psychoanalytic research. With *effectiveness*, we emphasize the need for the treatment to be registered in the consciousness of the patient. With *duration*, we note that the consequence of psychoanalytic treatment is cumulative, leaving its imprint over time. With *frequency of sessions*, we underscore the idea of therapeutic intensity. And, with *treatment relationship*, we affirm that the therapeutic effort is an intrinsically dialogic undertaking. In our 1999 study we sought to capture the common ground in our psychoanalytic community, if not the essence of the psychoanalytic enterprise. Just as we can speak of a foundational transference (Frankel, in press), with this study we develop a foundational psychoanalytic research undertaking.

In a recent review article based on a comprehensive meta-analysis of a wide range of studies, Shedler (2009) finds significant efficacy

---

[1] Adapted from Freedman, N., Hoffenberg, J. D., Vorus, N. & Frosch, A. (1999). The effectiveness of psychoanalytic psychotherapy: The role of treatment, duration, frequency of sessions, and the therapeutic relationship. *Journal of the American Psychoanalytical Association*, 47: 741–772.

and effectiveness with psychodynamic treatment. Two findings stand out: (a) "effect sizes for psychodynamic therapy are as large as those reported for other therapies" designated as "evidence-based" (p. 98); and (b) "patients who receive psychodynamic therapy maintain therapeutic gains and appear to continue to improve after treatment ends" (p. 98). In his definition of dynamic therapy, Shedler cites procedures which focus on the consciousness of the patient, such as raising affect awareness, emphasis on the therapeutic relationship, and concern with a patient's history, all of which are part of the psychoanalytic perspective.

Even within Shedler's exhaustive research, the hallmarks of the psychoanalytic therapy experience are excluded. The question of the relevance of duration and session frequency, and the nuances and impact of the therapeutic relationship and the transference are not studied. These aspects of the psychoanalytic psychotherapy experience are of interest and the question of how to study them and how to reconstruct the psychotherapy experience is an important one.

A brief history of psychoanalytic research

Psychoanalytic research has a history of its own. It began with Fenichel's (1930) account of the Berlin institute; Bachrach's (1991) summary of outcome studies reported by the Boston, Chicago, and New York analytic institutes; Wallerstein's (1986) iconic statement of *42 lives in treatment* at the Menninger Foundation; and the "RAPA" report introducing the field of process research highlighted by Luborsky's measure of the Core Conflictual Relationship Theme (CCRT) (Luborsky & Chris-Christoph, 1990). Frequency of sessions and duration of treatment have a literature of their own and all these have been reviewed in the 1999 study.

Of greatest interest for our present task was the definition and conception of outcome and we chose the "effectiveness model" as defined by Seligman (1996). Focusing attention on the issue of "how does the patient experience and evaluate the therapeutic process", we chose to launch an inquiry central to what we have defined as the foundation of analytic research. It needs to be stressed that this focus on effectiveness as a subjectively perceived or felt event does not imply a reliance on a one-person psychology. Rather it is an anchoring point that enabled us to trace over time the fate of the subjective/intersubjective matrix of experiences. Here we use an empirically-based instrument to evaluate just "how therapy lives on".

The measurement of "Effectiveness" at the IPTAR Clinical Center (ICC)

Outcome research has the quality of *Rashomon* in that it can be seen from multiple perspectives: the analyst observer, the independent researcher, and the direct experience of the patient. Earlier studies have focused on the first two; in this study attention was given to the latter criterion: the patient's experience of satisfaction, that is, the patient as consumer. Does the patient feel that therapy or analysis has made a difference in his or her life?

The impetus for this study came from the *Consumer Reports* (1995) nationwide study of psychotherapy experiences in the United States and Seligman's explications of those results (1995, 1996). In the *Consumer Reports* study, 4200 responders reported high satisfaction with their experiences in therapy, which increased as time in treatment increased.

Consumer Reports gave us access to their questionnaire (the Effectiveness Questionnaire) and scoring methodology (M. Kotkin, personal communication, 1998). Thus, this study was a replication of the *Consumer Reports* study on a new, independently drawn sample of patients with some pertinent methodological advantages. In this study, all patients were treated with psychoanalytic psychotherapy by therapists with analytic training from the same training institute. We compared the attributes of responders to the total clinic population and were able to evaluate a treatment modality within a single psychoanalytic community, as did Rogers and Dymond (1954) over four decades ago. Going beyond a replication effort, we treated the data in a manner responsive to issues of special concern to psychoanalysts. It is in this context that we present an empirical study of treatment outcome. It is an effectiveness study that relies on patients' perceptions of their mental health during and after psychoanalytic psychotherapy.

Clinic Setting and Population: The research was conducted under the auspices of the IPTAR Clinical Center (ICC), a component of the IPTAR Society in New York City. The ICC is a freestanding clinic whose therapists are either in training or are members of the IPTAR Society. The ICC was established in 1992 to serve a population that is in need but cannot afford ongoing psychological services. It is a low-cost facility and most treatment is paid for out-of-pocket, without third party payments.

The demographic profile as described in the early 1990s has remained essentially unchanged. ICC patients are an ethnically mixed group: 35% of patients were African-American, Hispanic, or Asian, and 25% spoke a language other than English as their primary language. Initial diagnostic impressions included neurotic and narcissistic character disorders, borderline personality, and a small proportion that suffered from more severe pathology. Fifty-two percent of patients were seen once per week, while 38% and 8% were seen twice and three times per week, respectively.

Procedure: The sample of patients for this study was taken from the patient population of the clinical centre. All patients, both past and current, were contacted by letter and asked to participate in a study of the effectiveness of psychotherapy they had received at the ICC. They were asked to complete the Effectiveness Questionnaire, which consists of 28 items asking the patient in simple language to identify:

1. The problems that brought them into treatment (depression, anxiety, family or relationship problems, stress);
2. Qualities of the treatment setting (frequency and duration);
3. Attitudes towards the therapist; and
4. Perceptions of the outcome of their treatment.

Two hundred and forty questionnaires were sent out and 99 were returned, representing a return rate of 41%. The demographic profile of the sample did not differ significantly from the general profile of the clinical population.

Method of Evaluation: The major outcome variable was the Effectiveness Quotient (EQ), which is identical to the outcome measure used in the national sample. This score is made up of three parts:

1. Patient satisfaction for treatment received;
2. How much help for the specific problem that brought them into treatment they received; and

3. A measure of change in emotional state, comparing how a patient felt at the beginning of treatment with how they are feeling now.

These three measures, each with a maximum weighted score of 100, are then added together to create an EQ score. The EQ can range from 0 to 300. For our patient sample, the scores ranged from 97 to 287 with a mean of 209.

The propositions stated and confirmed

A method for confirming or disconfirming clinical concepts has been suggested as an approach towards evaluating psychoanalytic process and thus avoiding reliance on meta-psychological formulations (see Hurvich & Freedman in Part II of this volume). We use the *Propositional Method* as it is directed towards evaluating treatment outcome as well, for inherent in each of the goals of analytic therapy is a clinical concept to be assessed. In what follows we state the outcomes of our work without statistical documentation as these can be found in the 1999 publication.

Proposition 1: Effectiveness of psychoanalytic therapy depends on an incremental treatment effect, with longer treatment exposure yielding incremental gains. It deals not simply with "before and after", or "treatment versus non-treatment", but instead with how much more effort yields how much more result.

In our study, we evaluated the impact of duration in successive phases. Comparisons were made for patients with varying lengths of treatment experience: less than 1 month, 1–6 months, 7–11 months, 12–24 months or over 25 months. The major findings were:

- There was an overall positive correlation between patients' perception of treatment effectiveness and length in treatment.
- There was no significant difference between patients receiving up to 6 months of psychotherapy compared with patients receiving 7–11 in perceived effectiveness (EQ scores).
- Significant differences were found in mean EQ scores between patients receiving up to 6 months of psychotherapy and 12–24 months and then again for patients receiving up to 6 months and over 25 months.

- Patients exposed to one year of treatment were less satisfied than those with two or three years; however, there was no difference between perceived effectiveness for two or three years. These observations were the first entry to confirm an incremental treatment effect over time.

Proposition 2: The effectiveness of psychoanalytic therapy relies upon session frequency regardless of duration. Comparisons were made between patients seen once, twice and three times weekly.

- Significant differences were obtained between once-a-week sessions compared to both twice and three times weekly, but not between two and three sessions per week; that is, patients in two or three times per week psychotherapy were more satisfied than those in once per week.

Continuing the study of the role of session frequency we examined the role of frequency among patients who had a *meaningful treatment exposure* (duration of seven months or more). We chose this cut-off for clinical reasons, as the first six months are often a turbulent period, whereas after seven months the treatment relationship tends to become more stable. We hypothesized that under more stable conditions added frequency would lead to greater satisfaction with treatment experience.

- Mean Effectiveness Quotient (EQ) for once, twice, and three times weekly sessions for patients in treatment seven months or longer paralleled the effect noted in the sample as a whole.

Thus, we can conclude that increased sessions make a difference and this is a finding which has specific relevance to psychoanalytic psychotherapy. The results speak to the issue of session frequency as a condition favouring intensity of treatment engagement and greater perceived satisfaction.

Proposition 3: While both treatment duration and session frequency were positively correlated with perceived effectiveness, they were not correlated with each other. This was understood as each variable having its own influence on perceived satisfaction with treatment. What then was their combined influence?

An index of Cumulative Facilitating Treatment Condition was developed where both conditions were given equal weight. This new measure of combined intensity of treatment exposure resulted in a more powerful statistical discrimination affirming that these quantitative indices influenced how the patient had experienced his or her treatment. This finding paved the way towards examining the qualities of the therapeutic process.

Proposition 4: The affective quality of treatment engagement defines the experience of effectiveness.

The quantitative findings thus far have affirmed the general proposition that more intensity yields greater gain. We turn to an evaluation of the treatment relationship as an indicator of a therapeutic object relationship and the conditions favouring the internalization of the therapeutic experience—a topic to be dealt with in Chapter Four. Such requisite conditions for effectiveness are primary themes of psychoanalytic reflections, be they termed transference, therapeutic alliance, or the *real relationship*. Here, we will be theory neutral.

A new measure was derived from the Effectiveness Questionnaire comprising three components: the Positive Relationship Index, the Negative Relationship Index, and Optimal Responsiveness Index. As to be expected, each of the three relationship indices was correlated with overall effectiveness. The Positive Relationship and Optimal Responsiveness Indexes added most to that treatment outcome. It has been our belief that increased therapeutic exposure contributes to the experience of greater affective intensity in treatment, and that such intensity facilitates a perception of the therapist as optimally responsive to the patient. Further, we maintain these conditions to be particularly important because of their role in facilitating a process of internalization that in turn supports the development of a relatively enduring internal relationship with the supportive and growth-enhancing aspects of the therapist.

Some gnawing problems: the Issue of cognitive dissonance

It could be argued that what we have observed is merely the effect of "cognitive dissonance" (Festinger, 1957). Simply put, one could assert that the idea that one has changed, that the belief that one's therapist is benevolent and supportive, and the awareness that one has spent considerable time and expense in therapy are all cognitively consistent with one another. To avoid an experience of internal dissonance, patients who have spent much time in treatment will tend to construct for themselves ideas about the relative benefits of therapy and the good qualities of their therapist. These perceptions then serve to justify actions the patient has taken, rather than reflect anything more meaningful about what has actually transpired in treatment or how it has helped. Clearly, this is an argument that undercuts the very rationale of this entire study.

In our view, the complexity of our data may well challenge the cognitive dissonance argument. When a patient evaluates their treatment as effective, then changes have taken place in their life and these changes can be attributed to what was offered during the treatment. While this is not an easy thing to show, it is an important argument. Several aspects of our study might constitute a response to the cognitive dissonance hypothesis, namely, the complex interactions between frequency, duration, patients' clinical syndrome, and perceived outcome that can not be explained away by cognitive dissonance alone.

The notion of cognitive dissonance assumes a singular motivation for the perception of improvement: the need for consistency between actions and attitudes. In challenging this view we looked for conditions of differential response, that is, we looked to see whether the treatment conditions of frequency and duration were related to differential patterns of response to treatment. We were now able to consider revising our earlier statement that more input or effort yields more results. It was likely that frequency and duration served different psychic functions. Along these lines, we wondered whether it was not true that selective and differential responsiveness due to patient characteristics also challenges the cognitive dissonance hypothesis. If patients with different clinical constellations respond more to one treatment condition than another, then surely something other than dissonance avoidance must be taking place.

Effectiveness, treatment conditions, and clinical syndrome: a factor analytic study

In the earlier discussion of cognitive dissonance we wondered whether patients with varying clinical symptom clusters would respond to differences in the characteristics of the therapeutic experience. To study this question, we first created meaningful clusters from the reported symptoms and complaints in our sample. We performed a factor analysis of subject responses to the question of why they "sought help from their therapists". Using orthogonal rotation, five factors were extracted:

- Factor 1: Eating Disorders (weight loss, anorexia, and bulimia)
- Factor 2: Anxiety (general anxiety, panic attacks, and phobias)
- Factor 3: Depression (depression, frequent low moods, and grief)
- Factor 4: Family Disorganization (problems with: alcohol and drugs, marriage or sex, children or other family members)
- Factor 5: Stress (job and stress-related problems).

Each patient was assigned factor scores based on their loading on the five factors and was placed into groups with respect to their highest factor score. We were now in a position to re-examine the impact of frequency and duration within distinct clinical constellations. Of the five factors derived, four showed meaningful patterns.

- Frequency and Effectiveness were correlated significantly for the Anxiety factor and the Eating Disorders factor.
- Duration was found to be correlated with effectiveness for those patients in the Family Disorganization and Stress factor.

In brief, this suggested that when the clinical syndrome is one of acute disturbance (as in anxiety and eating disorders), frequency, that is, higher intensity of contact, becomes relevant; and, when the clinical syndrome is one of chronicity (as in family disorganization and stress), duration of treatment becomes of relevance.

- No significant relationship between frequency or duration and effectiveness was found for patients in the Depression factor.

This lack of a finding was indeed troublesome as so many patients enter treatment complaining of depression. Clearly further exploration was required.

Two kinds of depression: Grief depression and anxious depression

The phenomenon of two kinds of depression has substantial support in the clinical literature (e.g., Blatt, 1998). From our patients' symptom checklists we distinguished two configurations: (a) *Depression with Grief* characterized by low mood and grief, and (b) *Anxious Depression* characterized by low mood and anxiety.

We wondered whether it was possible that these two groups, which differ in their phenomenology, also differed in the way they respond to treatment. Using questions from the Effectiveness Questionnaire we determined whether a patient indicated receiving help for a "specific problem that led to therapy", which we called "Focal Symptomatic Gains", or felt therapy helped with gains in concrete aspects of living, which we called "Adaptive Life Gains". Adaptive Life Gains included changes in "my ability to relate to others"; "being productive at work"; "coping with everyday stress"; "enjoying life more"; "personal growth and insight"; "my self-esteem and confidence"; and/or "alleviating my low moods". We now revisited the issue of the differential impact of duration and frequency in the treatment of Anxious Depression and Depression with Grief.

- Focal Symptomatic Gains: The anxious depressed group tended to show a positive response to both duration and frequency. For these patients help for the symptom that brought them into therapy increased with both increased time in treatment and increased frequency.
- Adaptive Life Gains: Both anxious depressed and grief with depression groups showed a response to duration but not to frequency; that is, both groups felt they got greater help in particular areas of life functioning with increased time in treatment.
- Grief Depression group: Duration of treatment was strongly related to perceived effectiveness of treatment.

We seem to be dealing with two constellations of depression. Patients in the Anxious Depressed group can name and recognize changes in their symptomatology, that is, symbolize their distress, recognize having gotten help for it, and derive benefit from intensity of treatment exposure. Patients in the Depression with Grief group, though unable to recognize symptomatic change, did acknowledge changes in their lives through treatment over an extended period of time (duration).

At first, through the factor analysis, we noted that patients with more acute disturbances seemed to report a more positive outcome with higher intensity, that is, increased frequency of sessions, whereas the patients with more chronic disturbances seemed to benefit pri-ma-ri-ly from longer duration only. Now turning to the two kinds of depression, we further noted that the very quality of outcome, whether there were merely symptomatic gains or perceived alterations in adaptive life style, suggested that what we had first simply called *effectiveness* may be shaped by complex psychic factors inherent in the treatment situation. This has implications not only for our argument against cognitive dissonance but also for future treatment design.

The recall validation study

Once we had a statistical analysis of the quantitative data on patients' perceptions of the effectiveness of their psychotherapy, we wanted to provide clinical validity. We took the step of recalling two of our subject patients to participate in a recall interview conducted by one of the authors. This interview was a forerunner of the Schedule of Therapy Remembered (STR) to be reported in the next chapter. Through these interviews we hoped not only to validate the Effectiveness Questionnaire, but to begin to understand how patients retrospectively experience their treatment, its impact on the quality of their life, and their current state of emotional health. Here are a few highlights.

The first patient, Ms A had an EQ in the high range and was in the anxious depression group. She was able to describe the benefits of treatment. She noted significant "focal symptomatic gains" and improvement in the ability to reflect upon areas of concern; was able to acknowledge the presence of the therapist within; and, in fact, seemed to have benefited both by frequency (two and three sessions per week) and longer duration (over two years). In contrast, Ms B, whose EQ score was in the lower range and who was in therapy once per week for less than two years, revealed a pattern of depression with grief and though she did not feel her depression was better, acknowledged that there were differences in her life, that is, "adaptive life gains" but these were expressed in concretized language. Friends said she was better but she did not recognize it.

The limits of the quantitative method

A careful, clinically informed reading of these two interviews suggested that the quantitatively expressed profile of psychoanalytic *effectiveness* was but a shorthand depiction of a complex intervening clinical process. We began with the notion that more effort yields more results—the quantitative foundations of analytic research. But now we need to offer a broader context which will allow for a more complete understanding of what is meant by *effectiveness*. Initially we set out to study three factors: duration, frequency of sessions, and an optimal therapeutic relation as a foundational frame to account for effectiveness. The quantitative findings supported these propositions but with the recall validation study, a fuller understanding of the transformations that might have taken place was suggested.

If we hypothesize the internalization of the therapeutic experience, then we would like to find a series of intervening psychic events to both describe and explicate it. For example, does a patient, as did Ms A, reveal the registration of the transference process? Is there a detailed description that is emotionally voiced both verbally and perhaps nonverbally? Did this experience remain active in working memory even after termination? And can such experiences be re-evoked within a new context and in new relationships during a post-termination phase? Those are the ingredients of *internalization* and to affirm such a process calls for a methodology of its own.

Having used our 1999 study and its robust findings of the effectiveness of dynamic psychotherapy as a baseline, our attention moved to developing innovative approaches that would lead to the reconstruction of the therapeutic process after termination with the aim of generating new insights into how psychoanalytic therapy process lives on.

CHAPTER TWO

Patients' representations of the therapeutic dialogue: a pathway towards the evaluation of psychotherapy process and outcome

Jesse D. Geller, Donna S. Bender, Norbert Freedman, Joan Hoffenberg, Denise Kagan, Carrie Schaffer, and Neal Vorus

The next three chapters explore the hypothesis that the operationalizing and measurement of the construct "representations of the therapeutic dialogue" can serve as a valid source of evidence about the outcomes of psychoanalytic therapy and the internalization processes whereby psychoanalytic therapy becomes and remains an adaptive resource in patients' lives after termination.

The research strategy we have adopted to explore this central idea is based on our shared commitment to three basic operating premises:

1. We conceive of representations of the therapeutic dialogue as the intrapsychic equivalents or analogues of the types of verbal and nonverbal exchanges patients have with their therapists. As early as 1926, Freud came to the view that the very essence of psychoanalysis is that it is a conversation in which "... nothing takes place between [the patient and the analyst] except that they talk to each other" (1926b, p. 187).
2. The processes that re-create on the intrapersonal terrain of self-experience the dialogic structure and functions of interactions

that previously took place during conversations with therapists, are to some extent available to introspection and self-report.
3. The narratives patients tell about the interpersonal aspects of their experiences in therapy offer a valid basis upon which to make inferences about the forms in which representations of their therapeutic dialogue enter awareness and their subjective meanings, the feelings that accompany their evocation and the functions they serve in patients' lives.

Methodological challenges

We begin by presenting an overview of the methodological challenges that must be addressed in order to obtain and present evidence that one's approach to doing therapy is "empirically validated". These include efficacy vs. effectiveness research and issues of time/space.

Efficacy vs. effectiveness

At the forefront of current debates about how to evaluate the outcomes of different approaches to therapy is the distinction between efficacy research and effectiveness research. Efficacy research refers to experimental or quasi-experimental evaluations of treatment outcomes that are conducted in laboratory settings. The *gold standard* of efficacy research is the *randomized clinical trial*. In the ideal randomized clinical trial, only patients who meet the criteria for a specific diagnosis are included and they are randomly assigned to manualized, fixed duration treatments or to control groups. Effectiveness research is the name Seligman (1995) introduced to refer to empirical studies in which the outcome of a particular form of therapy is evaluated retrospectively, that is, after termination as it is actually practised in the *field* rather than under laboratory conditions.

For many reasons psychoanalytic therapies do not lend themselves to being studied using procedures defined as *scientific* as those conducted under experimental laboratory conditions (Geller, 1998; Norcross & Goldfried, 2005). For example, in psychoanalytic therapy the problems patients bring to therapists are often characterological in nature rather than specifically symptomatic and, therefore, do not lend themselves to easy categorizing. In addition, time in treatment varies as patients continue in dynamic therapy for different lengths of time and terminate in many different ways based on decisions made mutually with their therapists. Furthermore, the moment to moment conduct of psychoanalytic therapy is not based on specific rules of procedure but rather upon principles best suited to patients' needs. Consequently, if psychoanalytic therapy is to be accorded the status of an *empirically validated* therapy, it will be necessary to create credible alternatives to assessing whether it *works* by way of efficacy- based evaluations.

In keeping with this position, we conducted the effectiveness study presented in Chapter One. It will be recalled that it documented, on the basis of variations in patients' scores on a modified version of Seligman's Effectiveness Questionnaire, that duration, frequency, and qualities of the therapeutic relationship have a positive impact on patients' assessments of the benefits they derived from therapy.

Time/space

The second methodological issue is the definition of the space between termination and evaluation—the consideration of *time/space*. The time that elapses between termination and the evaluation interview of this second study is a space in which the memory of the therapy can settle in. The impact of the therapy hour, while it registers during the session, lives on after the session, during vacation, and certainly after termination. Time/space refers to the reverberation of the events of treatment over time. There is much therapeutic activity going on even in the absence of the therapist (Geller & Farber, 1983).

The need to study the effect of time/space has several analogues in the empirical psychoanalytic literature. Pfeffer's (1963) work, which will be elaborated in Chapter Four, is a paradigm for the study of treatment after termination. He illustrated the repetition of the transference with his patients four years after termination. The phenomenon of transference repetition after termination has been noted in other studies (e.g., Schlessinger & Robbins, 1974), but the generative and reverberating aspects of time/space that might mediate a treatment effect have been reserved to studies of the psychoanalytic process—notably in Europe. For example, Sandell, Blomberg, Lazar, Carlsson, Broberg, and Schubert (2002), in the project of the Stockholm Psychoanalytic Society, found differential effects when comparing psychoanalysis and psychoanalytic psychotherapy across time. While there was no noted difference in outcome between the two directly after termination, differences were observed three years later, suggesting an effect that was only captured after time elapsed. However, this finding is limited in that the study relied only on psychometric appraisals (SCS-90). Leuzinger-Bohleber, Stuhrast, Rüger and Beutel (2003), in a major project of the German Psychoanalytic Society, obtained independent clinical evaluations of treatment six years after termination. In their approach reliance was placed upon qualitative interpretive psychoanalytic evaluations. In our present venture, we aim to combine the quantitative and qualitative interpretive aspects of these European projects.

In order to extend and refine our understanding of these provocative findings, we have pursued an alternative or complementary methodological approach. It is comprised of a research interview and a classificatory system that can be used jointly or separately according to a researcher's aims. We call these investigatory tools, the Schedule of Therapy Remembered (STR) and the Representations of the Therapeutic Dialogue Coding System (RTDCS).

Our research group evaluated procedures, protocols, and scoring systems over several years to develop these two new investigative tools that capture the essential aspects of psychoanalytic psychotherapy process. The STR is a semi-structured interview in which questions and prompts elicit a narrative that facilitates the remembering and re-remembering, telling and re-telling of interactions that took place within the context of a therapeutic relationship, and patients' judgments as to what was and was not achieved during a course of therapy. The RTDCS is a multidimensional framework that was designed to offer a profile of the material elicited by the STR. The manual provides detailed instructions for categorizing each narrative.

In order to set the stage for a more detailed description of these investigatory tools, their reliability, and early clinical findings, we will consider a concept which is fundamental to our work—the representational process.

On representations: psychoanalytic and cognitive perspectives

There are many psychoanalytic perspectives on the concept of representation. The importance we bestow on the concept of representation is based on a selective integration of the ideas contributed by psychoanalysts (e.g., Sandler & Rosenblatt, 1962), developmental psychologists (e.g., Piaget, 1954), cognitive psychologists (e.g., Bruner, 1964) and neuroscientists, (e.g., Olds, 2006). As Bruner (1968), a major voice in cognitive theory, put it:

> If we are to benefit from contact with recurrent regularities in the environment, we must represent them in some manner. To dismiss this problem as "mere memory" is to misunderstand it. For the most important thing about memory is not storage of past experience, but rather the retrieval of what is relevant in some usable form. This depends upon how past experience is coded and processed so that it may indeed be relevant and usable in the present when needed. The end product of such a system of coding and processing is what we may speak of as "representation" (p. 2).

According to our hybrid theoretical perspective, representations are externally unobservable mental activities, such as autobiographical memories, images, thoughts, expectations, plans, and fantasies. Unlike perceptions, representations do not require the support of immediately available sensory input to be consciously experienced.[i]

The psychoanalytic literature is rich in hypotheses about the ways in which representations of people and the way relationships with them proceed can facilitate or impede cognitive and emotional development throughout the life cycle. Freud (1921) anticipated the view that psychic reality is fundamentally interactional and dialogic in character, when he wrote, "In the individual's mental life, someone else is invariably involved, as a model, as an object, as a helper, as an opponent; and so from the very first, individual psychology, in this extended but entirely justifiable sense of the words, is at the same time social psychology as well" (p. 69).

We align ourselves with those theorists who share three related hypotheses about the interpersonal aspects of the "representational world" (Sandler & Rosenblatt, 1962):

1. The emergence of symbolizing capacities during the course of development makes it possible to employ images, objects, words, and actions to stand for or represent interactions with others who are not immediately available to the senses.

2. Representations of human interactions may be as varied in their complexity, emotional colouring, and functional significance as those existing between actual persons.
3. Whether representations of the self in relation to others are voluntarily brought into awareness or seem to appear spontaneously, individuals can use or react to them without conscious experience of their meaning or functional significance.

Concurrently, the understanding that patients' interactions with internalized representations of "therapy with their therapists" can influence important aspects of behaviour in a manner analogous to the "impacts" of in-session communicative exchanges with the therapist has become increasingly influential among psychoanalytic and cognitively oriented theorists (Atwood & Stolorow, 1980; Dorpat, 1974; Edelson, 1963; Geller, 1987; Kohut, 1971; Loewald, 1960; Norcross & Goldfried, 2005; Olds, 2006; Pine, 1988; and Strupp, Hadley & Gomes-Schwartz, 1977). According to our version of this expanded view, the therapeutic dialogue promotes the conscious retrieval of formative memories about the past, facilitates changes in implicit or procedural memory, and brings into existence new memories of experiences of therapy that can be used to build upon what was accomplished during therapy, after termination. Empirical research has not kept abreast of these theoretical developments.

Empirical studies of the representational process

Empirical investigations of how representations of the therapeutic relationship originate, evolve, and exert a regulatory influence on patients' experiential states and behaviours between sessions and after termination are, in fact, few in number. Earlier investigations by Geller, Behrends, Hartley, Farber and Rohde (1989) led to the construction of a network of open-ended questions and rating scales collectively known as the Therapist Representation Inventory (TRI). It is a self-administered battery of measures designed to investigate how often, in what forms, with what feelings, and to what ends, current and former patients remember, imagine, and dream about their therapists (Geller, Smith Cooley & Hartley, 1981).

Since 1980 the TRI has been used to study whether there are statistically significant linkages between the phenomenological and functional properties of current and former patients' representations of the therapeutic relationship and their judgments about the benefits they have derived from therapy. Full and partial accounts of our accumulating findings can be found elsewhere (e.g., Orlinsky & Geller, 1993). Here are selected highlights:

- Findings indicate that the tendency to recall or imagine conversations in which the therapist serves as a "dialogic partner" is commonly experienced by a large percentage of patients. These subjective experiences have been found to be comprised of different combinations of enactive, imagistic, and lexical representations. Statistical analyses carried out in diverse samples have consistently indicated that patients can be grouped and compared with respect to how their representational configurations blend visual images of the therapist sitting in his/her office, auditory images of the tonal qualities of his/her voice, thoughts about the words that were spoken or heard, and somato-sensory bodily experiences.
- Another reliable finding is that these inner dialogues are most likely to enter the ongoing stream of consciousness when patients are experiencing painful emotions (e.g., anxiety, guilt, loneliness); when desiring their therapist's approval; and when feeling insecure about their ability to make choices in ambiguous or conflictual situations (Orlinsky & Geller, 1993).
- A particularly suggestive finding is that the lengthier a therapy, the more likely a patient is to evoke representations that take the form of imagined conversations with the therapist to serve adaptive and reparative functions (Geller & Farber, 1993).
- Another recurrent finding based on the Therapist Involvement Subscale of the TRI has been that patients can be distinguished in terms of the relative predominance of the "themes" that organize the manifest content of their interactions with mental representations of their therapists. Factor analyses suggest that a patient's repertoire of themes can be reliably sorted into the following categories:
    1. Fantasies of establishing an extra-therapeutic relationship that attenuates the power differentials and status inequalities that separate the roles of patient and therapist;
    2. Wishes to control or master situations in which the therapist is experienced as frustrating or disappointing;

3. Fantasies of making physical contact with the therapist, particularly of a sexual or aggressive nature;
4. Doubts about the helpfulness of therapy; and
5. The felt readiness to use representations of the therapeutic relationship to build upon, preserve, and reinforce what was accomplished during therapy sessions and after termination for adaptive and reparative purposes.

In correlational studies, two clusters of themes have consistently had statistically significant relationships with patients' perceptions of the benefits they have derived from therapy. On the one hand, patients who have rated their therapies as highly effective have tended to be the same ones who reported entering into multimodal and benignly influential conversations with representations of their therapists in-between sessions (e.g., Farber & Geller, 1994), and after termination (Arnold, Farber & Geller, 2004; Wzontek, Geller & Farber, 1995) for adaptive and reparative purposes.

In other words, one of the most important findings to emerge from repeated administration of the TRI is that patients who believe that they have benefited from therapy are the same ones who strongly endorse the following statements: "When I am having a problem, I try to work it out with my therapist in mind"; "When I am faced with a difficult situation I sometimes ask myself: 'What would my therapist want me to do?'"; "I now find myself talking to other people the way I talk to my therapist"; "I try to solve my problems in the way my therapist and I worked on them in therapy"; "In a sense, I feel as though my therapist has become a part of me".

Conversely, self-reported negative treatment outcomes, among both current and former patients, have been consistently found to be correlated with the failure to create and use benignly influential representations of the therapeutic dialogue between sessions and after termination (e.g., Orlinsky & Geller, 1993; Geller & Farber, 1993).

Taken together, these findings support the conclusion that the ability to become conscious of representations of communicative exchanges with one's therapist that were experienced as "helpful" and "useful" strengthens the mental activities that promote self-determination and well-being, and should, therefore, be regarded as a reliable and important intrapsychic concomitant of what Seligman would designate as an "effective" therapy (1995).

This has strengthened our commitment to the central idea guiding our research project, namely, that the readiness and ability to continue the therapeutic dialogue, representationally, in the physical absence of the therapist, is both a marker of having benefited from therapy, and a vehicle for transferring the influence of in-session interactions to extra-therapeutic situations.

Yet, conclusions must remain tentative. We still have a great deal to learn about the forms in which representations of therapeutic relationships appear and reappear in awareness, their subjective meanings, and the functions that they serve in particular patients' lives during therapy and after the final session. There are many unanswered questions about the ways in which patient variables (e.g., security of attachment patterns), interpersonal variables (e.g., the status of the therapeutic alliance, or gender pairings of patient and therapist), and contextual variables (e.g., duration of therapy), singly and in combination, influence the ways patients encode, sustain, and re-activate cognitive-affective representations of the functional aspects of the therapeutic dialogue.

The schedule of therapy remembered and the representations of the therapeutic dialogue coding system

From the effectiveness study described in Chapter One, we derived information from patients reporting different levels of satisfaction with their therapy. A new question was posed: could we come to understand what in the treatments of these individuals accounted for the difference in the ways they evaluated their therapy? To answer this question we created the Schedule of Therapy Remembered (STR).

The schedule of therapy remembered

The STR is a 60 minute semi-structured interview that moves in a standardized sequence from open-ended to more focused questions and prompts, each of which offers a somewhat different approach to eliciting detailed retrospective accounts of patients' experiences in therapy. There are six major sections or "demand conditions" of the STR:

1. *Open-ended narrative.* The interview begins with the request: "I'd like you to speak for the next five minutes about anything that's on your mind. It could relate to thoughts about your therapy or your therapist, or to other relationships. Or it could be about anything that is important to you. I'll be sitting here listening, but I won't interrupt". Comparable instructional sets have been used to study: how the representation of affects becomes crystallized (Gottschalk & Geiser, 1969); the conceptual and emotional maturity of adults' representations of significant others (Bender, Farber & Geller, 1997; Blatt, Auerbach & Levy, 1997); and the processes of symbolization (Freedman, 1998).
2. *Referral issues.* The patient is then asked to describe what led him or her to therapy and what life was like at that time.
3. *Five adjectives.* The next phase of the interview has two interrelated parts. First, the interviewee is asked to "choose five words that reflect your relationship with your therapist." Then, the interviewee is asked to provide "examples that reflect the word that was chosen." This form of eliciting remembrances of the emotion-laden aspects of the process of therapy was adapted from the Adult Attachment Interview (Main & Goldwyn, 1998).
4. *Good/difficult moments and perceived outcome.* In order to evoke still other modes of remembering, participants are asked to describe "good" and "difficult" moments experienced during therapy and how they have impacted their current lives. The inclusion of these requests in the STR was inspired by the belief, held in common by many psychotherapy theorists and researchers, that there are significantly helpful and hindering "critical incidents" (Strupp et al., 1977) or "critical sessions" (Orlinsky & Howard, 1967).
5. *Dreams during treatment.* When dreaming and daydreaming we can create the illusion of being somewhere and with someone we are not. In order to examine the consistency or distinctiveness of representations of the therapeutic relationship occurring during wakefulness and those produced under the conditions of sleep, the STR includes an inquiry about remembrances of dreams experienced during therapy in which the therapist appeared

in the manifest content. About 38% of the therapist-patients who participated in a study conducted by Geller, Smith Cooley, and Hartley (1981) reported dreams portraying the therapist undisguised in the manifest content. Rohde, Geller, and Farber's (1992) investigation suggests that these dreams tend to express negative emotions and to depict a therapist who seemed malevolent as often as benevolent, and frustrating as often as gratifying.

6. *How are things in your life now*? The interview concludes by asking participants what their lives are like now. Answers to this question often provide a prism to understanding how former patients view the effects of their treatment.

In Chapter One, we reported that the STR is the methodological centrepiece of the second phase of a study of the effectiveness of psychoanalytic psychotherapy offered at a low-fee outpatient psychotherapy clinic staffed by psychoanalysts and candidates in the Institute for Psychoanalytic Training and Research (IPTAR). To date, 20 of the 99 patients from the original sample have participated in a re-evaluation study, at least one year after their treatment had terminated. They were administered the STR, another Effectiveness Questionnaire, the Therapist Involvement Scale, and questionnaires pertaining to annihilation anxiety, security of attachment, and depression.

While the STR was not designed specifically to elicit remembrances of communicative exchanges with the therapist, the data gleaned from verbatim transcripts of these interviews, which were conducted by a psychoanalyst, were found to be an invaluable resource and led to the creation and initial standardization of the Representations of the Therapeutic Dialogue Coding System (RTDCS).

The STR method yielded a rich narrative, capturing the process of representation cognitively and psychoanalytically defined, and represents a new lens through which to view effectiveness, first introduced in our 1999 study. The STR narrative is the vehicle for specifying the dimensions that define the representation of the dialogue and enable us to develop the RTDCS, which is the spine of our research methodology. In the STR we found an evocative reconstruction of the therapeutic narrative; in the method of the RTDCS we recreate the specific dimensions of therapeutic actions.

Endnote

i. Following Piaget (1954), we take the appearance of representations of the therapeutic relationship in conscious and preconscious thought as a reliable sign that a patient's experiences in therapy have been stored in long-term memory in the form of organized interpersonal "schemas". We have adopted the term schema to refer to knowledge structures that are not themselves directly showable to consciousness but whose enduring existence precedes and gives rise to representations, which are themselves inherently transient subjective experiences.

CHAPTER THREE

The RTD Coding System and its clinical application: a new approach to studying patients' representations of the Therapeutic Dialogue

Jesse D. Geller, Donna S. Bender, Norbert Freedman, Joan Hoffenberg, Denise Kagan, Carrie Schaffer, and Neal Vorus

The Schedule of Therapy Remembered (STR) produced a rich narrative of people's recollections of their therapy experiences. How to use this information to get a measure of patients' judgments about what was and what was not accomplished during a course of therapy now became the question to be answered.

The primary aim of Chapters Three and Four is to demonstrate the potential of the Representation of the Therapeutic Dialogue Coding System (RTDCS), as well as its operational definitions, scoring principles, and instructions. This will be followed by a presentation of the ways in which RTD scores can be analysed to be specifically responsive to the need for normative information about patients' retrospective reconstructions of the verbal and nonverbal aspects of the therapeutic dialogue. Included are the first steps in analyses of RTDCS data sets used on a case by case basis to arrive at highly particularized outcome criteria and to try to test the hypothesis that the likelihood of benefiting from a course of treatment is increased if a patient avails himself/herself of the opportunity to construct, remember, use, and identify with benignly influential representations of the therapeutic dialogue in the physical absence of the therapist.

Components of the RTD scoring system

In order to classify variations in patients' narrative accounts of their interpersonal experiences in therapy, the RTDCS was constructed from the verbatim texts of the STR. First, the transcript from the STR was divided into readily identifiable and meaningful segments or idea units following Stinson, Milbrath, Reidbord, and Bucci's (1994) procedure of reported reliability. Like a sentence, an idea unit makes a statement and is sufficient in itself. Idea units segment narratives into single frames or snapshots. One idea unit is delineated from another when there is a shift in any of the qualities that organize narrative accounts of interpersonal events. Members of our research team trained in this method have achieved levels of inter-scorer agreement ranging from 0.84 to 0.88.

Next, every idea unit was scored for the presence or absence of an RTD. An RTD, or Representation of the Therapeutic Dialogue, is the basic unit of analysis of the RTDCS. It is a statement in which explicit reference is made to a previously experienced interaction or communicative exchange with a therapist. Twenty scoring principles and examples are provided by the RTDCS manual to differentiate RTDs from descriptions of the therapist, evaluations of the therapist, and abstract generalizations about therapy. For example, "I felt angry at my therapist" is a narrative about the interactive aspects of therapy but neither communicative intent nor a discernible interaction is implied. However, the statement "I felt judged by my therapist but couldn't tell him" is *dialogic* and scored as an RTD (Bakhtin, 1981).

The third stage of scoring (see table 1) involves categorizing each RTD with respect to: (a) mode of remembering, (b) the channels of communication to which it refers, (c) its specificity, (d) its geographical location, (e) its emotional coloration, and (f) its capacity to function as an introject.

Forms of remembering

The scoring of each RTD begins by being labelled *Recalled*, *Inhibited*, *Longed for* or *Imagined* in its mode of remembering.

Recalled RTDs are reconstructed versions of dyadic exchanges that are remembered as having taken place during the course of therapy (e.g., "We spent a lot of time talking about my anxieties" and

Table 1. RTD scoring criteria.

Forms of Remembering the Therapeutic Dialogue

R – Recalled
In – Inhibited
L – Longed for
Im – Imagined

Modes of Communicating

V – Verbal
NV – Non-verbal

The Location of RTDs

IS – In-session
OS – Out of session

Specificity of RTDs

S – Specific communicative exchanges
C – Composite of conversations

Emotionality

P – Positive feelings towards the therapist
N – Negative feelings towards the therapist

Introjects

B – Benign
P – Problematic

"He asked me questions that helped me think in new ways about myself"). Recalled RTDs are not understood as "factual" renderings of "what really happened" in therapy. According to our constructionist perspective, Recalled RTDs are the complex creations of the intricate relations between remembering, and intrapsychic processes, such as imagining, thinking, and apprehending. We further assume that any attempt to translate the experienced qualities of a Recalled RTD into a coherent narrative would bring slippage from what an observer would regard as accurate. Then again, like poets, some patients *lie their way to the truth*. Like patients, we are primarily concerned with the meanings of and functions served by Recalled RTDs, and less interested in the question: can they be taken at face value?

Inhibited RTDs were never put into words with the therapist. They make known to the interviewer experiences previously concealed or kept secret in therapy, such as "I wanted to ask her how she felt about me, but I never did", and "I never wanted to talk about my childhood".

Longed for and *Imagined RTDs* are all private responses to dyadic interactions with the therapist. At the time they were originally experienced, they were left unsaid. *Longed for* RTDs convey remembrances of yearnings for particular interactions with the therapist that were *implicit* in the therapeutic relationship at a particular time. They draw on memories of needs and wishes directed towards the therapist, as in "I think maybe I wanted him to hug me", and "I used to hope that my therapist thought about me when he went on vacation". The manifest content of these RTDs concerns remembrances of as yet unvoiced desires, but unlike Inhibited RTDs, there is no direct evidence that the patient is censoring their expression.

An RTD is classified as *Imagined* if it makes direct allusions to remembrances of "what might" or "could have" been said to or by the therapist. Imagined RTDs make no reference to either unfulfilled longings or to that which could not be said to the therapist. Rather, Imagined RTDs are ways of remembering fantasies or suppositions about the therapeutic relationship. They are invented scenarios of "What would have happened?" or "What could have happened?" if the patient and therapist had interacted in a particular way. Examples of imagined RTDs are "I used to rehearse what I would say if I met him outside of therapy", and "Sometimes I asked myself, 'What would my therapist want me to do if I was unsure of myself?'".

Modes of communicating: verbal/nonverbal RTDs

Next, it is determined if the RTD makes use of verbal and/or nonverbal channels of communication. Questionnaire-based investigations have consistently found that representations of interactions with others tend to be experienced with varying degrees of vividness as blends of spoken words, vocal qualities, pictorial images, and body sensations, and that the ways in which these forms of representation combine vary from one individual to another (e.g., Geller, Lehman & Farber, 2002). To identify whether these variations manifest themselves in patients' narrative accounts of their experiences in therapy, the RTDCS manual provides guidelines for distinguishing between narratives that spontaneously make explicit reference to remembrances of what was said in words and/or to remembrances of perceptions of the therapists' gestures, postures, facial expressions, and tone of voice, that is, nonverbal references.

The location of RTD: inside and outside the session

In order to contribute information relevant to ongoing debates about the management of spatial and temporal "boundaries" which encircle the therapeutic process, our scoring system distinguishes between RTDs that took place "inside" and "outside" the therapist's office. Previous research (e.g., Geller & Farber, 1993) indicates that one of the most common ways of remembering the therapist is to imagine him/her "sitting in the office", and that some patients make use of representations of the therapist's office and its furnishings as symbols or functional equivalents of the therapy relationship. Except in emergencies or other special circumstances, therapists and patients only meet in the therapist's office. Clarity about where and when therapy is to take place is widely taken to be a prerequisite for establishing a safe therapeutic environment. Nevertheless, very little is empirically known about whether the outcome of therapy is linked to the types and frequency of interactions patients remember as having occurred outside therapy.

Specific or composite RTDs

Data from varied sources indicate that people's remembrances of interpersonal scenes and events vary in the degree of detail, clarity, and vividness (e.g., Geller, Farber & Schaffer, 2010). Our scoring system distinguishes between Specific and Composite RTDs and provides guidelines for examining their sequential arrangement. *Specific RTDs* are remembrances of single events that purportedly occurred at a particular time and place. The relationship scenarios of specific RTDs enable us to identify whether discrete events within sessions, or particular sessions were, from the patient's point of view, decisively influential in determining the course of therapy. *Composite RTDs* merge ostensibly distinctive and diverse experiences into some sort of "averaged typical instance". They are, in effect, generalizations about "what happened". In other words Specific and Composite RTDs bring to awareness episodic and semantic memories as they are called by cognitive researchers. Studies, like those derived from attachment theory (Bowlby, 1980), indicate that there is a wide range of individual differences in the ability to coordinate the relations between these different modes of remembering.

Main and Goldwyn's (1990) findings indicate that securely attached adults tell narratives in which their overall sense of relationships is integrated with vivid and realistic remembrances of individual moments, demonstrating the ability to coordinate Specific and Composite RTDs. By contrast, some insecurely attached individuals lose contact with memories of concrete moments, resulting in a vague and diffuse sense of their experiences and a loss of contact in the relationship. At the time of the STR, participants took the Calgary Attachment Questionnaire (George & West, 2001).

Scoring for emotionality: positive or negative RTDs

Each RTD is judged for the presence of positive or negative affect: "Does the patient make explicit reference to feelings towards the therapist and his/her actions?" Several questionnaire-based studies have found that each therapy leaves behind a legacy of representations of the therapeutic relationship that can be recognized and rated by patients with respect to their emotional content (e.g., Barchat, 1989; Quintana & Meara, 1990; Rosenzweig, Farber & Geller, 1996). Because the feeling states that accompany the evocation of an RTD may remain at a "tacit" level when translated into spoken language, we score for emotionality only those RTDs that include: (a) agreed-upon emotion words (e.g., happy, sad), (b) descriptions of the agreed-upon behavioural manifestations of feelings (e.g., laughing, crying), or (c) metaphors that are widely recognized as expressive of emotional experience (e.g., "I felt on top of the world when my therapist congratulated me", "I got a bad case of the blues when he misunderstood me"). Remembrances of emotional states are also characterized in terms of their valence or colouration. Thus, when affect is present we score RTDs as positive or negative with regard to their emotional content.

Identifying RTDs that function as introjects

The term *introject* in psychoanalysis has many varied interpretations and here we will offer a particular cognitive-affective definition: it must be infused with quasi-perceptual qualities, a sense of immediacy, and be capable of serving psychological functions in a manner comparable to "actual" in-session communicative exchange.

RTDs that are infused with these phenomenological and functional properties are deemed introjects and are scored as either benign or problematic. In their benign forms, introjects are pleasure-giving, supportive, clarifying, and enhance adaptive functioning. Examples of benign introjects include such RTDs as: "Sometimes when I'm unsure how to deal with a problem, I hear my therapist's gentle voice coaxing me to trust my own feelings", or "When I picture my therapist, I feel as if I'm with a comforting imaginary companion, kind of like I used to feel as a kid", and "I keep my therapist in my pocket, and when I need to talk to her I take her out". In their problematic forms, introjects are experienced as threatening, disapproving, malevolent, or persecutory and compromise efforts to cope with uncertainties and anxieties. Examples of problematic introjects include such RTDs as: "Like a voice in my head when I'm feeling ashamed, I hear my therapist's voice chastising me, and calling me by my formal name and not by my first name", "When I think of doing something selfish, I see my therapist's disapproving face in my mind's eye and I feel guilty".

When coding the dimensions used to characterize each RTD, we employed a decision-making process that identified the sources of disagreement among all the members of our research team, and rewrote scoring criteria accordingly. We repeated this process until most of the scorers were in agreement on all variables and consensus was easily reached by those whose scores differed. Next we examined the extent to which two of the manual's authors (working independently) would agree in their ratings of each of the RTD variables found in STR transcripts. Percentage agreements ranged between 84% and 98% for Type of Memory, Verbal/Nonverbal, Inside/Outside the Office, Specificity, and Benign Introjects. The judges did not, however, consistently agree in their ratings of the presence or absence of an explicitly expressed emotional experience. They agreed only 60% of the time. Unless and until the current level of unreliability is corrected, consensus scores will be used in all subsequent analyses.

Prevalence of RTD components

Scoring RTD profiles

Experientially the attributes that RTDs are scored for fit together to form more or less distinguishable configurations. Table 2 gives examples of verbatim quotes which illustrate the wide range of ways in which the therapeutic dialogue is remembered.

RTDs that are scored as Recalled, Verbal, Specific, and In-Session constitute a "domain of recollection" that can be readily distinguished from RTDs that are scored as Recalled, Nonverbal, Composite, and In-session. The latter combination highlights remembrances of the recurrent and predictable aspects of a therapist's communicative "style". The former recalls a therapist's utterances remembered within a specific session.

Once scored the RTD patterns of patients with a range of effectiveness scores were studied. To set the stage, we first summarize what we find normative about the ways in which the RTD variables, themselves, remain memorable after termination. Examining variations in their frequency of occurrence can serve as the database for correlational studies and group comparisons.

Sample

For this section of the study, patients who had terminated their treatments were recruited from our original sample (see Chapter One) to return and participate in an interview, conducted by a member of our research group, about their terminated therapy. Participants were offered US $50 and completed a battery of self-administered tests. All had been out of therapy at least two years. They were assured anonymity and that no information would be given to or solicited from their former therapist. To date 20 individuals have been interviewed.

RTDCS data (table 3 below) from ten patients have been used to conduct quantitative and qualitative analyses of the ways in which patients' representations of the therapeutic dialogue remain memorable and influence current functioning at varying intervals following termination.

Table 2. Scoring examples of RTDs.

Recalled Imagined Inhibited Longed for	Verbal/ Non-verbal	In session/ Out of session	Specific/ Composite	Emotion Positive + Negative −	Introject Benign/ Problematic
"In that session I felt judged by him but couldn't tell him"					
Inhibited	Verbal	In session	Specific	−	N/A
"Somehow she was able to find the right words to describe how I was feeling"					
Recalled	Verbal	In session	Composite	N/A	N/A
"Beforehand, I would try to figure out what I was going to talk about in therapy that day"					
Imagined	Verbal	In session	Specific	N/A	N/A
"I often wanted to know more about what he was thinking or feeling"					
Longing	Verbal	In session	Composite	N/A	N/A
"I often wanted to ask her about how she felt about what I was saying"					
Inhibited	Non-verbal	In session	Composite	−	N/A
"I felt I really needed to cry but I didn't want him to see me that way so I would really fight it"					
Recalled	Non-verbal	In session	Composite	N/A	N/A
"I felt judged and that was mainly because of his silences"					
Recalled	Non-verbal	Out of session	Specific	+	N/A
"I felt awkward when we ran into each other in the supermarket"					
Recalled	Verbal	Out of session	Specific	−	N/A
"Sometimes when I'm trying to make a difficult decision, I hear my therapist advising me"					
Imagined	Verbal	In session	Composite	N/A	Benign

Table 3. Percent of RTDs in STRI transcripts falling in various scoring categories, by patient number.

Patient #	217	97	450	199	176	243	89	13	73	284
Total of RTDs	26	36	85	34	77	30	42	46	15	71
Recalled	.85	.94	.56	.94	.79	.93	.66	.93	1.00	.76
Imagined	.04	.06	.05	.00	.14	.07	.09	.00	.00	.10
Longed for	.00	.00	.13	.00	.06	.00	.00	.02	.00	.01
Inhibited	.12	.00	.26	.00	.00	.00	.20	.02	.00	.13
Benign Introjects	.00	.00	.00	.00	.00	.00	.00	.00	.00	.06*
Verbalization										
Verbal	.04	.03	.13	.21	.75	.50	.04	.00	.00	.06
Nonverbal	.96	.97	.87	.79	.25	.50	.96	1.00	1.00	.94*
Location										
In-session	.92	.86*	.91	1.00	.93	.70	1.00	1.00	1.00	.85
Outside	.08	.14	.09	.00	.07	.30	.00	.00	.00	.15
Specificity										
Specific	.19	.25*	.27*	.29*	.33*	.60	.14	.20	.00	24*
Composite	.81	.75	.73	.71	.67	.40	.86	.80	1.00	.76
Affect										
Positive	.25	.11	.04	.15	.30	.23	.13	.15	.13	.08
Negative	.08	.14*	.24*	.24*	.62*	.37*	.09	.37	.13	.13
Either	.77	75	.72	.61	.08	.40	.79	.79	.74	.79
EQ Scores	170	190	202	203	210	223	255	265	263	263

*Scores are above the median for the category.

Results

Data from these ten patients reveal:

1. The total number of RTDs ranged from a low of 15 to a high of 85.
2. EQ scores: Patients' ratings of their therapies ranged from very positive, that is instrumental in transforming their lives in positive and needed ways, to rather negative, that is

moderately or highly dissatisfied with what they achieved in therapy. Degree of perceived effectiveness of therapy was neither a determinant of willingness to be interviewed nor was it related to number of RTDs as #73 who provided only 15 RTDs had the highest EQ score and #450 who had 84 RTDs judged her therapy less effective.
3. There is great variability in the extent to which the participants evoked and reported their experiences in therapy. Not surprisingly, verbally mediated RTDs that took place during therapy sessions were more prevalent in every protocol than any other configuration; psychotherapy is, after all, the "talking cure".
4. Content analysis of Recalled RTDs fell into two broadly distinguishable clusters: communicative exchanges that were considered as a source of gain and those viewed as a source of the obstacles that curtailed the ability to derive maximal possible benefits from therapy.
5. A defining feature of each patient's profile is the relative importance given to narratives about verbal exchanges versus accounts of interactions with the therapist that took place in the privacy of conscious thought. The latter category is the Inhibited, Imagined, and Longed for RTDs.

Five of the patients did not produce any Inhibited RTDs. The majority of those who gave recognition to memories of self-censorship spoke of concealing negative feelings towards the therapist or therapy. Four patients reported memories of having unvoiced wishes that were directed towards the therapist. The manifest content of their Longed for RTDs tended to centre either on longings to maintain bonds of attachment with the therapist or the desire to gain their therapist's approval. All but three of the participants recalled having imaginary conversations with their therapists that made no reference to either unfulfilled yearnings or to that which could not be said.
6. The percentage of RTDs scored as verbal exchanges ranged from 25% to 100%. Eight of the ten participants spoke about memories of communicative exchanges that took place through specific nonverbal channels (e.g., being observed by the therapist's smiling or disapproving eyes, listening to the soothing or forbidding tonal qualities of the therapist's voice, and being touched by

the therapist's restraining hands or embracing arms). There are substantial differences in the ratio of verbal to nonverbal RTDs found in their protocols. The ratios ranged from mostly verbal (97:3) to evenly distributed (50:50).
7. The majority of RTDs portrayed interactions taking place inside the therapist's office. Nevertheless, six of the participants spoke of interactions that occurred outside the therapist's office. In this group the ratio of in-session to out-of-session RTDs ranged from 92% vs. 8% to 70% vs. 30%. The out of session RTDs included remembrances of unanticipated encounters in the community or in the waiting room, telephone calls made between sessions, sending or receiving letters written during vacations, cards acknowledging holidays or important life events (e.g., marriage and graduation).
8. In all but one of the participants' protocols the percentage of RTDs classifiable as composite exceeded the percentage of RTDs that conveyed a patient's recollections of what was happening at a specific moment of relating. Specific RTDs ranged from 0% to 60% of responses. The percentage of RTDs that spoke to generalized memories of the therapeutic relationship ranged from 40% to 100%. Individual differences in the ratios of specific and composite memories are probably linked, in part, to the identifiable "cognitive styles" so well documented by ego psychologists. Some individuals tend to move from the general to the particular when narrating their experiences, while others tend to move from the particular to the general.

With regard to the ability to provide concrete anecdotes to substantiate abstract statements about the therapeutic relationship, Roy (2007) has obtained a noteworthy finding. He found that when therapy is experienced as effective, patients were more likely to remember specific events and verbal exchanges about their therapy experiences. This finding suggests that the linking or symbolizing function is also enhanced. He found that there were multiple sequences that linked composite to specific RTDs in four of the five patients whose EQ scores were indicative of a successful outcome, and no instances of such linkages in the protocols of the five patients whose therapies were deemed ineffective, according to scores on the EQ ($t = 2.96$, $p < 0.05$). When therapy is experienced as effective, then the patient is able to remember specific events and verbal exchanges about his

or her therapy experience. It seems this linking or symbolizing function is enhanced in effective therapies and is absent or diminished when therapy is perceived as ineffective.
9. Every participant's protocol contained RTDs having both negative and positive emotional valence. Not unexpectedly, Roy's (2007) correlational analyses revealed that patients with high EQ scores tended to produce more RTDs that incorporated the use of words clearly descriptive of positive feeling states.
10. All the patients left therapy with mixed or ambivalent feelings about their therapists and the therapeutic relationship. Patients' ambivalence quotients (ratio of positive and negative RTDs) appear to bear a complex relationship to their memory-based judgments about the outcome of therapy. For example, the patient (#217) who obtained the lowest EQ score produced far more positive (25%) than negative (8%) RTDs while the patient (#73) who obtained the highest EQ score produced equal numbers of positive (13%) and negative (13%) RTDs. We anticipate that measures of tolerance of ambivalence or of the ability to reflect rather than ruminate about the painful and pleasurable aspects of therapy will clarify the paradoxical nature of these findings. We share with many others the hypothesis that the capacity to acknowledge and tolerate ambivalence is a core aspect of maturity, and contributes to further maturation itself.

The identification of introjects

Until now we have reported on the frequency of occurrence of the constituent elements of RTDs. As previously noted, table 1 reveals how these properties can be combined to create units of analysis that give experiential primacy to the different ways in which what happened in the past can be selectively reconstructed.[i] At the bottom of table 1 are *introjects*. They can be distinguished in the following ways. They do not merely bring information about how the therapeutic relationship proceeded in the past. Rather they are imbued with the power to exert a direct and immediate influence on a person's current functioning, with or without his conscious consent.

Based on previous research (Kantrowitz, Katz & Paolitto, 1986; Pfeffer, 1993; Schlessinger et al., 1974), we anticipated that there would be some patients who had effective therapies and acknowledged consciously using "comforting" or "sustaining" therapist introjects for adaptation enhancing purposes since terminating. As can be seen in the table 3, contrary to expectations, only participant #284 reported having used a benign introject as a source of emotional support and guidance since terminating. In this quote from participant #284, we can hear the considerable importance he places on having access to images of seeing and being seen by his therapist's "calm demeanour": "Sometimes, but not always, a memory of Dr X is the catalyst for giving myself the liberty to have feelings, both good and bad ... what will kind of trigger a different way of thinking about something is not usually a particular thing he said it's usually just a feeling and like a visual image of just his face". When asked: "What is the feeling, do you know?" the patient answered: "I guess he always, he himself had a very placid and calm demeanour no matter what, and I guess I feel that way when I picture him calm, even though things might be very turbulent".

On the other hand, no RTDs that met the operational definition of a problematic introject were found in the protocols of the participants who had ineffective therapies. Are introjects as rare as these preliminary findings suggest? We suspect not. Clinical experience indicates that unless specifically asked, patients in therapy are not likely to talk about what they are learning about their therapists' attitudes and feelings towards them (Geller, 1984). We have wondered whether more patients would have reported scorable introjects if they had been asked about memories of "daydreaming" about their therapists. Daydreams commonly imply active involvement with images of persons not immediately present to the senses. Future versions of the STR will include questions about daydreams in which the therapist played a role and questions about the more somatosensory experiences brought to awareness by remembrances of interactions with the therapist in order to evoke introjects that might otherwise remain at a tacit or subliminal level.

Clinical application of RTD profiles

Case by case investigations of RTD profiles

There is a cumulative library of RTDCS derived from STR transcripts that enable us to conduct case by case investigations of questions that are central to the theory and practice of psychoanalytic therapy. For example, what types of therapist offerings do patients remember as facilitating or impeding progress towards the attainment of therapeutic goals? Are patients' judgments about the outcome of therapy and their remembrances of the pleasurable and painful aspects of the therapeutic relationship interrelated and do they influence one another?

In order to demonstrate the RTDCS's possibilities as an investigatory tool, we have chosen for analysis the narrative accounts provided by two participants who are designated #284 and #450: "Jim" and "Amy". We can now explore the RTD profiles of a patient who knowingly ended an effective therapy that had yet to yield maximal possible benefits and a patient who unilaterally dropped out of a therapy that was yielding symptomatic improvements.

The story of Jim's therapy—(patient #284)

Jim was 32, on the threshold of marrying and completing a PhD in the social sciences, when he ambivalently entered therapy for the first time at the urging of his fiancée. At the time of intake, he reluctantly proffered the following presenting complaints: "I was pretty happy but not happy enough", "I feared getting violent when arguing with my fiancée", and "Conflicts with my parents—I thought I was always trying to please them and that was getting in the way of pleasing myself". He was assigned to a male therapist with whom he met twice weekly for two years. Two months after his initial session Jim revealed that he also came to therapy because of a "shame ridden secret": "At the beginning of my therapy we talked a lot about my being concerned for a long time in a nagging way that I was somehow gay, that I had homosexual feelings".

Jim stopped therapy after discussion with his therapist at a time when he was completing his PhD programme and awaiting the birth of a son. During the STR Jim reported that he left therapy feeling: "I no longer worry about getting violent with my wife", "I guess some of my tense anger sort of defused", and "I'm a lot more open with my parents, and I'm able to stand up to them better, I think, and be openly critical, or just more independent". By the end of therapy, Jim felt confident that it "wasn't whether I was going to be gay or not—I'm almost certainly not".

Jim spoke throughout the STR with enthused satisfaction and gratitude about how he and his therapist worked together to realize these goals. Jim's EQ score, obtained two years earlier, similarly indicated that he judged his therapy to be highly effective. What his EQ score does not reveal is that although Jim stopped therapy after consultation with his therapist, he knew that the expectable benefits of therapy had not yet been obtained.

According to Jim, one of the major achievements of his therapy was the discovery that he was dealing with "fears of male intimacy rather than homosexuality, per se". On the way to the STR interview, Jim reported thinking that he had only taken initial steps towards "working through and conquering" his fear of intimacy with men when he ended therapy. Early in the STR Jim revealed that he is currently experiencing "a similar sort of obsessive anxiety about doing something sexually wrong with my newborn son". Jim concluded his initial narrative by saying:

> Because I ended it not having felt that everything was accomplished, um, I feel insecure about having ended it. It's not like my therapist had said, "Please don't end this". … I insisted on ending it. We both felt that it was a good time to end it and we might pick it up some time again. But I feel that I ended it with a lot left to do, I left with a lot of feelings about how it's not really over. It brought back the things I used to think about on the way over.

These complexities are captured by the adjectives Jim chose to characterize the essence of his experiences in therapy: close, intense, tense, warm, and incomplete.

Using these adjectives that Jim chose to portray his therapy we hope to point to both the types of communicative exchanges that may have contributed to the considerable gains Jim derived from therapy and what they reveal about the ways in which his fears of intimacy manifested themselves within the therapeutic relationship.

Sources of gain

Jim's protocol is rich in specific and composite recollections of verbal exchanges that have been deemed either "promising" or "probably effective" in the literature on empirically supported therapies (Norcross, 2004). He recalled questions that elicited feelings (e.g., "He asked me how I felt. That's not something I would take seriously for myself, I would be thinking about the events, not how it felt"). He recalled expressions of emotional support and encouragements to be more spontaneous (e.g., "He was always very open and very accepting when we talked about me being afraid of what would happen if I really let my desires go, and that felt very warm"). To illustrate why he felt "close" to his therapist, Jim recalled the following composite RTD: "There were times when he would say something about himself; very few times I felt our relationship was very close ... and that he was, I guess, trusting me that I could handle it".

In each of the following RTD configurations, we recognize the interpersonal conditions that are known to facilitate the development of a positive and durable therapeutic alliance (e.g., "He was really smart, and he was really patient, and a real pro ... in terms of letting me do things the hard way if I wanted to do them the hard way", and "Um, maybe I was a really good patient and made the most of it—I'm sure I was, but I also felt he was extraordinary and a really important person to me"). Here we would also include Jim's memory that his therapist's quiet silences conveyed non-judgmental emotional availability: "I never ever felt I was getting anything less than his full attention".

To illustrate why he characterized the relationship as "intense", Jim drew on composite RTDs of the many instances when his therapist helped him to make connections between domains of experience that were not evident to him before (e.g., "When I would talk about my childhood experiences, he would be able to bring them, or help me bring them together, into some kind of pattern"). What Jim remembers as a turning point in therapy was making connections between "standing naked in the shower with my father" and the realization that "it is not just a matter of fucking a man, but it is also a matter of male intimacy that I am dealing with".

According to Jim, "Coming to this understanding with my therapist felt good .... He helped me to realize what kind of person I really am". En route to acquiring this "life changing insight", Jim felt his therapist helped him to develop a new approach to seeking further self-understanding. Briefly, he recalled how being encouraged to "slow down" and to "tell and retell my memories" enabled him to "rethink things" and "to learn how to sort of take a second look in order to find out what my first look was". Thus, Jim left therapy with the conviction that his own abilities contributed to bringing about therapeutic changes, and that his therapist's efforts had strengthened his ability to interpret his own experiences. Consequently, it is noteworthy that RTDs that indicate that Jim and his therapist went on to explore the ways in which his conflicts about male intimacy manifested themselves within the "here and now" of the therapeutic relationship are conspicuously missing from his protocol.

Sources of incompleteness

With respect to the incompleteness of Jim's therapy, his RTD profile suggests that several interrelated factors may have been at work. Two thirds of the way into his therapy, Jim's therapist recommended that he see a movie "because he thought I would enjoy it". To explain why he had not seen it yet, Jim compared the unseen movie "to wanting to save a dessert … I'm not quite ready to give myself that pleasure". Jim also acknowledged that "there were things I wanted to know about him that I never knew and never asked. I need to give an example. Um, I noticed after two years that he wore a hearing aid, and I never said anything about it. I just wanted to ask him about it. I never did. I never learned of what his … all things about him, what his wife was like, his family was like. And I thought that made it incomplete, not just now, but then also". Thus, Jim left therapy knowing that his unresolved conflicts about "taking in" his therapist's presence and offerings were linked to what was not accomplished by his course of therapy.

In addition, Jim left therapy knowing that he had shied away from speaking honestly about conflictual engagements with his therapist. Although clearly in the minority, there are memories of disruptions of rapport and collaboration in Jim's profile. Thirteen percent of Jim's RTDs gave explicit expression to negative feelings about his therapist.

Tensions arose during the early stages of therapy when Jim felt: "He was just too hard on me", and when, "From the therapist's point of view I would be fighting him, and fighting the therapy". Later in therapy, Jim's conflicts with his therapist arose intermittently when his therapist "incorrectly" grasped the meanings of what he expressed: "Sometimes I felt he would distort what I was saying, that he would push things too far, and rephrase things in a way that I felt was too extreme. Whether or not he was right, I felt he was taking me to a place where I was feeling unsafe". As a specific example, Jim cited objecting to his therapist's saying that Jim was "terrified" as a rephrase of Jim's saying, "I was concerned and I was worried".

Perhaps further inquiry would have determined whether these "misunderstanding events" (Geller, 1984) provoked ruptures in the therapeutic alliance and whether they were discussed and resolved. Jim did, however, produce one Inhibited RTD that indicated the presence of conflicts that were never understood and mastered. Jim has an enduring memory of his therapist behaving in a "nasty" manner. It occurred when the therapist mistakenly saw another patient during Jim's hour, and insisted he wasn't wrong. After Jim consulted his date book he knew he was right, "But I just backed down ... I didn't want to have a conflict with him—in general".

Audio tapes of Jim's therapy might have told us whether he forgot or failed to report conversations in which he and his therapist connected his anxieties about male intimacy with his inhibitions about expressing curiosity about or conflict with his therapist. We are inclined to think that whether these communicative exchanges did or did not occur, their absence suggests that Jim left therapy before he took full advantage of the transformative powers of therapy. We take Jim's effective but incomplete configuration of change as confirming the hypothesis that the transformative powers of achieving insights will be incompletely activated to the extent that a patient has not come to understand the ways in which his/her intrapersonal and interpersonal conflicts, and their attendant anxieties and defences, are lived out within the context of the therapeutic relationship.

Also missing from Jim's protocol are RTDs devoted to the experiences he shared with the therapist after they agreed "that it was a good time to end it". Neither are there RTDs that focused on planning and implementing how to leave therapy at a time that coincided with other important endings and new beginnings. Jim's termination took place at a time when his son was about to be born. When he came in for the STR, Jim was dealing with a constellation of developmental tasks, which had yet to make demands on his adaptive capacities when he began or terminated therapy. Finally, there are no RTDs in his protocol that referred to conversations about what Jim could expect after he ended a therapy that was both "effective" and "incomplete". These absences are noteworthy given that the termination phase of therapy typically arouses a variety of problematic relationship issues, including facing the limitations of what *any* therapy can accomplish.

The story of Amy's therapy—(patient #450)

Amy, a 26-year-old single female dancer, reluctantly sought an appointment at the ICC at the urging of her friends. At the time of intake she reported that four months earlier she had been "crying a lot" and "couldn't get out of bed". Although "no longer as depressed", Amy reported that she was still feeling "stuck", "distracted", "unfocused", "very scattered", "very nervous", "helpless", and "unable to really cope with things". She was assigned to a male therapist. They met weekly for little more than a year until Amy unilaterally decided to stop.

The STR transcript indicates that Amy did not leave a therapy that was not yielding hoped-for therapeutic benefits, but that she had great difficulty taking pleasure and pride in the benefits she derived from her therapy at the ICC.

At the time of the research interview Amy was preparing to be married. She had recently been promoted to a managerial position in her dance company and she was continuing in a therapy she had begun shortly after "dropping out" of her therapy at the ICC two years earlier.

Amy's EQ score of 202 falls within the range of therapies deemed ineffective, but during the initial narrative, which she ended abruptly after three minutes, Amy reported, "I think originally I started going to therapy because I needed help with my coping skills. *But* now I think I've developed coping skills as a result of *it*, and now I go for therapy, um ... to learn as much as I can about myself and my relationships". When asked about the reasons that got her into therapy originally, Amy said, "I had a little bit of a workaholic mentality that, um, you know ... during the course of therapy I learned to let go of". In response to the question: "What do you feel you have taken from your therapy?" Amy said, "I think I've become more understanding and tolerant of other people. I feel like I have more control of my life and that I can cope better".

Despite these positive changes, what Amy most readily recalled during the STR were remembrances of what was uncomfortable, confusing, and disappointing about the therapy relationship. Four of the five adjectives she chose to characterize her experiences in therapy were charged with memories of painful feelings. The five were: awkward, distant, unsatisfactory, educational, and doomed. Similarly, as can be seen in table 3, 24% of her RTDs were scored as giving explicit expression to negative feelings about her experiences in therapy. Only 3% were scored as charged with positive emotions. The few pleasurable memories Amy recalled and reported dealt with what she called the "educational" aspects of therapy. The first made its appearance when Amy drew upon composite RTDs of verbal exchanges that helped her to clarify and name vaguely formulated feelings and thoughts:

> I would tell him something that was really aggravating me and he would ask me to describe my anger. And to, um—basically, you know, he would get me to figure out what was really bothering me. And then we would discuss why it was bothering me .... When I can identify the problem it's ... once I can identify it I feel like I'm pretty much on the road to either accepting it and dealing with it or getting rid of it if I can, if I need to. And, um, yeah he, uh, really helped me with that.

The second positively charged sequence of RTDs emerged as a preface to explaining why she found her therapy "unsatisfactory". Within this context, Amy acknowledged that "there were sessions that were very good and that really helped me". According to Amy, the "good sessions" that "really stuck in my head" were the ones in which her therapist "taught" her how to re-conceptualize her "trouble with negative thoughts".

> And like, um, I was afraid that I was influencing people by my negative thoughts, I was afraid that bad things were going to happen because I was imagining bad things happening. And he told me that thoughts were harmless—he basically really like got down and explained to me the difference between thoughts and actions—so that I didn't have to feel guilty for anything that I was feeling ... those were the kinds of things I thrived on, I think.

There are no RTDs in Amy's protocol indicative of communicative exchanges that enhanced her self-esteem—just the opposite. Her protocol is replete with remembrances within the context of therapy that deflated her self-esteem, for though Amy could receive and benefit from her therapist's "teachings", by her own admission she was unable to receive and integrate his caring concern.

> He was a very caring person and I never felt abandoned by him or that I couldn't rely on him. The one thing that stuck in my mind was that he told me—many times he told me—that I could call him anytime I needed anything, that, you know, that he had a voice mail and that I could always reach him on that. He really encouraged me to do that. I never did it. I just felt like he did everything that he could to help me and I just couldn't get past the fact that our relationship was just doomed. I just couldn't get past the fact that I didn't feel comfortable with him. And that I felt distant from him, what ... um—and I had all these questions I was afraid to ask.

Not surprisingly, Amy left therapy with an image of herself as having been insufficiently "self-disclosing". Returning to table 3, it can be seen that 26% of her RTDs were devoted to memories of what she stopped herself from showing or saying to her therapist. Their content indicates that a broad range of emotional experiences were self-censored (e.g., "I tried to hide any sign of weakness", "I couldn't tell him I was finding him attractive", "I never wanted to talk about sex", "I didn't dare ask him whether he liked me", and "I felt guilty about the things I withheld from him"). During the later phases of the STR, Amy acknowledged that she inhibited the nonverbal as well as the verbal expressions of her emotional reactions (e.g., "Well, whenever I would get very emotional, I would, um, I would, I, um, would not let myself cry because I didn't want him to see me cry. So I would really, really, really fight it. And, uh, that was difficult for me").

Amy's criticisms of her therapist, like many of her criticisms of herself, tended to focus on what he left unsaid. She recalled feeling disappointed that "we never discussed his training, philosophy of therapy, or practice". She also recalled, "I felt judged and mostly that was because of his silences", and "I felt very selfish and I felt very, um, I—it was just awkward for me to sit down and talk about myself and just have someone listening and not tell about what he felt". She remembered feeling that if he had revealed more of his private life to her, she would have felt less like a "case being studied" and more capable of "identifying with him". Her Imagined RTDs revolved around scenarios in which she and her therapist "compared what their mothers were like", and "talked about movies they had both seen".

As the following sequence of RTDs indicates, Amy also remembers that her therapist did not engage her in clarifying discussions about her tasks as a patient or the rationale guiding his choice of techniques.

> I, um, when he was waiting for me to do something I felt, um, I felt uncomfortable and, I don't know I never, I just never really knew quite how to start. Um, you know I would try to, I would certainly try to plan it, even beforehand I would go over my, what was going on in my life and try to figure out what I was gonna talk about in therapy that day, what was, you know what my priorities were but I *never* mastered the art of beginning and I felt like I always wanted questions to lead me into the discussion, rather than just me talking. We never discussed his tactics.

A theme that seems to link the RTDs that focus on her therapist is that much of what disappointed Amy about him was the particular cast of his conversational "style" (Geller, 2005). She left therapy feeling that her therapist had been insufficiently responsive to her need for a therapist whose style was more directive, verbally self-revealing, and nonverbally expressive of feelings and attitudes when listening. Research indicates that Amy's feelings that her therapist was insufficiently self-disclosing or active in structuring or guiding the therapeutic dialogue are not idiosyncratic (Farber, 2003). Moreover, her profile has encouraged us to believe that RTD data sets can be used to build upon Kantrowitz's (1986) finding that the "match" between a patient's unique communicative requirements and a therapist's style of participating in the therapeutic dialogue can exert a powerful influence on the outcome of therapy. Particularly striking is Amy's claim: "We never discussed our relationship." Her protocol does not contain any RTDs in which her therapist told her of his awareness of signs that she felt awkward and distant with him. Nor are there any RTDs in Amy's profile that indicated that she and her therapist explored why she harboured unvoiced wishes for and fears of closeness with her therapist.

Because of these accumulating burdens, Amy had been thinking about leaving therapy for several months when the following interactions took place during what she called the "last session":

> I was discussing some of the certainties, uncertainties I was having with getting engaged when he said to me something to the effect of, you know, you recall that I, um, told you you shouldn't do, do anything rash or make any hasty decisions without coming in and talking to me about it. I felt like he was scolding me for getting engaged, when he obviously felt I wasn't ready. So you know I asked him, I said, "Are you scolding me?" and he said, "Well, no, I'm not scolding you", and he got sort of, um, passive aggressive with me a little bit. If I remember correctly, I wanted to get into an argument with him. I wanted to fight with him, and, um, it just you know, didn't happen.

According to Amy, there was something about these events that "pushed me over the edge to switch therapists". In the next several weeks, she went on a business trip during which she was "supposed to call him every week". She did not. Instead, they exchanged "telephone messages". During the final telephone call made by Amy from a hotel room in another city, she said she "ended the relationship by telling him I was referred to another therapist". In the final moments of the STR she said of this decision: "I betrayed him by never returning to therapy with him".

In sum, Amy's RTDs indicate that, for her, consistently experiencing safety, comfort, and acceptance with the therapist was more a possibility to be imagined than a normative aspect of their relationship. Consequently, Amy has very few memories of gratifying involvements with her therapist to call upon when she calculates the value of what was accomplished during her course of therapy at the ICC. In tandem, she sees herself as bearing most of the responsibility for the failures of therapy, but not for its successes (e.g., "I can't think of a special time, but um, I felt that as the therapy went on, it became more and more a distance issue, and um, and I, but I felt that was more on my part than his"). It seems that Amy's guilt about how she ended therapy further detracted from her capacity to take pleasure and pride in what she did accomplish with her therapist.

The question arises: did Amy devalue the gains she derived from therapy when taking the Effectiveness Questionnaire which would explain her numerical ratings in line with her overriding sense that the therapy relationship was uncomfortable, frustrating, and disappointing? Amy's profile suggests that a therapy can prove successful from the perspective of eliminating specific symptoms, yet still be experienced as a failure if a patient leaves therapy with long-standing and largely unspoken dissatisfactions with his/her performance as a patient and with the therapist's style of participating in the therapeutic dialogue. Is it possible that the need to reduce cognitive dissonance can lead patients to underestimate as well as overestimate the benefits of therapy? Insofar as this is true, it challenges us to develop methodologies, like the RTDCS, that offer the possibility of disentangling patients' memory-based judgments about the benefits they derived from *therapy* and their memories of the painful and pleasurable aspects of the therapeutic *relationship*.

Conclusion

What we hope the stories of Jim's and Amy's therapies have conveyed is that information from the RTDCS provides insight into patients' judgments about the effectiveness of a particular therapy. For Amy and Jim, the ineffective and unsatisfying and the effective and satisfying aspects of their experiences in therapy aggregated in very different combinations.

By measuring directly and indirectly, what *was* and what *was not* accomplished during a course of therapy, RTDCS data sets can be used to conduct studies in which therapy outcomes are evaluated in terms of "configurations of change" (Blatt, 1998) rather than merely in terms of ratings of the extent of therapeutic change. Hopefully, our analyses of Jim's and Amy's profiles have demonstrated that the RTDCS can also be used to conduct systematic investigations of the psychological processes that contribute to the success or failure of therapy and the maintenance of therapeutic gains following termination.

It has been said that the final step in every scientific investigation is further investigation. Accordingly, we conclude with a list of the research questions that are guiding our ongoing research project:

- Which aspects of a patient's representations of therapy are most readily retained and re-experienced?
- How do remembrances of one's experiences in therapy connect with one's life-story schemas and identity?
- Do type and pre-treatment levels of psychological disturbance contribute to the manner in which representations of the therapeutic dialogue influence the processes within therapies that mediate patient-perceived satisfaction and outcome?
- Do patients' RTD profiles vary with varying post-termination durations?
- Do former patients revise their opinions about what was useful, helpful, and harmful in the months and years after termination?
- Is there a relationship between patients' representations of experiences in therapy and the subsequent capacity to build upon what was accomplished during the course of therapy?
- Is the manner in which patients make meaning out of their experiences with their therapists, as revealed by their RTD profiles, correlated with their scores on measures that are specifically designed to assess the capacity to reflect on internal experiences?
- Does the manner in which the therapeutic relationship is brought to a close influence the fate of the representations of therapy-with-the-therapist that were constructed during the course of therapy?

The empirical investigation of such questions will deepen our understanding of the processes that influence the degree to which the beneficial effects of therapy endure following the cessation of formal meetings.

Endnote

i. We are beginning to explore the possibility of using statistical techniques to form empirically derived constellations of RTD variables. For example, Green's (2007) factor analyses suggest that composite images of the therapist's gaze, postures, and gestures that coalesce with unvoiced negative feelings towards the therapist in the patient may be a particularly salient constellation.

CHAPTER FOUR

Representations of the therapeutic dialogue and the post-termination phase of psychotherapy

Jesse D. Geller and Norbert Freedman

The hope and expectation that the ending of an effective therapy will be a prologue to further growth and development occupies a central role in psychoanalytic theorizing. The primary aim of this chapter is to present preliminary findings of an empirically-grounded perspective on the hypothesis that patients *will* continue to build upon what they accomplished during the course of therapy after termination if they rely on enduring and benignly influential representations of the therapeutic dialogue to serve adaptive functions.

Some of the questions we have been thinking about are:

- How do memories of a relationship with a former therapist exert their influence on a person's current functioning?
- How do former patients continue to build upon what they accomplished during therapy after termination?
- What roles do the experiences of separation and loss play in shaping a patient's post-termination involvements with representations of the therapeutic dialogue that were constructed during the course of therapy?

- To what extent do former patients continue to grapple with the persistence of unresolved transference reactions evoked during therapy at varying intervals after termination?
- Did the ending of therapy usher in a period of mourning?
- Does continued use of therapist introjects for reparative purposes after termination postpone or interfere with the gradual relinquishment of emotional ties to the therapeutic relationship?
- Is there a period of time following the last session that should be conceptualized as an integral aspect of a patient's total therapeutic experience?

We hope to demonstrate how the STR-RTDCS methodology might be used to identify whether a former patient is using representations of the therapeutic dialogue to identify with the therapist's approach, to promote self-acceptance and self-understanding, to preserve an image of the therapist as a "sustaining introject" (Tessman, 2003), to grapple with the persistence of unresolved transference reactions, and to say goodbye or not say goodbye to the therapist.

In the pages that follow, we will take another look at Jim's RTD profile to determine to what extent this is true for him. We are guided by the hypothesis that as long as Jim remains emotionally involved with, attached to, or dependent upon representations of the therapeutic dialogue to serve these psychological functions he has not strictly speaking "terminated" therapy. Thus, the period of time after termination during which the representational legacies of effective and ineffective therapies continue to exert a regulatory influence on patients' lives might be accorded a status equal in importance to the beginning, middle, and termination phases of therapy. Following Rangell (1966), we shall refer to this hypothesized period of time as "the post-termination phase of therapy".

Representations of the therapeutic dialogue

One of the longest held hypotheses in psychoanalytic literature is that the beneficial effects of therapy persist after termination in the form of a newly acquired or strengthened capacity to reflect independently upon one's conflictual dealings with matters of survival, safety, pleasure, and goodness. The hypothesis that patients continue to build upon what they accomplished during therapy after termination was first expressed by Freud (1937) when he wrote that following a successful analysis, "the processes of ego-transformation will go on of their own accord and that [the former patient] will bring new insight to bear upon all subsequent experience" (p. 402).

In our view there are two complementary ways in which access to representations of what one perceived and admired about a therapist's approach to promoting self-understanding can support a patient's effort to continue to engage in insight-producing self-reflection after termination. In one way self-analytic mental activities can take the form of imaginary conversations with representations of the therapist's "felt presence". Few psychoanalysts (e.g., Kantrowitz et al., 1990; Schlesinger et al., 1974) have made systematic investigations into whether and how patients symbolically recreate the felt experience of participating in a collaborative and intimate dialogue with their former therapists in order to verbally think about the meanings and consequences of their motives and actions.

A second possibility is that patients' representations of a therapist's so-called "analyzing functions" can serve as the raw materials for the identificatory phase of the processes of internalization. Successive generations of psychoanalysts have given attention to the hypothesis that identificatory processes modify "how" patients engage in self-analytic activities so that they increasingly resemble the style in which the therapist sought to promote their self-acceptance and self-understanding. According to this perspective, identificatory processes give rise to "psychic structures" that de-personify and perform the regulatory functions served by representations of the self in relation to others, some of which were acquired through the processes of introjection. Giovacchini (1975) and Dorpat (1974) have written that until analyst introject fantasies are finally amalgamated as an aspect of the ego's executive system, the transformations involved in the internalization process have not been brought to an optimal conclusion. In other words, they share the view that analyst introjects are a way-station en route to internalizing the patient-analyst relationship. Some concern has been expressed, however, that former patients were being "dependent" or had not "completed" their analyses if they continued to evoke analyst introjects as an aid to self-reflection once they had benefited from constructive identifications with their analyst's approach to promoting self-understanding (e.g., Martinez & Hoppe, 1998).

Let us next turn our attention to Jim's RTD profile to examine these alternative perspectives on self-analysis.

Jim's uses of RTDs for self-analysis

Jim left therapy confident that he had acquired the "tools" required to gain non-judgmental awareness and understanding of his desires and conflicts with the important people in his life. He characterized his new approach to self-reflection as a "skill that I've taken away with me, that I can do all by myself". Many of his RTDs gratefully acknowledged that he would not have acquired this skill if his therapist had not encouraged him, in a variety of ways, to transform "how" he went about gaining intimate knowledge of his own personal experiences. As Jim sees it, he would never have developed the habit of paying serious attention to his feelings if it were not for his therapist's questions (e.g., "He repeatedly asked me how I felt: that's not something I would take seriously for myself, I would be thinking about the events, not how I felt"). He also credits many of the gains he derived from therapy to remembrances of communicative exchanges with his therapist that gradually transformed the manner in which he "looked inward". As briefly noted in Chapter Three, Jim reported:

> He helped me to realize I was the kind of person who has to rethink things in order to get to what I'm really thinking. That is, I often have to take a second look, in order to find out what my real response was because my first response was usually to cover up what I was feeling. Over and over again, my therapist encouraged me to "slow down" and to tell and retell my memories …. He would say, "Stop, what do you mean when you say…?"

RTDs such as these suggest that by recreating his therapist's approach to promoting self-understanding, Jim strengthened his own capacity to continue to engage in adaptation-enhancing self-analytic activities after termination.

Further inquiry would have been required to ascertain to what extent Jim's mode of self-analysis is dependent on a repetition of the dialogue with his therapist or has become part of the repertoire of the ego functioning, that is, internalized.

RTDs as sources of self-soothing

Although Jim has the representational capacities required to do so, there is no RTD evidence that he has entered into imaginary conversations with the felt presence of his therapist with the aim of acquiring further insights since terminating. However, as the sequence of nonverbal RTDs cited in Chapter Three indicated, Jim has taken comfort since terminating in being able to voluntarily recall consciously controllable images of his therapist's gaze and facial expressions as a source of emotional support and guidance. In other words, during the course of therapy Jim acquired the capacity to recreate, in the realm of somatic sensations, the sense of what it felt like being with his therapist when he saw how his therapist remained "calm", "open", "warm", "accepting", and "very attentive" as he spoke about his problems. This finding underscores how important seeing and being seen may be to the activation of the processes of introjection.

On the basis of their interviews with former analysands, Dorpat (1974), Giovacchini (1975), Kantrowitz et al. (1990), Pfeffer (1993), and Schlesinger and Robbins (1974) have similarly identified a group of patients who continue to rely on analyst introjective fantasies for the purposes of self-soothing long after termination. In the vocabulary of cognitive psychology, these patients transformed episodic and semantic memories into procedural memories that remind them of "how one does things" without being entirely aware that they are doing so (Tulving, 2002).

Jim gave no indication that he was encouraged or instructed by the therapist to summon visual images of his presence, when needed, to regulate his emotional experiences, both painful and pleasurable. What motivated Jim to create representations of his therapist's "placid and calm demeanour" and to imbue these representations with the need gratifying functions of a benign introject? One possibility is that Jim was motivated by the threat or actual loss of access to gratifying involvements while in the therapist's concrete presence while an alternative explanation might be influenced by Loewald's (1988a) notion of identificatory love. Others who emphasize the biological underpinnings of imitative learning (Bandura, 1977) and the discovery of the psychological functions of mirror neurons (Olds, 2006) have posited that the creation and use of benign introjects may also be a spontaneous and natural outgrowth of the experiential learning that takes place, outside focal awareness, while engaging in a mutually satisfying collaborative task with a more competent dialogic partner.

These formulations of the motivational origins of Jim's coping strategy are compatible with our basic operating premise that Jim transformed representations of what was done *for* or *with* him by the therapist into "psychological change tools" that enabled him to take responsibility for further healing into his own hands after termination.

According to our hybrid theoretical perspective, after termination a patient can only make constructive use of therapist introjects or benefit from the processes of identification if they can retrieve and make use of representations of the therapist's qualities and the functions he/she served in one's life.

Representations of the therapeutic dialogue and the work of mourning

For many decades, the following questions have been an important focus of psychoanalytic theorizing about patients' emotional reactions to ending satisfying therapeutic relationships:

- During the course of therapy did the patient transform what began as an instrumental relationship with the therapist into one in which the therapist came to be valued as a unique, inherently valuable, and irreplaceable person with a life of his/her own?
- What do patients feel they have lost when a therapy ends and what meanings do they ascribe to these feelings?
- Are grieving and mourning the final loss of the therapist essential preconditions for the completion of a deeply satisfying analysis?
- Is the absence of sadness and sorrow about ending an analysis a reliable sign that nothing of value was accomplished during the analysis?

Answers to these questions have emphasized the hypothesis that a psychoanalysis is not entirely over until a patient "mourns" the final loss of the analyst. Moreover, formulations of the concept of mourning have tended to analogize patients' reactions to the termination of a productive psychoanalysis to the psychological processes that are operative when a person gradually relinquishes their emotional ties to a person who has died or to the wishes for gratification from a love relationship that has ended.

A related assumption has been that achieving full "independence" from one's analyst following termination required the capacity to grieve for the absence of the physical presence of the analyst in one's life and a gradual relinquishment of dependence upon and attachment to the analyst's "inner presence". Schafer (1968) stated that continued use of memories of the therapist in the therapy to serve ego and superego functions after termination perpetuates "fantasized needful togetherness" and forestalls the work of mourning and the activation of the processes of identification.

Under ideal circumstances the decision to end a therapy is well planned, mutually agreed upon, and based on the fullest possible realization of the patient's hoped-for goals. But clinical reality is such that a large percentage of patients, like Jim, end therapies they know are "incomplete" at a time when many other endings and new beginnings are taking place in their lives.

There have been no systematic investigations of how ending a therapeutic process before it has been completed influences what Freud (1917a) called "the work of mourning" (p. 245). If Jim's responses are in any way representative, they suggest that regrets about "unfinished business" or "missed opportunities" and fantasies of recouping the therapist's need-fulfilling functions will play an important role in the post-termination mourning reactions of patients.

There were no RTDs in Jim's transcript that explicitly acknowledged that the ending of therapy ushered in painful states of grief. He did not speak about feeling sad about the loss of the therapist, or of missing him, per se. Using different methodologies with different types of samples, Craige (2002), Lord, Ritvo and Solnit (1978), and Tessman (2003) have found that mourning reactions can range from intractable to non-existent or non-discernible. Moreover, Craige's (2002) and Tessman's (2003) interviews with patients who were themselves analysts indicated that the absence of grief reactions was not an indication that nothing of value had been achieved during the analysis.

The few Longed for RTDs that Jim produced all dealt with a form of mourning that is rarely mentioned in the literature, namely a mixture of regret and nostalgia. Regret is mourning an account of lost opportunities that cannot be recouped, and the longing that one could have taken advantage of those opportunities.

As Jim put it, he is "regretful" because he left therapy before "mastering and conquering my fear of intimacy with men". It will be recalled that "incomplete" was the final word he chose to capture the essence of his experience of therapy-with-his-therapist. In other words, Jim's regrets are associated with unfulfilled ambitions, rather than with remorse and self-reproach about some wrong-doing or with frustrated wishes that his therapist had been different. Allusions to yearnings for a reunion with the former therapist made an early appearance in Jim's STR interview. He interpreted the fact that part of the route he chose to get to the interview took him through the neighbourhood where his therapist's office was located, as a sign that "half of me wants to be in therapy again, and half of me doesn't". As previously noted, he concluded the first part of the STR by acknowledging that he may return to therapy because he "doesn't understand" nor can he quiet an "obsessive anxiety" in which he ruminates about "doing something sexual to harm my son". Jim took these difficulties as further evidence that he had "discontinued" rather than terminated therapy. We take all of the above as evidence that Jim is still very much in the throes of the post-termination phase of therapy.

It seems that Jim's ambivalently held reunion wishes and fantasies are being fuelled by the recognition that he is unable to perform for himself the functions that his therapist previously performed for him and with him. His aside during the interview, "I looked forward to the interview as if it were another session," may be seen as a vivid example of what has come to be known as the "Pfeffer phenomenon".

In 1963 Pfeffer recognized that follow-up interviews of former analysands by researchers tended to recapitulate the essence of the interpersonal dynamics of their analytic experience, not with mechanical redundancy, but by evoking the unfinished business of the earlier analytic encounter. Green (2007) has demonstrated the feasibility of identifying whether there are similarities in the ways in which the interviewer conducted the STR with different patients and the relationship scenarios that organized patients' most prevalent and emotionally salient RTDs.

Concurrently, we are beginning to investigate how the representations of the therapeutic dialogue that are newly created during the course of therapy link up with the pre-existing representations of relationships that were acquired during formative interactions with caretakers and authority figures. Mayman's (1968) system is used to classify the early memories collected during the STR and the questionnaires administered at the time of the STR (e.g., the Calgary Attachment Scale). Previous findings (Bender, Farber, Sanislow, Dyck, Geller & Skodol, 2003) based on correlations between scores on the Therapist Representation Inventory and the Calgary Attachment Questionnaire support the hypothesis that the "informal working models" of securely and insecurely attached adults can create biases in the ways in which their experiences in therapy are constructed and retained in long-term memory.

We assume that the fate of representations that are newly created during therapy depends on whether they primarily serve as targets for the residual displacement of attitudes and feelings towards representations of internalized figures from the past or serve as catalysts for the transformation of these representations. The persistence of Inhibited and Longed for RTDs in the profiles of patients whose therapies were highly effective suggest that we will find that RTDs that evoke transference reactions are rarely, if ever, fully resolved, in the sense of disappearing, or made irrelevant during the course of extended and even highly beneficial therapies. This is supported by the results of the few follow-up studies that have tracked variations in the persistence of transference reactions following the completion of psychoanalytic therapies (Schlesinger et al., 1974; Oremland, Blacker & Norman, 1975; Tessman, 2003).

Data from a long-term follow-up study (Buckley, Karasu & Charles, 1981) suggest that one must allow for the possibility that a patient may still be working through transference issues five to ten years after termination. In a similar vein, Geller and Farber (1993) unexpectedly found that the frequency with which former patients evoked representations of their therapists tended to increase as a function of the number of years since termination.

With these considerations in mind let us weave in one final example of the ways in which Jim remains emotionally attached to and actively involved with representations-of-therapy-with-his-therapist. As noted in Chapter Three, Jim equated resisting the temptation to see a movie his therapist encouraged him to see to "wanting to save a dessert, I'm not quite ready to give myself that pleasure". In other words, by postponing the time when he will see the movie his therapist recommended to him, Jim keeps their relationship a part of his "living past".

Concluding comments

Many decades of research have led to the widely held conviction that the patient-therapist relationship plays an essential role in the processes that lead to the success or failure of psychotherapy (Lambert & Ogles, 2004). Along the way it was also concluded that the verbatim transcripts of actual in-session interactions can be used to reliably identify the recurrent patterns that organize patients' relationships with their therapists (e.g., Benjamin, 1974; Dahl & Teller, 1994; Luborsky, Popp, Luborsky & Mark, 1994).

What we hope this chapter has conveyed is that the RTDCS makes it possible to extract from the verbatim transcripts of structured interviews (STR) reliable, highly individualized, and quantifiable information about the ways in which patients characteristically interact with representations of their therapists after termination. Our primary aim has been to present preliminary findings as a means of demonstrating the flexibility and heuristic potential of the STR-RTDCS methodology. Of course we recognize that the number, nature, and sequencing of the RTDs obtained in any sample would be influenced by complex sources of variation inherent in the particular patients and their therapists, and that they would bear the imprint of the manner in which the interviewer and interviewee co-created what was and was not said. We further recognize that former patients' views of their experiences in therapy and their retrospective sense of what they accomplished in therapy will be, to varying extents, affected by the mindset of the present, and subject to change over large spans of time.

Despite these limitations, we believe that the analyses of RTD profiles that have been performed so far indicate that our investigatory tools can generate the kinds of empirical evidence useful to confirm or disconfirm hypotheses that occupy a central role in psychoanalytic theorizing about the ways in which patients' representations of their experiences in therapy link up with the processes whereby psychotherapy becomes and remains an adaptive resource in patients' lives after termination.

To date our emphasis has been on investigating the ways in which RTDs are retained in long term memory after the termination of effective therapies. We have yet to systematically examine the characteristics and changes that might take place in patients' representations of the therapeutic dialogue after the termination of a therapy that was experienced as ineffective or harmful (see the profiles of patients in table 3).

It has been said that the final step in every scientific investigation is further investigation. Accordingly, we conclude with a partial list of questions about patients' representations of the therapeutic dialogue and we invite readers and colleagues to join us in the search for answers.

Questions for future research

1. Do former patients revise their opinions about what was useful, helpful, and harmful in the months and years after termination?
2. Does the manner in which the therapeutic relationship is terminated influence the fate of the representations of therapy-with-the-therapist that were constructed during the course of therapy?
3. Are there connections between type and pre-treatment levels of severity of psychological disturbance and the manner in which individuals retain and re-experience representations of the therapeutic dialogue after termination?
4. How do remembrances of one's experience in therapy connect with one's overarching life story schemas and narrative identity?
5. What is the relationship between length of therapy, time since termination, and the likelihood that a former patient will reactivate representations of the therapeutic relationship for adaptive purposes?

6. What specific needs, circumstances, and personality dispositions motivate former patients to remain actively involved with representations of their therapists after termination?
7. How does the process of mourning retrospectively transform the qualities and functions of the representations of the therapeutic relationship that were constructed and stored in long-term memory during the course of therapy?
8. Does continued use of therapist introjects for reparative purposes postpone or interfere with gradual relinquishment of emotional ties to the therapeutic relationship?
9. Can retrospective reconstruction of the therapeutic dialogue illuminate the extent to which patients mourn the loss of their therapists as unique persons, or merely sense a loss of the psychological functions that the therapist served on their behalf?
10. Are there patients who may only be able to make "good use" of what their therapist had to offer when they remember sequences of emotionally charged interactions that were originally ignored or rejected?

CHAPTER FIVE

Reminiscing and recollecting

Jamieson Webster and Norbert Freedman

Another look at the Effectiveness Questionnaire and the post-termination interview

Let us revisit the Effectiveness Study where we encountered ten patients who elected to speak to Dr V, an analyst, about their earlier experience in treatment. The group had been divided in half with respect to their scores on the Effectiveness Questionnaire: five patients experienced the treatment as satisfactory and the other half reported a sense of dissatisfaction. Once more, we ask the question: what is meant by effective treatment?

In further studies of these patients and their recall narratives with Dr V, the division five and five holds over a number of telling categories with satisfaction correlating with measures of reflective functioning (Fonagy, 1995), secure attachment (Roy, 2007), absence of annihilation anxiety (Hurvich, 2002), and high referential activity, as measured by the referential process (Bucci & Maskit, 2007). One might conclude that satisfaction with therapy is a good quantitative indicator of the success of a treatment with all the concomitant benefits: more secure attachment to the therapist, decrease in anxiety, a widening of one's self-reflective capacities, and so on and so forth.

While as therapists we would be gratified to find such affirmation, let us pause for a moment and consider the difficulties of self-report and the dangers of taking global measures at face value. Furthermore, we would like to consider the consequences of the repetition compulsion, particularly when it comes to a question of understanding the laborious nature of structural change including the intricacy of measuring such an elusive aspect of the psyche.

In this chapter we will take a slightly different avenue from what you have read so far, going back to these ten patients' intake interviews to get a sense of them before treatment. If the five patients who report dissatisfaction also show a coherent host of other psychic traits like attachment difficulties and concreteness, and the five patients who report satisfaction tend to have high measures of reflective functioning, is it possible that they were concrete or reflective when they came to treatment? If so, has anything really changed? With a sense of this kind of continuity, a sense of what the patients bring with them to treatment, we might then have a clue as to how to look further into the idea of change.

As this is a study of therapy remembered and the process of remembering is at the heart of psychoanalytic studies of the mind, we decided to use memory as a means of assessing the patients before and after treatment. By widening the database to include the intake interview reports prior to treatment, and creating a method to convert these highly variable texts into a researchable form, we had a window to the manner in which these patients reconstructed the significant relationships of their past and to the interviewer.

Preliminary findings in the reading of the intake interviews suggest that it is possible to obtain a sense of a patient's memory structure. There were those patients who presented vague and pat images of their past and present lives. They seemed to be disconnected from events of the past, from their affect, from people in their lives, and also from the interviewer. Sometimes there was confusion. They spoke in global and over-generalized terms lacking specificity, and affect tended to be expressed in action more than in words. In contrast, there were those patients who offered detailed reports of early happenings, often defensively so, but at the same time added colour and context. There was a connectedness to the past, present, and interviewer, along with a specificity of memory and affective detail.

We called the first group of patients "prone to reminiscing" and the second group "prone to recollecting", a distinction introduced by Breuer and Freud (1895) in their *Studies of Hysteria*.

For Freud, hallucinatory wish fulfilment links satisfaction with memory and the first moment of Symbolization. Thus, for our purposes, we re-evoke these historical categories rather than the more recent contemporary cognitive concepts such as procedural and epistemic aspects of memory. What we found was that despite the variability of the intake interview, the method allowed us to distinguish five recollecting patients and five reminiscing patients and indeed these were the same satisfied and dissatisfied patients whom you have heard about. Reminiscing patients did not derive satisfaction from treatment, while recollecting patients did. *It would appear that satisfaction with the experience of therapy, as reported by the patient, was foreshadowed by the memory of satisfaction in significant relationships in the patient's biographical past*. While this may seem dismaying, we perhaps should not be surprised.

Now let us turn to the STR, the reconstruction of therapy after termination with Dr V. We start with the initial narrative, for in composing this narrative the patient once more was faced with a choice of imbuing meaning or not. For example, in the case of Amy, she simply stated, "I hate conversations" and proceeded to talk about a book of plays she was reading. In Jim's, he spoke of the ways his therapist helped him, including his issues with homosexuality, connecting this to the birth of his new baby boy. In the first instance the image of the therapist was hardly allowed existence. In the second, it was evocative and brought into the context of his present life.

These modes of linking allude to what we have called the process of Symbolization—a process that is intimately connected with memorial activity. In order to capture this phenomenon more systematically, our ten patient-subjects' initial narratives were scored on the scales of *Desymbolization* and *Discursive Symbolization* (for further elaboration see Chapter Seven and Postcript). It is the particular subsections of these scales that hold special interest.

To start, Desymbolization is a motivated act of destroying Symbolization, meaning making, and linking. It is not only a gap, but a gulf, born of psychic pain, a feeling of meaninglessness, confusion, and often the divisive aspects of sadism. It is an attempt to evacuate or eject meaning. The components of the *Desymbolization scale* are psychic equivalence, affect foreclosure, and disavowal. The two groups of patients differed sharply on the Desymbolization scale as a whole. The overall mean frequency for Desymbolization units for the low EQ patients was 11.2; for the high EQ patients, 3.2 ($p = 0.001$). All the low EQ patients had at least two or more units scored as "Psychic Equivalence"—concreteness or a flattening of meaning—whereas there were none for the high EQ patients. "Affect foreclosure" (which included a tendency towards vague event reporting as well as brief affect explosions) also was a quality more prevalent among the low EQ patients.

However, the two groups of patients did not differ on the incidence of disavowal. In fact, the most pronounced incidence of disavowal was noted among two of the recollecting patients. This last observation suggests an important corrective. While the thrust of findings points to the prevalence of Desymbolization among low EQ patients, it is the high EQ patients who may well reveal on closer inspection their own, more concealed, version of closing off meaning.

When we turned to our Discursive Symbolization scale, the focus was on Symbolization as manifest in spoken discourse as a space creating activity—linking to important others, times past, present or future, and through imagination and fantasy. What we found in general was that the high EQ patients revealed a higher level of Discursive Symbolization (total mean difference 6.28 as compared with 5.00, $p = 0.002$). This applied notably to the patients' ability to create temporal space in their representation of their recalled relationship to their therapists, that is, they created a distance and differentiation between past, present, and future. The particularity of this finding, along with the finding concerning disavowal, might make us wonder whether temporal space as an aspect of Symbolization serves a defensive function. Additionally, the high EQ patients, like the low EQ patients, were often very low in their scores on Symbolization in the dimension of fantasy space.

Keeping in mind that the high and low EQ patients also differed in the way their autobiographical past was reconstructed prior to treatment, now we observed that the meaning with which they endowed their terminated treatments, their Symbolization of that encounter, was also related to the expression of satisfaction with therapy. In other words, there appears to be a relatively constant memory structure or ego propensity that cuts across the treatment experience.

The fact remains that for the patients under study, even four years after intake and up to two years after termination, the same memory organization was retained. Clinically, the reminiscing patients seem to be the challenging and difficult patients. As already noted, they often do not derive satisfaction from therapy. And yet, the patients who reported satisfaction also showed a form of hidden disavowal. It is at this point that our clinical reformulation begins. It leads us beyond the effectiveness concept so that this study does not portray simply or merely a measure of constancy. We will search the post-termination interview for moments of contradiction, surprise, reversal, as it takes place in the gaps, and underneath the seeming clarity of these quantitative findings.

In Pfeffer's 1959 study, 15 patients showed that after termination within a recall situation with another analyst, the transference neurosis tends to be repeated. For any of these studies we must ask the thorny question: are the memories evoked in the recall study but an echo of life-long repetition or, alternatively, can we glean qualities of mind created by the therapeutic experience? Pfeffer opened the way for a second meaning of the effectiveness of treatment. The memory re-evoked is influenced not only by the time that has elapsed since the end of treatment, but, more importantly, by the dynamics of confronting the past now within a new transference–countertransference context.

On one side there is the comparison between the moment before (intake) exerting its impact upon the moment after (both the quantitative findings and the recall situation) separated by a linear notion of time and space. Here, for sure, we can find the stubborn persistence of mental structures. On the other side, working outside a linear model, we can observe the workings of time and space *in statu nascendi*. The hope is that we will find the transformation of those structures therein. By scrutinizing the recall process as it is told, step by step, we affirm a vision of internalization as a thrust towards ownership of a once forgotten/disconnected or remembered past. Thus, we need to look beyond repetition, towards the repetition of the repetition transformed.

Memory, structure, and process: an evolution of concepts

Our first conclusions represented a picture of the difficult patient and their failed treatment, as against that of the good patient and their successful and satisfactory treatment. Beginning with patients at the time of the intake interview, we could say the good patients get better and the bad patients do not. Moving away from this good/bad paradigm and the crude formulation that both or neither groups were successes or failures, we hope to develop a more illuminating picture.

As we surveyed the history of ideas on memory we saw two similar competing trends: in one there are two types of memory—one good and one not-so-good—in the other a more complex picture develops of two interlocking processes of remembering that involved a crucial relationship to Symbolization and the theory of unconscious desire.

Thousands of years before the advent of psychoanalysis in one of Plato's dialogues (1987), the *Theaetetus*, two models of memory in the form of wax tablets containing the imprints of past events are described. The object of the Platonic dialogue is epistemological—how do we know what we know? At the point where the wax tablets come in, the question of whether true perception is synonymous with knowledge is at issue. The first wax tablet is described as clean and the marks are of sufficient depth, plentiful and smooth. It has good memories and their imprints last a long time because their marks are clear and well-spaced; one would not mismatch perceptions and thoughts, and thus their knowledge would be sound. In the second tablet, there are impurities in the wax, and "it is unkempt and rough, a gritty sort of thing, contaminated and clogged" (p. 105). As the impressions are unclear, they are liable to make false connections; perceptions would be confused with thoughts and thoughts with perceptions: "[T]hese people invariably miss-see, miss-hear, and miss-think" (ibid.).

From this, one might suppose that true perception is knowledge. However, as is the Socratic way, this conclusion is contested. How do you know that a perception is a true perception as opposed to a false one? If knowledge is going to be linked to perception, one would have to know it is true in advance, which is tautological, that is, it is true because I know it is true. The dialogue breaks off in this aporia—obviously knowledge cannot be merely justification or opinion.

In a later dialogue, the *Meno* (2005), a similar question is asked: how can one come to know something as true, since one does not know it to begin with and therefore does not even know what to look for? This was called Meno's paradox. Once again memory is turned to and the famous theory of anamnesis is developed by Socrates wherein all knowledge must be a form of recollection since knowledge as acquisition has proved illogical. Socrates states that when we are born the eternal truths of the soul are forgotten and must be stirred up, roused by questions, reborn through dialogue, with the image of Socrates as a midwife. Knowledge, in this Platonic sense, is always a return, a repetition of something already known but forgotten, and the mind and its logical capabilities need only be followed truly. For Socrates, the two visions of knowledge are incompatible—it is the difference between truth as *doxa* or opinion, and truth as linked to the eternal forms, closer to what the Greeks would have called science.

Why have we gone back to such obscure and divergent beginnings? One reason is that it is remarkable to see the recapitulation of arguments that haunt psychoanalysis and mirror our dilemma. There was, even then, the impulse towards the dichotomy: good memory, good perceptions, and bad memory, bad perceptions. This system is overturned in making use of the inevitable gap in knowledge, the presence of false beliefs and false connections need only be unravelled in the direction of their truth. That this places forgetting at the core of being, and remembering as a kind of rebirth, is indeed close to the original psychoanalytic vision.

With respect to Freud's discovery of the unconscious, it is his clinical and logical acumen that demonstrates that the hysteric's reminiscences, the symbolic connections embedded in the symptom, are the key to the analytic structure. Despite the hysteric's "cognitive" difficulties, fugue states, and strange bodily symptoms, these first psychoanalytic patients were described by Freud (1905) as intelligent, incisive, witty, and determined. Psychoanalysis was predicated on this paradox—motivated remembering and forgetting.

After further investigation into other neurotic structures, Freud would conclude that for all of the "recollecting" abilities of obsessional patients, there the connections have been severed making the analysis quite difficult, more difficult in fact than with hysteria. They remember, but take no notice of what they remember. Freud would often note that it is to the hysterical core of the obsessional's symptomatic picture, the oldest portion reaching down into the earliest memories and affect laden symbolic connections, that one must aim (e.g., 1896), without being seduced by the "more conscious", "more recollecting" attitude presented.

If we now turn to contemporary developments, we see this same structure repeated in ego-psychology where despite clinical insight there is the dichotomous emphasis on a strong vs. a weak ego (e.g., Hartmann, 1956). Lewy and Rapaport (1944), for example, privilege representational memory over enactive memory despite the fact that enactive memory would be critical to any successful psychoanalysis and is part and parcel of the transferential experience. These two types of memory are often categorized as "passive-bad-id" dominated and "active-good-ego" dominated. This kind of categorization has often led to difficulties.

Today, once again one finds the expression of this division in contemporary psychology and cognitive theories. Fonagy's (1995) notion of mentalization at times puts emphasis on a hyper-reflective stance, where distinctions between self and other, past, present, and future are clearly represented, and the body does not make its appearance "too much".

For our purposes, in the initial study of memory, the term Symbolization proved useful in avoiding this dichotomous trap. Laplanche (1999), in his *Essays on Otherness*, notes that there are too many aporias in psychoanalysis between one thing and another (e.g., overdetermination and a vision of freedom; an emphasis on memory as factual reality, and traumatic vs. the emphasis being placed on fantasy, imagination, and desire; and, finally, the therapeutic effects divided between taking place as a reconstruction of the pathogenic past vs. a construction of something new). He says he would like to offer a way out.

He does so first by invoking the notion of the memory trace, in which both Plato and Freud speak about using the image of the imprint left on a wax tablet. He says in a psychoanalysis we re-encounter but a *kernel* of historical truth. The phenomenon of reminiscing viewed from the vantage point of trace theory signifies a kind of memory—"a memory cut off from its origins and from its access routes, isolated and fixed, it is reduced to a trace. It is a trace which is not on that account necessarily *more false*, but which contains a 'kernel of truth' that is more essential than the trivial conscious memory" (ibid., p. 154). It is this trace which forms the motivational base for what we call nodal transformation—the place where connections converge and which, in the therapeutic setting, functions as a provocateur for important openings or reversals in Symbolization. For Laplanche, it is not just new heights, but new depths—the trace acting like a hidden centre of gravity.

What we tentatively have then is a new concept of transformation. Nodal transformations allow the patient a measure of symbolized desire not previously embraced. A similar notion can be seen in the Kleinian (1975) idea of transformation where the chaos of the paranoid-schizoid position precedes the promised land of Symbolization in the depressive position. For Winnicott (1971) as well, transitional space and the encounter with paradox and the not-me ushers in potential space and the finding of a new symbol. Finally, in our own empirical work on the transformation cycle, Symbolization is followed by Desymbolization, allowing for a Re-Symbolization that is patently different from that which preceded it. We would now like to put this vision of transformation and the encounter with the memory trace to the test looking more closely at two cases from our ten patients.

The "Kernel of Truth" in the reconstruction of therapy after termination

Let us return to Amy, our low EQ, dissatisfied, reminiscing patient who starts her initial narrative declaring that she has a "different therapist now" and that she "hates conversations". As we know, she fills the last two minutes with a string of banalities—the movie she saw, the book she is reading, the tasks that lie ahead of her for the rest of day. She says nothing about the analyst she knows she is there to speak about except perhaps in total negation, and yet, the last remark she makes, seemingly innocent and logically tied to her annoyance with the wedding planning she has to do after the interview, might be telling. She is dreaming of eloping in Vegas. Yes, her initial narrative overall would be scored quite low on our scales of symbolizing space and quite high for Desymbolization, but what is more interesting than this global assessment is the jump in score she would have gained for her last remark in contrast to all the rest. In its singularity, it constitutes an opening or a break.

We look for these moments out of joint; the places where Symbolization creeps into her overall desymbolizing trend, and acts, as Laplanche called it, like an "agent provocateur" (1999). It is our contention that in these moments, we will discover her prior transference and its transformation. So, while we are not surprised by the five words that Amy chooses to describe her therapy—awkward, unsatisfactory, distant, educational, and doomed—again, she waits till the end to strike an evocative note. Doomed? What made it doomed, as if, in advance, it was already fated?

What we see, beyond her dissatisfaction with the "kind" of therapy she was getting is that there is something about the end of the treatment that is on her mind. She circles around the issue. Yes, there was something amiss in the relationship, but what happened?

Amy struggles with how much she wants to reveal. It often comes across as a litany of complaints. What eventually comes to the fore is that she wanted more and more from her therapist: to know him more personally, why he did what he did, why he asked about her dreams, what he wrote in his notebook after sessions. She started to withhold. She mentions quickly that she thinks she started to become attracted to him. She couldn't talk to him about any of this because she felt judged. This is what made the relationship doomed—because she couldn't get over the fact that there was this "distance". In the last session she wanted a fight, but it didn't happen. She asked if he was scolding her when she said she was getting engaged and he replied that she shouldn't do anything rash (elope). He said he wasn't. She left the session, then the treatment.

As we move further into the interview, Dr V asks about difficult moments in therapy and it is here that a real shift takes place. Interestingly, Dr V becomes uncharacteristically active, a countertransference phenomenon that signals the onset of something new. She begins,

> A: Well, whenever I would get very emotional, I would, um, I would not let myself cry because I didn't want him to see me cry. So I would really fight it. And, uh, that was difficult for me. And anytime when I found I didn't have anything to talk about, um, it was very difficult. I felt like it only worked when I had some sort of interesting experience or some sort of wild story to tell or, you know, something that I was very

angry about or something I felt very passionate about. And those were the good ones, when I, you know, when I went in there and I was feeling some sort of strong emotion. Unless it was something that I didn't want to be seen as, you know, like I'm not afraid to be angry as long as it's a strong angry. And I'm not afraid to be very happy as long as it's an empowered kind of happy. But if it's anything kind of weak, I didn't want him to see that. I didn't want him to see that side of me so I would fight it.

Dr V: Do you have any sense of why, why that was difficult or why you didn't want him to see that?

A: (pause) Because, um [pause] I think it might have forced him to really be there with me and, um, and that's—I know that's the thing I've been complaining about. But, um, it—I guess it was also the thing that I feared maybe. And, uh, also apparently because I—you know, I was attracted to him sometimes and I just didn't want, um, didn't want him to see me like that.

As she is led more and more to this image of what was difficult for her, how she wanted him to see her and how she did not want him to see her, notably not as weak, what emerges is the transference repetition and the transference fantasy. They are to be strong, excited, empowered, even wild, together. Such a feeling perhaps gets her away from her depression, away from that feeling of distance and doom. Re-evoking this fantasy helps her to see her own contradiction, one she clearly does not "understand" in the way one understands calculus, but that she knows, and which is unearthed in this interview—she could have forced him to really be there, she says that is what she wanted, but she backed away from it. She was afraid and she was attracted to him and those two things were somehow linked.

Being able to state her contradictory place in the impasse of the treatment appears to us as remarkable in contrast to her generally desymbolizing narrative. Remember, this is a woman who says she wants coping skills and thinks her problem is a chemical imbalance. How do we understand this contrast? What is important about the repetitive demand she is making towards the object? As we continue to listen, she is led to a scene—it pops into her consciousness, discrete and a seeming nodal point. It would be high on the Symbolization scales because of its vivid dynamic nature, but even more so because it provides a glimpse into her inner life. She says:

> It just made me particularly scared at those times because I really did not know what was going on and why I was being affected the way that I was. And, and, I remember a time, when I was really fighting it and I remember him almost, you know, getting excited. Almost, you know, like he had sat up a little straighter and was almost getting a little more interested in what I was saying. And it, it seemed like he was almost about to laugh because I think that he must have felt like he was so close to getting somewhere with me. And, um [pause] but it didn't, it didn't feel like very exciting territory to me so I held back. And, uh, you know, I didn't give him what I knew that he really wanted from me.

The rest of the interview, like the treatment, breaks off here. There is a great deal of provocative material that comes up here and there, but the STR seems to build up to this moment and trail off.

After this she tells about a dream where her therapist is there as she makes love with her fiancé; she giggles, admitting that this is when she first became aware she was attracted to him. She goes on from there to say she felt the therapist didn't understand the weight of her obsessive ruminations about the death of loved ones, including him. She has not worked out her estrangement with her father; she backed away from him when her brother died. The therapy, she thinks, gave her a better sense of control. She does not feel as pervasively helpless as she did during her first major depression.

She also has two early memories which are remarkable given what we have just read. The first is a scene after her mother has left and she sees herself having a rage-filled tantrum on the floor feeling abandoned. The second is of her locked in a crib looking out of the window at her father pulling into the driveway as he came home from work. She felt excited and proud of herself. Nevertheless, as provocative as these two images are—one of the rage at abandonment and distance and one of unconsummated excitement—along with the rest of the material in the STR, it is provocative precisely in light of the *nodal moment*. That is what that moment does—condenses material around it with a kind of gravitational pull. Unfortunately, we cannot draw any conclusions. It is only a series of pieces that follow on the heels of the transferential puzzle. The treatment was incomplete, that we know, but there at the place where it is articulated, she symbolizes with a sense of interiority and depth connected precisely to the transference.

The caveat that this is a one and half to two year psychotherapy at a frequency of once a week cannot be stressed enough. And yet, one would have to speculate about the kinds of gains this reminiscing and desymbolizing patient made, the inroads on her depression. She gets out of it more or less quickly now, she says, not sure how or why, but *we* know from this reading of the STR that it is directly linked to the therapeutic benefits of crystallizing some kind of unconscious truth in the transference. If she withheld and gained a kind of control over her own and the other's excitement, control through instigating an end in the face of disappointment and mounting tensions, then this seems to have carried into her life. Do we wish she had gone further? Of course! It is almost heart wrenching to read, and, yet, as a repetition, it is not just the stated disappointment but the gains of going to the heart of that disappointment, which are felt and analytically sensed as we go over this reconstruction of her treatment.

Let us now turn to Jim who is, for all intents and purposes, the opposite picture of Amy. Remember he is one of those patients who felt a sense of great satisfaction with his treatment, recollecting and symbolizing in his initial narrative. In contrast to Amy, Jim has a reflective mind; he is someone who thinks about himself. At the same time, because of his almost constant use of negation, his narrative becomes increasingly neutralized.

As the interview progresses what emerges is that the picture of his therapist must be clear, defensively so. One gets a sense that he would like the matter to be closed and as conflicting feelings arise in the STR, the only way he can keep his narrative together is through recourse to idealization. So the situation between Jim and Amy is reversed. She moves from a negativistic desymbolizing stance to one where she owns her own contradiction in her position with respect to her therapist. As she increasingly voices her desire, her symbolic capacities widen. With Jim, his capacities widen through a kind of narrowing—as his contradictory desires come to the fore, he is forced to rely on a primitive idealizing defence in order to keep unwanted thoughts compartmentalized.

This is not merely a signifier of dysfunction, but, once again, a repetition of the transferential situation. Nevertheless, it seems as if Jim was not able, in the manner of Amy, to allow this conflict to be absorbed into the transference and to say something about that experience. There is a move towards Desymbolization but not Re-Symbolization. While the tension mounted to a pitch between Amy and her therapist, Jim had ways of diffusing the conflict and pushing it under. We get the clearest demonstration of this, ironically, not when he speaks about his therapist but actually when he is asked about his dreams:

J: We rarely talked about dreams, I felt that his, uh, that he was really good at getting me to think productively about the dreams. Really—it was always a mind-blower, fantastic.
Dr V: Did you—did you see any—did that—did those meanings feel right to you? Did you see some other meanings?
J: Totally right. It felt really totally right. I—I—he was really working in a way that I didn't by myself. My writing about the dreams was a way to sort of, uh, disable—disable something. To bring out a lot of deep dark, you know, crazy feelings inside myself and get it out on paper and just disable them in terms of the power they might have.... I sort of put them back where they belong. And I don't need to take them out and tame them ... and I don't think them over so carefully now and sort of disembowel them, dissect them.
Dr V: Did you have frequent dreams about your therapist?
J: No, I—I wouldn't say it was a frequent occurrence but it wasn't terribly unusual. I don't know, I would maybe have a dream about him, I don't know, once a month maybe or maybe it was less sometimes, I don't know.

The ejection of his knowing in the final three "I don't knows" is striking for such a characteristically symbolizing and recollecting patient.

Again, the remainder of the STR reads like Amy's after the *nodal moment*. He says he always made his analyst look older in his visual memories, and traumas with male authorities spring up. He mentions suddenly that his mother had a mental breakdown and his father could not really handle it. He talks about his father's formidable power of denial. His final early memory is about being with his mother at the age of two at the butcher's with giant salamis hanging from the ceiling: he is, as is Jim's way, *not* scared, just looking. Knowing that he went into treatment because of how angry he gets at his wife, the appearance of his mother twice at the end of the interview gives us some sense of what was disavowed. There is definitive content kept out of awareness. He ends the interview with Dr V provocatively, saying he has been preoccupied with showing his analyst in a good light because he's grateful, but also because he paid a lot.

To conclude, as much as we get a sense of the incompleteness of a once a week therapy for two or three years, it is the recapitulation of the transferential dilemma that should catch our eye. While we would like to show the value of the STR for demonstrating the transformation that takes place in these treatments, here, we must point out, perhaps tentatively, that these findings reverse the conclusions wrought by the EQ study.

While Jim and Amy have two very different starting points, say as a symbolizer or desymbolizer, or with respect to the structural defences they began with, both patients moved in the necessary direction for the purpose of transformation as Re-Symbolization. Amy may have reached farther to the extent that she is able to say something definitive about her relationship to the analyst. With Jim, the transference remains mostly disavowed and displaced into the content of the therapy which is more easily undone.

Perhaps, to take this further, we need to take Freud more at his word when he says that hysteria and the symbolic connection embedded in the transference is the force behind analytic transformation. Again the caveat that this is therapy, not psychoanalysis, should be taken seriously, but it should not deter us from making a judgment on the benefits and difficulties of psychotherapy and a study of its transformative effects. At the very least, to know the limitations should reassure us as to why we conduct such time-consuming treatments as psychoanalysis. The transference as we know is easier to handle with greater frequency and our hope is not to break off the work prematurely but rather to carry it forward as far as it will go. But that is a matter for our other study (see Part III). Here, what is important is the way in which, through the STR, we get a picture of the benefits of bringing memory into the transference precisely as a moment of dynamic Symbolization.

COMMENTARY

How therapy lives on

Norbert Freedman and Joan Hoffenberg

These chapters address both the *that* and the *how* of therapeutic outcome research. It is stressed not only that psychoanalytic treatment has an ongoing presence in our patients' lives, but also how this may come about.

Beginning with a restatement of our earlier findings on effectiveness, we demonstrated that psychoanalytic treatment, with its foundational frame of session frequency and duration, results in the patient's perception of treatment as effective. When we further learned of congruent findings, derived from the meta-analysis of treatment experiences drawn from many quarters, then we were in a position to generalize beyond what at first had been the findings from a single centre—the IPTAR Clinical Center (ICC). These congruent findings were documented in a recent article by Shedler (2009), who reported effect sizes for psychodynamic therapy that were as large as those reported for other types of therapy, and also noted that patients who received psychodynamic therapy maintained therapeutic gains and appeared to continue to improve after termination.

Returning to our own database, the continuing aliveness of the therapeutic experience in the patients' subjectivity was compellingly depicted in the citations derived from the instrument, developed as part of this project: the Schedule of Therapy Remembered (STR). This is an open-ended demand situation evoking vibrant and varied recollections of therapy experiences. Geller's further explication of the Representation of the Therapeutic Dialogue (RTD) gives a compelling and vivid affirmation of the continuity of the therapeutic process, even in the absence of the therapist.

Beyond the affirmation of the "treatment as effective", these chapters raise further questions and introduce new lines of thought relating to issues of diagnosis, the post-termination phase, and the fundamental concept of internalization.

A discussion of treatment effectiveness cannot disregard issues of clinical diagnosis. Recent controversy has surfaced about the diagnosis and treatment of depression. In our 1999 study we noted two distinct types of depression: those with anxious depression for whom frequency of treatment was significant, and those with grief depression for whom only continued time in treatment made a difference. This distinction anticipated the discussions of the writers of the *DSM-V* manual. Ongoing commentary on the op-ed pages and in letters to the editor of the *New York Times* have confirmed what we noted years ago, namely that those who experience depression with grief do best with long-term psychodynamic treatment. Perhaps our findings might lead to a new designation in the forthcoming *DSM-V*: *Grief Depression*. Patients suffering from grief depression would benefit more from long-term psychotherapy, rather than from pharmacological intervention.

The concept of a post-termination phase is convincingly advanced by Geller. It is psychologically sound, strategically wise, and can be empirically verified. It is questionable, however, whether it is possible to identify distinct phases within the post-termination phase, as Geller suggests. On a practical level, the last "goodbye" handshake, whether mutually agreed upon or not, does not end the internal dialogue. Perhaps the concept "post-termination phase" speaks to Freud's idea of analysis as "interminable", for clearly, our patients continue to recall, interact with, remember, and make use of all aspects of their therapy experiences many years after termination. It is likely that the heuristic value of the post-termination phase lies in the fact that the former patient will in all likelihood become a future patient. This raises the question: does the post-termination phase inform or prepare us for the next analytic encounter? And if so, in what ways? This may be an issue of great practical importance.

The very concept of a post-termination phase invites consideration of a fundamental issue, that of the internalization of the psychoanalytic experience. In the two final chapters, we find two visions, both empirically rooted and persuasive. It is not coincidental that each author singles out one of the two characters, highlighted in the clinical observations: Jim and Amy.

Jim is Geller's ideal type for the understanding of "internalization". There is evocative literature, stemming from Europe, asserting that analytic thinkers tend to organize lines of thought around ideal types (Stuhr, 2002). Indeed, analytic thinkers have used ideal types as a way of advancing particular visions (e.g., the image of Oedipus). In the case of Jim, Geller views his RTD profile as portraying the internalization of the therapeutic dialogue. With an emphasis on "working memory", Jim is seen as actively reflecting, utilizing the tools for coping, and seeking to understand. He even gets comfort from nonverbal sources in his remembered therapy. He is also given to verbal thinking through imaginary conversations with his therapist.

Jim's "introjects", in Geller's words, are the hypothetical prototype of an inner dialogue, then and there, re-evoked in the course of the STR interview. It is tantalizing to contemplate that Geller's introjects, with their vivid images reflecting actions and counteractions, evoked by the STR, persist, as he states, in Jim's "working memory". Through Jim, he offers a portrait of an internalizing active ego.

Geller's ideal type is slanted towards the patient's capacity for cognitive competence, and, especially, towards the process of representation as a crucial element of working through. The analyst remained an adaptive resource in Jim's life, yet one wonders what was included or excluded in his remembered discourse. What was left out, as Webster suggests, is that which was excluded, dissociated. While the cognitive model for Jim is recollecting, for Amy it is reminiscing.

For Webster, Amy is the ideal type for internalization, and she understands Amy's style as one of reminiscing. This implies alternating states of consciousness: a nonlinear progression from dissociated or disclaimed memories to re-evoked memories or from desymbolization to symbolization. From material in Amy's STR interview, Webster describes internalization as a move from "repetition to repetition in the transference". The *nodal moment* becomes the repetition of a once forgotten, dissociated past. It is the repetition of the repetition transformed. For Webster, the issue is not simply one of capturing representations in working memory, but one of returning to ownership of unconscious desire.

The ideal type of Jim and the ideal type of Amy, as metaphors towards understanding internalization, has been at the forefront of psychoanalytic thought for many decades. It is encouraging to note that both models have led to an empirically grounded research approach which makes these ideas amenable to confirmation or disconfirmation. We will revisit this issue when we consider the process of *Progressive Symbolization* in relation to working through, developed in Part III of this volume.

PART II

THREE PATHWAYS TOWARDS THE MODIFICATION OF ANNIHILATION ANXIETY

FOREWORD

Marvin Hurvich and Norbert Freedman

Trauma, be it of developmental or adult onset, is a pervasive source of pathogenesis. During psychoanalytic treatment, signifiers of trauma emerge as indices of past traumatic moments. Such moments find their expression in Annihilation Anxiety, a threat to the survival of ego or self. Moreover, Annihilation Anxiety can change in the course of psychoanalytic treatment. It may ebb and flow in intensity and undergo modification in form, signalling not only a process of change, but sometimes one of *transformation*. The distinction between clinical change and change that is transformative will be highlighted throughout this volume.

The possibility that such markers of trauma can indeed be altered constitutes a profound challenge to all forms of therapeutic endeavours. However, such alterations, which we hope to document, depend on the clinical context in which they emerge, and indeed it is this context that may be determinative. Such mental reorganizations can be noted early in treatment, under the aegis of transference engagement or during phases of regression. We can also delineate alterations specific to long-term analytic treatment, stretching over years. Each set of observations affirms that transformations do indeed arise in the course of psychoanalytic treatment, delineates distinct pathways of change, and tells a different story—to document this will be the clinical yield of this project.

This, thus, is an empirically-based study of clinical change and clinical process. However, before spelling out the details we need to sketch out the line of thought that guides this clinical inquiry, the affirmation of clinical concepts and of clinical change. We will do so in the chapter entitled *The Propositional Method for the study of psychoanalytic concepts*. Then we will follow through by detailing our methods of observations in *Meet Mohamed and the method implemented*; only then shall we proceed with the details of our findings in Chapters Eight, Nine, and Ten. Each marks one of the three pathways of modifying Annihilation Anxiety during analytic treatment.

CHAPTER SIX

The *Propositional Method* for the study of psychoanalytic concepts

Marvin Hurvich and Norbert Freedman

The *Propositional Method* to be described in this chapter is being presented as a way of generating *another kind of evidence* for the study of psychoanalytic concepts. Propositions become vehicles for framing this other kind of evidence, for facilitating new clinical observations, and for offering a structure for comparative psychoanalysis. It is both propositional and generative.

The Method to be described is a procedure to highlight the key features of psychoanalytic concepts, through a reliance on clinical observations and clinical generalizations, and an effort to decrease metapsychological language and formulations. It is intended to facilitate a systematic study of psychoanalytic concepts, and their application to the psychoanalytic process.

The need for a new methodology for the study of psychoanalytic formulations

Concepts are not only elastic, changing over time, but they are also sources of controversy and conflict. They are statements evoking concordance, spelling out what we are thinking, doing, and inferring clinically, and they are sources of discordance. What we look for is a method that offers a genome that can encapsulate both the commonality and the diversity of thought, and then distil it so that it becomes available for analysis within a single frame. With the method in hand, we hope to find a coherent path towards confirmation or disconfirmation, thus enhancing coherence without succumbing to the search for universals.

Psychoanalytic concepts, while they represent the core of the psychoanalytic method, nonetheless in their actual use are prone to a number of inherent vulnerabilities that ultimately interfere with and undermine the accrual of psychoanalytic knowledge. They are prone to (a) over-generalization, (b) excessive adherence to psychoanalytic loyalties, and (c) their use sometimes neglects the specific clinical context to which they refer.

a. This strain in the evolution of analytic concepts can be traced to the very beginning of Freud's discoveries. As detailed in Bergmann and Hartman's *History of Psychoanalytic Technique* (1976), Freud's early discoveries were based on specific clinical procedures leading to observations and then to concepts. The first, the pressure method, was abandoned for that of free associations. The second was Freud's disappointment in, and subsequent modification of, his theory that neuroses were typically the result of sexual seduction of children by adults. The third was proposing the Oedipus complex as the nucleus of the neurosis. In each instance the technique and the observation came first and the concepts followed, be they the formulations about repression, the Oedipus complex, and so on.

Freud repeatedly added new concepts and modified existing ones on the basis of emerging clinical observations and also in light of theoretical inconsistencies. For example, in his 1895 anxiety paper, he correctly made the clinical generalization that many of his female patients who had anxiety symptoms also had sexual inhibitions. He later (1926a) revised the 1895 formulation that the anxiety was a result of the undischarged sexual energy being automatically transformed into anxiety. Additionally, his recognition of the negative therapeutic reaction was stated as a clinical observation in the Wolf Man (1918) case report. Later, in *The Ego and the Id* (1923, as cited in Bergmann & Hartmann, 1976), Freud used this earlier clinical observation as the basis for his theoretical concept of the superego.

A further instance of where Freud's recognition of a theoretical inconsistency led to a new focus and formulation involved a shift from the topographic to the structural model. An important reason for the shift was Freud's recognition of the inconsistency that within the system both "unconscious" repressed impulses and unconscious guilt were located. So, while he retained his key concept of the unconscious, the repressed impulses were now relocated in one psychic agency (the id) and unconscious guilt in another (the superego).

b. In the history of psychoanalysis and also in its current usage psychoanalytic concepts have been inherently elastic. This is the main thesis advanced by Sandler, articulated in his 1983 paper, who came to be considered the father of psychoanalytic conceptual research. Sandler illustrated the range of meaning through the use of the transference concept. At first, transference was simply a false connection, then it became a sign of resistance, a displaced edition of an earlier experience, and finally a direct communication to the person of the analyst within the analytic hour. When such a phenomenon appears, it gives conviction both to the patient and the analyst and reflects any thoughts and fantasies about the analyst in the here and now.

This wide range of meaning given to such a central notion illustrates conceptual elasticity. Historically, conceptual elasticity can be viewed to portray the changes in ideas and clinical issues that have permeated our discipline over the decades. But history aside, when divergent definitions of transference are encountered under the same name (i.e. transference), then which one of these formulations is correct? This is an issue still very much with us today: to wit, commitments to a Kleinian position, to Lacan, to Winnicott and Kohut and most visibly the ongoing dialogue in the United States between the Freudian and the Relational positions. At such points, it can be clarifying to find a clinical and research methodology that allows us to distinguish clinical observations apart from professional loyalties.

c. The phenomenon of conceptual elasticity can also be understood to reflect the particularity of the clinical situation in which it is embedded. Concepts are *context dependent*, Sandler (1983) reminds us. We use the trauma concept to illustrate this phenomenon of context specificity. As we shall show in the pages to follow, there is adult-onset trauma (torture suffered during the war in

Africa) or developmental trauma in early childhood (revealed through the cat dreams in the case of Ms K). Each will find its manifestations in the transference in moments of acute crisis and in moments of working through. Each manifestation of the traumatic has its own markers, its own qualities, and its own dimensions. To attend to this particularity of the manifestation of that concept gives richness and validity to the central notion and the clinical observation. Defining a concept along the lines of the context adds to the specificity of analytic inquiry. We have called this aspect of the method a *Modifier*, as will be described below.

To conclude this historical review, our discipline needs a set of pliable, context-dependent notions, which have a measure of generality so crucial to theory formation. Further, conceptual elasticity directs us to look at the specific properties that give rise to the concept, that is, specific dimensions about it. Then, we are also challenged to show the relationship among the dimensions so as to establish the definition of coreness and modifiers to expand the issue of particularity.

The Propositional Method

The *Propositional Method*, as pursued in this project, holds as a key tenet that psychoanalytic concepts be defined through the language of *clinical propositions*, as already stated, specifically, relying on descriptions of clinical *observations* and clinical *generalizations*. We further assume that these statements are best understood as probabilistic rather than as universal (Rubinstein, as cited in Holt, 1985), to be described below. It is an approach that encourages a specification of relevant conditions and variables. Whatever the concept under inquiry, it contains shared attributes discovered by analysts across the spectrum of theoretical positions, and these offer a basis for *common ground* as well as comparative psychoanalysis, which uncovers specific differences.

It was Waelder's (1962) seminal paper on the methodology underlying psychoanalytic inferences which forms the basis for our approach. In his essay, Waelder distinguished six levels of inference making: clinical observations, clinical interpretations, clinical generalizations, developmental formulations, metapsychological speculations, and sometimes aspects of Freud's philosophical pre-suppositions. We are limiting the present method to clinical observations and clinical generalizations, for this enables us to anchor all formulations in what is clinically and evidently present. By restricting the proposed method to these two levels, we are guarding against over-exclusion or conceptual conflation that has characterized the literature.

A brief consideration of the place of metapsychology highlights divergent views. As noted, Waelder (1962) placed metapsychological formulations at a high level of psychoanalytic inquiry, and offered as examples: cathexis, psychic energy, Eros, and Thanatos. For George Klein (1956), metapsychological formulations may obscure clinical phenomena that are starting points for observations and explanation. He favoured an emphasis on the clinical theory of psychoanalysis rather than on metapsychological formulations, as did Holt (1985). Here, we take account of a contrasting view that metapsychology is "the most fundamental component of psychoanalytic theory, the component that consolidates the most essential elements of a psychoanalytic conception of mental functioning, … [a theory] that enables us to account for specific clinical variations, using general and universal principles and processes" (Roussillon, as cited in Mijolla, 2005, pp. 1049–1050). We acknowledge the substantial inspiration for new clinical insights and for psychoanalytic thinking, reflected in Freud's delineation of the metapsychological points of view, famously expanded by Rapaport and Gill (1959). We additionally take note of the caution described by Loewald and Meissner (1976). They pointed out that, regarding the higher level of abstraction that characterizes metapsychological concepts, "[T]he distance [from the clinical observations] may become so great that theorists lose sight of what they are talking about. In this event, theory gains its own idiosyncratic momentum and is allowed to proliferate without response to or discipline by empirical data. It is then no longer grounded in communicable experience" (p. 162). In summary, when metapsychological formulations are remote from clinical observations, we either leave them aside, or seek to transform them into clinical observations. But we embrace metapsychological formulations that facilitate multiple perspectives on clinical processes.

While we have chosen to focus on clinical level observations and generalizations, we assume that the latter imply various assumptions and implications, and that some of these may qualify as metapsychological. More about this in the next section on the *Propositional Method* proper.

Apart from this focus on clinical process, as noted, such observations are always context-dependent. This is where the probabilistic issue enters, for the meaning of any given concept is influenced by the context in which it is observed. As one example, annihilation anxiety following the September 11, 2001 World Trade Center destruction was experienced differently by different individuals in relation to a number of factors, especially proximity to the site. But, additionally, it varied by other background factors including age, gender, ethnic background, the intrapsychic fantasies it triggered, and the history of previous psychic trauma. As we shall maintain, the context may modify the meaning of the concept.

We shall chart the steps of our method to follow: (a) the selection of the concept, (b) the definition of its coreness (or its presumed invariant nature), (c) its dimensions, and (d) its modifiers, through the introduction of intrapsychic, interpersonal, or cultural contexts. Before detailing these, we introduce some exemplars from earlier and current psychoanalytically-based work.

Earlier and current versions of the Propositional Method

The thinking behind our *Propositional Method* is not novel. Rycroft (1956), in a study of symbolism in which he compared the contributions of Klein, Winnicott, and Kubie among others, summarized his findings through a set of propositions: "For the sake of brevity my formulation takes the form of fourteen propositions" (p. 143). These propositions also pointed to succinct clinical observations. Thus, he sought to replace the concept of regression, with the term Desymbolization, which he felt reflected the clinical essence. We note that Rycroft relied on metapsychological formulations in his account because he felt that these alluded to valuable, implicit to be sure, clinical descriptions.

Horwitz (1974), with colleagues from the Menninger Psychotherapy Research Program, in the framework of a longitudinal, prospective study of both process and outcomes of psychotherapy and psychoanalysis, constructed a list of propositions where a key distinction was made between supportive and expressive interventions. The propositions were formulated as predictive and post-dictive assumptions, which were cast into testable hypotheses by clinical raters who had access to the clinical records at termination of the treatment. His method was both predictive and post-dictive, and he also included process issues. In his proposition, "In expressive treatment, transference attitudes toward one particular sex are experienced earlier toward a therapist of that sex", Horwitz is implicitly recognizing the extent to which his predictions would be modified by gender and by transference attitudes, reflecting an awareness of the probabilistic nature of his forecasting (p. 282).

Cramer (1998) used seven propositions, which she referred to as "pillars", to organize her findings on defence mechanisms, which spanned decades of work. For each pillar, she detailed empirical research findings that supported her propositions. These propositions reflect in their coreness the conflict theory of defence (originally formulated by Anna Freud, 1936) and each of the seven propositions mirror successively attributes or dimensions of this general theory. Thus, the propositions are concerned with experiences existing outside awareness; are developmentally organized; are adaptive and maladaptive; are stress related; are regulators of negative affect, and are imbedded in psycho-physiological processes. The structure and logic of this method, formulating a core idea and then spelling out its ramifications, is akin to the method about to be described.

A recent summary of research spanning many decades published by Holt (2009) utilizes propositions to spell out his views and evidence for primary process. He first offers ten statements aimed at summarizing the current psychoanalytic theory of thinking. He then delineates core propositions while distinguishing them from explanatory statements and commentary. He provides empirical evidence for his propositions, including from his own detailed studies of primary process thinking as reflected in the Rorschach responses. In his effort to take a fresh look at the psychoanalytic theory of primary process, Holt (2009) writes: "For the sake of clarity, I am going to reduce it to a set of propositions" (p. 24). He offers ten key propositions, and then details empirical findings that support these.

Bucci (1997) at first applied Kris's notion of the "good" and "difficult psychoanalytic hour" to the empirical study of analytic process. These formulations were translated into propositional language and evaluated through the method of the *Referential Process*. In 2007 Bucci and Maskit applied measures of the referential process to the study of recorded psychoanalysis. Comparisons were made between "integrative working sessions" and "non-integrated difficult sessions", which had been previously identified by Freedman, Lasky and Hurvich (2003). They predicted and found that working sessions could be identified reliably in terms of evocativeness, vividness, and specificity of affective experiences, compared to non-integrated, difficult hours. Crucial is that these empirical observations were used by Bucci to confirm her central theory of the cognitive linguistic regulation implied by *Dual Code Theory*.

Hurvich (2003) utilized a set of propositions with the aim of clarifying components of the concept of Annihilation Anxiety. A key underlying methodological and conceptual assumption was that differentiation facilitates integration. The advantage of listing the propositions is that this format provides, with a high degree of clarity, specificity, and succinctness, what is postulated, asserted, and hypothesized.

In all these preceding conceptually-guided and methodologically-driven vignettes, the defining characteristics of the concept could be seen at a glance. Observations articulated theory. This advantage, together with the detailed consideration of each proposition in turn, allows the reader to follow just what psychoanalytic evidence, with relevant comments and discussion, has been brought together and organized, to support the given proposition.

The Propositional Method *delineated*

Any given concept viewed through the lens of the *Propositional Method* shares these properties: its *perceived invariance*, its *dimensionality*, and its *clinical particularity*. To elaborate: each concept contains an essential kernel of similarity of what Bion (1965), in his book on *Transformations*, has termed *invariance*. It is this quality of perceived similarity, which allows us to define the coreness of a concept. Further, each concept makes its appearance in a variety of situations, which allows us to delineate a range of dimensional properties. It is this quality of invariance that offers the latitude for the study of transformation. Finally, as the concept comes to life through its inherent connections to clinical encounters, we can lend particularity to the notion under study. These are the anchoring points for the implementation of the method.

The thinking behind our *Propositional Method* is part and parcel of all empirical inquiry. Indeed, the idea of propositions formulated can best be understood within the context of hypotheses tested. To implement this process we offer the following four steps.

Defining the concept and its selected core

All inquiry begins with a concept selected. It starts with an observation that is clinically persuasive. It continues with the literature search of observations that have organized and captured psychoanalytic inquiry. Any such concept holds within itself a quality of coreness, which is defined as the concept's essence, a defining feature that is intrinsic and substantive. This quality of coreness was captured metaphorically by Bion's (1965) wonderful example of the image of a field of poppies and a canvas in front of the painter depicting a field of poppies. They both suggested, in spite of distinct differences in their modes of representation, an essential invariance. It is this invariance inherent in a given concept, its essence, which is a crucial first step for the *Propositional Method* and also for the study of psychoanalytic change.

However, coreness is only a relative anchoring point for the study of psychoanalytic concepts. Indeed, we speak of a *selected* core, akin to Bion's (1967) notion of a *selected* fact, which is the "creative integration of disparate facts into a meaningful pattern" (Britton & Steiner, 1994, p. 1070). Once more, for Rycroft desymbolization was a selected core replacing the notion of regression. For Cramer, the selected core was not only the notion of defence but its embeddedness in Anna Freud's *The Ego and the Mechanisms of Defense*. For Holt, it was not only primary process as hallucinatory wish fulfilment but shifts in cognitive functioning. Bucci places her observations not only in the general sphere of dissociation but in that sphere of knowledge dealing with Dual Code Theory of psycholinguistics. Closer to our endeavour, Hurvich's concept of Annihilation Anxiety has its historical roots in the selected core of Freud's trauma theory and the traumatic moment. He, thus, emphasizes one particular vision of Freud's, which has a deeper centrality to comprehend hitherto a wide range of as yet not acknowledged facts. For each of these investigators, the selected core became the launching pad for propositions about to be described.

We must hasten to add that each selected core is closely linked to a particular theory and indeed a given core is chosen to give voice to that theory. It is through the further elaboration of the core, via its dimensions and modifiers about to be described, that we elaborate the given concept.

The writing of the propositions

The goal in writing a proposition is to formulate clinical phenomena in a manner that is succinct, evocative, and translates the coreness of a concept into operational language. Much current research proceeds from empirical description to clinical generalization. That applies to many of the studies cited above, which are based on well-defined variables that become the basis for clinical generalization. The method of clinical propositions is also designed to aid the clinical investigator. To illustrate: the analyst, in clinical practice, can formulate propositions which clarify the impact of countertransference enactments; or a proposition that gauges just how metabolizing what was proffered may impact on subsequent clinical course. In Chapters Eight and Nine below, we have primarily written propositions which focus on the relationships among variables that are part of the clinical process. The writing of propositions can be a creative act. In formulating such a statement, we may wish to travel two pathways: that of using the moments of the session and translating them into clinical formulations, or the other way around. In both cases, the central task is the same: to translate a theoretical proposition into a clinically observable fact.

Ongoing controversies can be the occasion for a fruitful application of the *Propositional Method*. In the current theory of narcissism, two types have come to be recognized: the overt-grandiose (Kernberg) and the covert (Kohut). There are abundant clinical observations that illustrate each. A systematic depiction comparing each with the other can be achieved by writing propositions detailing key features of each. This process may generate new psychoanalytic knowledge, and is an example of Comparative Psychoanalytic study mentioned above.

This line of thought suggests that the *Propositional Method* can be a form of inquiry from clinical observation to empirical validation and back. It is a mode of consciousness that we might wish to recommend for the clinical observer. In each of our applications of our method cited in this volume, we travel a certain path: we begin with clinical description, formulate propositions, apply our categories of analysis, and then determine just how these propositions have clarified both the concepts as well as the clinical changes observed. In the case of Mohamed, a patient who experienced severe trauma and presented in this Part of the volume, we began with a history of terror, its modification in transference, and its eruption at the end of an interrupted treatment in a panic attack. In the case of Ms K, the patient indicating transformation during long-term psychoanalytic treatment, we also started with a terror dream, traced its vicissitudes in transference and countertransference over many years, and then examined how it was modified. Our categories of analysis, Annihilation Anxiety and its transformation through Symbolization, will document the "goodness of fit" between the concepts and the observed alterations in mental functioning.

Spelling out the dimensions

These dimensions are designed to bring to life the coreness of the concept. They enable both the clinician and investigator to render the concept operational, vivid, and evocative. They have something in common with the G-Factor and S-Factors of Wechsler's concept of intelligence. The G-Factor is the invariant core, while the S-Factors may be Dimensions of the concept, and Modifiers of the concept. A change in the dimension involves a change from one aspect of the core issue to another.

These dimensions may be illustrated in the development of Hurvich's (2003) notion of Annihilation Anxiety. The core quality of Annihilation Anxiety is defined by danger to the survival of the ego capacities and self-organization. But these survival strategies may be brought into focus and articulated by the dimensions. These dimensions comprise a range of psychic dangers: feeling overwhelmed, invaded, merged, destroyed, abandoned, and fragmented. These six overlapping dimensions are at the level *of clinical generalizations*.

They provide a succinct framework that highlights major areas under which most of the *clinical observations* regarding survival apprehensions may be included.

Each dimension is further spelled out by a series of key attributes. For illustration, we will include here nine attributes which characterize, at the level of clinical observation, the components of the concept of being overwhelmed: over-stimulated, swept away, buried alive, smothered, drowned, flooded, trapped, unable to function, and loss of control.

It is noteworthy that in the foregoing example all dimensions, and their attributes, were subordinate to the concept to be affirmed. Each dimension, and its attributes, defined the essence of what was meant by the *danger to survival*. In that sense, annihilation anxiety's relationship to its dimensions and attributes is a linear one.

Concepts differ in the shape in which the validity of the concept can be affirmed. Each concept has more or fewer dimensions and attributes. We just provided the example of the six dimensions and illustrated only one by providing nine attributes we have thus far isolated for overwhelmed. Regarding merged, we have included the attributes of absorbed, devoured/swallowed, and trapped. Cramer found six "pillars" that she considered crucial. Nonetheless, all dimensions and attributes must include "aspects" of a clinical observation deemed to be essential for that concept.

The modifiers and the probabilistic nature of the Propositional Method

In introducing modifiers, we attempt to make explicit the aim of the *Propositional Method*. To spell out the relevance of clinical observations to theory construction, we introduce two fundamental modifiers: limiting and transforming.

The modifier component takes account of the context, such as socio-economic status, race, and gender. Then, there are intrapsychic factors, such as ego strength variables, object relational variables, and self-integration variables. If we are writing propositions based on clinical observations in the treatment situation, then we specify whether the variable is intrinsic or extrinsic to that situation; that is, the modifier factor involves specifying the conditions under which the proposition holds or does not hold. We have identified two main groupings of modifiers: *limiting* (restricting and expanding), and *transforming* (desymbolizing and symbolizing). Regarding limiting modifiers (restricting and expanding), we include cultural, gender, or other such considerations, as well as various ego strength/weakness variables (status of reality testing, impulse control/affect modulation, and integrative capacity). For a gender-related modifier of the limiting/restricting kind, we cite the example given earlier in this chapter that transference attitudes in expressive treatment are experienced earlier towards the same sex therapist (Horwitz, 1974). Another example of a limiting/restrictive consideration is whether the clinical observation is based on a verbal or on a nonverbal, enacted manifestation. Regarding limiting modifiers, we specify when the patient experiences his psychic contents and emotions as intolerable, in contrast to being tolerable. An example of a transformative modifier is illustrated when annihilation anxiety appears in the context of psychic symbolization where the patient is able to compare, reflect, and imagine a danger. In this context, annihilation content has undergone a transformation. Once more, the limiting modifiers change the generalizability of the proposition, and this is what renders the *Propositional Method* a probabilistic one.

It should be stressed that we conceive of the processes of desymbolization/symbolization as major modifiers of Annihilation Anxiety. To extend the example just given: when Annihilation Anxiety appears in the context of desymbolization, of concreteness, or in a state of confusion, the full impact of the threat to survival may be omnipresent. When, on the other hand, the same affect-content appears in symbolizing space, when the patient is able to reflect, compare, and imagine the danger, then a new mental context is created and with it a transformation has taken place. Here, the same annihilatory threat exists in a new form, that is, it has been transformed.

Conclusions

We have described the *Propositional Method*: the task of defining the essential coreness of the concept, spelling out the propositions, defining its dimensions, and specifying the conditions under which they are modified has been delineated. In utilizing this approach, arguably more systematic and detailed than those historical examples cited earlier, we traverse level to level, from the core, to the dimensions and attributes, and then to modifiers. With each additional component, our assumptive base becomes more delineated and clarifying.

This method has a broad range of applications in the evaluation of psychoanalytic concepts. In all such endeavours the components of the method are the same, but the path differs. The empirical investigator applies the *Propositional Method* as a basis for hypothesis formulating, and then for testing, using the most available, reliable, and valid instruments. The systematic clinical observer formulates propositions from a body of available propositions and then utilizes them to make inferences about process. The practising clinician utilizes propositions as they emerge in the clinical encounter and translates them into clinical actions or interactions.

In the chapters to follow we shall apply the *Propositional Method* to two pivotal situations. They all involve the evaluation of patients in psychoanalytic treatment. All implicate the fate of the consequences of a *traumatic moment*, and Annihilation Anxiety in the tracing of change, but they differ widely in clinical context. The first case to be presented is an instance in which the patient, suffering from severe trauma resulting from torture in Africa, participates and is observed in the early phase of psychoanalytic therapy. The second is a case in which a patient suffering from early developmental trauma participates in psychoanalytic treatment stretching over a ten-year period.

CHAPTER SEVEN

Meet Mohamed and the method implemented

Marvin Hurvich and Norbert Freedman

The recorded psychoanalytic therapy of Mohamed, a refugee from torture in Somalia, treated in Oslo, Norway is the subject matter of this chapter. We begin with a brief portrait of Mohamed, sketch out our method of analysis of the transcripts of sessions,[2] present an account of the major variables of concern, Annihilation Anxiety (AA), and the symbolizing process (Symbolization and Desymbolization), and then return to the theme of our *Propositional Method* with the question: how to infer clinical change or a process of transformation?

Torture told, torture relived, torture anticipated, and then relived once more

Mohamed was a political refugee from an African country. He was in his early forties and was an active Muslim. He had a wife and six children at the time of his arrest in the mid-Eighties for his association

---

[2] The authors express gratitude to Dr Sverre Varvin of Oslo who conducted the psychoanalytic psychotherapy, arranged for the recordings of the sessions, and made transcripts of these available to us.

with groups opposing the dictator of his country. He was in prison for nine years, where he experienced severe torture, maltreatment, and under-nourishment, and was also sentenced to death. He was forced to watch the torture of his wife and one of his daughters, as well as to witness torture and other inhumane acts being inflicted on fellow prisoners, including children. A recurrent theme in therapy was his agony about what he had seen the soldiers and prison guards doing to others. This tormented him as did the physical suffering he himself had experienced. He managed, in spite of this, to find some comfort in his religious beliefs all through his time in prison. However, it was a hard blow for him when the authorities circulated a rumour that he had betrayed his comrades during torture.

Mohamed began therapy three months following release from prison and immediately upon arrival in Oslo, after being referred by the local non-governmental refugee agency, as they found his condition alarmingly severe. Varvin (2003), his therapist, gave this patient a diagnosis of Post-Traumatic Stress Disorder (American Psychiatric Association, 1994), with complaints of "pains, fatigue, depression, nightmares, re-experiences, avoidance, and hyper-alertness" (p. 219). He was in therapy for about one-and-a-half years, with a total of 43 face-to-face sessions, mostly once a week. The therapy was conducted in English. He missed only a few sessions, sometimes coming even if he felt ill. The psychotherapy was psychoanalytic, and he was instructed to express himself as freely as possible by saying what was on his mind.

The recorded psychotherapy of a trauma victim: segmentation analysis

All sessions were audio recorded. However, it was only possible to obtain typed transcripts of the four initial sessions and the four final sessions. On clinical grounds two initial criterion sessions were selected, sessions 3 and 4, which became the subject matter of Chapter Eight where we offer a detailed analysis of the events of early transference engagement. Then we present two final criterion sessions, sessions 41 and 42, which became the focus of Chapter Nine, a dramatic, unhappy ending in the form of a panic attack. Thus, this psychotherapy ended with a re-evocation of trauma in a phase of crisis.

In order to obtain an adequate gauge within each hour, we divided the sessions into successive scenes. A scene is a thematic episode that varies in length from two to four pages and is a natural division of the story told. For convenience, as we detail in the chapters to follow, each scene was given a descriptive heading by the investigators.

In order to obtain an estimate of the presence of each variable under study relative to verbal output, the entire transcript was also divided into idea units. Idea units are not syntactical constructs, but brief utterances that allow for segmentation of the text (Stinson, Milbrath, Reidbord & Bucci, 1994). The frequency of idea units within each session ranged from 199 to 307 per session. Our two major dimensions of psychic functioning, Annihilation Anxiety and the symbolizing process (Symbolization and Desymbolization), can be evaluated in terms of their presence relative to the idea units both within each scene and between the criterion sessions. These steps enabled us both to carry out an empirical study of the categories employed and to offer a descriptive/quantitative account based on our *Propositional Method*.

Defining Annihilation Anxiety and the symbolizing process

The propositions to be examined rely on empirical definitions of the major variables under study. In what follows, each of the two processes, Annihilation Anxiety and the Symbolizing process (with its two aspects, Symbolization and Desymbolization), are described first in terms of their coreness and then their defining dimensions and attributes.

Annihilation Anxiety: its core and its dimensions

Annihilation Anxiety refers to those specific aspects of psychic danger in which the patient experiences a threat to the survival of ego functions (Bellak, Hurvich & Gediman, 1973) and/or self. It corresponds to aspects of psychic dread variously described by psychoanalytic authors (e.g., Bion, 1962; Little, 1958; Winnicott, 1960), and has been given detailed description by Hurvich (1989, 2000, 2003). Moreover, the AA concept finds empirical definition in its specific dimensions.

The dimensions involve different degrees and qualities of helplessness. In their briefest designation, the overlapping annihilation dimensions are:

1. Overwhelmed
2. Merged
3. Disorganized
4. Invaded
5. Abandoned
6. Destroyed.

To elaborate:

Dimension 1: Overwhelmed. This is the most central attribute of Annihilation Anxiety, a key reflection of psychic danger from internal or external sources. It can be seen to subsume all the other dimensions. Particular components are apprehensions over loss of control, feeling flooded, bursting, immobilized, and unable to cope. The main psychic residues of massive psychic trauma are overwhelming affects, especially a mixture of anxiety and depression (Krystal, 1988). Individual differences are in the degrees of adaptive decrement, psychic disruption, and uncontrolled anxiety.

Dimension 2: Merged. This wish/fear involves feeling entrapped, devoured, engulfed, or absorbed. Merged fantasies represent danger when they imply threats to psychic separateness and loss of self. Many conflicts and inhibitions over physical and emotional intimacy result from the wish or fear of merger in people with weak structural boundaries. Issues of autonomy and therapist sensitivity to this need-fear dilemma (Burnham, Gibson & Gladstone, 1969) are centrally relevant, as well as connections with abandonment fears.

Dimension 3: Fragmentation/Disorganization of self, object, and ego functions. Both Anna Freud (1936) and Waelder (1960) included ego disintegration as a basic danger, and Kohut (1971) emphasized disintegration of the self as a key source of basic anxiety. Kernberg (1975) sees the central function of psychotic defences as attempts to protect against ego dissolution, and the loss of personal identity (Bak, 1943). Relevant patient fears include crumbling, falling apart, shattering, and going insane.

Dimension 4: Invasion. It includes feelings of being penetrated, impinged and intruded on, and sometimes feeling colonized

(Williams, 2004). Winnicott (1949) stressed early maternal failures in active adaptations to the infant's needs as factors in excessive responses to impingements. Interferences with "going on being" lead beyond frustration to a threat of annihilation. Individuals who experienced excessive impingements during early years are more vulnerable to intrusion experiences when they suffer psychic trauma.

Bick (1968) claimed that a sense of being overly vulnerable to penetration experiences is increased when there has been inadequate "adhesive identification" due to unsatisfactory skin contact during earliest infancy. This leads to fantasies of the self as porous, vulnerable to leaking out, and being unable to hold or to contain anything.

Dimension 5: Abandonment. This includes persons who respond with panic to the threatened loss of a significant person, and may be associated with fears of falling, and falling into a black hole. For some youngsters, excessive abandonment fears result in increased vulnerability to subsequent psychic trauma, and these also increase following psychic trauma.

Winnicott's (1962) concept of "unthinkable anxieties" (falling to pieces, falling forever, having no spatial orientation, and no sense of the relationship between mind and body) centre on failures in the "holding environment". Where inadequate techniques for self-regulation, self-care, and emotional self-reliance are present, annihilation anxieties are likely to ensue.

Dimension 6: Destroyed. This involves a tendency to respond with a life and death attitude to danger, perceived threat, or other situations that usually arouse some fear or anxiety. There is a focus on dying and on psychic death, on fears of world destruction, petrifaction (Laing, 1959) and on the "death imprint" (Lifton, 1976). A catastrophic mentality is a frequent response to psychic trauma, and may be associated with a "doomsday orientation" (Krystal, 1988), a dread and even conviction that sooner or later there will be a return of a fate worse than death, because lightning does strike twice in the same place.

In addition to Annihilation Anxiety dimensions, we make a distinction between annihilation *content* and annihilation *mode*. A differentiation is made between an active and passive *mode*. Thus Annihilation Anxiety (e.g., being overwhelmed, invaded, or destroyed) may be expressed as an *activity* of the ego or self, inflicting injury upon the other; or conversely in the *passive* victimized position in which the patient experiences annihilatory dread. A further distinction is made between *active self* and *active other*, that is, when destructiveness is implemented either by the subject himself or by others (i.e. persecutors). Similarly, *passive self* and *passive other* denote when victimization or persecutory experiences are attributed to self or others. It will be noted in our findings that the active/passive attributes, a circumstance which defines the *agency* of annihilatory experiences, have been found to be closely coordinated with the process of Symbolization and Desymbolization, respectively.

Symbolization: its core and its dimensions

Symbolization is a process of meaning making, of symbol formation. When it arises during a therapeutic hour, it marks a process of psychic integration. But we also recognize the opposite, a process of non-integration, of *Desymbolization*. Each has its own dimensions and deserves its own definition.

The core of symbolization entails the processes of linking. Linguistically, symbol formation finds definition in three terms: the bringing together of the symbol, the abstract signifier, and the thing being signified by an interpreting subject. Clinically, this process of linking has been defined by Loewald (1983) as follows: "Symbolization may be described as an imaginative act: two different items of experience are linked in the mind in such a way that one represents the other". Such a process of integration can also be thought of as a process of creating symbolizing space. There are numerous versions of this symbolizing process to be found in the psychoanalytic literature and their highlights are summarized in the Postscript at the end of this volume. They each meet the central core, but here, applied to the study of Mohamed we have singled out three dimensions: object relational, fantasy, and temporal space. These describe what we consider to be crucial components of symbolization.

Dimension 1: Object Relational Space. In this configuration the patient gives voice to the presence of another; recognizes a person with definable attributes, that is, as having a mind of his or her own, having an impact on the other, and having attributes different from the subject himself or herself; and experiences others in a vivid and evocative manner. The other is understood in multiple and in contradictory ways.

When we observe an alteration in the direction of object relational space, it affirms Klein's (1930) contention that symbol formation entails a shift in the patient's position vis-à-vis the object. It is an objective confirmation of what she had termed the shift in the direction of the depressive position—the site of symbol formation.

Dimension 2: The Space of the Imaginary. In this configuration, the patient is able to insert the quality of the "as if" into the narrative. The patient's language makes use of metaphors, allusions, dreams, daydreams, fantasies, or fantasy-based thinking itself, explicitly related and reflected upon as such. It includes explicit recognition of a fantasy, with reference to its determining effect on other aspects of mental functioning. This dimension of linking spoken language to the imaginary has its roots in the writings of Winnicott (1971) who holds that the symbolic is born in the sphere of a particular state of consciousness, a transitional state of uncertainty, of the potential, a world of allusion where new meanings are created.

Dimension 3: Temporal Space. In this configuration, time is a crucial signifier of inner space. The patient's utterances reveal the interplay between three temporal points: past, present, or future. Temporal space implies triangular space, for the patient chooses between what is, what was, and what might be. It is a special case of triangulation in which the patient chooses not only between two points, which are present, but also an excluded unknown other. It is this kind of triangulation, according to Green, which is a precondition for reflective functioning and with it symbolization.

These three dimensions constitute an estimate of what we have termed a symbolizing process. It is empirically related to Bucci's notion of the referential process (see Ms Y study in Part III), and conceptually to the notion of reflective functioning (Fonagy & Target, 1995, 1996, 1998).

Desymbolization: its core and its dimensions

Desymbolization is not simply the absence of the symbolic, but has its own definable qualities. An overriding consideration that underlies all forms of Desymbolization is that of equivalence. While the core of Symbolization is that of *linking*, the core for Desymbolization is that of *equivalence*. When all is equal, there is no choice to be made. New meanings are foreclosed and the subject is confronted with a loss of signification. It is an experience that is desymbolized. However, there are gradients in the paralysis of meaning, and these are reflected in the three dimensions to be described. The rationale that guides this organizing concept and its dimensions is once more detailed in the Postscript.

Desymbolization in clinical discourse is encountered in three ways: in psychic blankness, symbolic equation, and frozen constellation. Further, these three dimensions of Desymbolization leave their mark on the manner in which emotions can be processed, and so all show a tendency towards affect disregulation. In the reading of clinical material, we scored signs of the three dimensions, and also indicators of affect disregulation.

Dimension 1: Psychic Blankness. The term psychic blankness is borrowed from Andre Green's (1975) "blank psychosis" and refers to a mental state characterized by emptying, deletion of the mind contents, and a blank hole or inner void, destroying all efforts at symbolization. In terms of affect disregulation, psychic blankness may be revealed through disfluency of speech, perseveration, globality of affect, and psychophysiological manifestations of unnamed affect. Psychic blankness can be activated by a single word or phrase (e.g., fire alarm as in the panic attack in session 42).

Dimension 2: Symbolic Equation. This term is borrowed from Klein and Segal's notion of *symbolic equation*. In the word, *equation*, we find the roots of the destructive aspects of meaning making, and in the word, *symbolic*, the communicative, even constructive, pockets that can facilitate a therapeutic object relationship. However, in our clinical material, this phenomenon is largely revealed by part-object representations and by the body objectified. Desymbolization as symbolic equation is of a more oscillating nature in contrast to psychic blankness.

Dimension 3: Frozen Constellation. In symbolic equation it is the facts that are equated, but now it is the emotions that are rendered equal in a frozen symbolic constellation. It is the affective force that homogenizes perception. One can find traces of this in the way that Fonagy and Target (1996) hesitatingly designate psychic equivalence as a process of mentalization where affect leads the way. Frozen constellation can reveal itself in two extreme forms: (a) the repetitive use of intense affect naming (e.g., Frosch's (1995) pre-conceptual emotional organization), and (b) event reporting in which emotions cannot be named, repeatedly observed in the case of Mohamed. This process has components of alexithymia.

Scoring of Annihilation Anxiety and the symbolizing process

We are now ready to apply the scoring categories just outlined to an evaluation of the transcripts previously segmented into scenes and idea units. Our frame of analysis was identical for each of our variables, Annihilation Anxiety, Symbolization, and Desymbolization. For each we can make a statement of their prevalence, their dimensions or saliency, and their intensity. This manner of categorizing the text will inform all further aspects of our quantitative findings.

Prevalence. This is a statement of either presence or absence of each of the variables contained within a given idea unit. Prevalence can be expressed as a percentage of the presence of each variable relative to the number of idea units contained within each scene or in the session as a whole.

Saliency. Having identified the presence of a variable (be it Annihilation Anxiety, Symbolization, or Desymbolization), we then asked what was the profile of dimension choice the patient expressed within each scene and in the session as a whole. For Annihilation Anxiety, once present, we determined whether it was: 1. overwhelmed, 2. merged, 3. disorganized, 4. invaded, 5. abandoned, and/ or 6. destroyed. The saliency score is the percentage of each dimension present relative to all dimensions utilized during each scene or session. Such a profile can be derived for the respective dimensions of Symbolization: object relational, temporal, and imaginary space; and Desymbolization: psychic blankness, symbolic equation, and the frozen constellation.

Intensity. The notion of intensity incorporates two ideas: a quantitative and a qualitative one. From a quantitative perspective, we give weight to the repeated presence of a variable within an idea unit. From a qualitative perspective, we recognize the presence of a range of different dimensions within an idea unit. Both the repeated use of a dimension and the use of different dimensions speak to the issue of intensity. Hence, the properties are evaluated on a Likert Scale based on three anchoring points: 1. presence of only one instance of one dimension within an idea unit; 2. presence of multiple instances of one dimension within an idea unit; and 3. presence of two or more dimensions within an idea unit. The result of these ratings yields a mean intensity score for each of our variables: Annihilation Anxiety, Symbolization, and Desymbolization per scene and the session as a whole.

This evaluation was carried out by two experienced observers well versed both in the theory and the coding of the variables under study. The ratings were based on consensual agreement. Ratings by independent judges, accompanied by inter-rater reliabilities using more detailed scoring manuals are a next step here. Ratings of annihilation anxieties based on Rorschach responses, with independent inter-rater reliabilities have been published earlier (Benveniste, Papouchis, Allen & Hurvich, 1998).

Targeted clusters and the method of visual analysis

In an effort to supplement the quantitative findings for the entire session covering multiple scenes, we also sought to highlight significant patterns within each session by selecting targeted Annihilation Anxiety clusters. As will be described in Chapters Eight and Nine, a targeted cluster is defined by clinical judgment and involves peak Annihilation Anxiety activity within a given session. The targeted cluster, for each session, was selected by consensual agreement by two investigators. Through this step, we were in a position to articulate the mutual interplay between Annihilation Anxiety and the Symbolizing process, Symbolization and Desymbolization.

Each targeted cluster was studied through the method of Visual Analysis. This method permitted us to track the contiguity or discontiguity of each of our three variables across successive phases within the analytic hour. This method is cited as an approach to the study of clinical change within a single case design[i] (Kazdin, 1998).

Transformation or mere clinical change? A return to the propositional method

This entire project was not simply confined to affirm the clinical validity of the Annihilation Anxiety concept as it registers trauma communicated in analytic therapy, although it will certainly do that. Neither was it confined to depict changes in the Symbolizing process revealed through the patient's position within the transference, although we will note that as well. Rather, the central theme had been the broad proposition that there may be a transformation of one central danger situation, Annihilation Anxiety, as this is mediated (or modified) by another clinical experience, namely the capacity to symbolize. Such research goals lead us to address the question: when is clinical change just that, change, or alternatively when does it deserve the assertion that something has been transformed? Can we make an empirically-guided distinction between clinical change and that type of change that we might term trans-formative? To clarify this issue we need to make a detour on the notion of transformation drawn from analytic writings.

Transformation viewed historically

The alteration of a mental function from one form into another has been the hallmark of analytic thought from its very beginning. It can be anchored in Freud's (1917b) classic work "On Transformations of Instinct as Exemplified in Anal Erotism", and Ferenczi's (1916) contribution "The Ontogenesis of the Interest in Money". In Ferenczi's memorable paper, from the first play surrounding sphincter control and the expulsion of faeces, he traces the impact of such activity and interest on to a child's playing with mud, then with sand (nice and white), then with pebbles, then with beautifully coloured marbles, onwards to coins, paper money, monetary symbols, an interest in investment, and to capitalism. A single theme was retained throughout development, yet appearing in an altered context. Then there is Bion's (1965) classic example in his book on *Transformations* demonstrating the phenomenon of invariance as he compared an actual field of poppies with a painted representation on the canvas. What is intrinsic to these examples is the notion of the core component of representation appearing in varying contexts, which takes on new, as yet undefined qualities. The demonstration of a transformative phenomenon is a requisite of all studies of significant change in psychoanalysis. It is also crucial for our studies of the transformation of Annihilation Anxiety in the course of psychoanalytic treatment. There we can observe a persistent experience of survival threat appearing recurrently, yet in a new form.

Application to the study of Annihilation Anxiety

Transformation of a core concept, in our case Annihilation Anxiety, depends upon the context in which it is embedded. In Chapter Six we emphasized the general view that all concepts are highly context dependent and that the context may be external, situational, or intrapsychic. Along the same lines we will have ample occasion in the material that follows to show how Annihilation Anxiety varies from session to session, but, more significantly for us, from scene to scene. With each encounter in a new context there is also a renewed opportunity for alterations to arise. Ricoeur (1970) had offered the general formulation that transformation is a dialectical process and entails the encounter with antithetical forces. In previous work, Freedman (1985) advanced the proposition that for transformation to occur the context must stand in an antithetical relationship to the psychological function undergoing alteration.

When we apply such a formulation to our study of changes in Annihilation Anxiety, we can ask the question: does the concurrent surfacing of symbolization create a new context that merits the designation of a transformative event? Indeed, the more a context is antithetical to the dominant pathological mode, the more likely it is to disruptively evoke new experiences leading to new forms of adaptation. Annihilation Anxiety is a situation of danger in which the patient experiences a threat to the survival of ego or self, while symbolization, especially as a gesture through which the patient reaches out towards the other and discovers new aspects of self, is an affirmation of the survival of ego or self. A new psychic context has, thus, been created and, indeed, we can speak of transformation. Now, annihilatory concerns can be reflected upon, viewed in past or future contexts and, indeed, have become more transference intensive. When this occurs, the earlier deeply frightening moments can live on within a new arena of experiences.

However, in this study we focused on transformations that may take place in two directions: positive ones, exemplified by Symbolization, and negative ones, in the form of Desymbolization illustrated by a turn towards regression. Modifiers are a way of offering an operational definition of the transformative process[ii] (we remind the reader that the notion of modifiers was spelled out in Chapter Six). When an annihilatory fear, which is verbalized and communicated, leads to a state of psychic blankness and inability to think, that too is a transformation, albeit in a negative direction.

As we shall be tracking changes of mental functioning in the course of analytically-based treatment from session to session and from early to later phases of Mohamed's therapy, we will observe the ebb and flow in the intensity of Annihilation Anxiety as these come to life through its dimensions. However, with the superimposition of processes of Symbolization or Desymbolization new contexts are created through a process of divergent modifications, either positive or negative. Specifically, when in the course of treatment, there arises an accentuation of Annihilation Anxiety and then concurrently there is an upsurge of symbolizing activity, we can infer that a positive transformation has arisen (e.g., session 4 and session 41). When, conversely, an upsurge of annihilatory fears is preceded or embedded within a process of Desymbolization then a modification in the direction of ego regression has set in (e.g., notably in session 42).

We conclude that the context in which Annihilation Anxiety occurs offers a challenge to the possibility for transformation. The theme of this part of the volume (Part II), "Three Pathways towards the Modification of Annihilation Anxiety", where each pathway occurs in a different clinical context, speaks to this issue. The term transformation as used here is a crucial event in the process of *working through*, as will be spelled out in Part III of this volume.

Endnotes

i. In this and all further analyses of data we will present descriptive statistics supplemented by the method of Visual Analysis. Additional statistical analysis is in progress and will be the subject of a future publication.
ii. In addition to the transformative modifiers, we recognize also "limiting modifiers", that is, clinical considerations that specify the conditions under which a proposition holds or does not hold.

CHAPTER EIGHT

Annihilation Anxiety and its transformation during early transference engagement: sessions 3 and 4

Norbert Freedman, Marvin Hurvich, and Alexandra Petrou

This early phase of transference engagement comprises two salient sessions which are distinctly different in character. Session 3 offers a retrospective account of the traumatic situation which we label "trauma retold". Session 4 is a retrospective report now revived in early transference engagement, termed "trauma relived". The reader is alerted that this early phase of the first month stands in sharp contrast to the situation a year later when Mohamed had been confronted with a series of disappointments, failures, and crises, followed by the anticipation of a panic attack and then a panic attack proper in the treatment situation. In each circumstance, Annihilation Anxiety dimensions and Symbolization processes reveal a distinct interplay between Annihilation Anxiety and its modification through a process of Desymbolization and then, Symbolization. It is with this perspective in mind that we enter the detailed examination of sessions 3 and 4.

Sessions from this early treatment phase were four in number, but appointments 1 and 2 were primarily concerned with mental status evaluation and historical review. A reading of the transcripts suggested that beginning with session 3 there was a more intense expression of current concerns. Then in session 4 there was an added component, namely the patient's explicit attempt to draw the therapist into a more intense interaction. Hence, the two sessions were quite different from the vantage point of transference engagement. We shall begin with session 3.

Session 3: trauma retold

We divided the transcript of this hour into six scenes. The main themes contained within each scene were abstracted to highlight them. These are included so as to orient the reader. Those selected passages underscoring major themes that illustrate the presence of the various dimensions of Annihilation Anxiety are in italics.

Scene One: Historical Account of Mohamed's Participation in the War. Mohamed opens with a factual account of his participation: "In the war of 1977 ... I was supporting an infantry unit and leading artillery and rockets in a mountainous region between Jidija and Harrar" (*dimension 6*). He tells, "Whenever the four to six Somali soldiers tried to go out of the place and attack, they got shot in the head" (*dimension 6*).

Scene Two: Danger Discussed in a Cultural/Familial Context: Affirmed, Denied or Disavowed. In this scene Mohamed offers a repetitive account of cultural customs in Somalia. He does so in spite of the therapist's inquiry about his "problems". In Somali tradition, problems are told ... as to what has happened: "We are nomads and when we come to each other, eh, we first give praise to each other, but never start with problems.... So when we say we are fine, it's fine but there are always problems.... In Somali tradition people help each other. Your relatives and friends are like a family insurance and then you get helped."

Scene Three: Danger Relived Subjectively. Mohamed is particularly upset when talking about the loss of his previous family (*dimension 5*) and the impact that recall of his torture (*dimension 4*) has on his current family. In general, when he recalls what happened to him, he has a difficult time thinking about it (*dimension 1*). Mohamed restates how sad he feels when listening to other people's problems and talking about his own. He talks about how hard it is to see that someone needs help, and he starts shivering when he sees someone with problems (*dimension 4*). Mohamed then begins to speak about a difficulty in the refugee camp. He talks about a man who he is sure used to work for the military police and used to kill innocent people in the northern region of Somalia (*dimension 6*). Mohamed describes a dispute between this man and a Somali woman with a few months-old baby whose husband is in Somalia. The man began insulting her and threatened to kill her (*dimension 6*). Mohamed reports that he tried to help although it makes him sick to even look at the man (*dimension 4*). He describes a conflict resolution meeting with the man, the director of the camp, himself, and others, and states that in the meeting, he was really shivering, being very nervous thinking about the murderer (*dimension 4*).

Scene Four: Danger Revisited: Meeting the Torturer in Oslo. When he discovered the former torturer in the Oslo asylum camp, he experienced neck pain and hand numbness: "I was sitting in a wooden chair and I was feeling neck pain and pain on my right side. I felt like a person in torture.... When I am in the house or when I can walk a bit just because of that back pain I can lie on the bed, but suppose if I just sit like that constantly I am feeling this pain. How can you resist when you know that there is such a bad person, a man of dispute.... The whole thing was too much and I felt neck pain" (*dimension 4*). The analyst is able to elicit the patient's awareness of anger and a strong wish for revenge underneath the feelings of terror and accompanying the somatization, which feels like the earlier experienced torture (*dimension 4*). The physiotherapy, however, seems to be helping. Mohamed describes how he is sleeping better, and even though he is still in pain, he has been helped. "Before it was difficult for me to touch that place but now since I have started the physio, I can touch it" (*dimension 4*). He has been noticing how the numbness in his hands is connected to the muscles in his back. "Everything is connected."

Scene Five: Sources of Current Irritability: Smoking, and Scheduling. Therapist asks Mohamed whether he keeps up-to-date with the political situation in Somalia. Mohamed provides a brief report to his therapist, but notes that he "does not like hearing problems". He would like to watch sports on television "so that I at least can forget". But he cannot watch television in the camp because "they smoke in the place". He does not like smoking and becomes very nervous and irritated (*dimension 4*). He then describes phobic aversion to cigarette smoke and to smokers at the train station coffee shop, which again, has an invasive quality (*dimension 4*). This experience prevents him from enjoying any activity. He appreciates having a coffee, but does not like sitting in coffee houses because everyone smokes (*dimension 4*). He relates to his therapist that a week ago after visiting his physiotherapist he felt very ill: "I get headache and I get pain in all my muscles" (*dimension 4*). He could not take the train to his other appointment because "I was so sleepy that I could not resist my urge to sleep." By the time he recovered he was late for his other appointment, which he realized was at a different time, "so I get confused because of the appointments and because I was very, very tensioned, and then I just forget everything" (*dimension 1*). His therapist asks him if he has heard any news concerning his application for immigration. "No," he responds, "no, I have not. It's really, it's torture to me. … I get very, very tired and I always feel pains in different places of my body" (*dimension 4*).

Scene Six: A Prophetic Dream by his Previous Wife. His thoughts drift back to Somalia before he was arrested. He walked into his house late one night and his wife woke up and told him that she had had a dream: "I have seen three men came to us, and they were carrying a pistol, and they arrested you" (*dimension 4*). He further notes, "When I have been arrested, it happened just like she dreamed." He then asks his therapist if he could talk to his surgeon because he is experiencing pain in his testicles: "When I am tensioned or when I am ill, the testicle it is very hard, and I am feeling pain on the artery" (*dimension 4*).

Summary of the clinical description of the session

In summary, in session 3, Mohamed describes the dangers he faced. Initially he reports incidents of killings, reflecting a concern over destruction of life (*dimension 6*), but the locus and focus is external to himself with the annihilation experience being somewhat ego distant. Then, as he gets in touch with the torture memories, there is somatization of psychic pain, accompanied by invasive experience that constitutes persecutory anxiety from internal sources (*dimension 4*), with overwhelming anxiety (*dimension 1*), which leads to interference with areas of ego functioning, especially, confusion and memory loss, and interference with the ability to function. As he focused more on present time problems, the indications of being overwhelmed decreased.

Concurrently with this progression towards higher levels of Annihilation Anxiety and, specifically in the experience of being invaded, we can also observe a progression in the disruption of meaning making. We advance the proposition that with greater verbalization of annihilatory content in the form of being invaded, there also occurs an accentuation in the disruption in meaning making.

Quantitative empirical observations concerning Annihilation Anxiety and its modification

The findings from session 3 will be presented in three ways: (a) The pervasiveness of Annihilation Anxiety (AA): prevalence (sheer presence), saliency (occurrence of specific dimensions), and intensity (the frequency and range of dimensions within a given idea unit). Cumulatively, these constitute the core of the AA concept as we conceive of it. (b) The Symbolizing process: this process is presented in its two aspects, Symbolization and Desymbolization. Each is marked by prevalence, saliency, and intensity. We hypothesize that the two sub-processes (our two main AA modifiers) are inversely related to one another. And (c) targeted AA activity cluster, which is clinically defined, and always involves peak AA activity and its specific pattern. This targeted segment highlights the impact of this unique AA activity on the Symbolizing/Desymbolizing processes; it constitutes salient AA moments, moments of consequence. The process will be delineated through a particular methodology, the Visual Analysis of graphic representations, introduced in Chapter Seven.

The pervasiveness of Annihilation Anxiety for the entire hour: empirical findings

The prevalence of AA activity for session 3 was 25%: thus a quarter of all idea units contained at least one reference to annihilatory anxiety. The saliency of dimensions emphasized the themes of invaded (58%), destroyed (21%), and feeling overwhelmed (18%). The intensity/range mean was 0.32. For a detailed description of AA prevalence and mean intensity scene by scene, see table 4.

The symbolizing process

There are indications that session 3 is a predominantly Desymbolizing one. When we examined the incidence of the two components of the Symbolizing process, we found that there were 72 scorable

Table 4. Descriptive statistics for session 3 as a whole and scene by scene.

	Total	Scene 1	Scene 2	Scene 3	Scene 4	Scene 5	Scene 6
AA Prevalence	25%	19%	4%	34%	29%	23%	27%
AA Saliency	Invaded 54%	Invaded 0%	Invaded 50%	Invaded 43%	Invaded 90%	Invaded 68%	Invaded 77%
AA Intensity	0.32	0.31	0.11	0.43	0.34	0.29	0.31
Symbolization Prevalence	6%	0%	0%	12%	0%	0%	11%
Symbolization Intensity	0.21	0.13	0.68	0.31	0.09	0.04	0.22
Desymbolization Prevalence	25%	0%	4%	24%	57%	27%	20%
Desymbolization Intensity	0.33	0	0.04	0.33	0.66	0.41	0.24

instances of Desymbolization compared with 54 for Symbolization in this session. When we further considered intensity, the trend was once more in the same direction: Desymbolization was 0.33 compared to 0.21 for Symbolization. Hence, when one of these variables becomes dominant, the other typically becomes subordinate.

Targeted cluster analysis through the method of Visual Analysis

In the targeted cluster analysis we define the interplay of three sets of variables: their contiguity, their covariation, and their discontiguity. Through this method we are able to define the structure of the Annihilation Anxiety process during a given session (see figure 1). The focus now will be on scenes three, four, and five.

The saliency of AA activity defined by the dimension of Invaded reflects the height of the AA cluster. For each of the three criterion scenes (scenes three, four, and five), AA expressed through the dimension of Invaded leads the way and we see it as the dominant organizer of this phase of the session.

We note that Desymbolization co-varies with feeling Invaded. Moreover, in scenes 3 and 5, the intensity of total AA is close to the

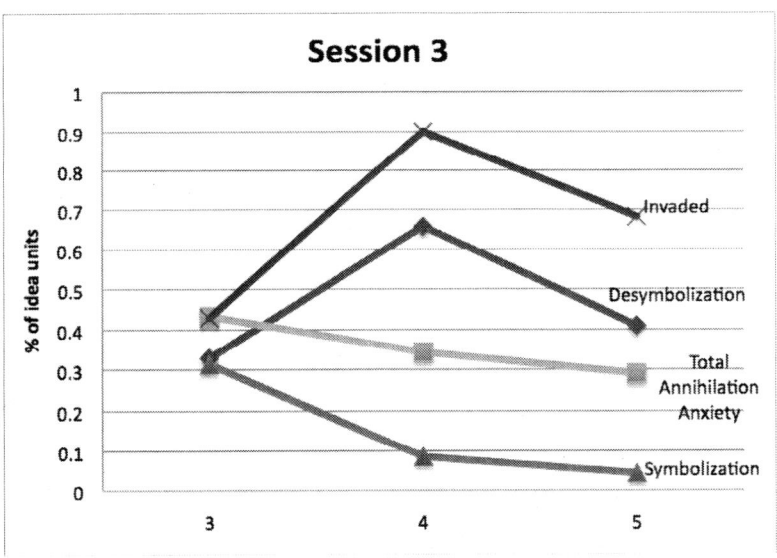

Figure 1. Targeted Annihilation Anxiety cluster for session 3.

intensity of Desymbolization. These data show that the degree of relationship between Desymbolization and the various manifestations of AA co-occur to varying degrees.

As we look at figure 1, Symbolization is found to be substantially lower than AA as reflected in the Invaded dimension, as well as overall AA, and also Desymbolization, for each of the criterion scenes. Moreover, while the shape of the curve for Desymbolization mirrors the shape of the Invaded dimension of AA, this was not the case for Symbolization here.

This configurational display using the method of Visual Analysis hints about the structure of the hour. It supports the view that this is a Desymbolizing session, that is, that Desymbolization co-varies with the Invasion dimension of AA. It supports the view that here AA is discontinuous with Symbolization, the meaning making process, and that the Symbolization and Desymbolization processes here are inversely related.

Quantitative empirical documentation and clinical validity

This targeted cluster analysis so far based on quantitative data reflected crucial moments during this analytic hour. What have we learned from these quantitative findings about the impact of Annihilation Anxiety activity on the Symbolizing process? We have already established that Annihilation Anxiety highlighted by the dread of being Invaded reveals not only saturation but also an intensification beginning with scene three and peaking in scenes four and five. As we listen to Mohamed during these moments, we hear: "I was like a person in torture". He was suffering from pain; he thought of a person in camp, a former torturer whom he hated and who "was a very bad person." These thoughts culminated in a state of "I became very very, very, very, very ill!" Clearly, there was a sense of torture, of persecutory ideation, torture at the hands of the persecutor, and once more suffering in the sense of feeling invaded—a perforation of his body self.

Then, when he was faced with the full force of hatred and produced persecutory themes in scene four, Desymbolization appeared in the form of part-object representation, the body objectified (that is the moment in which Annihilation Anxiety activity and Desymbolization peaked): "But the pain on the muscles, is still existing ... and ... it has a connection with the pain on my back". Furthermore, when we looked at the quality of Desymbolization in scene five, the emphasis shifted to a series of event reporting, the focus on specific schedules. Now affect had become frozen as he was recounting minute events. The affect experience had thus been defensively avoided.

Concluding remarks for session 3

We had said on the basis of our quantitative observations and Visual Analysis that Annihilation Anxiety during this hour had become Desymbolized. We can be more specific now. It is a shift in the direction of concretization and finally to a frozen constellation of emotions. We think of this as a process of petrification and concretization of the thinking process. A very different set of events arises only one session later, when the transference context has shifted.

Session 4: trauma relived

In session 4, nine days later, the second session we examined, there was considerable focus on reliving the trauma that he had suffered, where he told, now in emotional terms, of food deprivation, of inadequate medical care, and absence of creature comforts. It was a session that was also marked by a change in attitude and position by Mohamed towards the therapist, and concurrently, heightened therapist activity. Hence, we describe this session as one of increased transference engagement. We divided the transcript into five definable scenes and applied the same method used in session 3 detailed above. Here are the highlights.

Scene One: Hospital Treatment as Torture: Comparison of Mogadishu and Oslo. The session begins with Mohamed informing his therapist of an upcoming minor surgery on his testicle (*dimension 4*). He will be hospitalized, but will go home the same day. Mohamed remembers a surgery when in prison also with a brief hospital stay, but knows this is not the same situation. When the therapist notes that the prospect of a short hospital stay makes him anxious, Mohamed responds: "I was informed that in Norway people don't stay in the hospital. Doctors send patients home after operating on them. But it's not torture. In Somalia, it was part of my torture" (*dimension 4*). Further, Mohamed relives his earlier trauma in the here-and-now by relating how at that time he had an infection in the stitches on his testicle (*dimension 4*), but was released from the hospital anyway because someone had paid them for the hospital bed.[i] "It was to their advantage that I was ill, because when I'd asked for help, then they'd say I could have drugs for my illness but only if I signed something first. That was the only way I could get the medicine I needed. And the doctor that looked after me was part of the torture group."

Scene Two: Requesting, even Imploring Permission for Revenge. His therapist wants to know how he feels about being tortured. Mohamed describes it as a bodily experience, more primitive than words: 'It was a very bad thing and when I think about it, it makes me feel something that I can't put into words.... I feel something in my body. ... (*dimension 4*) It was so inhuman, but they were doing worse than that; they were torturing women and children' (*dimension 4*). Mohamed asks his therapist: "What would you advise me to do if I see someone from that torture group in Norway?" The therapist responds to his question by asking Mohamed to reflect upon his choices. Mohamed persists by asking repeatedly, "Do you think you can give me advice? Is it not legal for you to give advice?" He then laughingly says that he wants to see how the therapist thinks about it first, "Because I want to know if someone who has not been in the problem would think of it differently than someone who has." Mohamed uses the metaphor of swimming. "Suppose someone doesn't know how to swim but tries to. He starts sinking ... but just before he is about to drown, someone saves him" (*dimension 6*). When Mohamed later talks about his experience, he can describe how he felt when his legs were stuck in the sand, what he was thinking about at the time, about life, etc. (*dimension 6*). Someone who has been through the actual experience would be able to describe more accurately what it is really like. "But I'm wondering, since you probably haven't been through what I've been through, what the difference is in what you would do if you saw someone from the torture group" (*dimension 4*). The therapist gives no advice here.

Scene Three: Conception of Torture: Islam and Christianity. The patient then focuses on religious doctrines of Muslim and Christian theology, as well as appealing to the therapist's physician role, in an attempt to further pressure the therapist to approve his vengeful wish. Mohamed invokes the Koran to tell his therapist that "If you decide to do something, it's better to ask your companions, your friends or your relatives or your parents" because "if there is any mistake, then they can fix it and that is something good." Mohamed argues that he wants the therapist's opinion because he is the doctor—a psychiatrist who hears lots of problems and is not like the ordinary man in the street. "But maybe you really don't want to get involved in this." Mohamed adds that people ask such things of elders because they are experienced in dealing with problems. "Or, we ask such questions of people we trust, like brother or father. Or, someone like a doctor, because they always advise something good. Their career is helping people."

Scene Four: Torture Re-Visited, and Implemented in the Here and Now in Oslo. Mohamed again recounts details of his earlier torture experience, stimulated by the recently discovered presence of the former torturer. He tells the story of when he and several others were released from prison and were living in Mogadishu. Some of the people in the torture group came to them soliciting money: "They didn't know that we knew they had been the torturers (*dimension 4*). It is hard to put into words what I was feeling then. One could think of killing them (*dimension 6*). I saw them torture children (*dimension 4*). So it is very, very difficult when someone that you know who tortured you or your wife, comes to you for money. One could kill him" (*dimension 6*). Mohamed progressively acknowledges the difficulty he experiences in controlling his behaviour. As a result, Mohamed decides against the taking of revenge, with the idea that he would be no better than his tormentor: "If you try to get revenge, you are becoming like that person. But when I see such people, I feel very sad and I have to control my personality and my feelings, try not to react, or kill him, or torture him (*dimensions 4 and 6*). It's not good to solve a wrong with a wrong. Because then you're just like him. If someone knocks your head, and then you knock his head, you are both just fighting—doing the same thing." "An eye for an eye," the therapist interjects. "Yes," Mohamed responds, "and it also exists in Islamic law. If someone cuts your hand you can cut his hand but it's not exactly like that (*dimension 4*). If someone cuts your hand, you have to take him to a mosque or a judge and tell what happened. If you can forgive him, then the man goes free, but if you can't, then the judge can order that his hand be cut like yours. So it's not exactly like you can just quickly retaliate."

Scene Five: Re-experiencing Details of the Original Torture. Mohamed remembers his small cell in jail and how he was being denied the food that his relatives provided him. The guards would demand any money he had for food. "And so I would give it to them. If I didn't, I wouldn't be allowed to eat or to go to the toilet. I was getting increasingly nervous and angry and very violent (*dimension 1*). Now when I get very angry I feel pain in my body (*dimension 4*). Sometimes I feel numbness and headaches and tired (*dimension 4*). I try to keep myself calm so the other person does not know what I'm feeling."

Summary of the clinical description of the session

The manner in which the annihilatory fears were told differed markedly in this session. It began with reliving the original trauma, the terror of being invaded. But he also linked it to the anticipated surgery. This anticipation set the stage for a series of pressures to get explicit approval for his vengeful wishes from the therapist. Mohamed became assertively persuasive, utilizing an imaginary swimming scene and a comparison of religious metaphors. Once more, as he relived the original trauma, he was dreading not only psychic invasion but also being destroyed and overwhelmed. It is at this point that apprehensions of being invaded and overwhelmed shifted from a passive to an active mode.

Concurrently, it was also possible to observe changes in the mode in which meaning was communicated. Through the use of imagery, qualifications, expression of intent, and the implementation of metaphorical thought in the form of religious icons, there are indications of a Symbolizing mode of thought. A reading of this text is consistent with the hypothesis that now annihilatory fears had been modified through processes of Symbolization.

Quantitative empirical observations concerning Annihilation Anxiety and its modification

The steps outlining quantitative findings for session 4 will parallel what had guided our presentation for session 3. Once more we will present our observations in three steps: (a) The pervasiveness of Annihilation Anxiety (AA): prevalence, saliency, and intensity. (b) The Symbolizing process: Symbolization and Desymbolization.

Each is marked by prevalence, saliency, and intensity. And (c) targeted Annihilation Anxiety activity cluster, which is clinically defined and always involves peak AA activity and its specific pattern. Again, this process will be delineated through the method of Visual Analysis.

The pervasiveness of Annihilation Anxiety for the entire hour: empirical findings

The prevalence of AA for session 4 was 33%, higher than it was for session 3, which was 25%. Once more, Invaded was the most prominent theme for expressing psychic danger, and it was higher than we observed it to be for session 3 (73% vs. 54%). Then the intensity mean of AA was 0.47, suggesting the use of a greater frequency and range of AA dimensions within idea units. Finally, in terms of active/passive mode, the expression of AA appeared predominately in an active mode. All quantitative indicators suggest that during this session Mohamed showed a trend of expressing the danger in a more pronounced fashion, both in content and in his use of images during the hour. For a detailed description of quantitative observations scene by scene, see table 5.

The symbolizing process

Clearly, in session 4, the Symbolization process was dominant, not only in the number of scorable instances (104 compared to 24 for the Desymbolizing process) but also in the use of dimensions. Whereas object relational space was the primary theme (57%), it was complemented by the presence of both imaginary space (35%) and temporal space (22%). This trend was also reflected in the intensity measure: Symbolization had a mean intensity of 0.61 whereas Desymbolization a mean intensity of 0.14. We hypothesized that for the session as a whole there will be once more an inverse relationship between Symbolization and Desymbolization.

Targeted cluster analysis through the method of Visual Analysis

Once more we selected a salient AA targeted cluster to articulate the structure of the hour. Based on peak AA activity and clinical observations, we selected scenes two, three, and four and represent the findings revealed through Visual Analysis.

Table 5. Descriptive statistics for session 4 as a whole and scene by scene.

	Total	Scene 1	Scene 2	Scene 3	Scene 4	Scene 5
AA Prevalence	33%	52%	40%	0%	33%	37%
AA Saliency	Invaded 73%	Invaded 100%	Invaded 61%	Invaded 0%	Invaded 77%	Invaded 58%
AA Intensity	0.47	0.66	0.63	0	0.54	0.43
Symbolization Prevalence	39%	34%	69%	63%	42%	0%
Symbolization Intensity	0.47	0.34	0.91	0.73	0.53	0
Desymbolization Prevalence	11%	24%	23%	0%	1%	16%
Desymbolization Intensity	0.14	0.28	0.29	0	0.01	0.25

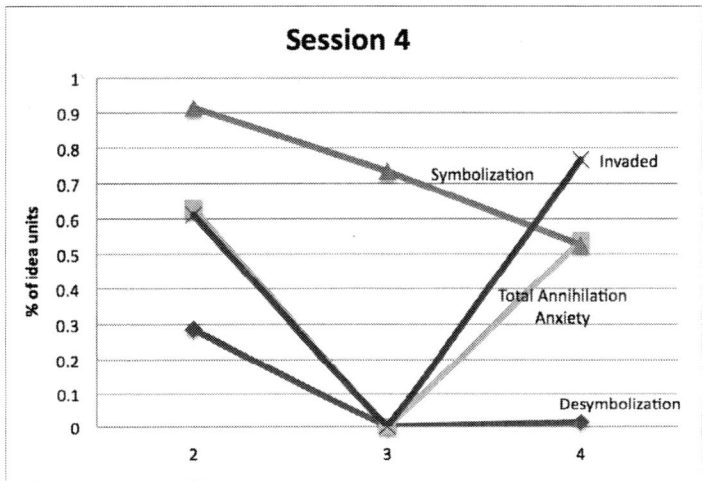

Figure 2. Targeted Annihilation Anxiety cluster for session 4.

During session 4 the structure was dramatically different from session 3 since AA demonstrated an oscillating pattern: it peaked, declined, and then peaked again. Furthermore, this time, AA covaried with Symbolization during peak moments. Indeed, Symbolization was a defining marker throughout the hour.

Total AA shows a peak during scene two, a dramatic drop in scene three, and a peak once more in scene four. Unlike in session 3, in session 4 we use total AA activity as the organizing variable because there were more dimensions present in this part of the hour, not simply Invaded.

Symbolization is high in all three scenes, in spite of the negative slope from scenes two to four. For scenes two and four Symbolization is either higher or matches the total AA process. Moreover in scene three, Symbolization is present albeit AA activity is absent.

Desymbolization was consistently low or absent in the targeted cluster. Furthermore, it was substantially lower in scenes two and four compared to AA in those scenes. For this hour, it appears to be disconnected from AA when the latter occurs. Desymbolization again is inversely related to the Symbolization.

Once more, this method of Visual Analysis focused on the interplay of our three variables, which define for us the structure of this hour. It justifies the designation of this hour as a Symbolizing session. Furthermore, when AA peaks, it is associated and contiguous with Symbolization. Further, when AA activity is absent, Symbolization persists. Figure 2 once more reaffirms that Symbolization is inversely related to Desymbolization.

We advance the proposition that in this session, in spite of an increase in the expression of AA, the character of the hour had been altered. The Symbolizing space had now become predominant. We hypothesize that the presence-absence-presence of AA created a psychic context during which Symbolization could emerge.

Empirical observations and clinical validity

Once more, we learned from the quantitative analysis of session 4 that it is a symbolizing hour, and that the particularity of the modification (here, transformation) that took place comes to light most clearly when we consider the oscillation of the targeted areas: scenes two, three, and four. It would appear that the presence-absence-presence of Annihilation Anxiety reflected the appearance of a transference context during which Symbolization could emerge. For each scene, we need to look at the juxtaposition of Annihilation Anxiety activity and the appearance of the Symbolic mode.

For each of these scenes, through a qualitative reading, distinct aspects of the symbolizing process can be identified. In scene two, Mohamed relives the trauma (and indeed he had just told of betrayal in an earlier scene). But this time he redirects his grief and aggression to the analyst. He not only recalls the torture, but presses for support from the analyst for his urge to kill the torturer. As the therapist, in preserving the therapeutic frame, maintains an analytic stance, Mohamed attempts to understand the therapist's thoughts. He then evokes a metaphor of a drowning person to ask the therapist whether someone who has not experienced the horror of dying was able to apprehend the dread of it. In terms of our scoring, through the use of this metaphor, Symbolization has taken the form not only of object relational but also of imaginary space.

In scene three, significantly, in the context of a dialogue with the therapist, Annihilation Anxiety content disappeared completely and was replaced by religious imagery. In creating a comparison between Islam and Christianity Mohamed used the principle of an eye for an eye, verbalized by the therapist, as a vehicle that might help him restrain his murderous impulses. Once more the therapist refrained from offering advice. What now follows in scene four is *torture relived* through the invocation of specific memories of betrayal and the recognition that the torturers were not aware of the fact that they were recognized as torturers.

To summarize, the targeted scenes two, three, and four from session 4 with oscillating Annihilation Anxiety activity demonstrate that in scene two torture was first relived in object relational space, then in scene three in imaginary space, and in scene four in temporal space.

Commentary

What we have just described within the frame of the symbolizing process mirrors Bucci's work on the referential process (Bucci & Maskit, 2007). For her, the sequence of arousal-symbolization-reorganization is an icon of a "good psychoanalytic hour". In the oscillating sequence of session 4 we also observed such a sequential alteration of mental functioning, from recognition, to imagination, to memory, associated with working through a sequence of mental functioning. Thus, for Mohamed, arousal was already present in scene one as he relived torture involving injury to his testicles. Then, Symbolization was present both in scenes two and three with the drowning metaphor followed by the imaginary invocation of God. Then, reorganization was present at the end of the sequence of Symbolization, when Mohamed recalled past details of torture, now told in temporal space.

Concluding remarks for session 4

For this phase of the treatment, we can affirm the phenomenon of "the Symbolization of Annihilatory Anxiety". Empirically, it was defined by apparently higher levels of Annihilation Anxiety and Symbolization intensity as compared to session 3. The quality of Symbolization that we witnessed also suggested a shift in the targeted Annihilation Anxiety cluster, which was oscillating from high, to absent, to high Annihilation Anxiety activity. Within this cluster we could observe just how symbolizing evolved from the use of object relational to imaginary and then to temporal space. We hypothesized that these were the conditions which created an inner context in which terrible dread could now live on within Mohamed's consciousness. This example of transformation was a transitory occurrence, but, nonetheless, of considerable theoretical import. A parallel finding will be reported in the study of the recorded psychoanalysis of Ms Y (see Chapter Seventeen).

Comparison of sessions 3 and 4—constancies and modifications

That annihilatory anxieties, a menace to psychic survival, should be a theme in the psychic content of the psychotherapy of a patient who has endured severe trauma is definitional. However, through fashioning a way of operationalizing the spectrum of annihilatory anxieties with its profile of dimensions, we were able to witness how these signifiers of menace became embedded in the therapeutic engagement even during the first few sessions.

Our descriptive empirical observations have already affirmed that annihilatory anxiety was markedly present in both sessions 3 and 4, that the experience of dreading invasion was paramount, and, most noteworthy, while the annihilatory fear formed a relatively constant presence in both sessions, its modification was markedly distinct in each hour. The direction of this modification was highlighted in the distinct structures of each hour, as seen through our method of Visual Analysis. There we observed that session 3 was essentially a desymbolizing session, that is, a mental structure in which Annihilation Anxiety was embedded in the process of concretization, and dissociated from the process of meaning making. In contrast, session 4 had the structure of a symbolizing hour in which the meaning making process was contiguous with the experience of annihilatory dread in the context of heightened transference engagement, and even persisted when Annihilation Anxiety was absent. Each of these two structures also had its defining clinical markers which were contained within the account of Symbolization and Desymbolization.

These structural differences were affirmed through a direct comparison of our main defining variables, as already shown.

In session 4, the symbolizing hour, Annihilation Anxiety was more frequent and showed higher intensity. Concurrently, it demonstrated higher prevalence and intensity in the symbolizing process. In contrast, for session 3, the desymbolizing hour, Annihilation Anxiety was somewhat lower. Yet, Desymbolization was paramount, both in prevalence and intensity. An additional scene-by-scene analysis indicated that for session 4, five out of five scenes revealed higher Symbolization scores compared to Desymbolization; for session 3 this was observed for only one of the six scenes. Conversely, in session 3, five of the six scenes had higher Desymbolization scores than they had Symbolization. This saliency of each of the two modifiers underscores the significance of these two variables in shaping the Annihilation Anxiety process.

Furthermore, in this predominately symbolizing session, session 4, we discerned a different pathway, namely Annihilation Anxiety becoming embedded within the pulls and pushes of the transference dialogue, and that this may have led to new symbolic forms. As mentioned, our microanalytic method allowed us to generate new clinical propositions. Thus, as we tracked targeted Annihilation Anxiety clusters, we noted a distinct path that suggested how such modification could take place within the therapeutic hour. The microanalysis of session 4 revealed that as Mohamed relived the trauma within enhanced transference engagement, new lines of clinical inquiry were suggested. There we noted how the particular moments evoking the dread of past memory through a shift in transference demand elicited fantasies, memories, and even culturally poignant metaphors, which appeared to give life to past suffering in an ego syntonic mode.

This dynamic vision of the Annihilation Anxiety concept embedded within the broader frame of the dynamics of working through has been spelled out by Hurvich (2011) in a rendition of the new developments of the Annihilation Anxiety concept within the analytic situation. These processes are further articulated in the next chapter as well as in the account of the recorded psychoanalysis to be found later in this volume (see Part III). In the next chapter we will demonstrate how this reverberation between anticipated loss of meaning and confrontation with destructiveness are part of the genesis of a panic attack.

Endnote

i. The fact that there are recurrent references to surgery on his testicle and specific severe pains related to the experience in camp suggests that the torture may have included experiences of actual physical assault on his genitals.

CHAPTER NINE

Termination crisis and a panic attack: sessions 41 and 42

Norbert Freedman, Marvin Hurvich, and Alexandra Petrou

About a year and a half after the phase of Mohamed's early treatment engagement, the psychotherapy came to an abrupt halt. The analyst described how the earlier sessions reflected a process of rapprochement in the phase of the working alliance, next a middle phase of depression and hopelessness, and then a final phase which necessitated a return to his home country. The anticipated departure was a subtext that defined the last two recorded sessions (see Chapter Seven). It is in anticipation of despair that our final observations of the recurrence of Annihilatory Anxiety and its transformation will begin.

Throughout this year of treatment the themes of past torture, torture remembered, and torture relived permeated these sessions: the torture in camp, undernourishment, having been sentenced to death, and recounting what prison guards had done to others. Once more, however, a reading of the clinical material (as well as the therapist's comments) suggested that the impact of trauma progressively permeated the patient's state of consciousness, and led us to consider sessions 41 and 42 to reflect a process of cumulative trauma. When these memories were revived in therapy, they peaked once again in the anticipation of panic, and this concern was activated in session 41. But then, through the coincidence of a fire alarm, the total spectrum of terror was activated and relived during the therapeutic hour. That becomes the central theme of session 42. It is for this reason that we designated session 41 to be anticipatory of the panic attack, and then session 42 became the panic attack proper session. Once more we will offer the highlights of each session scene by scene.

Session 41: trauma anticipated

In keeping with our methodology, we begin with clinical observations contained in the successive scenes of the hours, to be followed by clinical generalizations described in summary form. These culminate in the confirmation of the clinical propositions through documented empirical observations. As in Chapter Eight, the transcript of this hour was divided into six scenes, and the main themes contained within each scene were abstracted so as to highlight the themes of the hour. These are included so as to orient the reader. Those selected passages highlighting major trends that suggest the presence of the various dimensions of Annihilation Anxiety are in parentheses.

Scene One: Everyday Life Makes Mohamed Tense. The session begins with resistance towards therapy: lateness, travel, and inconvenience. Memories of the sun affecting his body lead to a series of physical complaints: "Because I am feeling cold, I am getting the pains, and I am getting this mental tiredness" (*dimension 4*). He expresses concern over his wife's helplessness regarding being locked up in the hospital: "She was very ill" and could not leave the hospital; "She was trapped" (*dimension 1*). He worries about his wife's inability to speak English or to understand Norwegian. Finally, he expresses anticipated tension even over keeping his therapy appointments.

Scene Two: Forbidden Foods. In an effort to help the patient deal with his emotional upset, the therapist responds to the patient's request for coffee and sugar. The therapist continues to accommodate Mohamed, and this leads to a discussion about tea and coffee in Somalia, and then a comparison with food habits in Norway. The "use of sweets" in the raising of the children arises. He relishes the eating of chocolates and coconut, but is disgusted that Norwegians use pig fat in chocolates. The disgust continues concerning the use of animal fat in bread. Then he voices repulsion about alcohol in chocolates: Note that there is no manifest Annihilation Anxiety here.

Scene Three: The Cat, a Close Companion. The patient reports a cat emerging from the forest near his residence. The cat shocked his son; it was not aggressive, but the boy thought it was harming him. Memories of being in jail are re-evoked: swamped by cats that were "climbing on the walls and the trees and 30 or 40 of them came down to us, putting their legs inside the fence to get some food." He remembers feeding the cats: "It was as if somebody was with me and somebody was eating with me." He recalls eating with his family; eating alone is torture to him: "When I am alone, I could not eat." In the Mogadishu camp, the security officer became annoyed and ordered members of a tribe that Mohamed likens to gypsies to kill the cats (*dimension 6*). These gypsies laugh together, dance together, and only eat meat. They hunt by using a net in which the animals get stuck: "They break the legs and kill them with knives, and every family collects what goes in the net" (*dimension 6*). Then the leader is asked to "collect the cats and kill them" (*dimension 6*), which Mohamed feels, "It was an inhuman act. He was beating the cats with a hard club" (*dimension 4*). A dream is evoked. A cat came during the night, was beaten, but came back, and begged for food. "When I saw the cat here in Norway you know I remember that day when they were beating and killing the cats in the prison" (*dimension 6*).

Scene Four: Memories of the Old Man and his Boy, and Torturing Children. Mohamed tells the story of an old Somali man, a sailor, who lived in London with his son. Upon his return from London, the man was arrested but not his son. In jail, Mohamed and the old man witness the torture of children: "They were beating them and they were held. They tied a rope to their hands, and then hung them from a high place, until they got what they wanted from them" (*dimension 4*). Mohamed voices shame about the torture carried out by his own countrymen and tries to convince the old man that these actions were justified.

Scene Five: Political Menace and the Recognition of Kindness. The patient reflects on the stability of the Norwegian government and of the United Nations. He reports on starvation and chaos in Somalia. He repeats his shame that "We did it to ourselves. War criminals continue to create problems." He feels angry and tired. He hopes that respect for the law will lead to kindness by the administration. Here we note shame, and much guilt, with little manifest Annihilation Anxiety.

Scene Six: Persecuted in his Own Home. "The authorities who are responsible for our safety also did the crime." He speaks of a complaint letter by his landlord, presumably accusing Mohamed of disturbances and of loud noises. Mohamed felt it was a very bad letter, and a betrayal. He reported feeling disturbed by unfair treatment, and that it was unjust for his not having been consulted beforehand. He was threatened with possible eviction from his house. He is known and respected by the commune. He feels judged, and that it was an "inhumane judgment". "We don't make any noise," he says as he repeatedly declares his innocence. He needs to find a new house. In the midst of these disturbing events, he faints during the evening, and becomes very angry and ill (*dimensions 1 and 4*). Pain leads to sleepiness. "New pains are coming. I have got new pains on parts of my neck, and new pains upon my chest, and the previous pains remain" (*dimension 4*). He fears an illness of the heart, alluding to emotional distress linked to feelings of anger over injustice (*dimension 4*). "I am cut off from my breathing" (*dimension 4*). He cannot take care of his wife and children. "I want to live alone for a while." He has a dream in which he saw a man walking out on his family. "I would be like a devil." He has thoughts about leaving the family because the responsibilities now feel overwhelming to him (*dimension 1*). Our hypothesis that session 41 involved signs of an anticipation of the panic attack that materializes in session 42 merits some additional elaboration. As described, the patient was quite upset by the news of a possible eviction, which he experienced as a betrayal, and a narcissistic and moral injury. There was also a wish to be free of now burdensome family responsibilities, and the experience of breathing difficulties, heart concerns, fainting, and excessive anger. These reflected a general lessening of ego stability, and a state of increasing mental fragility. All this occurred in this last scene of the session, just prior to the one where an announcement of a planned fire alarm constituted an external triggering event that was followed by a panic attack.

Summary of the clinical description of the session

In the initial phases of this session, Annihilation Anxieties remain quite distant from conscious concerns. Indeed, they are hardly mentioned. Rather, the focus is on health and food, including affects of distaste and disgust, and finally reflection on cultural comparisons. The negative transference needs to be recognized. Then a veritable explosion of affect was evoked, as he told of an encounter between his son and a cat. This incident was the launching pad for a sequence of associations. First, there was a memory of cats encountered in jail, followed by torture executed by a gypsy clan ordered to exterminate the cats. He then related a dream dealing with an old birth-giving cat that was tortured and yet survived. The allusion to further torture scenes also deals with his suspicion of the Norwegian culture as he was seeking to protect his son. In sum, he was full of contradictions between Norwegian culture and Somali culture, between torture and survival, and between loyalty to his wife and abandoning her. Permeated by shame, he ends the session with persecutory anxiety and conflict for wishing to abandon his wife, and his fear of being like a devil.

The intensity of the affect depicted in this session is modified by various aspects of symbolization, at first defensively through the images of food, of cultural distinctions, and then, through the cat metaphor. Metaphorical thought is expressed first through memories, then through two dreams, but then he also experiences guilt and remorse. In spite of the affect modulation associated with symbolic functioning, the session ends with overwhelming threat to his safety—a feeling of despair and of persecutory anxiety.

Quantitative empirical observations concerning Annihilation Anxiety and its modification

The steps in outlining quantitative findings for session 41 will parallel what had guided our presentation for session 3. Once more we will present our observations in three steps: (a) The pervasiveness of Annihilation Anxiety (AA): prevalence, saliency, and intensity.

(b) The Symbolizing process: Symbolization and Desymbolization. Each is marked by prevalence, saliency, and intensity. And (c) targeted AA activity clusters, which are clinically defined and always involve peak AA activity and its specific pattern. Again, this process will be delineated through the method of Visual Analysis.

The pervasiveness of Annihilation Anxiety for the entire hour: empirical findings

The sheer magnitude of AA—its prevalence, saliency, and intensity—is not characteristically different from what was encountered a year earlier in sessions 3 and 4. In session 41, prevalence was 26% and mean intensity 0.36. What is striking, however, is the curvilinear distribution of AA activity during this hour, in terms of prevalence and intensity (see table 6). In these two aspects, there is initial abatement of AA (even absence in scene two), then a peaking in scenes three and four, and an abatement once more towards the end of the session. Of great interest is the apparent saturation of AA activity in scenes three and four, which alerted us to the designation of the targeted cluster. However, in scene three the dominant dimension was "Destroyed", whereas in scene four, it was "Invaded". At first, Mohamed has to tell the story of destruction, and then continues with how he felt himself to have been invaded.

The symbolizing process

Directing our attention to the prevalence of Symbolization, what is striking is the shift from scene to scene and the fact that it is a curvilinear progression once more. Symbolization was relatively absent in scenes one and two, peaked in scenes three and four, and abated towards the end of the session. What is noteworthy is the overlap in this session between high AA activity and Symbolization, both occurring at the same time. We can already suggest that during this phase of the hour AA had become symbolized. Furthermore, the unfolding Desymbolization sequence was the obverse of Symbolization: high at the beginning, low in the middle of the hour, and then resurgence towards the end of the hour (table 6). Moreover, when we look at the pattern scene by scene, we find in table 6 that for the first two scenes Desymbolization was substantially higher

Table 6. Descriptive statistics for session 41 as a total and scene by scene.

	Total	Scene 1	Scene 2	Scene 3	Scene 4	Scene 5	Scene 6
AA Prevalence	26%	33%	0%	30%	39%	16%	27%
AA Saliency	Invaded 39%	Invaded 60%	Invaded 0%	Invaded 13%	Invaded 65%	Invaded 0%	Invaded 32%
AA Intensity	0.36	0.35	0	0.45	0.63	0.19	0.35
Symbolization Prevalence	22%	7%	0%	32%	33%	6%	15%
Symbolization Intensity	0.24	0.07	0	0.35	0.37	0	0.15
Desymbolization Prevalence	14%	26%	27%	1%	2%	6%	24%
Desymbolization Intensity	0.18	0.28	0.34	0.01	0.02	0.06	0.34

than Symbolization. The pattern of the two middle scenes shows that Symbolization was superordinate to Desymbolization and then Desymbolization became prominent once more for the last two scenes. The sequence affirms the previously noted inverse relationship between symbolization and desymbolization.

Targeted cluster analysis through the method of visual analysis

In view of the curvilinear distribution of AA activity during this session, it was scenes three and four that stood out and were defined as the targeted cluster and became the focus of our analysis (see Figure 3).

Once more, as in session 4, it was the mean intensity AA score that was the salient variable. What is of interest is the peak moment of AA activity during this hour, as can be seen in figure 3, as well as the relative contiguity of AA with the height of Symbolization as contrasted with the level of Desymbolization. In addition, it can be seen that as the patient symbolizes, the intensity of verbalized AA increases. But this trend is short-lived. Soon, Desymbolization will become dominant.

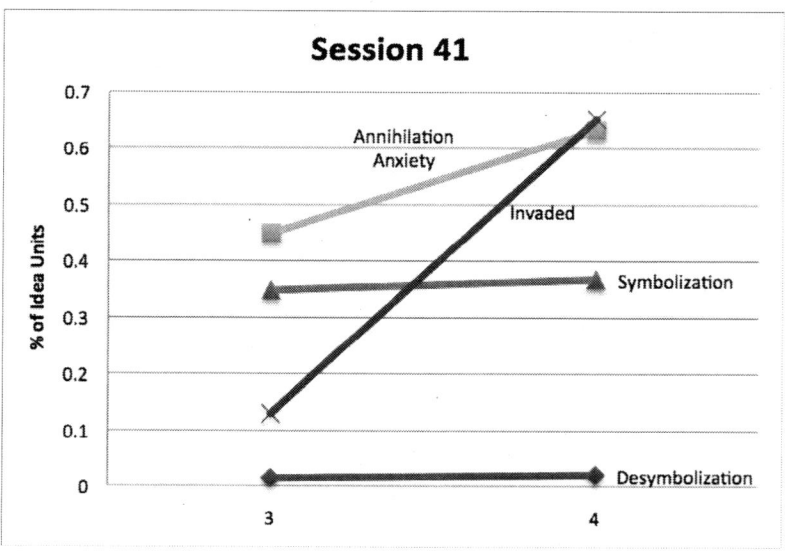

Figure 3. Targeted Annihilation Anxiety cluster for session 41.

Empirical observations and clinical validity

These empirically-based findings raise two issues that deserve separate commentary. The first addresses the phenomenon of the "symbolization of the annihilatory experience", as we had encountered it in the previous chapter in relation to session 4, where we observed the Symbolization of Annihilation Anxiety during heightened transference engagement. We now notice a similar pattern of a targeted peak of Annihilation Anxiety prevalence and intensity during scenes three and four. Even though this is the session just prior to the panic attack, the presence of a scene with metaphoric dimensions is dramatic.

The stage is set by the image of a wild cat, but Mohamed's thoughts wander to a cat as a companion, a cat to be nourished, and a cat endangered. Object relational space gives way to fantasy space and to temporal space. This is a sequence that we have encountered both in session 4 as well as in our studies of recorded psychoanalysis on the process of working through (see Chapter Eighteen).

Symbolizing activity was further accentuated in a noteworthy progression where each symbol was followed by another one: the son, the memory of the cat, the gypsies, the cat dream, memories of earlier torture, memory of the old man, and ending up with pervasive feelings of shame. The Symbolization context was embedded in an aspect of Annihilation Anxiety, which reflects an active mode.

The second significance of the quantitative findings is that they portray the unique temporal profile of an upcoming panic attack, which we hypothesize as a prelude to the panic proper. It is defined by the curvilinear, normal-type distribution of absence-peak-absence of Annihilation Anxiety, which can be better understood when we account for the prevalence of Desymbolization in scenes one and two, as well as scenes five and six, preceding and following the symbolizing phase.

The expectation of future dread was first introduced by various forms of Desymbolization in scenes one and two of session 41. Mohamed was absorbed by invasive memories of discomfort: pain, coldness, mental tiredness, needing sleep, weakness, the body objectified, and an aversion to pig fat in his diet—for a Muslim, a source of disgust.

Following the evocative process of Symbolization in the middle phase of the hour (scenes three and four), persecutory fears mounted. The session ends with the resurgence of Desymbolization: a memory of fainting in his house. In this fainting scene there is an instance of petrification of an AA experience—possibly preparatory to the panic attack.

In summary, we can now formulate the profile of anticipatory Annihilation Anxiety, which can be crystallized into four propositions: 1. Anticipatory Annihilation Anxiety is expressed in its characteristic sequential form: initial apparent absence, peak, and abatement. The significance of this oscillating Annihilation Anxiety pattern will be further discussed below. 2. There is a prodromal form (perhaps reflecting the weakness of Mohamed's ego) of anticipatory Annihilation Anxiety manifest in Desymbolization. Here, concreteness and the body objectified signal the imminent surfacing of explicit annihilatory themes. 3. There is a transitory surge of Symbolization invoking the imaginary and connecting to significant objects, which temporarily transforms the annihilatory dread and leads to a peaking of that experience. And 4. the anticipatory Annihilation Anxiety attack ends with a petrification ("I can't think") exemplified by disfluency, perseveration, body objectified, and paralysis of thought, where once more Desymbolization reflects a frozen constellation of psychic experiences.

This last set of observations suggests the more general proposition that both Symbolization and Desymbolization selectively transform and modify Annihilation Anxiety during specific stages of the therapeutic hour, as fundamental traumatic moments are reworked in consciousness.

Session 42: panic attack proper

We divided this session into seven scenes, and once more here are the highlights and a clinical summary.

Scene One: "I Am Tired! I Am Tired!" Mohamed tells the therapist about the house in which he and his family live together with other Somali community members. Mohamed feels different from the rest of them, and thinks his problems are more difficult than those of others. He feels overly tired, overwhelmed, tense, nervous, and helpless from the family obligations, wife problems, taking care of the kids, and dealing with their illnesses. In all this he feels there's no one on whom to rely (*dimension 1*). Cold weather and slippery conditions result in his feeling afraid of falling (*dimension 5*) and of injuring his son. All these feelings lead to tiredness and pain (*dimension 1 and 4*). Mohamed is yearning for a rest and for household help.

Scene Two: Therapist Responds to Tiredness. Mohamed is caught in a state of increasing despair and psychic tiredness as he reaches out to his therapist to help him apply for added health insurance benefits. "I know you understand. I am feeling you can help me." The therapist provides the patient with a detailed account of past and present health benefits and actions he should take to meet his medical needs. The therapist also urges Mohamed to request a home help. He responds with gratitude, "I think you are the right person here."

Scene Three: Yearning for Family Support. Mohamed's thoughts go back to Somalia. He is concerned about his wife's family because they are in danger and he cannot help them. He feels "physical tension" which he tries to overcome by immersing himself in the problems Somalis are facing in Oslo, regarding which he can have no impact. In fact, he feels even more nervous and tense and fears losing control of himself (*dimension 1*) when with his family. Talking about his problems with the Somali community makes him feel deeply ashamed because he appears needy. At the same time though, he maintains that he needs someone to help him, as he is overwhelmed by his role as a father and husband (*dimension 1*). He hoped that family members from Somalia could come to Oslo to help him, but he is pessimistic. This "makes me feel very nervous and I get afraid of my pain" (*dimension 4*). With despair, he describes having trouble controlling his young son as he plays aggressively with his sister. He concludes, "I cannot resist anything." He wanted to create a club for Somalis in Oslo, but he was forced to delegate leadership to others because "I am always very tensioned" (*dimension 4*) and he has great difficulty relaxing: "I need someone who helps me."

Scene Four: The Plight of Somalis. He compares Oslo to Somalia. In Somalia, he had no rights. The police "did whatever they wanted, and they were killing and torturing people". Things are different in Oslo, but "it's not that much better". He is in need of help, but he does not see how to get the help he needs. He talks of the exiled Somalis who are not able to "live together with other people". They have all gathered in Oslo where they share their worries about the families they left behind. He comments on cultural idiosyncrasies: Somalis never sit down and they talk while standing. But he is different: he has more problems and is isolated from them. He cannot tolerate social interactions, although he recognizes that his isolation is not good for him.

Scene Five: Panic Attack Proper. The therapist alerts Mohamed that a fire alarm is scheduled to go off at 12 o'clock, as he does not want Mohamed to be surprised. Mohamed then complains that he "feels very tired. I am feeling pain all over my body" (*dimension 4*). He pauses while breathing heavily (*dimension 1*). The therapist, seeing the panic attack beginning to fulminate, urges Mohamed to breathe slowly, but Mohamed announces, "I cannot breathe" (*dimension 3*). The therapist instructs Mohamed on breathing. Mohamed requests a cup of coffee, and the therapist brings it with sweeteners. Mohamed reports that he is feeling tired and the therapist responds that the fire alarm has not sounded as yet. Mohamed denies feeling overwhelmed by the mentioning of the fire alarm and comments that he felt "tensioned" when he came out of the house in the morning. He is feeling pain in his neck and remembers having "breathing problems" in the past (*dimension 4*). The text here is interrupted by incomplete sentences, abortive utterances, long pauses, and silences.

Scene Six: Attempts at Recovery through Externalization. Mohamed remembers an earlier fire alarm—which took place at five o'clock in the morning—when his wife became very shocked, confused, and started crying. "Now everything seems okay, it's normal," suggesting the positive impact of the therapist's interventions. The fire alarm sounds at this moment and the discussion centers around sweeteners and their function. Mohamed feels that he has put on weight, as he is no longer as active as when he was a sportsman, a soldier, and an officer back in Somalia. He has tried losing weight, but he cannot "resist his hunger". If he does not eat, he feels tension; in fact, everything he does makes him feel tense. "Everything I do is affecting my brain (*dimension 1*)."

Scene Seven: Therapist Joining the Recovery. The therapist provides detailed instructions to Mohamed as to what to do when he has problems breathing in the future. The therapist informs Mohamed of the physiological underpinnings of panic attacks and the resulting somatic symptoms.

Summary of the clinical description of the session

Embedded within the seven scenes there appear to be four clinically meaningful phases that highlight the evolution of the panic attack:

First, there is a prodromal phase, where Annihilation Anxiety is combined with what seems to be a state of extreme dependency. The therapist is drawn to respond to the patient's requests for help, and the therapist offers relevant information (scenes one and two). This was marked by high physical fatigue, inability to cope, and despairing yearning for help from the therapist, who becomes actively engaged.

Then, in a second phase, there is a veritable burst of verbalized Annihilation Anxiety with abortive containment (scenes three and four). Now, despondency continues in the form of acute shame, then feeling trapped, culminating in a sense of loss of control. These successive themes, regarding multiple relationships in the past, are acutely present in the patient's current experience.

In a third phase (scene five), there was a peak in the panic attack proper. It took place after he was alerted to a previously scheduled fire alarm, but occurred before any alarm had as yet sounded. "I cannot breathe, I cannot breathe." It was expressed with utterances of Annihilation Anxiety, but it focally surfaced through psychophysiological signs, which suggested a state of psychic blankness. Once more it impelled the therapist to intervene actively and behaviourally.

There was a final phase of abortive recovery. It had two aspects, first within the patient and then within the therapeutic couple (scenes six and seven). At first the patient recalls past encounters, then the therapist becomes actively involved, offering and providing physical comfort to soothe Mohamed, who is in a state of disequilibrium.

Quantitative empirical observations concerning Annihilation Anxiety and its modification

Previously, we presented our findings successively along three lines through which we evaluate salient features (i.e. AA, Symbolization, and Desymbolization). Now it seems most parsimonious to give the highlights of the entire configuration, in contrast to the three preceding sessions considered separately. Here are the highlights for session 42 (table 7). While the overall mean prevalence and intensity scores are not different from the other sessions, it is the persistence of AA activity, the lack of relief from scene to scene, that defines this hour. Within AA, overwhelmed becomes the salient dimension (61%).

In terms of Desymbolization, this qualifies as a desymbolized session marked by nonverbal expression. The prevalence

Table 7. Descriptive statistics for session 42 as a whole and scene by scene.

	Total	Scene 1	Scene 2	Scene 3	Scene 4	Scene 5	Scene 6	Scene 7
AA Prevalence	28%	28%	0%	32%	23%	39%	25%	29%
AA Saliency	Over 61%	Over 58%	Over 0%	Over 75%	Over 50%	Over 30%	Over 100%	Over 0%
AA Intensity	0.36	0.3	0	0.36	0.36	0.7	0.3	0.29
Symb Prevalence	6%	2%	8%	4%	9%	0%	20%	0%
Symb Intensity	0.09	0.02	0.08	0.04	0.09	0	0.2	0
Desymb Prevalence	27%	30%	0%	28%	23%	39%	15%	43%
Desymb Intensity	0.34	0.37	0	0.32	0.27	0.74	0.15	0.43

for Desymbolization was 27% and the mean intensity was 0.34. Correspondingly, Symbolization is quite low: prevalence was 6% and the mean intensity was 0.09.

Targeted cluster analysis through the method of visual analysis

We will present session 42 both in terms of its peak activity in scene five, as well as the session as a whole. This is portrayed in Figure 4.

In figure 4, we note a persistent high level of AA activity. One exception appears to be scene two, when there was no patient speech as the therapist felt impelled to intervene. Furthermore, this is indeed a desymbolizing hour, for, as we note, Desymbolization is higher than Symbolization in five of the seven scenes and is contiguous with AA. It is clearly not a symbolizing hour as this quality of mind is persistently absent throughout, with the exception of scene six, at a point of an abortive recovery from the panic attack. What is visually seen is the simultaneous peaking of AA and Desymbolization as the visual marker of the panic attack in scene five.

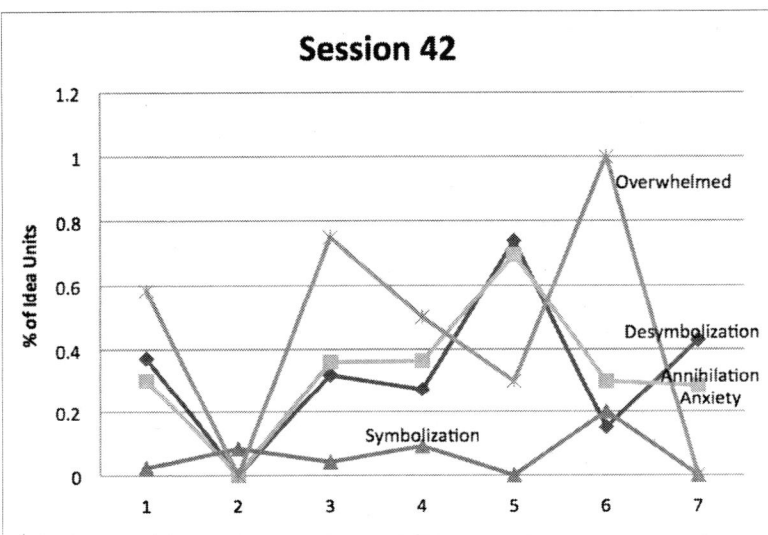

Figure 4. Targeted Annihilation Anxiety cluster for session 42.

Empirical observations and clinical validity

Clearly, Annihilation Anxiety as well as Desymbolization are important features of the entire session. What needs to be articulated is just how Annihilation Anxiety is modified, predominantly by Desymbolization, in the successive phases of this session.

In phase one, the prodromal phase, Annihilation Anxiety in the form of being overwhelmed was relatively prominent, but was absent during the second phase when the therapist became active. The therapist felt impelled to be helpful, sensing a coercion of despair on the part of the patient. Concurrently, Desymbolization was markedly pronounced in both scenes and was manifest as concreteness, the body objectified, pleading utterances, and calls for help.

The burst in phase two revealed a mounting of verbalized Annihilation Anxiety activity in the form of feeling overwhelmed and experiencing the dread of destructiveness. A high level of Desymbolization continued, this time in the form of speech disfluency, and perseverative cries for help. This concurrent Annihilation Anxiety activity, together with Desymbolization, was temporarily mitigated by recourse to cultural comparisons between Norwegians and Somalis.

Phase three, the panic attack proper, depicted in scene five, represents the targeted area, as it has been dramatically shown in figure 4, with the simultaneous peak of Annihilation Anxiety and Desymbolization. Qualitative analysis revealed that here Annihilation Anxiety intensity peaked not only in terms of frequency, but also in the multiple use of Annihilation Anxiety dimensions in close proximity. Now, the quality of Annihilation Anxiety emphasis shifted from feeling overwhelmed to feeling invaded. Furthermore, the most prominent sign was a very marked prevalence of desymbolization expressed in different forms. Specifically, during this phase of the session, there was disruption in affect regulation in the form of long pauses, which appeared to be the most evident sign of psychic blankness. There were also utterances reflecting the concretization of bodily experiences (neck tension). With this cumulative presence of forms of Desymbolization we can also speak of a phenomenon to be termed *Enacted Annihilation Anxiety*, a psychic state that has already been described in the method section in Chapter Seven.

In phase four, the phase of abatement, formulated (verbalized) Annihilation Anxiety declined, but there was still a prevalence of feeling overwhelmed in scenes six and seven in figure 4. Concurrently with Annihilation Anxiety, both Symbolization and Desymbolization appeared: Symbolization reflected in the recall of a previous panic attack, and Desymbolization in the form of concreteness. In scene seven, since the therapist spoke predominantly, there were few instances of patient utterances.

In sum, the evolution of the panic attack proper can be described along a timeline: a prodromal phase, a formulated phase, an enacted phase, and a phase of recovery through therapist activity.

How the panic attack revealed itself through the lens of empirical observations

The close interplay between high Annihilation Anxieties and emotional schemas, reflecting massive physiologic, visceral, somatic and motor images, has been previously described by Hurvich (2002) in an article exploring relationships between Annihilation Anxiety and Symbolization/Desymbolization in the description of the panic attack of a different patient. He stated:

> The panic attack description can be seen to constitute an organized nonverbal emotional schema, split off from the verbal system, a mental representation that includes mental and massive somatic, visceral, physiologic, and motor images. It thus reflects the somatization and deverbalization that have been found associated with desymbolization (p. 357).

Here we have spelled out one unfolding event sequence applicable to the way Mohamed processed the sphere of total psychic helplessness.

First, we noted the increased expression of despair on the verbal level exemplified by the term "overwhelmed"; secondly, a gradient of mounting Annihilation Anxiety intensity, from scene to scene; and thirdly, the peaking of Annihilation Anxiety in the form of that kind of Desymbolization we have termed psychic blankness. There appeared a point in the genesis of panic when spoken language had become insufficient, thus confirming Hurvich's (2002) earlier formulation based on clinical data.

Furthermore, we stress the anticipatory nature of the onset of the panic attack. To paraphrase Suzanne Langer (1942), the panic attack was suggested to Mohamed, to his analyst, and to us as observers, before its explicit appearance. Here we are emphasizing that the appearance of the overt panic attack is partly based on current contextual factors, in addition to the year of cumulative stress. It was the therapist's notification of the expected impending alarm which served as the immediate trigger for the panic symptoms, in addition to the year-long weakening of the patient's psychic equilibrium.

The manner in which the actual attack is expressed in scene five of session 42 suggests that its potential comes about through an aura as this has been portrayed in the successive phases just described. This aura was composed of cumulative trauma, including cumulative Annihilation Anxiety. It began with what might be called an avoidant dissociation, concretization of the body, helpless dependency on all sources of support (in which the analyst participated), and then the burst of feeling overwhelmed, helpless, and invaded, as formulated in spoken language. When the attack did arrive, it was revealed not simply verbally, that is, formulated, but in a surge of psychic blankness, that is, nonverbally as well. When Annihilation Anxiety appeared to be resolved, it had become not just more transference-but also countertransference-intensive. At this point the analyst was challenged to intervene. This spillover of the Annihilation Anxiety experience within the frame of the transference–countertransference dialogue situates the Annihilation Anxiety experience as a pivotal mental organization in this analytic process.

The second pathway towards transformation: from anticipated annihilation dread to panic attack proper

Comparison of sessions 41 and 42

During early transference engagement, described in Chapter Eight, we offered an account of the first pathway towards transformation. During this phase of heightened transference engagement the analyst found himself embedded in Mohamed's treatment, as seen in the shift from session 3 to session 4, when the patient was telling and then reliving his tales of torture. Annihilatory fears here were prominent. But what we also observed was a shift of what we shall designate as divergent modification, namely that a high level of Annihilation Anxiety can evoke Desymbolization in one context and Symbolization in another. During the initial hour, session 3, annihilatory fears were desymbolized, that is, concretized. During the next session, as the analyst found himself affectively embedded in the therapeutic dialogue, annihilatory fears had become symbolized. There we could note the emergence of metaphoric thought and a progression from telling, to imagining, and then to the evocation of memories. It appeared as a brief, albeit significant moment of working through. This first pathway of transformation, thus, was documented in the previous chapter.

Now it is noteworthy that a year and a half later, under very different clinical conditions, where regression was prominent, Mohamed was harassed by internal and external stressors. He revealed a similar pattern of divergent modification as this emerged during sessions 41 and 42. These two sessions could be distinguished on several counts. In session 41, Annihilation Anxiety was segmental and peaked only during the middle of the hour (scenes three and four), while in session 42, Annihilation Anxiety was high and pervasive throughout the hour, and was accentuated by the feeling of being "overwhelmed". Also, in session 41, Symbolization was present, albeit primarily during the middle of the hour, but in session 42, Symbolization was absent. It was Desymbolization which held centre stage, as it peaked during scene five, the panic attack locus.

Of interest here is that in both sessions there were moments during which Annihilation Anxiety surfaced and peaked. The patient deployed the same content, the same dimension (feeling invaded), but the consequence was a very different form of mental functioning. In session 41 (scene four), Mohamed evokes the image of an old man and then children being tortured. These events are told in detail with the evocative emotion of shame, while he made connections between past and present events—he was symbolizing. But then in session 42, faced with the signal of an anticipated fire alarm, he felt he could not breathe, could not think, and his mind became blank. Annihilatory content in many ways seemed to be similar, but the ensuing quality of mind was highly divergent. What was different was the total clinical context. Once more it is the context that gives shape to how the manifestation of clinical concepts can be modified.

These two modes in which the annihilation experience can undergo modification can also be thought of as two modes of defence. The confrontation with threat to survival of the self can readily evoke a process of dissociation. It is possible to distinguish here between two forms of dissociation: an adaptive and a fragmented one. In session 4, Mohamed, after reliving the torture of his imprisonment, makes demands on his therapist. Here he evokes an imaginary drowning scene, resorts to religious icons, and then creates new mental forms that introduce a shift in his relationship to his therapist. It is an adaptive solution. Similarly in session 41, as he evokes memories of the old man and of the children being tortured, he also links himself to psychic reality. This too was adaptive. But one week later, with the impact of the panic attack, his thoughts became disorganized and throttled. He was unable to breathe, and his mind was in a state of blankness. We can then speak of fragmented dissociation. Annihilatory fears had won the day. We, thus, conclude that symbolizing modifiers are adaptive ones, while desymbolizing modifiers tend to be fragmented, although this is not necessarily so. The issue of considering Annihilation Anxiety as a source and a mode of defence, evoking patterns of dissociation, is further touched upon in the Commentary section in Part II of this volume.

Having traced the shifts from session 41 to 42, from Symbolization to Desymbolization, from adaptive to fragmented dissociation, we describe the second pathway of transformation of the Annihilation Anxiety experience. Clinically, it ended in a downward slope in spite of valiant efforts by an engaged and sensitive therapist. It was the last session of the therapy. Yet, there is another path to come. It deals with modification of Annihilation Anxiety in the course of long-term analytic treatment—the topic of the next chapter.

CHAPTER TEN

Transformations in long-term psychoanalytic psychotherapy: the case of Ms K[3]

Rhonda Ward, Norbert Freedman, and Marvin Hurvich

In the two preceding chapters, it has been shown how a patient's psychic functioning can reorganize dramatically in diverse directions with the presence of Annihilation Anxiety. It was noted in Chapter Eight how, within the first four weeks of psychotherapy, Mohamed, a severely traumatized patient, revealed such a transformation. His telling of extreme torture, at first desymbolized and concretized, appeared within a new context during active transference engagement. This was a transformation arising through a symbolized transference.

In Chapter Nine, a clinical regression was described and an alteration in the opposite direction was noted. During the "eye of the storm", the panic attack proper, there arose an accentuation of Annihilation Anxiety, a regressive transformation, creating experiences of psychic blankness. Under these conditions of helplessness,

---

[3] A sketch of "The Transformation of Annihilation Anxiety and its Symbolization", containing an early version of this case material, was first presented at the Berlin IPA congress in 2007 by Freedman, Hurvich and Ward, and was subsequently published in German.

thinking came to a halt. As an epilogue to this second pathway, a fleeting moment of recovery appeared in conjunction with a countertransference enactment, thus depicting the nonlinearity inherent in psychic transformation.

These two pathways towards the transformation of traumatic moments, intriguing as they are, raise a host of questions when generalizing beyond the confines of the severely traumatized patient. To what extent can the foregoing conclusions apply to patients suffering not only from adult onset trauma, but from derivatives of severe developmental trauma? Further, can transformations be observed, not only in brief, but in long-term psychoanalytic therapy? Is there a distinct quality of mental transformation that tends to come with long-term treatment and is therefore observable in psychoanalytic practice? To explore these difficult issues, let us turn to yet another study, another database.

The case of Ms K

We focus now on the tracking of critical psychic events and their sequelae within the context of a ten-year period of psychoanalytic psychotherapy. While in the Mohamed case, audio recordings and session transcripts were used, here reliance was placed upon the analyst's process notes. In both cases, the material was traced and evaluated using the dimensions of Annihilation Anxiety and symbolization, spelled out in Chapter Seven.

At the time of this study, Ms K, a married woman in her mid-thirties, had been in twice-weekly psychotherapy for ten years. She had evolved from a struggling graduate student with occasional panic attacks, to having been awarded a doctoral degree with distinction. Despite her intellectual gifts, Ms K revealed in her therapy a core dread of deadness and of being killed off. But through the evolving transference, she developed the capacity to establish a libidinal connection to her analyst, which in turn became a vehicle for the transformation of her dread of deadness into symbolized and reflective forms.

A series of dreams about kittens, occurring during distinct phases of the treatment, portray this transformation. They reflect a range in representation from death occurred, death escaped, to death owned. Let us elaborate.

Cat dream #1 (year 1)

"An egg crate has been delivered with a kitten inside. It was dead because it had not received any nourishment." In this dream, death has occurred, immediately signalling the overwhelming presence of Annihilation Anxiety. The clinical material from this phase of the treatment supports this notion. There were fantasies of poison being emitted from a gland near the ear, fears of having a flesh eating disease, and explicit images of sharks going after bloody meat. The patient often reported states of panic and concerns about keeping herself together. Translating these clinical observations into propositional language, we find Annihilation Anxiety dimensions of feeling overwhelmed, invaded, self-disorganized, and destroyed. Interpretively, the survival danger appears to be one of oral deprivation.

The process notes from this phase also revealed numerous manifestations of Desymbolization. There were restrictions in the associative process: "I don't feel verbally awake. ... I can't remember what I talked about in the last session." The patient's state of consciousness was often qualified by boredom and the numbing of excitement. The analyst was frequently experienced as deadening to the patient. No matter what was offered, the patient could not feel nourished. Additionally, organ speech often dominated the picture (nausea, pains in the forearms, and back aches), thus illustrating the extent to which Ms K was driven at this point by unmetabolized affects.

There is support here for our general view of an inverse relationship between Annihilation Anxiety and the symbolizing function: when there exists a pervasive threat to the core self or body self, the symbolizing function is throttled. For us, this first phase of Ms K's psychotherapy involved the transformation of Annihilation Anxiety in the direction of a desymbolized, regressive transference.

Cat dream #2 (year 3)

"Ms K has escaped the Holocaust. She has a tiny kitten which she is trying to nourish. A maternal figure (her former therapist) is attempting to prevent nourishment, but Ms K finds a way and the kitten is getting bigger." While in this dream Annihilation Anxiety persists, there is greater distance from the immediate threat (escaping the Holocaust) and there are beginning signs of its symbolization.

In propositional language, the dream reveals the saliency of the Annihilation Anxiety dimension of abandonment (the maternal figure preventing nourishment), as well as the dimension of destroyed (the Holocaust).

This dream also depicts a gesture towards symbolizing space. We find the invocation of object relational space in the dialogue between the maternal figure opposing nourishment and the patient providing nourishment, and the introduction of temporal space in the reference to the therapist of the past. Some distance has been created between Ms K and death.

Now the process notes from this phase also revealed an important and unexpected phenomenon. Within the patient's utterances, there was a decrease in references to Annihilation Anxiety. However, this shift was accompanied by a surprising phenomenon involving projective and introjective mechanisms: the Annihilation Anxiety found residence in the consciousness of the analyst, who noted an intense affective engagement that mirrored the patient's transference. At this significant juncture, the analysing function of the analyst was experienced as having been annihilated. While the patient was showing signs of a beginning symbolizing transformation, the analyst was experiencing a regressive transformation. This we are calling *Projected-Introjected Annihilation Anxiety*. Here we find the beginnings of the deepening of the transference and the accentuation of the intersubjective field, manifest in the transformation of Annihilation Anxiety within the consciousness of the analyst.

Cat dream #3 (year 9)

For reasons of confidentiality, this dream material cannot be detailed; however, a condensed version of the salient features will be offered. This dream appeared during an important phase of transition, where the content of Annihilation Anxiety (particularly the dimension of entrapment) was embedded in images of enactment. The traumatic past and the present were woven together in the dream elements, and the clinical material surrounding this dream was marked by evocative scenes affectively told. The analyst noted an emerging aliveness in the analytic dialogue and no further disruptions in the analysing function were reported.

Cat dream #4 (year 10)

"Ms K, her husband, and her parents are in a mobile home. A fire has broken out and they are trying to escape. Ms K attempts to take her two cats with her, but mother is interfering." The annihilatory content in this dream is more direct. It involves the actuality of an immediate danger, the fire; it is in the room, threatening her actual family and her own cats. The interfering maternal object is the actual mother, not the maternal substitute as in the second cat dream. Here annihilation is more owned.

As signalled by this dream, the cumulative presence of Annihilation Anxiety still persisted in this phase. In Ms K's waking life, Annihilation Anxieties took the form of apocalyptic-like apprehensions about the future of the earth, panic in relation to finishing her dissertation, and fears related to entrapment. But these Annihilation Anxieties were cast within a new context, as symbolization had more fully entered the process.

Thus, the clinical material from this phase reveals how Ms K's associations moved more freely from current concerns to memories from the past, with descriptions of object relations more vivid and affectively palpable. Her destructive tendencies towards "the frame" abated to a large degree. Her mentor, once a feared and harsh judge, became a supportive helper with standards to be valued. The analyst was no longer experienced as the depriving, non-nourishing other, but as a more complex other—idealized, at times devalued, and a strong competitor. A more benign internal object inhabited her thoughts.

This new inner landscape was expressed in yet another dream from this phase: *"I am watching a tennis match. On one side is an older Chinese woman with no legs. She has an old fashioned tennis racket and is persistently manoeuvring around the court on a kind of skateboard. On the other side are three women, whose bodies are joined together. Between them they have all of their arms and many racquets, and one pair of legs. I say to myself, 'Is this fair?'"*

These two dream images, taking place on each end of the tennis court, reflect two mental processes at work. They give the annihilatory promptings a new direction. The image of the legless, yet adaptive tennis player, suggests a revision of the transference object into an admired, challenging, persistent, resourceful, yet castrated and potentially castrating object, in contrast to the earlier "killer mother", who permitted starvation. Secondly, the fused threesome at the other side of the court depicts an emerging thrust towards object choice within a triangular context, the image, partly fused, partly moving towards action, framed within a mode of reflectivity. Indeed, the patient reflected upon and took actions in her life at this point that underscored this thrust. She had mobilized the active aspects of her ego.

* * *

In the preceding material, we can observe transformations specific to long-term psychoanalytic treatment. We have noted shifts that transcend what we found in the Mohamed study, where we observed the symbolization of Annihilation Anxiety during early transference engagement. The nature of transformation in the above tennis dream is so evocative, scintillating and complex in reorganization, that it suggests a measure of *working through*. Linguistically, the dream has the properties of a presentational mode of thought (Langer, 1942), as well as high referential activity (Bucci & Maskit, 2007). These symbolic forms when they occur, providing a new context for annihilatory fears, portray an aliveness antithetical to the theme of deadness, implied in material dominated by the presence of Annihilation Anxiety. It is this very antithesis that defines a symbolizing transformation of Annihilation Anxiety (see Chapter Seven).

These observations also bring to light the process in which transformation arises within the analytic dyad. The process notes, telling us not only what the patient experienced but what was registered in the analyst's consciousness, were most informative. After cat dream #2, there were periods in which manifest Annihilation Anxiety diminished in the patient's utterances, but then appeared in the subjectivity of the analyst. Hence, the alteration of Annihilation Anxiety did not occur only in the subjectivity of the patient but also within the dyad. Once more, we hypothesize here a process of *Projected-Introjected Annihilation Anxiety*. This suggests that Annihilation Anxiety may be activated in the consciousness of the analyst. Here we are reminded of the intersubjective component of *Progressive Symbolization*, a multi-dimensional concept that embodies our understanding of *working through* and which will be developed in Part III.

A final note

With the depiction of these successive dreams, the reader may be impressed with the linear nature of Ms K's mental transformation, and that would be misleading, for psychoanalytic process is nonlinear. We have seen this, not only in Ms K, but in Mohamed as well. In the case of Mohamed, the nonlinearity appeared within the patient (from a symbolized transference to a panic attack and momentarily back to a recovery). In the case of Ms K, the nonlinearity was most evident in the countertransference of the analyst, where a symbolized countertransference was transformed into one of an experience of annihilation, that is, a desymbolized countertransference, then back to one that was symbolized. Indeed, this overall trajectory within the analyst can be viewed as a signal of things to come within the patient. In Part III, the nonlinear aspects of psychoanalytic process will be further elaborated.

CHAPTER ELEVEN

Severely traumatized patients' attempts at reorganizing their relations to others in psychotherapy: an enunciation analysis

Sverre Varvin and Bent Rosenbaum

Several attempts in psychoanalysis have been made to arrive at a comprehensive understanding of symbolization processes leading from "raw" sense and perceptual impressions to mental representations, and further on to the establishment of emotional and symbolic meaning. The understanding of these processes is highly important when it comes to trauma. Post-traumatic states are dominated by deficits in mental processing and disintegrated images, thoughts, and feeling states that haunt the traumatized. The personality changes as a result of adaptation to these changes in the mental condition. This tends to diminish or incapacitate ego-functions, such as the ability for emotional regulation and symbolization.

In dealing with trauma it is of central importance that our psychoanalytic understanding covers the whole range from nonverbal, not-understandable, unconsciously sensed or apperceived mental states to a narrative integrating capacity with contained emotions, subjective truth, and the ability to take a third position, that is, the ability to reflect on one's own mental states.

Freud portrays *binding* as a basic process whereby drive excitations, being a source of (automatic) anxiety, become bound into complex mental representations. When binding fails defensive measures may be necessary in order to avoid catastrophic or automatic anxiety in the patient's subjective experiences. These defences, for example dissociation, denial, encapsulation, and projection, then restrict the ego's capacities. In many traumatized patients the balance between binding and unbinding forces are constantly threatened. External stimuli that provoke anxiety and aggression thus lead to destabilization (beyond normality) of the function of the mind.

Mohamed came to treatment shortly after he had been released from a nine-year stay in prison under very harsh conditions and consequently had fled to another country. In one of the therapy sessions he tried to talk about his prison experiences, including his own torture and the maltreatment of children. The analyst asked him to say more and he then had a breakdown.

Vignette 1

Mohamed: Sometimes when I am feeling these pains I don't feel any problem in my head, but now I am sitting here I am feeling, I am feeling, eh, this pain here on my head—this place. I don't feel always. Now I am feeling just on my part, on this part of my head I am feeling itching, something like itching, some sort of unordinary feeling. ... It's really in the back of the head, and this time I feel [...] some sort of tension, some sort ... [breathes heavily for 15 seconds] I don't know, it just came [...]. [He breathes heavily.] [One minute pause.] Please can I [...]

Analyst: You want to lie down?

Mohamed: Yes, [breathes] ... It's not a pain, it's some sort of feeling, then I feel pain in all my body, I am like a shocked person and, eh, something is running in my body, something electronic, some sort of feeling, I don't know why I am weeping, I don't know [breathes heavily, cries]. I am not [...] I don't know what will happen I don't know ...

Analyst: It's difficult to find [out] what. I think emotionally many things are happening inside you, so, eh, which will take time to put into words and to find out what it is. And of course it is ... [Patient interrupts]

Mohamed: It is a sort of feeling, which comes to me more and more, this kind of, eh, feeling, eh, eh, and it's [...] something coming more and more. The first time when I felt this pain in my hand and my neck it was some sort of a fear and I don't know when I feel this, when I feel like [...] I am worried and very tensioned and become very emotioned I am feeling *cold*, very cold ... [Mohamed is now calmer and more coherent] and then I don't know how I will be, what will happen and [sobs], I don't know whether I will be treated or not, I don't know what sort of illnesses is inside, I don't know about my future.

Mohamed had little capacity to bind the anxiety evoked by memories of his prison experience. The analyst's question was probably experienced by Mohamed as too demanding, not supporting, and without an affirmation of his desperate mental experiences. Gradually, in the interaction with the analyst, who became more and more supportive and affirming of the patient's desperation, a certain reorientation towards a real dialogue with his analyst was achieved. To some degree the excitation became bound to socially meaningful expressions, such as crying (even though he did not "know" why he cried), and the patient's narrative became more coherent as the deictic[i] anchoring of the content of his thoughts about present, past, and future became less confused.

The understanding of "binding of excitation" in the example with Mohamed implies a conception of an interface between mind, others, and body in a culturally mediated context. This process of binding is in accordance with the concept of mentalization described by Lecours and Bouchard (1997) as a linking function: "connecting of bodily excitations with endopsychic representations" (p. 855). It is a process of transformation whereby "unmentalized" experiences are changed into "mental contents within a human interpersonal and intersubjective matrix" (ibid., p. 857). The concepts of binding and mentalization also stress the role of the analyst participating as mediator in this process. The analyst has to speak, dream, and think from a position without which a binding process may not be established. In the example above, the analyst, by being demanding, first contributed to the breakdown and confusion of the patient, and thereafter mediated a possible transferential field with his words and with symbolic acts (providing a couch for him to lie on and a subjectively experienced safe space within the analyst's mind).

What concerns us here is thus this ongoing process of binding excitation and reorganising bodily and psychic experience, and establishing meaning. What may be learned from the study of traumatized patients in therapy is how these processes go both ways. In the above example with Mohamed we saw a disintegration provoked in the process followed by a progressive process of reorganization, even though it was very rudimentary at that stage. We will later show a similar process occurring in two early sessions of his therapy. One main question is: what brings these processes about?

Traumatized people act as if they were partly outside the cultural realm of common sense. Their experiences are often short-circuited by the process of cutting off the cultural mediation by signs; seen in a Peirceian frame of reference (Peirce, 1955) the interpretants of "logic" are not available in the traumatized part of the personality, which is another way of saying that traumatic experiences may be mediated by dissociated fragmented or encapsulated representations in, for example, implicit memory, and lead to derealization or depersonalization, as the culturally-based meaning of experiences becomes less accessible.

According to this viewpoint, trauma is pathological precisely because of this damage to the link to the cultural and social mediation of experience, a damage that curtails the process of transformation of bodily excitation to mental content and also reduces the further reorganization of levels of mental representation. The importance of the culturally mediated symbols for transforming what may be called bodily memories of trauma into coherent and comprehensible narratives becomes accordingly more problematic for a person in exile who is estranged from his cultural roots.

Culturally symbolic expressions provide protection against "raw experience", and they are the medium through which we construct our reality. Traumatized individuals have had experiences that are "beyond the imaginable" and these are alternatively (a) not signified at all (leading to confusion); (b) badly signified (for example, only as images or bodily sensations (signs); (c) action-tendencies (e.g., fight-flight or freeze) that are stored in the "traumatic, implicit memory"; or (d) only partly signified. The various symptoms described in the diagnosis of Post-Traumatic Stress Disorder (American Psychiatric Association, 1994) may in this context be seen as lower level mentalization, which functions as a protective device in the attempt to avoid images of unnameable and unowned frightening experiences often with grave Annihilation Anxiety.

In the example of Mohamed the analyst was mainly affirmative, but he also introduced a possible time dimension for "finding meaning". This seemed to help the patient to conceptualize the idea of a future, although tentatively. The analyst's attitude in this process may be seen as a basic and very common culturally-determined response to pain, reflecting or resembling a mother's holding attitude, which contains the possibility that pain will disappear with time. It may be seen as a maternal response that refers to cultural codes for dealing with pain, exemplified in the proverb "time heals all wounds". It also represents the decisive function this primary relation has in providing a secure deictic structure (orientation in time, space, and awareness of self) for the experience.

Trauma results in a de-differentiation of affects, that is, "a loss of ability to identify specific emotions to serve as a guide for taking appropriate actions" (van der Kolk, McFarlane & Weisæth, 1996a; Hoppe, 1971; Krystal, 1978). Affects do not in themselves need verbalization to be made conscious and thus differentiated (Chiozza, 1999). The problem is thus not the simple "labelling" of affects, but the differentiation via a working through of the emotional experiences. At one end, there is the transformative process that changes bodily excitation into mental qualities, and at the other end, there is the culture as "supplier" of adequate schemas and symbols for making emotional experience meaningful.

Following, we will present an analysis of fragments from two early sessions of Mohamed's therapy based on a semiotic model of enunciation. This model aims to take into consideration the dialogic character of emerging semiosis (the intersubjective meaning making process) in trauma therapies (Leiman, 1998). The hypothesis is that this may provide a window to question how symbolization takes place and might also provide insight into therapeutic action.

Enunciation analysis: investigating symbolizing processes of the psychotherapeutic space

Theoretical background

Hurvich and Freedman (see Chapter Seven) define three dimensions of the Symbolizing space: object relational space, temporal space, and the space of the imaginary. In a similar key, Hurvich and Freedman define three dimensions of Desymbolization: psychic blankness, symbolic equation, and frozen constellation.

Enunciation Analysis (EA) can be considered as an addition to the Symbolization/Desymbolization analysis of Hurvich and Freedman. EA takes into consideration the details of how the analyst (whether speaking or listening) and the patient (speaking or listening) from moment to moment shape the therapeutic relation and its dialogical nature.

The French linguist, Emile Benveniste (1902–1976), originally defined enunciation as actualizing language in reality through an individual act of speech (1970). He pointed out that the personal pronouns are at the same time empty and indispensable positions in language. *Empty* because anybody can make use of them, and *indispensable* because they determine the direction and aspect of the utterance in the actual situation. The concept of direction implies conscious and unconscious intentions as part of the message and its content (who is saying what to whom; who evokes and invokes what from the other), while the concept of aspect concerns the character and quality of the content as it should be (intersubjectively) understood in the concrete situation of the speech act. These positions in language get their significations only through the concrete utterance of them. Uttering a statement saying, "I want to ..." or "I feel that ..." or "I think that ..." immediately makes a bodily impact (on the other) and sets into motion series of possible significations—implying both a conscious, reflective level of speech, and an unconscious immediate, pre-reflective level of speaking. The speaking "I" is at the same time also a spoken "I". The speaking "I" is never totally in command of the speech act. The meaning that appears in the utterance is always also unconsciously determined as part of the internal object relationship. Both positions are bound by unconscious and intersubjective structures, insofar that the "I" invokes, or is evoked by the other. Thus, the speaking "I" is always already, intersubjectively, linked with the other.

This view is in accordance with the Russian linguist Bakhtin's idea (1986; see also Leiman, 1992; Volosinov, 1973) that an utterance is always an answer. It is an answer to another utterance and it qualifies the prior utterance to a greater or lesser degree. It is also in accordance with Peirce (1955) who states: "All thinking is in a dialogical form." For Peirce signs can be symbolic or non-symbolic thought-signs (icons and indices). And the phenomena of the dialogue can be seen as being immediately present ("Firstness"), can be understood dynamically as action-reaction ("Secondness") or as something which has to be interpreted ("Thirdness").

The theoretical ideas of both Bakhtin and Peirce are in accordance with psychoanalytic ideas of transference–countertransference and the ways the transference dynamics are weaved into textual (and fantasy) material of present, past, and future nature (Priel, 1999; Steiner, 2007).

Specifying enunciation as a model in its own right

Enunciation Analysis is a thorough investigation of the communicative interplay between positions of the "I" and the "You". The "I" may describe daily situations or phantasies, or may be free associating, hallucinating, and so on, but implicitly or explicitly these expressions of the "I" are always directing (itself) towards an explicit or implicit (internal) other. When the "I" relates to the internal other and at the same time is communicating with persons in the environment, then parts of the other (internal and/or external) are shaped by the projective identifications.

In the psychoanalytic perspective the Enunciation Analysis can thus be seen as an investigation of object relations and fantasies brought to life in the transference–countertransference dynamics of the analysis. Enunciation analysis emphasizes five "I-You" dimensions in which the subject may pose itself in relation to internal other(s).

The first dimension, D1, is characterized by an immediate, unconditioned emotional expressivity of the subject (body-proper phenomena).[ii] Examples of this dimension would be expression of mental pain, cries, outburst, fragments, incoherence, isolated clichés, and encapsulations, and also nightmares, flashbacks, and hallucinations connected to the traumatic situation. The other (second person perspective) in this dimension, D1, is the analyst creating a holding environment and acting as container in the phase of receiving the signs of the patient's pain. The analyst, in such moments, is catering for ego needs, until the patient may have sufficiently introjected the ego-supportive analyst-mother functions as a more coherent imago.

The second dimension, D2, concerns the subject's situational relation to the other (internalized and/or external friends, family members, or analyst). Phenomena in this dimension are expressed as staged scenarios, that is, descriptions of situations, locations, and interpersonal events.[iii] The patient may tell about a situation that has taken place either by participation of the patient himself or by somebody else, either in fantasy, fiction, or reality. The account of a dream-sequence also belongs to this dimension. The staging can be characterized as one-, two- or (more seldom) three-dimensional (using these terms in a common sense way).

These two dimensions constitute *the imaginary mode of speech and experience*. The imaginary mode of experience presents itself as embodied and immediate reactions to a situation in which the meeting of two subjects has to be understood.[iv] The utterances and responses are often concretely anchored in the atmosphere and volatile dynamics of the meetings and they have references to "here-and-now" or "there-and-then". The imaginary mode of speech (and experience) is descriptive and not mediated by reflective thoughts and psychological insight. D2 is preserved by iconic, interpersonal, and mirroring characteristics, and D2 is then more symbolized than D1 (repetitive, fragmented, and with uncontained projections of mental pain).

The third dimension, D3, is constituted by expressions characterized by "institutionalized" or common social knowledge. This concerns the expression of general and popular ideas and culturally accepted logic, mentor-like (superego) points of view and explanations, or socially accepted clichés whether they have abstract qualities or are just idioms. Utterances are based in introjected self- and object-representations. Feelings of reduced safety of the self-representation lead to rigidity in thought and speech-patterns.

The fourth dimension, D4, presents the subject as a genuine dialogue-partner, proposing an opinion, point of view or observation, and at the same time dialectically allowing the other's opinion to have a space or standpoint. Self- and object-representations are relatively stable and safe, emotions are expressed, but in an integrative way. This dimension implies the ability to contain a mind-state of not-knowing, and to carry on a dialogue in spite of the frustration of no-agreement between involved parts, and the uncertainty about (the desire) of the other's desire.

The third and the fourth dimension of the enunciation capture *the symbolic mode of speech and experience.* These dimensions contain the ground for symbolic transference–countertransference interventions (confrontations and interpretations in symbolic terms). They are based in group- and culture-bound psychological narrations, and are temporally organized and Other-oriented. Their functions demand internalizations of mental experiences and are more reflective and integrative than the functions of the imaginary mode. Discrepancies, not immediately understandable ideas, "not-knowing" or gaps in mutual understanding, are overcome on the level of dialogue.

This distinction between a language of equivalence, immediacy, and action (imaginary modes of experience), as contrasted with a language of self-awareness, thoughtfulness, reflection, and stable identity in the communication (symbolic modes of experience), runs through most theories of symbolization of the mind. The imaginary and the symbolic modes can appear separated. But since the human experiences and ways of expression can "swing" back and forth between these two modes then they are also linked to each other. The two modes belong to the same model, so to speak. But face to face with the patients, listening to different parts of their narratives, the analyst will experience that one mode of experience may be more active and predominant than the other.

The link of the imaginary and symbolic modes is responsible for the unconscious processes linking "Thing-representation" and "Word-representation" into Object-representation, and responsible for transforming sensory impressions and thoughts into thinking. The imaginary mode is basic—it exists in all utterances and we cannot escape it regardless how healthy or pathological we are. The link between the imaginary mode and the symbolic mode may be more or less functional or dysfunctional. Dysfunctionality means that the linking function is not based on an "average expectable environment" (Hartmann, 1939) and that it does not sustain "competences" of the extended consciousness.[v] On the other hand, functionality of the link implies anchorage of the utterance in "common sense" and in "stable self- and object-relations". Functionality also means that the identity-feeling of the person—the sense of identity grounded in his/her internal self-object relations—is based in the social and cultural we-ness rather than exclusively in a narcissistic dyad. Functionality of the link between the imaginary and the symbolic modes of experiences is thus the precondition for being able to work symbolically in analysis (free association, making use of interpretations, and the working through of the mourning processes).

In the Enunciation Analysis functionality/dysfunctionality of the link is scored in the utterances in a binary mode (as working + or not working –).

Two sessions of Mohamed's therapy in light of imaginary and symbolic modes of speech and experience

We have chosen to analyze session 3, scene five, and session 4, scene four, as there were marked differences regarding Symbolization/Desymbolization and Annihilation Anxiety (see Chapters Eight and Nine). We also found significant differences seen from an enunciation perspective. In session 3, scene five, enunciation analysis revealed that there is a much heavier emphasis on the imaginary mode of speech and its dimensions of communication (D1 and D2). In the analysis of the utterances, D1 scores appear often in session 3, but seldom in session 4. The same pattern is seen for both the analyst and the patient, which may indicate a predominance of projective identificatory processes either as countertransferential empathic communication with the pain of the patient expressed in enactments where the analyst takes part in a traumatizing scenario or as a defensive mirroring of the pain. For the patient we now and then see scorings of dysfunctionality in the link between the imaginary and the symbolic mode to such an extent that it sometimes would be more correct to say that symbolicity is not in play.

* * *

In session 3, the patient starts talking about rumours of war and the analyst comes with affirmatory statements showing attempts to follow the paths that the patient, in his "story-telling", wants the analyst to pay attention to. In this initial part of the session the enunciation follows a descriptive mode without reflection. Unconsciously the patient's memories attract his story-telling towards a description of how people in his surroundings smoke and that he is compelled to go where there is a lot of noise. These two words, smoke and noise, seem anchored in a past context, which is still very present in his mind, evoking bodily unpleasant feelings. Under the influence of these feelings the enunciation of the patient is more and more pushed towards raw emotional expressivity of mental pain (D1)—with an unclear address of the utterance, with utterances consisting of half sentences or few words, sometimes coherent and at other times rather incoherent and fragmented indicating that he is losing anchorage of the communication in a basic trusting atmosphere and that his anxiety (Annihilation Anxiety) is no longer contained. This may indicate that the analyst is merely mirroring his anxious state of mind without modifying his mental pain.

During the end of the session hope and support are introduced by the analyst, but again only with a few, positively supportive words in an attempt to guarantee a better future (D4). Even though the patient grasps the possibility of getting away from the unpleasant feelings of smell and noise—disgust in a narrow and wider sense of the word—he does not succeed in bringing himself out of the imaginary grip of the sense impressions and fragmented thoughts.

* * *

Session 4, scene four, starts out very different from session 3. Even though the patient is telling about very unpleasant events he is able to unfold his utterances in a longer coherent narrative. The weight of the enunciation is on the descriptive mode (D2), but there is a strong attractor towards a dialogical dimension (D3 and D4).

In the parts of session 4 where emotional expressions (in the D1) appear on the surface it seems as if the flow of the description of situations and scenarios (D2) helps the patient to re-integrate, by his own force, his first-person positions in his memory and ways of organizing his accounts of his life. It is possible for the patient to engage himself and the analyst in the atmosphere of a dialogue, although this engagement was not yet stable over a longer time-period and thus must be described as a restrained one. But the patient does not, as in the former session (session 3), become passive and overwhelmed by the sense impressions. Instead the analyst is tacitly invited to take part with his interventions (statements, ideas, understanding). The analyst is led towards co-construction of the described scenarios and he (analyst) finds it safe to lead the patient towards a shared understanding of them. The analyst is here not only mirroring and enacting in a traumatizing scenario but is in a position where emotions initially are worked on and modified, and the digested material is then internalized by the patient.

Subsequently the analyst feels that it is safe to talk about the possible emotions that the patient may harbour, and he helps the patient to speak about these both with reference to the time when the dreadful events took place and with reference to the here-and-now with the analyst. The analyst intervenes with symbolic interventions that the patient may think about (D4), and this helps the patient to remain reflective to a certain extent. However, it does not last long. The balance between being in the symbolic mode of experience and in the imaginary mode is still very delicate. It is still easy for the patient to slide back to the imaginary mode (D1 and D2) where he needs the analyst as a holding and containing, non-demanding, and nourishing partner of the dialogue.

Conclusion

It seems from this analysis that the traumatized person's main problems lay in the balance between the imaginary and symbolic aspects of mental functioning. The analysis showed how the patient tended to function and be imprisoned in imaginary modes where the implied other was unstable and often almost disappearing. In these situations he needed the active affirmative presence of the analyst as a containing, environmental mother. When the analyst took a more active stance challenging the patient on a dialogic, symbolic level, the patient was able to meet him on this level, and to start a work of integration, at least for some time. This analysis points at two factors that are important in understanding traumatized patients while being able to relate and intervene with them in therapy.

1. The analysis confirms that traumatization, especially severe traumatization, leads to serious instability and deficiency in the symbolizing capacity (Grubrich-Simitis, 1981, 1984; Krystal,

1971, 1978; Küchenhoff, 1988; Laub, 1998; Varvin, 2002, 2003; Varvin & Rosenbaum, 2003). This appears in the Enunciation Analysis as deficiencies in upholding a balance between D1-D2 and D3-D4. Clinically, we see this when a traumatized person in a response to a neutral or helping comment from the analyst slips easily into dissociated states of mind dominated by the imaginary mode of experience in which the comment is felt as an immediate stressor affecting his/her relation to others and the apperception of the environment. The traumatized person's core problems with symbolization of emotions and sensations appear in his/her mental work with the problems and stressors of everyday life. The past is evoked as schemas that function as templates in order to make meaning of present stress.

2. The analysis implies that in the treatment of traumatized patients the analyst/therapist has to take utmost care to listen to and follow the embodied and the non-rhythmically, disharmonious, and fragmented messages from the patient. These messages may carry with them confusion and persecutory anxiety which may change the patient's states of mind abruptly from seemingly symbolic modes of experience to imaginary modes. In the former, the patient is able to explore and find out what the meaning is of self and other's statements and actions. In the latter, the patient is in a situation of need and confusion, an existential crisis, so to speak, where internal basic trust is not working and where safety and emotional nourishment has to be supplied from the environment/analyst. In the symbolic mode of experience, the analyst can instigate exploring activities with interpretations, for example of transference and countertransference. When the patient is functioning in the imaginary mode, without anchorage in a stable internal and external environment, the analyst's activity must secure the patient. Affirmative interventions must then be the main strategy (Killingmo, 1995).[vi] The analyst must expect from time to time to be an all-embracing container and at the same time keep alive a creative reverie function.

As a conclusion of this work we hold that the analytic setting providing a stable frame and the analyst's functions as an environmental "mother" are preconditions for bringing the patient out of a predominant imaginary mode of functioning. We are aware that this is not enough in practice and that, for example, aggression and distrust has to be met by containing and working though projective identifications.

Endnotes

i. Deixis means "to point at". It concerns how elements in speech organize time, place, and space for that which the utterance refers to. It orients communications in a "I-you-here-now" perspective, and gives the uttered sentence subjectivity at the same time as the sentence then refers to something outside language (Rosenbaum, 2000).

ii. Lacan proposed the terms "body-proper" and "body-of-the-other or imago" to signify the positions of the alienated subject finding itself in the mirror-image constituted by the other, that is, the severely traumatized person who looks into the mirror and either cannot recognize him/herself ("I know who I am, but this is not me" [body-of-the-other]) or cannot emotionally feel him/herself as being the one in the mirror ("I cannot feel myself any more, even though I might be the one that I clearly see in the mirror" [body-proper]). The two positions—of the body and of the imago—never fully coincide, but the attempts to bridge the gap—rather than being swallowed up by the gap—open the possibility of expressing oneself symbolically. Being overwhelmed by anxiety of the gap may, on the other hand, lead to desymbolization.

iii. Seen from a linguistic/pragmatic point of view (Lepper, 2009) elements of speech that the analysts may be listening to and investigate are: time, space, deixis, coherence of themes and narration, embeddedness of the utterance in a larger context, and linking concrete bodily (preverbal) expressions with symbolic meaning of the communication.

iv. One must understand that the meeting taking place on the conscious level always runs simultaneously with a process of overcoming the gap of not-being-able-to-meet-fully on the unconscious level.

v. Antonio Damasio (2000):

- The ability to consider the mind of the other
- The ability to sense the minds of the collective
- The ability to suffer with pain as opposed to just feel pain and react to it
- The ability to sense the possibility of death in the self and in the other

- The ability to value life
- The ability to construct a sense of good and of evil distinct from pleasure and pain
- The ability to take into account the interests of the other and of the collective
- The ability to sense beauty as opposed to just feeling pleasure
- The ability to sense a discord of feelings and later a discord of abstract ideas, which is the source of the sense of truth.

vi. Affirmative interventions relate to basic existential dimensions (e.g., the need for safety and predictability). Affirmation is affective, somatic communication mainly mediated nonverbally. Affirmation implies the presence of an empathic other, a communication that somebody cares.

COMMENTARY

Three pathways towards the modification of Annihilation Anxiety

Marvin Hurvich and Norbert Freedman

In the course of the preceding chapters and the three successive pathways of modification we have encountered several issues concerning the structure of the annihilatory process and its relation to Symbolization, which are not specific to each chapter but have a general relevance to our entire enterprise. Here are some of the salient issues.

On the context specificity of Annihilation Anxiety

That the meaning of a psychoanalytic concept and its clinical implications vary with the clinical or social context in which it appears has been a tenet of the Propositional Method (Chapter Six). The very title of this essay, "Three Pathways towards the Modification of Annihilation Anxiety", implies three clinical contexts: pathway 1—early transference engagement; pathway 2—clinical regression one and a half years later; and pathway 3—revisiting a traumatic episode after ten years of psychoanalytic work. In all three situations Annihilation Anxiety, its prevalence and intensity, was essentially high; it was a relative constant. Annihilation Anxiety indeed is a constant confrontation with dangers to psychic survival. What changes vastly are its modifiers.

It is the modifiers that become the signifiers of mental transformation. In this study, we have focused on two major modifiers: Symbolizing, and Desymbolizing. In the Symbolizing mode, Annihilation Anxiety could co-exist within a context of meaning making whereas in the Desymbolizing modification meaning was throttled.

On the modes and dimensions of Annihilation Anxiety

There remains the task of distinguishing two aspects of the Annihilation Anxiety process: its dimensions and modes. In the dimensions we have spelled out a profile of subjectively felt experiences signifying a fundamental threat to psychic survival. In the mode on the other hand we have specified that ego quality that depicts a patient's ability to process the impending menace.[i]

Indeed it is the active mode of coping with Annihilation Anxiety, which reflects a Symbolizing form of thought. It is a state of consciousness in which the patient not only confronts, speaks of the impending menace, but anticipates it, imagines it, now or in the past, thinks about it, uses it in relation to the other, and endows annihilatory fears with psychic life. Every instance of a *symbolized* Annihilation Anxiety was also in the active mode.

It hardly needs emphasizing that Desymbolized Annihilation Anxiety may have considerable clinical significance, and that Desymbolization and Annihilation Anxiety tend to be more often correlated than Symbolization and Annihilation Anxiety (Hurvich, 2002).

On the symbolization of Annihilation Anxiety and the position towards the object

In our observations of instances of symbolized and desymbolized Annihilation Anxiety we observed not only changes in mental functioning (i.e. reflectivity, the imaginary, and memory), but also shifts in the position towards the therapist. Hence, from an object relations point of view, our findings are an empirical documentation of the Kleinian distinction between the Paranoid-Schizoid and the Depressive positions. Conversely, a regression of Annihilation Anxiety in the direction of Desymbolization reveals a regressive transformation in the direction of not only fragmentation of thought, structural de-differentiation, and a paralysis of the symbolizing function, but also persecutory ideas as an expression of negative transference.

On Annihilation Anxiety and the mobilization of defence: dissociation

Annihilation Anxiety with its signification of survival threat reflects not only the state of the ego or the patient's position towards the object, but reactivates early derivatives from infancy. What is activated is a primitive mode of defence: dissociation. As a way of keeping terrifying experiences out of consciousness, to disavow them, dissociation has application not only to trauma cases as we have seen here, but to a broad clinical spectrum of patients. Even in highly symbolizing patients, as was evidenced in the case of Ms K, dissociation is likely.

On a gradient of dissociative defences in the Annihilation Anxiety process

Analysis of the Annihilation Anxiety process in our three pathways has also suggested the manner in which dissociative processes can be integrated into consciousness. Bucci (2007b) has distinguished two forms of dissociation, adaptive and avoidant, and we have added a third: fragmented.

In Mohamed's panic attack, we see an instance of fragmented dissociation. In the instance of projected Annihilation Anxiety, in the case of Ms K, when the patient did not experience Annihilation Anxiety, but the analyst did, we have spoken of an avoidant Annihilation Anxiety. But when the patient was able to reflect the implications of the Annihilation Anxiety within the working transference (tennis game dream), then we spoke of an adaptive Annihilation Anxiety. The dread had become part of analytic work. This gradient of Annihilation Anxiety once more suggests a process of transformation. However, we must remind ourselves that even in its most adaptive form, it is an experience that is not easily obliterated.

An alternate vision: enunciation Analysis

Our analysis of modifiers has rested on the distinction between a Desymbolizing and Symbolizing mode of thought. From a different point of view, that of Enunciation Analysis (Chapter Eleven), this distinction as found in the writing of Varvin and Rosenbaum describes an alteration from the Imaginary to the Symbolic. The crucial implication of that difference in language rests on the assumption that even the Imaginary (which we classify as Desymbolization) is dialogic in nature. This definition rests on a basic philosophical issue related to the understanding of binding. The question is to what extent binding is based on the maternal connection and to what extent it is due to synthetic/integrative functioning, that is, to aspects of primary ego autonomy. This volume is enriched by the inclusion of the enunciation point of view.

In spite of the profound conceptual distinctions introduced through Enunciation Analysis, there was a remarkable convergence with our findings which relied on the notion of Desymbolization and Symbolization of Annihilation Anxieties. In their depiction of session 4 (in contrast to session 3), which we have termed a symbolizing one, Varvin and Rosenbaum emphasize that "[T]he patient ... engages himself and the analyst in the atmosphere of a dialogue. ... The analyst is led towards co-construction" which leads to a shared understanding. It is gratifying that except for the different terminology, their clinical observations overlap completely with those advanced here, while described in another psychoanalytic tongue.

Limitations

As a final note, it is necessary to emphasize that all generalizations are based on a small selected lens of observations and are based on methods derived from single case design. It goes without saying that replication is essential. Moreover, when we speak of modifiers, we have selected one set of modifiers, namely Symbolization and Desymbolization, while not including others, especially limiting modifiers.

We are further aware that many generalizations can be limited or revised by selective clinical instances that counter our observations. We demonstrated that Symbolization of Annihilation Anxiety tends to be associated with greater transference engagement. But notably in borderline patients, heightened transference engagement can be associated with regression and Desymbolization. In part these observations affirm the probabilistic nature of our *Propositional Method*.

However, when our observations on a single case can be replicated in other instances, and can be related to parallel situations in the literature, to that extent the proposition has been affirmed. Clearly, empirically-based propositions must not only be generalized, but must be grounded and modified by other clinical studies.

With a number of the formulations contained in these pages, the issue of causality arises. Thus, when there is a positive relationship between Annihilation Anxiety and Symbolization, it may well be that Annihilation Anxiety, through its vivid imagery evokes symbolizing activity. Conversely, symbolizing activity may evoke new qualities of Annihilation Anxiety. We have attempted to keep both possibilities in mind, and to look for details in the contextual material as clues to likely cause-effect relationships.

Endnote

i. In this discussion we are paying special attention to the active self-mode. We are leaving aside Annihilation Anxiety (AA) attributed to others who have become the agent of destructiveness. In the first instance (AA-self) destructiveness is owned with a sense of agency while in the second instance (AA-other) the subject finds himself in a victimized recipient position.

PART III

A SPECIMEN OF WORKING THROUGH

CHAPTER TWELVE

A very broad concept seen through a very narrow lens

Norbert Freedman and Rhonda Ward

What we are about to explore is a very broad concept seen through a very narrow lens. The concept is *working through* and the lens is a specimen from a recorded psychoanalysis. The concept has evolved over decades of psychoanalytic experience and clinically can cover years of analytic work. The lens comprises 25 sessions from the third year of a four-times-a-week psychoanalysis. The concept gets at the very heart of the efficacy of psychoanalytic work, but the lens, hopefully, pinpoints those ingredients that matter. One of those ingredients we have discovered and believe is essential to working through is termed the *nodal moment*.

In the course of this specimen, the repeated theme of *torture* can be heard. Torture is desired, feared, dreaded, confronted, imagined, reflected upon, and resolved through contrition. For Ms Y, the patient, torture appears within the context of an anticipated inner *storm*, a theme running like a red thread throughout the specimen, representing an effort towards transformation.

Working through is repetition transformed. What matters is not only the recurrent confrontation with moments of dread or despair, or with what feels intolerable, but also a progressive embeddedness of these moments within an ever-widening context of psychoanalytic communication. The aim of this project is to spell out such progressive forms of transformative activities. To this end, in an effort to make the broad concept of *working through* amenable to psychoanalytic inquiry, we will advance our concept of *Progressive Symbolization*.

A historical perspective on working through

The effort to capture the essence of *working through* needs no justification. Freud (1914) introduced the idea in a simple, apparently unambiguous phrase, "remembering, repeating and working through". While this phrase appeared only once in his writings after 1914, the *working through* notion ultimately became known as a "period" or "phase" of working through (1926a, p. 159). This concept has been an abiding challenge to psychoanalytic thinkers for almost a century. Its generic notion, *remembering* through repetition, has been amply demonstrated in clinical reports, though the clinical necessity for *recovered memory* has been questioned. The path towards the ownership of pathogenic *moments* has also been a continuing and often controversial preoccupation of our field (e.g., Berlin IPA Congress, 2007).

In an extensive review article, Brenner (1987) reminded us that the *working through* concept was initiated by Freud to provide an answer to the gnawing question: Why does analysis take so long? He noted Freud's original assumption that what must be overcome is repetition derived from fixations and resistances from id, ego, and superego. Tracing the views of analysts across the decades on this subject, Brenner identified a series of manifold, preferred aspects of conflict considered pathognomonic. He believed these views had one thing in common: the task of analysis is one of confronting the patient with the pathogenic roots of compromise formations, and their interpretation is enhanced when situated within the frame of the transference. When analysed, compromise formations are dynamically indistinguishable from symptoms. Beyond the statement that compromise formations must be interpreted and analysed, there seems to be no suggestion of the specific forces that lead to their transformation.

The specimen approach

Despite Brenner's sombre view of the broad concept of *working through*, we set ourselves the task of discovering those ingredients inherent in analytic work that might be considered transformative, and we cast out a net aimed at finding a method of inquiry that would be both clinically persuasive and lend itself to empirical documentation. We turned to the origin of psychoanalysis and our ego ideal of psychoanalytic inquiry. This starting point was Freud and his patient, Irma (1900). Her actions registered in Freud through disguised dream content (the specimen); he subsequently interpreted the specimen through his self-analysis, and used this is a launching pad for his theoretical extrapolations. Such a sequence was dramatically extended in Erikson's also classic monograph, *The Dream Specimen in Psychoanalysis* (1954), from which an innovative arena of thoughts about mental functioning and mental transformations evolved.

In Erikson's inquiry into the dream specimen, four levels of observation can be discerned: (a) the factual, though much reconstructed background of Freud's highly conflictual, even traumatic encounter (mostly revealed in the correspondence between Freud and Fliess) with Irma (who had undergone a "bloody" surgery); (b) the dream text itself, that is, the telling of the events surrounding Irma's surgery as represented in Freud's dream specimen; (c) Freud's detailed associations and summaries about his own dream experiences—a well-spring of thoughts that formed the basis for his monumental theories of transformation from primary to secondary process thought, as well as his formulations on female sexuality; and (d) Erikson's further rendition and re-contextualization in which he singled out and examined the surface structure, that is, the formal, linguistic properties of the dream specimen, considered how the dream was told by the dreamer, and explored its meaning as a move towards ego synthesis within the evolving inter-subjectivity of the transference. Here Erikson injected his vision of the social "actuality" in which Freud, the dreamer, was embedded, and the object relational context, leading to inferences about the analytic process. We consider levels 1 and 2 instances of clinical observation; level 3, clinical generalization; and level 4, the contextualization of observations into psychoanalytic theory (Waelder, 1962). In these distinctions, we find the frame for a methodology of a specimen study, our guide throughout this monograph.

This then is a specimen study, not of dream work, but of *working through*. It embraces the detailed examination of audio recordings and transcripts of *criterion sessions* from the third year of a psychoanalytic treatment, a sample from many years of analytic work. Like Erikson, we began with a specimen (the criterion sessions), subjected it to formal empirical evaluation, and then sought to draw conclusions about the process of working through, and as shall be developed, *Progressive Symbolization*.

The structure of the lens: the transformation cycle and its components

Our specimen offers an unfolding sequence describing a transformation cycle, a shift in mental functioning from integration to non-integration and back to re-integration. The sequence begins with a veritable emotional transfusion, born of conflict and presented in formulated language, which we have termed the symbolizing phase. This phase, in paradoxical fashion, contains the onset of a transference regression and with it, ego fragmentation, leading in a downward slope to a desymbolizing phase. Amidst desymbolization, signs of reversal appear in the form of what we call *nodal moments*, moments that suggest the beginning of an upward slope. (Throughout the specimen, *nodal moments* become the immediate precursors to and signifiers of mental re-organization.) Finally, a series of enactments pave the way for a phase of re-symbolization and the culmination of the upward slope. This phase contains the recapitulation of earlier experiences in a new form, a spiral, where new heights as well as new depths are reached, facilitated by an encounter with the *extraordinary countertransference*.

The transformation cycle exemplifies *Progressive Symbolization*, our organizing concept for this study. Progressive Symbolization is a process that is not linear, but a dialectic process, one of thesis, antithesis, and synthesis. In this progression, new symbolic forms are preceded by successive forms of desymbolization, followed by a reactivation of the symbolizing function. Thus, in the specimen, critical moments arise that become the preconditions for new psychic attainment: facing the dread of object loss during transference regression; re-finding the object during *nodal moments*; and confronting and tolerating the actuality of the object during a period of countertransference crisis. We might say that, in the inevitable oscillations in states of consciousness faced by every patient, darkness precedes dawn.

In most general terms, our notion of *Progressive Symbolization* alludes to a process of ego synthesis (Nunberg, 1931), a concept which has been part of the analytic literature from its early beginnings. Progressive Symbolization involves the ingenious translation by the ego of one symbolic form into others; it is the ego's attempt at mastery; and it involves a shift from passive to active, and a move towards synthesis, thus creating psychic space for new structural configurations. The hallmark of *Progressive Symbolization* is ego activity, that is, overcoming a state of helplessness (what has been termed "primitive mental states"), within a frame of transference and object relatedness.

Returning to the structure of the lens, the transformation cycle, several components are contained therein, which are crucial to *Progressive Symbolization*. Each component offers a phenomenology that can be documented and translated into clinical propositions. It is a multidimensional concept embracing multiple perspectives: it is situated within the experiencing subject; it involves the participation of both members of the analytic couple; it has its temporal nonlinear gradient; and it has its spiralling effect. Hence, in the propositions stated below, we will note the intrapsychic, the intersubjective, the nonlinear, and the spiralling aspects of *Progressive Symbolization*. The fourth component, that of the spiralling effect, suggests the overriding motivational forces at work, which will be spelled out in Chapter Eighteen.

Proposition 1: Progressive Symbolization, working through, involves a shift from an unintegrated to an integrated mode of mental organization; an enhanced connection to one's inner processes—a move towards a *symbolizing mode of thought*. In spite of the intrinsic dialogic nature of analytic work, distinct forms of change are registered within the subject. During a given hour, specific qualities of mind can be discerned. When utterances are marked by repetition, and redundancies, revealing concreteness and equivalence of thought, when affect is foreclosed or throttled, we call this a desymbolizing, unintegrated mode of mental functioning. In contrast, when experiences are expressed vividly, evocatively, with specificity, when there is metaphoric thinking and imagination, when memories from the recent and remote past are stirred up and reflected upon, we refer to this as a symbolizing, integrative mode of mental functioning.

We shall offer a psychoanalytic view of symbolization: the unification by the ego of fragmented object representations into more differentiated transference experiences. Above we described the symbolizing phase as a veritable affective transfusion born of conflict. As we placed empirical findings beside the evolution of analytic thought, we noted that in symbolization, there are affective bursts reflected upon, a reliance on the imaginary, an effort to find space to reach the other, and a position towards object choice. In desymbolization, we find not simply the absence of the symbolic, but its destruction: the wish to confuse, to destroy meaning, to disavow significance, and in this to face the abyss of object loss. These forces oscillate during *Progressive Symbolization* and clearly both experiences are critical for working through. When there is only symbolization, there may be merely redundancy; and when there is only desymbolization, there is stasis, even impasse (for more details see Postscript).

Our general proposition that analytic work moves in the direction of more symbolized thought is intuitively persuasive; nonetheless, it is the gradient of change and its qualities that will hold our curiosity, as we examine the material to come.

* * *

Proposition 2: Progressive Symbolization, working through, is marked by the intensification of intersubjectivity. It is evident that the shifts just described find registration not only within the subject and within the analyst, but within the analytic couple as well. This shared attunement occurs incrementally, and as treatment continues we would expect not only a synchrony of content but also of mode of thought. At peak moments of treatment intensity, there arises that point where both members of the couple are drawn into a joint state, described as an "analytic third" (e.g., Ogden, 2004). Such a cumulative reciprocal engagement follows Bach's (2006) premise that the analytic process must involve the experience that each participant exists in the mind of the other. We were on the look-out for objective indicators of such mental events in our specimen.

The intersubjective process is affirmed when the patient's mode of thought finds its mirror in the analyst's utterances. Mirroring, a notion introduced by Kohut (1971), at its core reflects the analyst's ability to apprehend the patient's intent. More recent discoveries

A VERY BROAD CONCEPT SEEN THROUGH A VERY NARROW LENS   197

(mirror neurons) have corroborated such early psychoanalytic visions on the neuro-physiological level. It has been demonstrated that shared activation of emotions and actions takes place in the analytic dyad so that one can sense the other (Gallese, Eagle & Migone, 2007). Whether or not such a process can be affirmed by our data may be questioned; nonetheless, when we looked inside the hour and compared the patient's level of symbolization (reflected in her spoken language) to the analyst's symbolization (reflected in both her spoken language and nonverbal vocalizations), we found a match, affirming a basic synchrony. Such observations led us to believe that a shared intersubjective process was alive in the analytic dialogue. These findings will be reported in Chapter Thirteen.

Another way of gauging the interpenetration between patient and analyst was through the tracing of the analyst's working memory. Our method involved what we call the *clinical scan*, a brief taped account by the analyst at the end of each session of her reflective reconstruction of the hour. The scan offered a basis for comparisons between what was recalled and what had actually transpired. It was a valuable window into the role of the analyst's participation in the symbolizing process, as it allowed us to discern whether the analyst recalled the essentials that characterized the session, heard the signs of symbolization, or conversely, heard concreteness during a desymbolizing hour. Such findings, indeed observed, were reassuring. It showed that, by and large, the method of the scan can yield a valuable estimate of the entire session, and that in this specimen the analyst was generally in "sync", capturing the essential qualities of the hour.

But there were also important deviations from this pattern of interactional synchrony. A systematic scrutiny of the scans for deletions and/or distortions of the session material revealed inferences of ruptures, even *extraordinary* countertransference reactions. This additional use of the scan allowed us to gauge the impact of discontinuities in the analytic process on the ensuing work.

The very phenomenon of countertransference rupture leads to questions concerning its impact on the symbolizing process. A simple linear hypothesis would suggest that such ruptures have a deleterious impact on symbolization; however, the reverse may be the case, for, surprisingly, such ruptures may lead to more differentiated thought. Here, the synthetic function of the ego cannot be discounted and such instances indeed were observed in our specimen (see Chapter Seventeen). To understand this further, we turn to our third proposition of *Progressive Symbolization*.

* * *

Proposition 3: Progressive Symbolization, working through, arises through successive phases of analytic work, which are nonlinear and paradoxical in nature, and which give rise to *nodal moments*. These are moments of reversal, of transition; they are linked to countertransference enactments, and are shifts, which suggest the motivational base for clinical change.

That analytic work proceeds in definable phases has been a major theme for decades in the teaching of analytic technique. Freud's (1926a) premise that transformative psychic actions arise at specific fixation points and that these are moments during which the ego is challenged has been affirmed in the literature. While authors emphasize specific theoretical predilections, they often point to events that occur during specified phases of analytic work.

To select some prominent illustrative highlights: for Winnicott (1955, 1956), as well as Khan (1960), a phase of regression, evoking a state of absolute dependence, is considered a necessary precondition for *working through*. For Britton (1998), following Klein, working through is a process of confronting the challenges inherent in triangular (early Oedipal) conflict. Sandler (1976) describes a phase of "countertransference enactment" in his classic vignette, where he fails to reach for a tissue box, an action he considers a manifestation of role responsiveness. Other writers highlight the crucial moments of working through during the termination phase of analysis. Dewald (1990), writing within the frame of Classical Conflict Theory, notes: "When the core of psychic structure has been exposed, the earliest compromises have been made conscious, and there is movement toward modification of the core, the analytic process enters the termination phase" (p. 703).

Now we are suggesting that the surfacing of such pivotal transformative experiences can be observed even within the limited time frame of a single specimen. Such transformations mark a paradoxical change in mental functioning as the patient experiences a shift from one state of consciousness to another. Indeed, the predominance of shifts in the symbolizing process was found to be an organizer of the transformation cycle. As stated above, we identified four phases: a *symbolizing, working* phase; a *desymbolizing*, regressive phase; an *enactive* phase; and a phase of *re-symbolization*.

In Chapter Fourteen, we will show how a *working phase*, with the symbolizing function dominant at first, was transformed into a transference regression leading to the surfacing of desymbolization. In this phase, the patient initially worked within a symbolizing and integrative mode of analytic engagement, but increased signs of identity diffusion and reliance upon the body self emerged. During this downward slope, a state of dependency was created and the patient faced the full measure of object loss. But towards the end of the phase, however, the first *nodal moment* emerged, signalling the potential for reversal.

Then only a few sessions later, in the midst of the desymbolizing phase, further signs of reversal appeared, as the patient began to face her conflicts in *triangular space*. In Chapter Fifteen, we will describe three successive *nodal moments* arising during this phase. These moments of mental reorganization pointed to an upward slope and each successive moment revealed a greater intensity of transference engagement.

In the enactive phase, a series of analyst- and patient-induced enactments arose in four successive sessions, the implications of which are detailed in Chapter Sixteen. There we show how disruptive acts and counteracts, often outside the consciousness of the participants, led to another *nodal moment* and a shift in the direction of the symbolizing process.

In the final segment of this specimen, the resymbolizing phase, we meet with an explicit erotic transference, which evoked an unambiguous countertransference enactment, followed by a return to symbolic synthesis. This marked a temporary, to be sure, but striking crystallization of the patient's core, unifying an awareness of her conflicts, her ideal (who she would like to be), and the mortification of who she is.

Thus, in this progression of symbolized forms of experiencing, moving from phase to phase, we can chart the path of *Progressive Symbolization*. To comprehend this sequence more fully we turn to the last aspect of working through, the role of repetition and the spiralling function.

* * *

Proposition 4: In *Progressive Symbolization, working through,* cyclic repetition leads to spiral transformation. Here we observe the full measure of the transformation cycle, where *Progressive Symbolization* reaches new depths and new heights through the recapitulation of crises previously encountered. As we shall develop, it is in this spiralling aspect that we find the motivational source for clinical change.

The phenomenon of a transformation cycle has been widely recognized by many analytic observers. The regularly occurring phases in analytic work, shifts from higher levels of mental organization to lower levels and back again, have been frequently observed in our literature. Expressed in different language, Loewald describes a shift from integration to disintegration and back to reintegration; Winnicott writes of unintegration phenomena and reintegration; Kohut of the repetitive encounter with empathic failure; Tronick and Stern of messiness in the transition from rupture to repair; and S. J. Ellman speaks of transference cycles. Perhaps the most comprehensive and articulated expression of cyclic oscillation can be found in the Kleinian notion of shifts from the paranoid-schizoid position and back to the depressive position. This was given a poetic vision by Britton, in his reference to movement "from the wilderness back to the promised land" (1998). Stressed in this Kleinian view is that this alteration is not simply a descriptive clinical phenomenon, but that it has dynamic force, the recognition of which, for us, is of crucial importance for the understanding of *Progressive Symbolization*.

The full appreciation of the concept of the depressive position is not simply exhausted by the fact that it marks the recovery of symbolic functioning, but further that it is nourished, as it were, by the events of the preceding *paranoid-schizoid position*, that is, the world of chaos and desymbolization. Britton (1998), in his essay, "Before and After the Depressive Position", spells out this notion of the impact of the intervening phase of apparent chaos, noting that the depressive position, following the paranoid-schizoid position, is qualitatively distinct from that which preceded it. In our findings (Chapter Thirteen), we shall affirm precisely such an effect when we compare a session from the re-symbolizing phase that follows a phase of desymbolization, to a session from the initial symbolizing phase.

However, we wish to go further than this. The path to re-symbolization is more than simply the encounter with desymbolization (or for that matter, the paranoid-schizoid position), but through the confrontation with object loss, the ego assimilates difficult moments successively. Thus, *Progressive Symbolization* is not only the incremental attainment of higher symbolic forms, but more significantly, includes the oscillating emergence of an active ego. This occurs first in the form of bearing the helplessness of object loss, in re-finding the object (albeit ever so briefly) during *nodal moments*, and in engaging the *real* object during the enactive phase.

The net result of such oscillation is not simple repetition but a spiralling effect. Here the work of Laplanche comes to our aid. If there is simple repetition, analysis goes nowhere. Using the metaphor of astronautics, Laplanche (1999) suggests that we must supplement the notion of a cycle with that of a spiral. As already stated, the depressive position that follows the paranoid-schizoid position differs from that which precedes it. Or, in our language, the phase of desymbolization and its oscillations leaves its impact on subsequent symbolization and integration. Through empirical observations, we indeed confirm that during the last session of our cycle, following a new countertransference crisis, new symbolic forms emerge not previously reached. The analytic process is, thus, alive.

To give flesh to this overview of our quantitative findings, we conclude this introduction with some highlights from the final hour of our specimen, session 257. The full measure of the spiralling function took shape during this session. The opening was marked by not only affective arousal, but nightmares, play, and the expression of a frankly erotic transference. A phase of impasse developed—the patient having pulled the analyst closely into the interaction—and a disruptive, *extraordinary countertransference* evolved. But after the evocation of another *nodal moment* and the survival of the crisis, the session ended with the patient embracing her ego ideal and musing with reflectivity and contrition about what had taken place. Here we find an exemplar of working through as repetition transformed.

CHAPTER THIRTEEN

Method and findings: the case of Ms Y: the patient and her analyst within the context of a recorded psychoanalysis

Norbert Freedman, Richard Lasky, and Rhonda Ward

At the time of this research, Ms Y was a professional woman in her thirties, and a mother of a three-year-old boy and a newly adopted infant daughter. She and her husband were residing in a suburban community in the US Midwest, enjoying a secure income. About six years prior to this study, she began a twice weekly psychotherapy and in her second year of treatment converted to a four-times-a-week psychoanalysis.

According to the analyst, the tone of the treatment shifted dramatically during the first two years of the analysis. The initial transference, one of non-engagement and affective withdrawal, developed into a sadomasochistic transference and then into one that was explicitly erotic. This intensity, one of over-engagement, seemed to have been a defence against the initial schizoid-like position, though, as the treatment progressed, acute neurotic conflicts also surfaced. It was at this stage that we entered the study of the treatment process.

The centrality of the sadomasochistic conflict was highlighted at the beginning of Chapter Twelve, and is a theme that will surface in the chapters to come, as we discuss a *symbolizing phase*, a *desymbolizing phase*, an *enactive phase*, and the erotic transference of the *re-symbolizing phase*.

The analyst and the frame

The analyst, a graduate of a psychoanalytic institute, had 12 years of analytic experience at the time of this project. With great consistency she sustained a treatment frame, guided by the "classical" analytic method. During the analysis, Ms Y was seen on the couch four times per week, and interventions ranged from empathic reflection, guided mirroring, to explicit interpretation. Even though the patient's initial clinical picture (that of a kind of schizoid defence) showed the presence of primitive ego organization, the analytic frame was sustained.

At the end of the second year of the analysis, the analyst introduced to the patient the idea of tape recording. She explained the research objective and obtained her written consent. Thereafter, taping was rarely an issue, and even when it became a vehicle for the expression of conflict, the taping did not prove an obstacle to the development of the treatment. For a discussion on the impact of audio recording on analytic process, see Bucci (2005).

The clinical scan

An important research tool in this study was the "clinical scan". At the end of each session, the analyst taped about five minutes of her impressions of the session, covering aspects of object relations, self-states, anxieties, transference and countertransference themes, and a free ranging estimate as to how the session had evolved. The "scan" method was developed at the Downstate Medical Center by Berzofsky, Wilke, and Freedman (2000) and has been in use for some years in the evaluation of psychotherapy process. For the analyst, the scan can be a time for reflection, even emotional discharge, when the dynamics of both patient and analyst are active and linger on. A splicing procedure makes this a powerful research instrument. Listening to the development of an analysis in one sitting can be quite pleasurable. From the treatment of Ms Y, we currently have about 260 sessions from three years of the analysis, and 60 of those sessions from the third year (sessions 201–260) form the basis of this report.[i]

Clinical scans from two criterion sessions

Now let us glimpse into two sessions from our specimen, viewed from the perspective of the analyst.

METHOD AND FINDINGS: THE CASE OF MS Y

Transcript of scan for session 232: an integrative session

Analyst: "Patient began the session by reporting that she was emotionally numb. Then she reported conflicts with her mother, specifically in regard to food during her mother's current visit. She went on to report that her mother had surprised her by doing something that indicated she had in fact heard the patient, which is something the patient is not used to doing. It was good that she admitted it and it shows progress that she admitted it. She has long history of never noticing this kind of thing. My assumption is that it's likely that she is being more observant at this point because she is bringing her attention to more of the details that are occurring in her interactions with others. She is also reporting positive feelings towards her father. Then she talked about decision-making regarding purchasing a new home and went on to talk about how she doesn't want to go back to being in suburbia, the way her parents raised her and her siblings. Then she reported a dream and at that point in the session, she returned to the transference and, speeding up the pace, started talking to me about how she doesn't want to depend on me. There was no acknowledgement at all that this was perhaps derivative of the earlier material she had talked about in regard to her parents. But she was very much involved in a pretty high transference stream at this point of the session. What was so interesting was that there were very highly conflictual expectations and wishes for me. That she both wanted to depend on me and didn't want to depend on me. How she wanted me to react to her and she didn't want me to react to her. I suggested to her at that point in the session—I guess it was about three quarters of the way through the session—that to let herself have any feelings about me at all while she was feeling so very much, is a very difficult thing for her to do. That in fact she wards off her feelings towards me because they feel so intense. After that comment, she told me that she was really very angry with me. She said that my stomach had growled earlier in the session, and she wouldn't dare tell me that when it happened. She talked about how she doesn't really want to torture me but she feels to let me off the hook is something she doesn't want to do either, until she understands why she's got me on the hook. I felt very much that I was in this maternal transference at this point, although I chose not to interpret that. Well actually it wasn't a choice because I didn't realize it until after the session how much I was in the maternal transference. I think it needs to develop more fully before it can be interpreted."

Transcript for scan of session 245: an unintegrative session

Analyst: "The theme of today's session was that the patient is feeling immobilized by the need for her to make a decision in regard to whether the family is going to put a bid on a particular house and move, or hire an architect to draw plans to add an additional addition to the house they live in now. And, she is responding to the feeling of being stuck, by being very depressed. Her husband has put the ball in her court and she is reluctant to make the move for similar dynamic reasons that she struggles so much with dieting. Her fantasy is that if they move into this house with all this space, somehow she'll become this voracious consumer and fill the house with all this junk and incur all this debt and she'll lose something unique about herself. She'll turn into her parents. And she is overwhelmed by that thought and really depressed by that thought that she wouldn't be able to contain herself in the same way as when she tries to diet. If she has one extra tenth of an ounce of ham on a sandwich, then she feels, well forget it, everything is ruined and I can eat anything that I want now. She began the session by starting to criticize me, and it was interesting the way she was criticizing me. She liked the clothes that I had on but she thought that my top looked heavier than my bottom, and she speculated that maybe she criticized my top because she admired the way my legs look and she is very critical of her legs. And she really kind of splits her body and my body into all these part objects. And she went into this really kind of masochistic technical analysis of her own legs, dissecting the calf from the ankle and the thigh, and clearly, she has thought about it and has opinions about like every line and curve of her leg. And how she never wears short skirts and she won't wear suits with skirts. So self-punitive. And then she also became critical of her daughter at that point. She said, she had the thought that her daughter was going to be squatty. And she very quickly moved away from that and then the bulk of the session was about trying to make a decision about this house and becoming increasingly depressed. But towards the last section of the session, realizing that she needs more time to pursue some of the obstacles that stand in the way for them adding an addition to the current house. And once those obstacles are surpassed or overcome, she'll feel good about moving ahead. And if those obstacles weren't overcome, then she also would be able to accept the alternative, because she would know that she couldn't do what she planned to do. But the session was ... she was actually quite flattened in the session, really quite depressed."

These two snapshots offer an entry into our propositions on *Progressive Symbolization* outlined in Chapter Twelve: that a given hour may be characterized by different modes of mental functioning, that such modes may reverberate in the mind of the analyst, and that such configurations appear in distinct phases, even in a single session (e.g., session 232). The fourth proposition that there might be a spiralling effect cannot be evaluated until we reach session 257, the end of our specimen.

54 Sessions in the course of a psychoanalysis: defining salient psychoanalytic hours

In his *Essays on Otherness*, Laplanche (1999) remarks that in the tracing of the transference, or for that matter, the analytic process, what is important is not the familiar or ordinary session, but the extraordinary, the unusual session. We have taken this advice to heart—a wise approach not only in clinical practice and supervision, but also in psychoanalytic research. For what we hope to find is not only the trajectory that defines psychoanalytic change—its peaks and troughs, but also the unforgettable moments—the beacons that highlight salient issues. So we set out with 54 sessions from the analysis of Ms Y to discover defining sessions. Our approach was initially both qualitative and quantitative.

Capturing the immediacy of the analyst's experience of the hour: the A and Z properties

The starting point of our method was the analyst's clinical scan. These scans were our first anchoring points towards distinguishing two modes of mental organization that might characterize a given session. Through listening to the scan, the clinical investigators (RL and NF) provisionally designated a session to have either *A* or *Z* properties. These abstract terms were chosen so as to avoid an evaluative dimension. A or Z did not mean "good" or "bad", but referred to different qualities of mind. A qualities generally represented processes of integration, developmental progression, and relatively stable object relations, reflecting a range of functions such as the awareness of transference, affect communication, reflective functioning, and the ability to receive interpretations. Z qualities were associated with processes of unintegration, regression, and destabilization, and functions associated with the experience of impasse.

Further delineating A and Z properties

These global qualities were translated into specific rating procedures. Several judges were enlisted to further delineate the properties of A and Z. For example, a scan containing "distance from raw affect", and "a sense of relational immediacy" depicted an A session, whereas "fragmented object representations" and "counter-aggression felt by the analyst" suggested Z functioning. These items were to be used in a global fashion. We did not rate the items individually, since our interest was in the analyst's overall feel of the hour.

Reliability of A and Z ratings

The initial clinical investigators, each working independently, listened to the scans of the 54 sessions, and made a quantitative judgment about the analyst's experience of the hour. The investigators came to the task with differing familiarities with the case. One of the investigators, R L, had a supervisory knowledge of the treatment, though at no time had the sessions in the study been discussed with the analyst, while the other investigator, N F, was completely unfamiliar with the patient's history or clinical picture.

Each investigator gave the scans two ratings: one for A (integrative) and one for Z (unintegrative), using a ten point scale. The inter-judge reliability for the A ratings for the 54 scans was 0.78, and for Z, 0.84. Mean A and Z score, reflecting the best estimate of the joint ratings by the two investigators was arrived at and the correlation was -0.84 (Bucci & Maskit, 2007). We could readily say that when the treating analyst described a given session as high in integrative qualities, she was also likely to have described the same hour as low in unintegrative qualities and vice versa.

We had the first confirmatory evidence that over the course of 54 sessions, scans could be reliably judged as containing specific psychoanalytically defined forms of process encompassed by the designation of A and Z qualities. We then sought to answer three questions which determined our subsequent procedures: how can clinically "unusual" (criterion) sessions be identified?; to what extent do the A and Z ratings of the scan reflect the psychoanalytic process in the actual session?; and in what way can A and Z be considered signifiers of the symbolizing or desymbolizing process?[ii]

Discovering criterion sessions

Was it an unusual A or Z session? This question led to further scrutiny of our data. From the pool of 54 sessions, we sought to identify those that could be considered unusual and statistically extraordinary. Since it had become possible, from the ratings of the scans, to discern the character of a given session, those scores were converted into standard scores and criterion sessions were selected as those showing a score of at least one standard deviation above or below the mean. Hence, a session of at least one standard deviation above was called a criterion A session, and any session one standard deviation below the mean, a criterion Z session. The result was 16 criterion sessions, 9 A sessions and 7 Z sessions. These 16 sessions could certainly be called statistically unusual, but whether or not they were clinically unusual remained to be seen.

The two further questions: whether these criterion sessions, based on the scans, were really A or Z sessions, and whether these hours could be designated as symbolized or desymbolized, led to further inquiry. The first issue was readily answered through the available transcripts of the sessions. For any given criterion session, we were able to determine the correspondence between the scan and the session through an independent evaluation of the transcript. The answer was in the affirmative (Freedman, Lasky & Hurvich, 2003). But the further question of whether such sessions could be considered symbolized or desymbolized, reaches the heart of our conceptual issue. At this juncture, having established a database of 16 criterion sessions, we were in a position not only to inquire as to whether the sessions were symbolized or desymbolized, but also, whether the sessions were mirrored in the mind of the analyst, whether they revealed successive phases of psychoanalytic engagement, and whether there were changes of a spiralling nature over the course of these sessions. At each point of inquiry, we looked for new empirically-based methods to investigate our clinical hunches, seeking to confirm or disconfirm them. Let us elaborate.

The propositions of Progressive Symbolization empirically evaluated

Proposition 1

Proposition 1 holds that *Progressive Symbolization* involves shifts in mental organization ranging from an unintegrated (desymbolized) to an integrated (symbolized) mode of thought. Empirically, this means that a particular hour or a part of that hour is marked by a predominance of either symbolization or desymbolization. Some brief reflections on the concept of symbolization are called for here.

Symbolization is a process of meaning making, where the unification of diverse experiences leads to an integrated third form. It involves linking in triangular space—a process of connecting two items of experience stemming from distinct spheres of the mind, where one represents the other. There are different forms of symbolization (Cassirer, 1955), which influence each other incrementally, even progressively, as we shall develop, and are stepping stones in shaping one's internal reality. The alteration of symbolic forms provides the frame for the study of clinical change.

Symbolization is a highly overburdened concept, Fonagy suggested in 1998. Indeed, different dimensions of this symbolizing process are articulated in the psychoanalytic literature, addressing distinct aspects of treatment, and these dimensions will be spelled out in the Postscript at the end of this book. However, an ingenious empirically-based vision of symbolization has been developed by Bucci, in her concept of the referential process (Bucci & Maskit, 2007). This concept is derived from a cognitive-linguistic understanding of spoken language, it addresses issues vital to the analytic process, and is the basis for a method that allows for a quantitative (computer generated) evaluation of transcripts from recorded analytic sessions. In this study, we used the measures of the referential process as a best quantitative estimate of a symbolizing process.

The concept of the referential process and its measurement

The referential process involves the unification of the emotional schema, registered in sub-symbolic form, with formulated symbolic form. It marks the integration of affective experiences not previously formulated, in a manner that is both apprehended by the speaker and penetrates the listener. The process is exemplified by the use of "metaphor", where the speaker offers a discrete image that captures sub-symbolic emotional affects, while at the same time evokes corresponding emotions in the listener. Change in the referential process implies a change in psychic functioning, and this can become manifest in the transference. Bucci & Maskit (2007) describe distinct phases of the referential process within a given session: arousal (the surge of affect from the emotion schema), symbolizing (the act of connecting the image to the words), and re-organizing (reflecting on the material evoked). When there is high referential activity, these three steps repeat themselves within sessions and over the course of several sessions. Thus, symbolizing here is not just a single event but a sequential process—precisely what we observed in our *A* criterion sessions. This cumulative process is generative and affirms the progressive nature of symbolizing activity.

The referential process finds codification in the *Discourse Attribute Analytic Procedure* (DAAP, Bucci & Maskit, 2007). In the scoring of transcripts from recorded sessions, the spine of this method is in the measure of Referential Activity (RA). Referential activity reflects the patient's ability to capture through language, nonverbal images, in a manner that can be apprehended by others, images that are specific, evocative, and even provocative. The variable of referential activity comprises a large part of the variance of any given text. Additional measures of the referential process, that is, "dictionaries", have also been developed for: affect (positive, negative, and neutral); reflectivity; disfluencies of speech; somatosensory speech; as well as for "nonverbal vocal responses" (e.g., mm-hm), the latter applied to the analyst's speech only. There have been two important recent additions to this scoring system: the "high RA" is a score measuring the intensity of the referential process, and the measure of covariation reflects the extent to which one aspect of the referential process precludes the other. More about this later.

It is fortunate that in Bucci's conceptualization of the referential process, aspects of the symbolizing process are captured within a single empirically-based measure. Her notion, based on the theory of Dual Code, is psycho-linguistically defined, depicts the mental life of a patient "beneath the surface" of consciousness, and matches in many ways psychoanalytically driven notions about the symbolizing process. Hence, when there is high referential activity in a given session, we would expect to find the patient's language affectively charged, evocative, perhaps provocative, inviting reflectivity, and evoking selective distancing.

As stated above, Bucci holds that these forms of referential activity shift during the course of a given hour. For her, a symbolizing hour involves alterations from a phase of arousal, to symbolizing, and to a phase of re-organization. This pattern can be seen in the scan of session 232 presented previously (an integrative session), though it is absent in the scan of session 245 (an unintegrative session). In the scan of session 232, the analyst noted the patient's experience of cooking with her mother (arousal), the telling of a dream (symbolizing), and then the reflection upon her relationship with the analyst (re-organization). No such progression was noted for session 245.

Empirical observations

The typed transcripts of the 16 criterion sessions (9 *A* and 7 *Z*) were evaluated by the computer assisted analysis of the referential process (DAAP). An initial comparison of the resultant profiles revealed sharp distinctions between *A* and *Z* hours. This initial data analysis was subsequently carried out in a more systematic fashion by Bucci & Maskit (2007). In this work, they deployed the variables of the referential process to obtain what they call an "imaging profile", which tracks shifts, minute-by-minute, during each session, to determine the ups and downs of each variable. Here is what was expected and observed:

- In general it was expected and observed that the level of referential activity would be higher in the 9 *A* sessions, whereas disfluencies signalling a sub-symbolic process would be more pronounced in the 7 *Z* sessions. During the *A* sessions the patient told her story vividly, evocatively, provocatively, and even with

urgency. During the Z hours, there was a prevalence of disfluency of speech, signalling the presence of a sub-symbolic process not as yet symbolized.
- It was expected and observed that in the A hours the covariation between referential activity and reflectivity would be a negative one. This means that in those sessions, the patient experienced a greater separation in time between narration and reflection. This finding, showing how one kind of psychic activity is separated in time from another distinct one, highlights the interplay between two spheres of mental functioning and with it, the creation of symbolizing space.
- It was expected and observed that in the A sessions there would be a positive covariation between reflectivity and disfluency of speech. This relationship suggests that the patient was disfluent while reflecting, indicating that reflections occurred with new formulations, that is, new statements were arrived at rather than previously formulated thoughts repeated. It implies that symbolizing is not only expressive space creating, but is also generative.

We concluded that the A sessions, previously described by the clinical investigators as "integrative" hours—hours where paradox was integrated and brought into the transference—could be designated as symbolizing sessions. For when the session transcripts were subjected to the measure of the referential process, it was confirmed that the A hours revealed a narrative that was affectively alive, reflective, and generative. In such sessions, the process of symbolization was marked by arousal, symbolizing, and re-organizing. Henceforth, we shall speak of an A session, a session high in referential activity, as a symbolizing session.

But does low referential activity suggest desymbolization? There remained the gnawing problem of defining and confirming desymbolization. For us, desymbolization is a psychic event, suggesting not just the absence of the symbolic, but a motivated and definable psychic activity: the wish to destroy meaning, eschew, and even annihilate significance. Here our views depart from those of Bucci. For her, the absence of referential activity (low RA, low symbolizing) is a sign of the nonverbal sphere, the sub-symbolic, and the impact of the emotion schema. In our clinical observations reported in subsequent chapters, we note that in those hours marked by low referential activity, there indeed are identifiable mental functions, which we describe under the general heading of desymbolization (see Postscript for dimensions of desymbolization).

Proposition 2

Proposition 2 affirms that symbolization and desymbolization reverberate in the mind of the analyst. In Chapter Twelve, we suggested that *Progressive Symbolization* is not simply a quality of mind that resides within the subject, but is created during the interchange of the analytic couple. We also suggested that this interplay can be confirmed in two ways: first, by tracing just how the patient's symbolized or desymbolized experiences are absorbed in the analyst's consciousness after the hour, and secondly by examining how such joint participation can be noted through the way the analyst's speech is reflective of the patient's speech during the course of the hour. The first relies on the analyst's scan, signalling just how the session lives on in her consciousness, while the second on a computer analysis of the session transcript, revealing how the profile of the referential process finds its mirror in the analyst's spoken language.

As we have indicated, the analyst's registration of the salient features of a given session, as demonstrated in her reconstruction following the hour, can indeed be a good indicator of what actually transpired during that hour. The reader will recall from the scan of session 232 just how the analyst perceived the session highlights—the moments of "arousal" in the beginning, dream episodes reflected upon, and the powerful transference image related to torture at the conclusion. This was precisely the sequence in the actual session. For the desymbolized session (session 245), the repetitive morbid quality was also captured in both documents. This correspondence between material reconstructed and material from the transcripts was affirmed by the positive correlation between *A-Z* ratings of the scans and the computer generated measures of the referential process for the corresponding sessions. Through statistical analysis, we affirmed provisionally that by and large, the analyst was able to re-create and absorb the essence of the hour (Freedman, Lasky & Webster, 2009).

There was another line of inquiry that further clarified the quality of the analyst's engagement, namely, her nonverbal vocal responses.

A crucial determinant of the character of the hour was not only the content of the analyst's speech, but a specific nonverbal form marked by the familiar utterance, "mm-hm" (NVR). This NVR is not just a nonverbal vocalization, but, when there is attunement, it tends to be well timed, may arise at the peak of a patient's affective burst, or during pausing. It is a manifestation of phonemic rhythm. There exists in the literature independent evidence that when during a clinical interchange, rhythmic organizers are accompanied by bodily movements such as hand movements or head nods, and when this occurs, new forms of thought are likely to be generated in both participants. These are audible and visible events that function as precursors to the symbolizing and referential process (Gilani, Bucci & Freedman, 1998). In the analytic situation, they can be regarded as markers of "interactional synchrony", and following the writings of the Boston Change Process Study group, suggest a process of implicit relational knowing (IRK) (Stern et al., 1998). Turning to our findings from the case of Ms Y, the presence of the "mm-hm" turned out to be a powerful correlate of the referential process, and, for us, of symbolization. There were substantially higher frequencies of NVR uttered by the analyst during the symbolizing sessions as compared to the desymbolizing hours. We might say that the symbolizing process had become inter-subjective.

It will not be surprising that during these symbolizing hours, while the analyst was offering her synchronous interactive "mm-hm", her spoken language had a distinct symbolizing quality. The analyst's speech revealed higher levels of referential narrative, affect, reflectivity and the negative covariation between reflection and referential activity. We might say that as she resonated with her patient, as she shared and reflected upon images, and as she delayed her thoughts before speaking, she indeed mirrored and deployed the same language forms used by her patient.

But what was the role of the analyst during Z hours or Z moments? The statistical findings regarding interactional synchrony reported earlier came mostly from the nine symbolizing hours. But these findings might be misleading. Such findings rely upon the pull of high referential activity as a provocative phenomenon, pulling the analyst in. It does not account for the low symbolizing sessions or for the "difficult" moments within A sessions, which can be a source of rupture. Again, we took recourse to the scans and sought to match those moments of disruption in sessions with the analyst's registration of these moments in the scan. Were they affirmed, distorted, or even deleted? If distorted or deleted, an impasse, if not rupture, in the analyst-patient relationship is suggested, and such findings become a challenge to the proposition that symbolization in the patient reverberates in the mind of the analyst.

A qualitative analysis of the criterion sessions revealed there were five instances of such deletions, where the analyst did not register moments in which the patient was regressive and desymbolizing. Did such events re-enforce a pull towards regression, or alternatively, did the apparent rupture start a process of reversal, even repair? The first is a linear process, the second a paradoxical process—one that serves as a modifier to our main proposition. This finding implies that even the confrontation with rupture may activate synthetic functions in the patient, launching the process in a new direction. To clarify this complex issue, we inquired just how such reversals might be embedded within the phases of analytic work—the subject of our next proposition.

Proposition 3

Proposition 3 advances the notion that specific phases of analytic work are the sites of transformation. We next investigated the trajectory of the clinical course. Were the 16 criterion sessions distributed at random across the course of the specimen? The answer was a decided no, for when we situated the criterion sessions within the context of the entire 54 sessions, there appeared a definable time trend. Session 205 (the first criterion session) began a definite A phase, followed by a dip towards Z at session 221, and then a return to A at session 227. Even more striking was a second sequence: there was marked A activity from sessions 232–243, pronounced Z activity from sessions 245–249, and an A peak at the 257 mark. The distribution appeared to be cyclic in nature. The most pronounced cycle occurred from sessions 232–257, the most persuasive evidence for a transformation cycle. This cycle became the focus for the remainder of our specimen study.

Within this span of analytic hours there were four definable phases, identified by levels of A and Z activity and by the scores of the referential process. From sessions 232–243, there was a predominance of *A* activity and, as expected, referential activity was high; we considered this a symbolizing phase. From sessions 245–249, *Z* activity was predominant and referential activity was markedly low; this seemed to be a desymbolizing phase. From sessions 252–255, *A* activity was neither high nor low, though referential activity moved upward. In these particular sessions, qualitative findings revealed that enactments were prominent and we, thus, termed this segment the enactive phase. Finally, there was a renewed predominance of *A* activity in sessions 256–257, reaching a peak of both *A* and referential activity in session 257; this we called the re-symbolizing phase. As a whole, the defining of these phases provided us with a launch pad for the study of the dynamics of *Progressive Symbolization*. In what follows, we shall offer highlights of our qualitative findings and clinical inferences for each phase, with details to be found in the next four chapters. But before doing so, we need to introduce a further methodological step.

The method of sequential specification

With the discovery of these four phases, a new level of inference making was introduced. In evaluating propositions 1 and 2 we relied exclusively on "objective" empirical data, that is, the *A* and *Z* ratings or levels of referential activity. Indeed, this reliance was equally true in defining the four phases just described, for each phase had its own "objective" marker. However, when we wished to trace changes from one phase to another, for example from the symbolizing to the desymbolizing phase, a new level of inference making was introduced, which included the qualitative analysis of subjective states, both within the patient and within the analyst. We, thus, introduced the method of sequential specification (Freedman, Lasky & Hurvich, 2003).

In this method, while inferences were also grounded in empirically-based observations of recorded sessions, we took the further step to integrate such observations into the language of psychoanalysis. Each event, moment, phase within a session, entire session, or even the whole specimen is described and evaluated from three perspectives: the patient, the analyst, and the interpretive clinical observer. We began with the patient's speech, including both verbal and nonverbal expressions, as well as pausing (the recordings and transcripts), continued with the analyst's perception of the hour (the scan), and then, as interpretive listeners, proceeded to summarize and translate the events into the language of psychoanalysis (listeners' observations and commentary). The reader will find the listeners' observations and a commentary section following the presentation of the clinical material contained within each chapter. This is a *Rashomon approach,* where looking at the same phenomenon from multiple perspectives yields a new synthesis. Here is a brief summary of our phase specific findings.

The symbolizing phase was also the site of a downward slope, a gradient of change, and with it the first instance of transference regression. While symbolizing activity was initially high, levels of symbolization (referential activity) progressively declined, indicating a downward pull. Such a gradient of change suggests a transition from one state of consciousness to another. This shift implies the challenging phenomenon of "transference regression", where the patient is successively confronted with the raw material of disorganizing conflicts. Most important, its more intense affect can also be a communicative act, pulling the analyst into the patient's inner psychic reality, signalling a first step in the direction of *Progressive Symbolization.*

Now this gradient of change, empirically defined, nonetheless is a paradoxical transformation. We asked, "Why should the patient, engaged in creating symbols, telling dreams, reflecting and recollecting, concurrently be harassed by thoughts that interfere or confuse?" In brief, what is the nature of the implicit downward pull in the face of an explicit upward push? We returned to quantitative observations and identified a particular intervening process manifest in spoken language (derived from the referential activity profile), "somatosensory thought" (organ speech), which functioned as a mediator in this downward pull. In Chapter Fourteen, we shall describe and interpret these findings, and consider their relevance to the writings on "transference regression" by Macalpine, Winnicott, and Khan, as well as McDougall.

The desymbolizing phase was a time of quite profound regression, yet within this phase we discovered what we termed *nodal moments,* reversals signifying another kind of paradoxical transformation and the beginning of the upward slope. *Nodal moments* are brief, memorable, often occur late in the hour, and can be reliably distinguished from their surrounds. Such *moments* suggest that working through has taken a new direction where psychic events, initially implicit and unformulated, can become explicit and formulated or, in our language, a phase of desymbolization can be resolved into symbolized form.

We first discovered *nodal moments* through a critical reading of the transcripts; they were then confirmed by the quantitative empirical method of *Segmentation Analysis* (see Chapter Fifteen). These empirically derived critical moments provided an arena for the scrutiny of how confrontation with triangular conflict can initiate reversal and create the path towards mental re-organization. We found *nodal moments* in three sessions of this phase (sessions 245, 247, and 249), and noted how they depicted different patterns of triangulation. In the emergent content, the patient became increasingly able to express desires, explicitly and more directly. In form, these wishes became embedded in a more symbolized mental landscape, became more vivid, were told in a presentational mode of thought, and had enactive qualities. This vivid narrative coincided with memories recovered and told with imagination. During these moments of "triangular working through", the relationship to the analyst became explicitly interactive and even confrontational. As per our earlier discussion on "metabolizing", these *nodal moments* were often preceded by instances of countertransference ruptures.

As we further considered the quality of these *nodal moments* they contained different renditions of the triangulation process, matching in turn models of triangulation reported by such psychoanalytic writers as Kernberg, Britton, Steingart, and Rose. These models will be elaborated in Chapter Fifteen.

The third phase was the "enactive" phase, sessions 252 through 255. Following the series of *nodal moments* of the desymbolizing phase, this sequence of sessions appeared, which were not classifiable as either predominately A or predominately Z, and were, thus, neither symbolized nor desymbolized sessions, though the referential activity scores for these hours moved upward. Another "objective fact" alerted us to a potentially informative event, namely that the analyst's scans for these sessions increased in length. Once more, this finding was based on an empirical "fact", but interpretive listening led to various lines of thought. This shift might signify that the patient had more to say and/or that the analyst was more engaged, but whatever the interpretation, there was a veritable surge of the analyst's commentary during this period.

In these successive sessions, we observed the context for different forms of enactment, be it patient-induced, analyst-induced, mutual enactment, or enactment symbolically resolved. The empirical facts were the guide and the context led to a psychoanalytic understanding consistent with the writings of Ellman, Smith, and Katz. For details see Chapter Sixteen.

To summarize, embedded within each of the phases described thus far—the symbolizing phase, the desymbolizing phase, and the enactive phase—spanning approximately seven weeks of analytic work, were processes of change marking a downward and an upward slope. Here then are juncture points of clinical change that parallel the line of thought advanced by many voices in our literature. While our formulations of change are based on a specimen with a very short life-span, the formulations in the literature are inevitably based on months if not years of clinical experience. However, the methodology of our specimen approach highlights the notion that small and brief changes can signal major events to come, and this also challenges us to find the motivational sources that move towards clinical change. We locate these in the processes inherent in the transformation cycle.

Proposition 4

Proposition 4 asserts that cyclic repetition leads to spiral transformation. We discovered distinct phases within our specimen having a cyclic pattern, revealed in the downward and upward slopes. Such unfolding cyclic patterns offer not just a description of the event, but imply a dynamic process as well. To understand the phenomenon of a transformation cycle, it becomes necessary to emphasize the motivational force implied by the terms, Symbolization and Desymbolization. We hold that the ability to symbolize is defined by a patient's position vis-à-vis the object. During the downward slope, through the invocation of transference regression, the patient is "dragged down", resulting in the process of desymbolization. But paradoxically, while facing the "abyss", a reversal takes place and with it a move towards re-finding the lost object. This is the onset of the upward slope. It begins with the emergence of *nodal moments* and following an enactive engagement, new heights of symbolization can be reached. Such a sequence underscores the impact of regressive experiences on subsequent functioning. We return to Laplanche's (1999) advice concerning the spiral function of clinical change. The cyclic process may be entirely repetitive, but in analysis we expect more than a cycle. A move "beyond the cyclic" is demonstrative of the process of *working through*. In the spiralling function, mental organization may appear to return to the point of origin, but does so at a level both less and more organized, so that experiences become symbolized in a new way. The *working through* process entails the superimposition of the spiralling function on the ordinary cyclic repetition of analytic work.

Empirical observations

We examined both the cyclic and spiralling functions within this transformation cycle. Comparisons were made between sessions 232 (the "before" symbolized session), 245 (an unambiguous desymbolized session), and 257 (the "after" symbolized session). When we considered both the mean A-Z ratings, as well as the mean referential activity scores, as overall indicators of symbolization, we found the expected dip during the desymbolized phase. Most importantly, the levels of symbolization defined by mean A-Z and RA scores were the same in the "before" and "after" sessions. Such a match confirmed the cyclic alternation but not the spiralling hypothesis.

However, when we considered more subtle aspects of referential activity, namely, the "high RA" scores and nonverbal vocalized responses (NVR), a different pattern emerged. As previously stated, "high RA" represents the components of referential process within a single passage, where there is an intense coalescing of images expressed vividly, evocatively, with specificity, strongly impacting the listener. The "high RA" score was substantially higher in session 257 as compared to that for session 232. This supports a spiralling hypothesis and suggests that in the final phase of this transformation cycle, the re-symbolizing phase, a new level of psychic activity was attained.

Moreover, there was another unexpected observation. When the measure of nonverbal vocal responses (NVR) was considered, the level of the analyst's interactional synchrony was actually lower in the after session then in the before session. This suggests the possibility of a disruptive countertransference at the very point when heightened patient affective engagement was present.

Thus, both observations support the spiralling hypothesis, for the patient appears to be more excitedly and emotionally engaged, while signs of disruptive behaviour on the part of the analyst were also present. Indeed, it marked the superimposition of the spiral on the ordinary cyclic alternation. In Chapter Seventeen, this spiralling function will be translated into clinical language, as we will examine the erotic transference, the extraordinary countertransference, and the survival of the analytic process.

Endnotes

i. The original sample consisted of 60 sessions, but six sessions were inaudible.
ii. These reliability findings were corroborated in a joint study by Bucci and Maskit (2007).

CHAPTER FOURTEEN

The induction of transference regression during the symbolizing phase: sessions 232 to 243

Norbert Freedman and Rhonda Ward

In 1950, Macalpine published a memorable paper on the nature of *transference*, in which she asserted that a regressive transference is not only inevitable, but is evoked and actually induced by forces inherent in the frame of the psychoanalytic process. For us, the regressive transference is a paradoxical situation in which the patient may feel received, even supported, yet at the same time confronted by an enigmatic force that pulls in a downward direction. This precise situation was encountered by Ms Y during the symbolizing phase of this transformation cycle.

Macalpine's statement, based on an extensive review of the cumulative psychoanalytic knowledge up to 1950, raises for us two fundamental issues deserving separate consideration. The first concerns what we might call the *induction hypothesis*, the other we will call the *reverberation hypothesis*. Regarding the *induction hypothesis*, Macalpine spells out a series of specific transference forces, mobilized by the explicit and implicit analytic frame, which activate a pull towards a lower level of mental organization. This implies a paradoxical situation: the patient experiences an enigmatic force, pulling in the direction of lesser differentiation, and occurring at the very point of feeling heard and received. In the *reverberation hypothesis*, what we call *regression* is not only experienced by the patient, but is also communicated to and experienced by the person of the analyst, lending depth to analytic work.

Before proceeding further, the term *regression* needs justification. Innerbitzen and Levy (2000), in a major review article, develop the thesis that *regression* is an outmoded, concretized, often confusing concept, diffuse in meaning, vague, contradictory, and a concept which should be abandoned. They prefer the term "transformation" for those processes that are regressive. Notwithstanding their critique, the term *regression* has remained an indispensable descriptive clinical designation over the decades for analysts with wide-ranging perspectives. Bromberg (1979), writing from a relational perspective, notes that regression, the patient's confrontation with raw affect, is essential for analytic work. The deeper the regression, the more profound the clinical change. Bach (2006) believes regression is inevitable and finds the term useful when describing altered states of consciousness, particularly in the treatment of narcissistic patients. He notes that regression, a form of dissociation, might feel like a "death of the self" and may continue unabated unless the patient encounters some kind of healing environment. Much earlier, Rycroft (1956) uses regression and desymbolization equivalently, but prefers the latter term as a designation for what is at work. We believe that the regression concept should not be abandoned, but, in agreement with Rycroft, we feel the concept should also encompass the notion of *desymbolization*. This is the meaning we shall give *regression* in this chapter.

Let us return to the *induction hypothesis*. Descriptively, the *downward slope* implies a linear path of change and we assert that progressively, in the course of a *working phase*, a decline in the symbolizing process occurs (what we term Progressive Desymbolization), leading to an altered state of consciousness. But such a shift raises the added question: what makes such an alteration possible, that is, what is the motivational force underlying such a move towards de-differentiation? We speculated that even within our specimen this altered functioning could be traced to the concurrent, yet incompatible (paradoxical) forces that emerge. We looked for a gradient of change that might reveal that during the symbolizing phase, a rise in *anti-symbolic* processes could be observed. Hence, in the midst of a symbolized transference, the breeding ground leading towards de-differentiation might be found. It is in this sense that we say that the *downward slope* during a symbolizing working phase of treatment is a paradoxical phenomenon. We set ourselves the task to delineate, even to discover such a process.

Now to the *reverberation hypothesis*. Induced regression during the *symbolizing phase* is not only a subjective experience, but also becomes a communicative act. As the patient begins to voice regressive despair, the addressee is pulled in. For example, when the Rat Man, in a moment of crisis, speaks to Freud as "Captain", he condenses the painful image of his torturer (contained in the subjectively felt horror story) with the momentary image of his analyst, probably intending to pull the analyst in (Freud, 1909, p. 169). Such regressive moments are not only raw in form, but by definition have a sense of urgency. In this way, the patient comes closer to his/her psychic reality, while making increasingly explicit and implicit demands on the analyst. These demands include a quest for empathy, for rescue, to tolerate confusion and despair, to surrender, in short to contain all that which is unbearable at the moment. These implicit demands evoke profound alterations in the countertransference, for as the relationship intensifies, the analyst is either pulled in or resorts to flight.

Regression induced or regression reverberating

Judging from the plethora of creative ideas on regression, it seems almost impertinent to select three anchoring voices that have organized our thinking, yet, as Sandler (1983) has noted, psychoanalytic concepts are elastic. The following voices reflect the evolution of the concept of regression since 1950. Macalpine embodies the spirit of the structural view of American ego psychology from Rappaport to Arlow and to Brenner; Khan resonates with the British object relations vision of therapeutic regression, articulated in the writings of Balint and Winnicott; and MacDougall, a spokesperson for French psychoanalysis, resonates with contemporary Freudian analysts in her emphasis on the implicit role of the unspoken presence of interpenetration inherent in the analytic process.

As already noted, Macalpine makes the most explicit statement of the induction hypothesis. It is the analytic situation, *analysis as situation*, which creates transference, a situation construed as unreal, infantile, regressive, produced by "a reduction of the analysand's object world and denial of object relations in the analytic room" (Macalpine, 1950, p. 522). Analysis is a therapeutic method in which an infantile regression is induced, and analyzed.

Macalpine describes the many factors inherent in the frame, which we believe account for a surge in the experience of paradoxical moments, moments which in turn create impasse and the throttling of symbolic functions. The experience of being seen while not seeing the analyst, the rule of abstinence, the fixity of the routine, the frustration created at times by silence, the atmosphere of timelessness, the frequency of visits, all promote a dreamy state of consciousness, the sense of being both infant and adult, of being loved and hated, and of being rational and irrational. According to Macalpine, the sole explicit nourishment is that of interpretation.

Macalpine's paper is of historical interest. Her general conclusion, articulated in such a scholarly manner, cannot be rejected. The analytic frame indeed intensifies the yearning for being loved and the fear of being rejected or hated, and creates experiences of equivalence implying object loss. These intense, often unconsciously felt inner states, initiate the path towards what we have termed the *downward slope*. This line of thought implies a general clinical proposition, namely, that the psychoanalytic situation can facilitate the downward slope.

* * *

What is not addressed in Macalpine is the vision of the "ego in environment" that has emerged during recent decades, notably the shaping role of the other within the analytic dyad especially during states of regression. Hence, there is the concept of role responsiveness (Sandler, 1976), that is, the analyst's pre-floating, pre-conscious response, the "useful" countertransference stirred up by the patient's demands during moments of stress. There is Laplanche's notion of *alterity*, which implies the continuous search by the patient for the enigmatic other (1997). Most crucially, contained in the writing of Winnicott (1955), is the idea of regression as a move towards primary dependence, emphasizing not object loss, but a yearning for object presence. To these considerations we now turn.

* * *

Khan (1960), in the spirit of Winnicott, emphasizes the theme of regression as a state of absolute dependency. Regression, or for Winnicott, non-integration (1974), is a way for the patient to connect to early developmental processes, where there is a struggle to overcome impingements, and an opportunity to connect to instincts, passions, and hope.

In his clinical essay, "Regression and Integration in the Analytic Setting", Khan (1960) set himself the task of showing how a patient's analytic regression presented itself and made specific demands on his countertransference. He describes a three year treatment with distinct phases, a phase of manic activity, a phase of intense grief and regression, and a phase of reintegration. Although Khan's patient regressed to a level more primitive than that found in our specimen, he nonetheless described periods of despair, increased withdrawal, and the stirring of the body ego, elements reminiscent of Ms Y's downward slope. Such elements suggest that a distinctly different psychoanalytic universe has been reached.

In the course of his patient's "controlled regression", Khan was able to trace the analytic process through bodily references. There occurred a week of physical illness, a critical time of crisis which the patient could not articulate psychically. There were childhood memories of pulling out and eating her hair, nibbling food, and promiscuity in adolescence. For the analyst, these were signifiers of need, helplessness and loss of control, but also of attack, defiance, and a demand to be contained. It was an indication of object seeking, within the kernel of a regressive episode.

The patient's affective process led to a total sense of loss and then to a collapse into hopelessness, a "just being nothing" (1960, p. 139). Khan described a session where the patient "started to cry, quietly, gently, and with the whole of her body. I could feel its reality and pain *in myself* [italics in original]. There was nothing of her strength left, she felt; and this also I could feel." Khan continues, "It is hard to define this in words, as in my countertransference experience I registered it with the whole of my mental and body sensibility. In this phase I had to learn more and more to rely on and use my body as a vehicle of perception in the analytic setting. By my body I mean the body-ego" (ibid., pp. 139–140). As the patient fell into a state of absolute dependency, Khan's role in the analytic situation was "to be there, alive, alert, embodied, and vital, but not to impinge with any personal need to translate her affective experiences into their mental correlates" (ibid., p. 140). The patient easily registered whether or not Khan was fully there in his body attention and Khan sensed this registration through a subtle change of affective rhythm.

During the regression proper, Khan became the mother of need and the mother of care. The patient received the embodied representation of a supplementary ego. She "needed and borrowed my flesh and bone to hang on to" (ibid., p. 141). As the analyst pulled the patient into a different state of consciousness, the patient shifted "from a false, to a true self" (ibid., p. 142). As Winnicott (1956) notes, "Good enough adaptation by the analyst produces a result which is exactly that which is sought, namely, a shift in the patient of the main site of operation from a false to a true self" (p. 387).

We find in this dramatic example the foundation for a second general clinical proposition, namely, that within the inevitable induction of regression, a transference demand, expressed through the body ego, is communicated implicitly to the analyst, and in turn reverberates in the analyst's subjectivity, creating an alteration in the analyst's state of consciousness.

We wonder, while the patient felt protected from impingement and felt the presence of the analyst in so tangible a fashion, what is the motivational force that impelled her to move? Perhaps we will find an answer in yet another voice.

* * *

In Macalpine we cited the phenomenon of transference regression, induced by the frame, and in Khan the role of transference–countertransference reverberations in the nonverbal sphere of the analytic dialogue. In the writing of McDougall, however, both aspects of regression are met within the sphere of the early body self, which signifies both desymbolizing as well as potentially creative aspects.

In "The Psychosoma and the Psychoanalytic Process", McDougall (1974) alerts us to a state of profound impasse of meaning making in the symbolic chain, mirroring some of the earliest traumatic moments in infancy, where deprivations are shunted aside onto the sphere of the soma. In such a regressive state, the patient experiences a fall-back to traumatic preverbal moments of life, where symbolic connections never developed, leaving a frozen constellation of the body-ego. Such constellations, when reached in moments of regression, signify not simply defences or a retreat to absolute dependency, but the inherent capacity for symbolic functioning and the creative. In the evolving transference, these constellations manifest themselves as pockets of concreteness, of "operational thinking" or *pensée opératoire*, preventing the emergence of imagination and fantasy.

In *A Plea for a Measure of Abnormality*, McDougall (1980) widens the horizon, suggesting that the "barren calculus of the soma" can also be the path towards the "magic" of infancy; that addictive voraciousness implies a thrust towards creativity, and that it can involve an affective explosion as the patient, facing a terrifying void, seeks to achieve control over herself or over the object through surrender or provocation.

The apparently *regressive body-ego* offers the analyst a Janus-faced challenge, for it contains the signals of concreteness as well as the potential for creative imagination. Through the language of the body soma, the analyst not only hears the quest for provisions, evoked by a state of absolute dependency, but is also confronted by a dual task, to receive the patient in the depth of her being, as well as to attain a broadened perspective on her actuality. This stance of interpenetration is stressed by Grunes (1984). For the Kleinians, this process is one of simultaneous alternations of introjective-projective identifications. For us, it marks the emergence of a process of *Progressive Symbolization*.

In this path to finding an internal tie to the other, the patient may pass from confusion, to renewed concreteness of the body soma, and then to a flight towards an imaginary paradise. This idea was captured in Laplanche's (1997) notion of the search for the enigmatic other. We believe that this is one of the earliest and most pervasive cravings, which may well have a role in moving the patient towards the lost or even never found symbolic good object. As we shall see in the clinical material to follow, feeling stuck in a concretized body self can be resolved through religious yearning. Such a turn of events can be a source of spiralling alteration. In Suzanne Langer's (1942) words: "Nature speaks to us, first of all, through our senses; the form and qualities we distinguish, remember, imagine, or recognize are symbols of entities which exceed or outlived our own internal experience" (p. 93).

McDougall's notion of the creative aspect of the regressive experience inspires a third clinical proposition, namely, that in a state of desymbolization, the patient can find a source of repair through the evocation of belief (Bion) or the enigmatic other (Laplanche).

* * *

Our three voices are clearly rooted in very different theoretical perspectives, although they all adhere to the classical analytic frame. Their patients reflect distinctly different forms of psychopathology, yet each offers a window into what appears to be an induction of regression, or in our language, desymbolization. Furthermore, they all acknowledge a process in which such experiences can reverberate within the analytic relationship.

Now comes our perhaps audacious proposal: each type of regression can be found in the treatment process. Moreover, each can be discerned within a specimen of an analysis, within a phase of that specimen, and during successive sessions of that phase. These assumptions lead us to our empirical study, and hopefully will further our understanding of the process of working through.

The gradient of the downward slope—empirically defined

Time is an organizer of psychoanalytic change. The induction of regression, referred to by Macalpine, evolves over months or even years. The regression in Khan's example took place two years into the three year analysis. In our specimen, the subtle incremental shifts leading to a frank *regression* occurred over about three weeks of analysis during the predominately symbolized phase. Now we will put to the test the proposition that inherent in the process of associating, remembering, being listened to, and telling dreams, mental forces are set in motion that lead to a desymbolizing mode, involving the as-yet-unformulated aspects of one's inner life.

Two sets of observations confirm this proposition. The first comes from the analyst's clinical scans. For sessions 232, 238, and 243, the *criterion* sessions for this phase, the analyst felt the patient was quite engaged in her analytic work. Yet the A and Z ratings of the consultants suggested that there was a steady decline in these sessions towards non-integration.[i] Equally conclusive are the findings concerning changes in the referential process, derived from the transcripts of the entire session. Referential activity declined steadily from session to session as Ms Y's spoken language became less affectively evocative, more global, and less reflective—in our language, the depletion of referential activity is a signifier of desymbolization (see Postscript).[ii] The induction of a downward gradient was affirmed. A process of transference regression appeared to be in play.

One of the important corollaries inherent in the notion of transference regression during a *working phase* is that with the decline of the symbolizing function, there apparently arises concurrently an increase in *anti-symbolic* processes, creating the subjective experience of paradox and with it, concreteness and desymbolization. We set out on a voyage of discovering these anti-symbolic forces, for we had no ready-made empirically-based dimensions to guide us.

Taking recourse to the available database, generated by the analysis of the referential process language variables, we conducted a computer search. The aim was to discover the dimensions within a given hour that might reveal a shift in certain mental functions, concurrent with a decline in the referential process (the symbolizing function). We arrived at such a finding, which brought to the fore a process that made sense both empirically and theoretically. The variable in question was *somatosensory thought*, that is, the language of the body ego.

Somatosensory, as it is referred to in the scoring category of the Referential Process, has its clinical and historical origin in the term, "organ speech". The phenomenon of organ speech has a long history in the chronicles of psychoanalytic ideas. It is one of the core components of anxiety neurosis (Freud, 1895). There we find numerous clinical descriptions: "bodily functions as primitive forms of thought"; "utterances anticipating regression"; "concrete and magical forms of thought", and "using the body as an alien presence". When organ speech is embedded in an associative context, the ego can either reflect, or becomes overwhelmed by the impingement of the body ego. When the body experience is disconnected, even dissociated from the symbolizing context, this becomes a signifier of the depth of regression.

Here are the highlights of our findings, and out of necessity we need to be somewhat technical in our report. Somatosensory speech was prominent throughout the symbolizing phase, but from session to session its association with both affect and reflectivity varied.[iii] In session 232, the hour with one of the highest levels of referential (symbolizing) activity, somatosensory experience appeared to be integrated with the capacity to reflect upon it.[iv] Indeed, it seemed that Ms Y was able to coordinate experiences of her body self with emotions felt towards objects. By session 243, a much reduced A session, somatosensory language remained prominent, though linked to negative affect and disconnected from reflectivity. At this point in the downward slope, the language of the body ego had become a dominant yet alien presence, probably throttling reflectivity. A spiralling process seems to have been set in motion, but in a downward direction.

These findings support one of our hypotheses of transference regression: during analytic work, there is a decline in the symbolizing process and a concurrent increase in the confrontation with paradoxical experiences. This is consistent with the induction hypothesis and would invite agreement from our three analytic authors. It particularly lends support to McDougall's vision that transference regression implies the loud participation of the language of the body self. However, it is not clear whether we are only dealing with an intensification of regression, as well as a move towards increased dissociation, or alternatively whether each criterion session signifies a particular type of induced regression articulated by our three authors. At this juncture we have reached the limits of quantitative empirically-based inquiry and need next to turn to the more nuanced details of clinical observations. We shall start with the beginning of the symbolizing phase, session 232.

The gradient of transference regression clinically defined

Session 232

Ms Y begins the session with a vivid and conflict laden episode about preparing a meal with mother during her parents' recent visit. Although a power struggle brewed between them, evoking memories of a similar experience with grandmother, she gave mother "a lot of credit for avoiding the conflict", experiencing her as "really trying to help". Father, too, was felt as "really being there" for her, his efforts to help "really sweet", efforts that triggered memories of his help with her first child. Ms Y speaks of experiencing the analysis as a "strong hold" during the visit, a place where she had gained insight rather than feeling "swept away" by her relationships with her parents. After a 14 second silence, Ms Y alludes to thoughts about her analyst, but then spends another 15 minutes obsessing about a house for sale before returning to the "emotional subject", her upset about their relationship. She then thinks of a frightening dream remembered while driving to her session. In the dream, she was being mugged in a parking garage by a Mafia type and she was yelling, "Help me!" She associates to a child's toy noticed in the analyst's garage after the previous session, but how feelings of being shut out by the analyst had left her feeling "unemotional", fearful of depending, and unsure if the analyst were "really there".

* * *

Listeners' Observations: Though this session begins with ingredients of a *symbolized session*, the atmosphere becomes noticeably conflicted. Idealizing allusions become intertwined with persecutory images of seeking help and being shut out by the analyst.

* * *

Then a series of prolonged silences ensue, the last stretching over 54 seconds: "My mind is kind of blank" [30 second silence]. Following the analyst's interpretation about how the patient was feeling understandably protective and unsafe, the patient states: "You know, you're still you and I still love your voice and I still am attracted to you in that we have a rapport, but I feel like I've been had in a way [10 second silence] because I was told it would be okay and it wasn't" [12 second silence]. Then taking recourse to metaphoric language: "You know, I'm feeling very tender right now and I just got this mental image of myself sticking my big toe in the water." The analyst acknowledges Ms Y's bravery and after more than three minutes of silence, the patient states: "I'm angry at you [25 second silence], I'm angry because I'm hurt [31 second silence], and I'm a little confused, [1 minute silence] and I don't want to torture you, but on the other hand, I think I don't want to let you off the hook too easy either until I understand."

* * *

Listeners' Observations: The blankness, a temporary paralysis of overwhelming aggressivity, is contained through a process of metaphor, followed by registration and repudiation ("I don't want to torture you"), leading to a moment of reflectivity. Ms Y's state of being "kind of blank" can be seen as a prelude to a more profound state of psychic blankness (seen in session 257), but here she is able to apprehend the dimensions of her own destructiveness and interpret this for herself.

Commentary on session 232

This session has many of the qualities of Kris's "good hour" (1956). First, there is a chain of associations, memories, and a dream leading to an impasse, followed by the explicit transference. It has the shape of a symbolizing, working session. This quality of mind dominates the hour, although there are also signals of impending regression.

The potential for the downward pull suggests itself by the impasse with the long silences, the search for words, leading to the utterance, "My mind is kind of blank." This experience of "blankness of mind" calls for interpretation. There seems to have occurred a blocking of thought, an inhibition of the functions of representation, a state where good and bad objects could not be combined. The patient resorts momentarily to a "homogenization" of inner experiences, a compromise in which all parts are equivalent, and none can be chosen (e.g., Green, 1975). Here we find paralysis born of paradox, a move towards psychic equivalence. This is the nucleus of *Desymbolization*, a process which will become more pronounced in subsequent hours (see Postscript: *On Desymbolization*).

There also emerged the bursting forth of a persecutory idea aimed at the analyst: "I feel I've been had," leading to a surging desire for revenge in the form of a negated wish to torture the analyst. As we have stated, variants of this torture theme will appear in succeeding sessions. Now, however, haltingly to be sure, the hovering conflict is resolved through the final compromise formation.

The use of a somatosensory image in arriving at this compromise highlights that this is an integrative hour. The phrase, "sticking my big toe in the water", suggests the use of the body ego, deployed in metaphoric form, as a vehicle for reconciling conflictual longings. This illustrates the empirical findings in this predominantly

A session: the negative covariation of "body language" with reflectivity. It highlights a process of the recovery of the symbolizing function.

Now Ms Y was able to give voice to a complex thought not previously spoken: "I don't want to torture you, but on the other hand, I think I don't want to let you off the hook too easy either until I understand." The word "understand" deserves emphasis, for it expresses a wish to preserve the object tie in the face of the love and hatred felt towards the analyst. In her clinical scan, the analyst appreciates and acknowledges this resolution. Here, Ms Y was not as yet in a regressed state of dependency, demanding to be heard, though she will be a few sessions later.

In sum, this stepwise progression suggests a move, a minimal one to be sure, towards a transference regression. The frame, the associative process, the ongoing presence of the analyst may well have initiated this downward slope, thus supporting Macalpine's induction hypothesis. This was a controlled regression, pointing to the resiliency of Ms Y's ego. Through silence she gathered strength to formulate her wish for revenge, an explicit expression of desire within a moment of safety. Contained was the full blast of the torture fantasy, which will be elaborated later within the intersubjectivity of the analytic dialogue.

Session 238

This session opens with a dream in which Ms Y is driving a car and being blocked by a crossing guard, who is protecting a group of elderly pedestrians. She associates to her "ferocious protectiveness" towards her young children, her critical thoughts regarding how her sister-in-law had recently "cared" for her infant daughter when babysitting and the uneasiness she feels about her anger at her. Associations move next to the analyst and the conflictual feelings she has about the anger expressed towards her in a previous session. Pauses and sighs begin to punctuate the narrative as Ms Y approaches the following thoughts:

> But I was thinking how [8 second silence] you know y … you made a comment about how I had these thoughts that just intrude and they, they, this was I think the last session and it

just happened again. Because when I said the word "thinking" it, the, the, the ... ing or something got caught in my throat and it sounded, to me like it was a very, um, it sounded like a Jewish inflection the way that I said "thinking" and then I was, thinking about asking about [laughs] then I was thinking about, a, a, a Jewish accent and what if you had a, a thick Jewish accent and how would I react and I just, I got all off on this—it would be, it would be—you know, I, I love— [sighs] the way you speak it would be a very different [laughs] experience I'm thinking like a very thick, not Brooklyn but you know very, it, it wouldn't be as pleasant to listen to, I don't find it as melodious, and now I'm, concerned because I feel like I'm treading on thin ice because, I feel like my comments are starting to sound prejudicial or, or, um ... judgmental.

Ms Y then begins to feel off track and articulates the inner regressive pull she is experiencing:

The thing that keeps getting in my way is feeling pulled to you and [sighs, 27 second silence] which I know is part of my problem but it's sort of as if your presence keeps, well what I'm doing with your presence keeps, it feels like it's hindering my progress [15 second silence]. As if I was trying to tell myself "keep, keep separate, keep" almost like "keep my emotions for you out of this" and then I'll be able to focus on me and my problems and, and, uh and learning about myself.

* * *

Listeners' Observations: While the hour opens with a measure of symbolizing work, organ speech becomes linked to persecutory ideas in the transference, leading to confusion and diffusion of identity. Here we find the genesis of a deepening thrust towards desymbolization.

* * *

Ms Y returns to the idea of sounding prejudicial, which evokes a deeply troubling thought. Does "prejudicial" refer to her adopted baby daughter, who has dark skin? Ms Y is suddenly overcome by a scary conflict of equivalence: is she prejudiced not just towards the analyst but also towards her little baby daughter? Does this anticipated "distance" repeat that felt towards her mother? This startling experience of equivalence ushers in an altered state of consciousness.

A string of self-accusatory thoughts burst forth about her overeating, her unhappiness with how she looks, and how sick she is of repeating her destructive behaviour "over and over and over and over". Ms Y is confused about her feelings for her daughter, her analyst, and herself. Now, the dread that all is equivalent has invaded her sense of identity, has created confusion in her thinking, and has brought forth helpless rage directed at herself: "I'm so off track in a way I—can hardly see my way clear to getting back on track and I don't know what has thrown me so. And I don't even know if I'm going through a storm."

* * *

Listeners' Observations: The terrifying thought of being prejudiced against, even perhaps hating her baby daughter, evokes a feeling of confusion, a sense that everything is equivalent. Ms Y feels overwhelmed, unable to think, to choose, and impelled to go on and on and on. The pain and shame left her unable to sort out her thoughts.

Commentary on session 238

This criterion session, six sessions after session 232, carries the earmark of a more profound transference regression. The underlying dynamic force remains the desire to torture, carried out now through the vehicle of somatosensory experience. First, bodily experiences are played out as *a thing apart*, not integrated with reflectivity. For example, the phrase, "Something got caught in my throat," passed through successive states: it was initially a concretely felt physical discomfort (caught in the throat); then the physical experience became conflated with a negative self-image (a stereotyped Jewish accent); which was projected onto the analyst ("What if you had a Jewish accent?"), and finally it became explicit as a frightening idea of being prejudiced against her own baby daughter. This sequence sheds light on our empirical findings. It illustrates just how the *organ speech* became linked to negative affect, forming an alien desymbolized presence. But in the unfolding transference, as this unbearable thought suddenly reached consciousness, the sequence peaked with a self-state of confusion and despair.

With this sequence we can offer an interpretive account of Progressive Desymbolization. Initially, there is a dissociation of aggressive desire, registered in the body self; the alien presence is introjected, then projected onto the hated analyst, leading to a sense of loss of identity; and finally, there is an introjective identification, where Ms Y becomes conscious of the horror of her prejudice against her daughter. This sequence leaves her in a state of helpless, repetitive, desymbolized confusion.

Surely this is an account of induced regression, but the question arises: how do these events reverberate in the analyst's consciousness? To obtain a glimpse of this dimension, we now turned to the analyst's scan.

In the scan, the analyst failed to register the anxiety-provoking episode concerning the Jewish accent, as well as how much difficulty the patient was having in keeping herself "separate" from her. Consequently, the analyst joined the patient in a disavowal of the "storm", when she comments, "She is not in a storm as she describes it now," though she did take in that "There's something really off about her and this causes general discomfort." The analyst did empathically receive the patient's struggle with her aggression towards her baby daughter, and indeed captured her horror at having hatred in relation to the darkness of her skin. Thus, in spite of the patient's implicit attack upon her, the analyst was able to receive the patient and the essence of her paradoxical feelings. Reflecting upon the session, the analyst wondered just how very guilty the patient must feel. In this scan, there is evidence that reflective symbolization, not available to the patient, was carried forth by the analyst. We have termed this elsewhere, the symbolizing countertransference. This is a countertransference in that it counters the patient's transference, but it is also a symbolizing act, in that essential connections are made by the analyst at the very moment the symbolizing function is paralyzed within the patient (Freedman, 1997).

We end our reflections on session 238 with a clinical proposition: within the frame of the downward slope, when the patient is faced with Progressive Desymbolization, it is the analyst's symbolizing countertransference which offers a path towards the deepening of the analysis, a path towards working through. The language of the body self, initially appearing as an alien presence in the transference, can elicit the raw material of traumatic early origins, creates a "measure of abnormality"—to use McDougall's language—yet when such a moment can be contained within a symbolizing countertransference, the patient is helped to tolerate a paradox that may eventually become integrated.

In sum, while it may be in question whether or not Ms Y was in a state of absolute dependency during this session, surely she was in a state of absolute despair. Further, while it may be in question whether or not the analyst was able to absorb the despair on a somatosensory level, as did Khan with his patient, surely she was able to metabolize Ms Y's profound guilt over her prejudice, and in that sense, the analysis was carried forward.

Session 243

Ms Y opens with thoughts about how focused she is lately on her relationship with the analyst and the "reverberation" between them. Clearing her throat, she wonders if this in part is still about her anger at her from several weeks ago and the fact that it is so sustained. She associates to "contortions" she has been going through for a couple of days involving a phone message she left for a female friend. After several minutes of obsessing and "not knowing", she is ultimately able to articulate her worries that her aggression had come through. She feels that "spiked roadblocks" get in the way when she tries to get close to others and tries to connect within herself. Having stated this, she wishes the analyst would give her some confirmation that she had just said something insightful, and this reminds her of the previous session in which she wanted to hear more from the analyst but experienced her as not there.

* * *

Listeners' Observations: The patient opens with *reverberations* of sustained anger, isolation, neediness, and experiencing the analyst as absent.

* * *

Next, a series of confused and concretized exchanges occur between Ms Y and her analyst, where the patient alludes to worries that the analyst is "pissed" at her, though the analyst does not directly address this. Then Ms Y reaches for another vehicle of the body self: the word "heart". This word is at first used in a repetitive and concretized fashion: "I'm afraid you'll give me what I'm asking for and open up to me, which in my heart I know is not the best thing for me, because it's not you, it's me." Regarding her spirituality, Ms Y states: "I have a slight sense of being comfortable enough sharing with you things like that, mainly because of [clears throat] clues that I have from all that I am privy to. One is just where you live. A part of my heart is here. I really love where you live." But the idealization breaks down: "When I meet with that silence from you, it feels more uncomfortable than ever, because it chips away at the belief in what I said to the point that I begin to doubt what I said. It unnerves me a little bit." A few minutes later, the heart image appears again in relation to her troubling feelings towards her daughter: "And I was so upset about feeling so completely un-bonded with my daughter and feeling so hardened somehow. Like my heart was hardened in a way, I just didn't want to give."

* * *

Listeners' Observations: Up to this point, the heart image is used as a concretized expression of despair.

* * *

From a sense of being "hardened", "pissed off", and at a point of complete "distraughtness" over her relationship with her daughter, Ms Y employs again the heart image, this time within the context of hope. She speaks of turning to God in prayer: "I just prayed that God would come into my heart and open up my heart toward her." She describes attending church and receiving communion while holding in her arms her baby daughter, dressed in a beautiful yellow sweater, a "sweater of faith", which evoked feelings towards her of being "special" and "a gift". "I felt so moved, because I could feel my heart opening up to her. ... God was answering my prayer." She temporarily felt united with God, with herself and with her little daughter.

* * *

Listeners' Observations: Despite the despair, there is a temporary respite of hope.

* * *

The session concludes with Ms Y returning to anger and disappointment about not feeling responded to, this time in relation to two close female friends. She remembers a sign on another church and she paraphrases it: "Sometimes God will not help unless you pray." (We might say that she will be healed by God but not by the analyst.) She ends in a state of confusion, wishing she were more reflective, more able to reach out to others for help, and less action oriented.

Commentary on session 243

This session reveals a further intensification of the transference regression, spearheaded by the increase in negative affect and somatosensory communication. Through the dual use of the word *heart*, first deployed in concrete fashion, then used metaphorically as an expression of care, even salvation, a three pronged significance can be gleaned. For embedded in these utterances is not only the incremental deepening of transference regression, but also an increased pull on the countertransference, as well as a striking turn towards symbolized thought in the form of a *nodal moment*.

First, the *heart* image conveys paradoxical aspects of Ms Y's position towards herself and towards her analyst. *Heart* was fashioned in the form of a "Klang association", as Ms Y worked herself more and more into self-denunciation and despair, reaching a peak when describing her heart as hardened. She felt unloving and unlovable. Then there occurred a momentary reversal, where *heart* became linked to an idealized image of love from God. Her self-representation became transformed into that of a loving mother. Out of the disdain for her analyst, a new imaginary *good object* was found. If the analyst was unable to heal her, then God could. Here we are reminded of McDougall, who notes that in the very confrontation with feelings of profound disconnection, there may arise promptings towards integration, creativity, and alterity.

This paradoxical attitude found its mirror in the countertransference, suggested by the clinical scan. On the one hand, it was a symbolizing countertransference, similar to that of session 238. The analyst took in the patient's awareness of the reverberations of anger in their relationship, as well as the tremendous relief she felt when connecting to her baby in church. Nonetheless, there is evidence of a desymbolizing countertransference, as the analyst failed to register the heart image in general, and particularly the horror of the "hardened" heart and the self-destructive aspects related to it. Additionally, the analyst felt compelled to tilt the session material in the direction of the positive, noting: "She didn't seem particularly anxious in today's session. I think she's working her way out of the agony that she's been going through since the baby has arrived." She also seemed to disavow her countertransference by stating: "It felt to me like my countertransference was under control today." But was it? We know that the patient will be in a frank regression only two sessions later. Despite the transference regression and the disavowal in the countertransference, there was also a striking, brief move by the patient towards finding the symbolic. This remains a challenging phenomenon to be explored.

On transference regression

The phenomenon of transference regression, Progressive Desymbolization has been confirmed. In the course of analytic work, while the patient was heard and received, an alteration in mental functioning in the direction of desymbolization was noted, both quantitatively (through empirical observations) and qualitatively (through an interpretive reading of the text). A corollary notion, that simultaneously an anti-symbolic process manifests in the experience of the body ego, was also substantiated. These propositions, rooted in highlights from the analytic literature (Macalpine, Winnicott, Khan and McDougall), found resonance in the clinical material. As aspects of regression became more pronounced, as somatosensory experiences became more disconnected, so did the patient's demands on the countertransference. Therein lies an affirmation both of the induction and the reverberation hypotheses.

A crucial moment of reversal

In spite of the regressive trend, and perhaps activated by countertransference, there arose towards the end of session 243 a moment of reversal. It was a change of state, finding expression in the dual manner in which the word *heart* was used.

Let us briefly revisit this phenomenon, for it illustrates in the structure of spoken language the transformation of which we speak. In one mode, *heart* was used as index, that is, repetitively, mechanically as it were, suggesting concreteness; a single sound quality pointing to a motivational state of profound disconnectedness and psychic equivalence. The recurrent, repetitive use of the thinking apparatus, body as implacable computer, seems to reflect an underlying state of psychic deadness. Yet, in a subsequent mode, *heart* was also deployed as a private symbol of multiple signifiers, that is, *heart* expressing shame, disappointment, coldness, and ultimately representing a path towards hope and even religious redemption. This is a voyage of reparation, in which the dread of objectlessness is moved through magic and belief towards refinding the inner object.

This moment of reversal, the church scene, is a moment that highlights the nonlinear nature of clinical change. It is what we will call a *nodal moment*, a signal of the upward slope, and it is a remarkable phenomenon that will hold centre stage in the sessions to come.

Endnotes

i. This decline is expressed in the measure of A (integration) minus Z (non-integration) difference scores: for session 232, the A-Z difference is 8; for 238, the A-Z difference is 7, and for 243, the A-Z difference is 6. This gradient suggests that the integrative functions still remain dominant, yet it also points to a successive decline.

ii. The mean referential activity (WRAD) scores for sessions 232, 238, and 243 are 0.48, 0.47, and 0.44 respectively. In spite of the apparently small changes, these shifts can be considered to be substantial.

iii. The covariation between somatosensory experience and reflectivity shifted from session 232 (−0.23) to 243 (−0.06) suggesting an alteration in the direction of lesser integration; somatosensory experiences with affect (notably negative affect) revealed a covariation from 0.08 (session 232) to 0.23 (session 243), also suggesting that the difficulty in integrating somatosensory experiences are accompanied by negative affect.

iv. The reader is reminded (Chapter Thirteen) that a negative covariation implies an integration between aspects of the referential process, signifying that two functions do not co-occur. Thus, when in session 232 there is a negative covariation of −0.23 between reflectivity and somatosensory experience, the former appears to be integrated with the latter function. This seems to be diminished in session 243.

CHAPTER FIFTEEN

The emergence of *nodal moments* during the desymbolizing phase: sessions 245 to 249

Norbert Freedman and Rhonda Ward

While in church after communion, connecting within her heart to God, holding her baby on her lap and feeling love for her, Ms Y encountered a moment of a coming together of meaning, of uniting disparate parts within herself, be they a linking of hallucinatory wishes to reality, subjective self-awareness with objective self-awareness, or the splits arising from triangular conflict. This scene from the end of session 243 (Chapter Fourteen) was a *nodal moment* preceded by a transference regression. It was a moment of unification, marked by a surge of libido, a crucial ingredient of ego synthesis. When such a *nodal moment* occurs during a regression, it is a first step in the direction of the upward slope and of *Progressive Symbolization*.

Nodal moments highlight paradoxical transformations at work. These crucial events are preceded by episodes of desymbolization, where the underlying meaning is implicit and unformulated. But when the *nodal moment* appears, meaning becomes explicit, formulated, symbolized. It is in the transformation from the unformulated to the formulated that the paradox can be discovered, processed, and confronted.

Nodal moments have the contour of a triangular challenge. During regression, with the morass of equivalence, concreteness, and sameness, triangulation looms as a vitalizing alternative. Whether it is the choice between the included or excluded *other*, the revival of Oedipal fantasies evoking the desired, hated, or feared inner object, or the confrontation with contradictory states of consciousness, from objective to subjective self-awareness, the witness looking in from without or the participant immersed from within, each is a condition of choice likely to create triangular space, and is the subtext for the emergence of the *nodal moment*. Each is the context for evolving symbolization and reflective functioning and is what we observed in the desymbolizing phase, leading to the upward slope of this transformation cycle.

What are the mental processes in the course of an analytic hour that might impel a patient to embrace a new mode of thought in the direction of symbolization? This question was raised and answered in a thoughtful paper by Friedman (2003), where he suggests that symbolization arises during analysis specifically in those moments when the patient feels compelled to enter a new and unexpected object relationship. The patient is confronted by an altered transference position, a new abstraction is created, and a new mode of symbolizing thought can be formulated. Stated more generally, symbolization appears to be heralded by a shift in transference expectancies.

Friedman's view has many forerunners in the history of psychoanalysis. The most evident is that concerning the classical Oedipal triangle, in which the patient feels confronted with the choice between the desired and the hated other and impelled to resolve the conflict through symbolization. More cogent is Klein's assertion that symbolization arises specifically with the onset of the depressive position. A symbolizing mode of thought becomes the defining event at this juncture, marking a new stance towards the Oedipal object. (Klein considered this one of her most lasting contributions (Steiner, 2007)).

The foregoing line of thought guides a general clinical proposition to be examined in the course of this chapter: when during an analytic hour marked by desymbolization, the patient experiences a shift in transference position, a *nodal moment* emerges and with it, a reversal pointing towards new, more integrated, symbolic forms.

THE EMERGENCE OF *NODAL MOMENTS* 247

This vision of unification asserts that a triangular object relationship can impact an evolving symbolizing process. But triangulation takes inevitable and distinctly different forms, and these can have identifiable reverberations in the ensuing treatment process. We are less interested here in articulating different triangulation paradigms per se, or in affirming one view over another, but rather, in discovering how a particular triangulation form may be revealed in a given *nodal moment*. Triangulation is essential, for as we shall see, it allows for increased differentiation, first within the subject, then within the dyad, and finally within the shared consciousness of both.

Perspectives on triangulation: Kernberg, Britton, and Steingart

Abelin (1975) notes that triangulation entails the awareness and organization of mutually opposing forces inherent in the Oedipal triangle, and has as its consequence the enhanced integration of cognitive and affective experiences. This paradigm is also implicit in Kernberg's (2001) vision of the analytic situation, notably in his affect theory, where he views the Oedipal situation as one of the basic structures of human experience.

This view of triangulation stresses the stark choices of living: to love and feel included or to hate and feel excluded. Such choices inherent in triangulation can evoke overwhelming fears, castration and annihilation anxieties, or conversely, wishes for libidinal satisfaction. The manner in which these affects are resolved differs in clinical groups, for triangulation can result in a splitting process in borderline patients or can become a pathway to integration in the narcissistic disorders.

Kernberg's (2001) view of triangulation as a process that invites strong affective valences, also embraces an interpretive frame. For him, interpretation is the mutative factor, with the analyst as organizer of the patient's mental life and the vehicle for the resolution of the triangular conflict. We see aspects of this triangulation model in the clinical material from sessions 243 and 245.

* * *

Triangulation also entails the creation of an inner mental space and with it the emergence of thirdness in analytic work. While Britton, in his writings, also recognizes fundamentally conflicting psychic forces, he views them more as a clash between that which is felt to be subjective—the participant moored to the inner world, and that which is felt to be objective—the participant as witness. Significantly, Britton (1989) does not use the term "triangulation", but speaks of "triangular space" (p. 86). He notes, "[This space] includes, therefore, the possibility of being a participant in a relationship and observed by a third person as well as being an observer of a relationship between two people" (ibid., p. 86). This is a potential space born of early Oedipal struggles, and in it we find the linking functions of the early caring maternal object. In analysis, it is facilitated by the containing functions of the analyst. A third force is created, heralding the attainment of a "new" object relationship.

The closing of the gap within triangular space is both a promissory note and an arduous task. Britton (1998) illustrates this challenge in his discussion of Rosenfeld's thin-skinned and thick-skinned narcissists, the former moored to subjectivity, the latter to objectivity. Neither can tolerate the third area, and when faced with the opposite, are overcome with chaos, emptiness, helplessness, and fragmentation, or in our language, desymbolization. In the face of nameless dread (Bion, 1962), symbolization becomes impossible. Although these are extreme types, they describe alternating positions, oscillating states of consciousness found in all analyses.

Britton speculates that inherent in these extreme types, there exists a profound antipathy, a kind of atopia, preventing the coming together of two minds. He gets closer to reconciling this puzzle, however, in his essay, "Before and After the Depressive Position" (1989), where he suggests that moments of containment can create reversals in analytic space. Britton notes that a sequence may start with an organized regression, offering the opportunity for the unfreezing of a frozen situation. He describes a sequence taking only one week of analysis. The patient moved from "fragmentation and confusion in the pre-depressive paranoid-schizoid position" to an "arrival" in reflectivity and moral responsibility, the "depressive position", and finally to a post-depressive position including uncertainty but also hope. All were movements taking place in a developmental progression, but rather interestingly, each sequence included a return to another state of chaos and despair, a movement consistent with our observations below. For a brief moment, Britton's patient was able to create triangular space in the direction of the upward slope, only to collapse once more.

By substituting the term *nodal moment* for depressive position in this example, we might say that in just one week of treatment, the latent agony could be briefly formulated. Following Britton's line of thought, a *nodal moment* arising in intersubjective space signifies a readiness in the patient to experience being both observer and being observed. This is a unifying experience, a third area, integrating the tension between subjective and objective self-awareness. During an episode of desymbolization, the patient clings to objectivity, two minds disconnected from one another; or alternatively, clings to subjectivity, only one mind in a state of merger. The *nodal moment* becomes a release from emptiness. Only in the play of triangular space can these polarities be reconciled.

This triangulation model adds a new dimension to the understanding of symbolizing space. The reconciliation of the subjective and the objective is unthinkable without the invocation of the imaginary. Here, conflict is not denied, but appears in a new form giving access to new versions of mental functioning, that is, the evocation of recent memories, memories of early vintage, and the implications of these memories within the transference. This process is illustrated in session 247 below.

* * *

As triangulation arises in intersubjective space, the symbolic itself can become the source of mental transformation. In Steingart's concept, the "enacted symbol" (1995), we find a vehicle for a further step in *Progressive Symbolization*. The enacted symbol is not an enactment per se, not necessarily motorically manifest, but a preconceptual, concretistic, symbolic organization, a form of *pathological play* driven by action, imposing counter-action on the other. Whether appearing in motoric form or in spoken language, the enacted symbol has one abiding function and force: it signifies an urge to create an alteration in the subjectivity of the other, thus forcing a shift in the analytic relationship. The enacted symbol clearly affects a change in the symbolizing space and with it the transference–countertransference dialogue.

A similar line of thought has been described by Rose, showing how the symbolic, first in a primitive mode, becomes the source of, even the impetus for, new symbols. He terms this process "progressive triangulation", akin to our notion of *Progressive Symbolization*. In his essay entitled, "Symbols and their Function in Managing the Anxiety of Change: an Intersubjective Approach" (2000), Rose seeks to bridge the impasse created by the exclusion of the subjective and/or the disavowal of the objective. In this sense, Rose's work marks an extension of the line of thought spearheaded by Britton. Yet he goes further. For to him (as well as with Steingart), the symbolic does not reside only within the subjectivity of the patient, but is further borne in the interaction between two minds. New subjectivity is created out of intersubjectivity. The symbolic, when created, changes the state of consciousness of the analytic couple. The symbolic may be born of the conflicts of early origins, as implied in the writings of Kernberg, and comes to life in triangular space, as spelled out by Britton, but as Rose notes, in the emerging analytic frame, new unifying symbols are created, having a generative impact on subsequent thought.

The mode of representation in this kind of transition is of great consequence. Langer (1942) introduces the notion of a presentational mode of thought, a form of emotional communication relying on iconic and imagistic forms, suggesting thoughts that we know before we are sure we know them. Through a process of symbolized experiences, momentarily translated into an enactive mode, a specific impact is experienced in the transference and countertransference. Thoughts and affects are communicated in a forceful, evocative manner, altering the direction of analytic communication and marking the staging scene for a phase of reintegration.

In sum, this third triangulation model also signals a progression of previously unformulated thought. It is a model that is explicitly linked to the transference and relies upon the play of memories and fantasies. Added is the measure of enactment in presentational mode, directed towards the analyst. As a result, it is a triangulation model that is the most relational expression of inner conflict, and functions to alter the transference–countertransference dialogue. This is exemplified below in the material from session 249.

* * *

Now we have described three visions of the triangulation process by recent psychoanalytic thinkers. These three theories reflect three qualities of mind that can be noted during *nodal moments* within a single specimen. Three clinical propositions suggest themselves:

with Kernberg, we assume that triangulation signals a formulation of previously split-off affectively charged desires, revealed in the transference. With Britton, we expect that triangular space, an intersubjective dialogue in the transference, will be marked by a greater tolerance for the inevitable conflict between objective and subjective self-awareness. In this intersubjective dialogue, a third integrative force can be created, protecting the patient against regressive disorganization. With Steingart, we hold that an enacted symbol will shape a new kind of intersubjectivity, allowing the patient to progressively formulate an inner experience previously unformulated, and altering the state of the transference.

Nodal moments *empirically defined*

The transformations we will be describing arose during a phase of quite profound regression—a phase affirmed through the evaluation of the clinical scans. For the three criterion sessions (245, 247, and 249), the *A* minus *Z* scores pointed in a negative direction, affirming that a predominance of non-integrative themes was heard by the clinical investigators (Chapter Thirteen), although the level of regression seemed to remit somewhat during session 249.[i] When the level of referential activity (WRAD) was considered, the picture was similar, although with one notable exception: WRAD was depleted for sessions 245 and 247, but not so for session 249, at variance with the clinical ratings suggesting that Ms Y appeared to be emerging from the more regressive episode.[ii] Furthermore, as detailed below, we took recourse to a more sensitive measure, which pointed to a process of non-integration towards re-integration— the very phenomenon we wish to describe. This measure consisted of the covariation between the referential process and other components of the referential profile described earlier (Chapter Thirteen).

In general, a negative covariation points towards integration, whereas a positive covariation suggests a process of non-integration. When the patient reflects, plans, and then offers a narrative, thoughts are coordinated and arise in sequence, yielding a negative covariation. When, however, these same functions occur simultaneously, an impasse, a *traffic jam*, may ensue and a positive covariation results.

Such sequences distinguish different parts of an analytic hour and mark the distinction that highlights the *nodal moments*.

Nodal moments: *segmentation analysis*

We set ourselves the task of identifying *nodal moments* in our three criterion sessions, manifest in discrete moments within the text and standing out from the surrounding field. Two investigators (NF and JW) began with a clinical reading of the sessions. With even a cursory glance, we were able to set off such moments by drawing a line marking the onset and a second at the apparent end. The investigators were able to arrive at consensual agreement. We then marked off material preceding the *nodal moment* (identical in word count to the *nodal moment*), the *nodal moment* proper, and its sequella. Each presumed *nodal moment* was brief, appearing towards the end of the session. With these demarcations, we were in a position to move towards a more empirically-based definition of *nodal moments* and the processes playing a role in mental transformation.

In our next step, we sought to confirm the *nodal moments* objectively, asking whether they were differentiated in structure from the preceding material, as defined by the components of the *referential process*. These empirical observations were made possible through the use of a feature of the DAAP. This enabled us to obtain separate profiles of the referential process for the session in its entirety, the *nodal moment* proper, and its sequella. The focus of analysis was on the covariations of the referential process with the other language functions such as affect verbalized and disfluency of speech, as well as somatosensory functions (organ speech). We were guided by the general hypothesis (Bucci & Maskit, 2007) that a negative covariation between Referential Activity (RA) and the other language functions suggests an increased integration in the flow of communicated thought. The more the patient is able to separate the ongoing referential narrative from other affective or sensorimotor experiences, the more the symbolizing process is preserved. We looked for the emergence of negative covariations during the *nodal moments* and determined whether this represented a shift from the material immediately preceding it.

Statistical analysis lent general support to these expectations (Freedman, Lasky & Webster, 2008). For the total of nine comparisons

THE EMERGENCE OF NODAL MOMENTS 253

(three variables per session for each of the three criterion sessions), there were more negative covariations within each of the *nodal moments* as compared to the preceding material, suggesting three configurations. Further, when we considered the shifts from the antecedent material to the *nodal moment*, there tended to be positive covariations during the antecedent, shifting in the direction of a negative covariation during the *nodal moment*. Such observations lend support to the view that there arises a greater integration of specific language functions with the symbolizing process, be they affect verbalized, interrupted speech, or the voicing of the body self, as indexed by the referential process. These negative covariations can be construed as rapid fire, alternating peaks and troughs of diverse but coordinated mental functions, during this crucial but brief moment of analytic communication. They stand in relief from the positive covariation during the preceding clinical material.

These generalizations call for elaboration. The negative covariations that marked the *nodal moment* implicate different psychic experiences depending upon what the patient was concerned with during a given session. For session 245, it was primarily the communication of affect that made a difference; for session 247, it was not the content but the fluency of speech that needed to be integrated; and for session 249, the accent fell on themes surrounding the body self.

These empirical observations have affirmed that a *nodal moment* can be reliably identified and that it reflects shifts in cognitive-linguistic functioning. More surprisingly, these covariations revealed patterns specific to each of the three sessions, be they affect named, fluency of speech, or somatosensory functions, which played a role in the greater integration of the referential process. Since these selective functions work in bringing about a process of symbolization, we ask whether each has a particular relevance to the different models of triangulation cited above. This leads us now to take recourse to the qualitative and interpretive evaluation of the criterion sessions.

The nodal moments *clinically defined*

The segmentation analysis enabled us to affirm our most general clinical proposition that during a regressive phase a *nodal moment* is evoked, having a distinct mental structure and creating a reversal from the preceding context. Yet, the further statement that a *nodal moment* may signal a new thrust towards psychic agency calls for psychoanalytic interpretation. In each of the three criterion sessions to follow, Ms Y initially found herself in a predominantly unintegrated, desymbolized, and *regressed* state. As analytic work in the session proceeded, she became increasingly faced with incompatible forces. In each case, an impasse, silences, and a change of affective climate ensued. Then came the *nodal moment* and with it a more differentiated mode of thought.

Session 245

The patient begins the session in conflict about sharing her erotic, envious, and critical thoughts about the analyst:

> When I, uh, pulled up in the parking space just outside the garage, I just caught, uh, just caught a glimpse of you walking to, uh, over here ... and I saw that you were wearing a dress I liked, and then it [sighs] you ... like my criticism was that it's the same old thing, sort of, like, "You look heavier on top ... you're not like five foot ten and, and, and ultra-thin and svelte or, or something," and, and then I thought, "You're short and dumpy," and then I got horrified by that. You're not short and dumpy ... and then I thought, "Well, wha ... what do you like about her?" and then I thought, "Oh, I love your legs. I love your legs. ... I wish I had your legs." I hate my legs. I just have heavy calves and thick ankles. My thighs are not too hot either. ... Well actually each half from the thigh to the knee and from the knee to the ankle, both are equally pretty poor.

The patient then begins to speak about a decision she has to make regarding buying a house she has recently seen or renovating the one in which she and her family currently live. Her affect is flat, and her voice is a monotone. She spends about 30 minutes describing the various rooms of the house for sale, explaining how the rooms could be utilized and detailing the numerous steps involved in an alternative plan to renovate her present house. She obsesses about the decision, wishes the whole thing would "go away", and declares that she has to deal with it but is just not dealing with it. She says that the thought of living in the house for sale "just, just immediately makes me feel, uh, lifeless, kind of lifeless and depressed and upset." She describes the house for sale as "staring me in the face", and regarding what she feels are her only two choices, she says, "It's very black and white, how I'm looking at it."

The patient's ruminations eventually lead to increased disintegration: "I don't know, I'm really kind of stuck here [53 second silence, sighs loudly]. I, I start spinning in circles even as soon as I start thinking a thought. I, I can't even articulate it because it, it gets all, uh [37 second silence] ...."

* * *

Listeners' Observations: Ms Y's initial intense focus on the analyst's body and clothing suggests a sticky over-involvement and hypercathexis, highlighting part-object representations, reflecting a state of desymbolization. The space of interactional synchrony is throttled. She appears to be confronted by an experience of paradox, as she states, "It's very black and white, how I'm looking at it." The ensuing impasse evokes a further process of disintegration and confusion of thought.

* * *

Nodal Moment: Then, about 15 minutes before the end of the session, a dramatic shift takes place. The conflict is at first revealed nonverbally: the patient pauses for 17 seconds. She then states, "I don't feel as upset now because I feel I know what I want." She remarks that she and her husband, in their discussions about the houses, have been reminded of past fantasies of moving out of state. The patient then directly expresses her feelings towards the analyst: "But ... I wouldn't want to leave you. .... I thought ... 'I can't, um. I'm tied here to you.' ... I can't, I can't move before I, I mean I have to finish, this process, it just feels like a priority to me and I, I, I wouldn't tell Jack that, but, um, [20 second silence] that's a pretty strong tie."

* * *

Listeners' Observations: The patient's mounting anxiety was momentarily reduced through an expressed desire towards object relatedness—a tilt in the direction of self-reflection. She also hints at triangular conflict involving her husband, who represents an intrusion into her primary commitment to the analyst as object.

* * *

At this point the analyst remains silent. In fact, the analyst's activities throughout the session were minimal, limited to a few exploratory questions and supportive comments. No interpretations were offered.

The session ends with the patient expressing feelings of confusion: "My mind is a blank." She declares that she is "whacked out", that she cannot stop eating, is totally depressed, does not know what to do, and that she is driving her family crazy. Furthermore, she feels like she is going to buy a house she hates. It all reminds her of her despised childhood. She dreads voracious consumption, being technologically menaced, and out of control.

* * *

Listeners' Observations: The patient's affirmation of relatedness offered only scant repair. The moment of desired union was not consummated.

Commentary on the nodal moment

With this *nodal moment*, there occurred a transformation from a profoundly desymbolized state, occupying much of the hour, born of paradox and impasse, to a more symbolized state, where form was given to desire, conflicts acknowledged hesitantly but with force, all directed to the person of the analyst. In structural terms, Ms Y moved from repetitive, fragmented self-experiences during which somatosensory thought could not be integrated, to a shift towards object choice and the symbolic order. This *nodal moment* corresponds to the classical view of Oedipal triangulation emphasized by Kernberg: the analyst is chosen as the organizer of psychic conflict, and in this way, effects an alteration in the analytic relationship.

To be sure, this *nodal moment* has the contours of a prototypical negative Oedipal situation, where the husband is excluded, even devalued, the analyst included, desired, and the object of affection. The expressed tie to the analyst could be seen as a reaction formation against the *horrifying* aggressive thoughts towards her.

However, what appears to be Oedipal may not be so Oedipal after all. This *nodal moment* could be seen as an expression of perceived invariance (Bion, 1965). Ms Y could have sensed in her analyst's passivity an absence needing to be rectified. Thus, she might have created an experience of perceived invariance (defensive sameness): "That's a pretty strong tie," giving voice to a yearning for symbiotic union.

This last view addresses an inescapable observation, namely that a *nodal moment* can occur in spite of a temporarily distant analyst. But whatever its dynamic origins, this *nodal moment* affirms our general proposition that such an alteration is derived from a shift in the patient's position towards the object.

Session 247

This session is highlighted by the recovery of memories. It begins with Ms Y discovering an unfamiliar couch in the waiting room, which reminded her of an unexplained massage table she had also seen there before. (Note: a massage table will find its way into an erotic fantasy by session 257.) Thinking of these possessions of the analyst "disoriented" her and she had difficulty holding a train of thought.

Ms Y then tries to speak about the previous session and how the analyst had given her something she wanted, but once again she feels "distracted". She tries again to elaborate: she had felt upset since the day before, but a "good kind of upset" as she had thought a lot about the "meaty" intervention of the analyst's, "something meaty I could sink my teeth into". Her pain about her difficulty centering and calming herself leads to images of recent tornadoes in the US Midwest. The analyst links these images to tornadoes within the patient and a childhood reminiscence of being "very scared" comes to mind.

The patient continues that she's been feeling like she's just "bobbing along" like "I've become a victim to my—I can't think of the word … impulses … it feels like I'm, I get dragged along … a … and I'm crying and I just get dragged along, putting myself through things that I don't, I'm exhausted I don't really want to go through them and I just … don't feel like I have a choice [17 second silence] …."

Ms Y seeks to regain a focus by turning to the decision she needs to make concerning buying a house or renovating the one in which she lives. She oscillates between the two houses, and expands the oscillation to a decision about going with her husband out of state to a wedding versus staying home to have sessions with the analyst. She gets some temporary relief as she enumerates the options facing her, but to no avail. It leads her "into a confused circle". She feels in "limbo-land". "I feel nervous," she states. "I feel depressed and really anxious over this house thing [34 second silence; sigh; 10 second silence]." She wonders if she is "tormenting" herself. Then after a 19 second silence Ms Y states, "I feel inside like a mouse that's running around in a maze and doesn't know where to go and I keep reaching all these dead ends ... [33 second silence]." The mouse metaphor leads to the reclaiming of yet another, more poignant memory, this time from years past, and the beginning of the *nodal moment*.

* * *

Listeners' Observations: Here we observe a somewhat different version of regression and desymbolization. In comparison to session 245, where the regression rests on concretized, part-objects and "thing representations" (such as body parts and the houses), this part of the hour is unambiguously marked by feelings of being overwhelmed, a diffusion of focus, and a sense of loss of cohesiveness. Of great interest from a structural perspective is the memory of the analyst's intervention from the previous session. Ms Y is grateful, but unable to make use of what the analyst offered. In the *nodal moment* to follow, another memory is introduced, this time from early adulthood.

* * *

Nodal moment: Ms Y recalls a scene from college, where she was drinking heavily at a bar with her psychology professor, discussing research studies on mice. Somehow she wound up at his house. She recalls with embarrassment throwing up: "He was a funny guy, I liked him, he was quirky and I remember I liked him as a teacher, and however it happened that we ended up drinking together I can't understand but there was a certain point in that evening where, I couldn't just, uh, sit there discussing psychology or whatever with him, you know, I had to, drink, so much so, that I threw up at his house ... and it's just at the moment ... where I just feel inadequate or I feel, um, that I can't deal with something [sighs, 9 second silence], there's a skill that just, kind of eludes me, and I just kind of give up."

* * *

Listeners' Observations: This memorial process lifted Ms Y to a new level of reflectivity. A triangulation process was at work, though differing from that of session 245. Yes, there were three characters: the professor, the analyst, and Ms Y, but this *nodal moment* is reflective of a distinctly different triangulation process. First, however, the aftermath.

* * *

Briefly Ms Y remembers an outing with friends from the day before and is critical of herself for not connecting enough with them. During a 20 second silence, she hears the analyst's stomach growling and is conflicted about talking of her reaction. At first she forgets the analyst's question about it, and then, "It's almost like, I want to say, to your stomach, 'Don't do that', or mine either, because I don't want to, I don't want to, uh, deal with what I do with it." She ends the session with thoughts about how her analysis is very "consuming" lately, leaving her with little energy for anything else.

* * *

Listeners' Observations: Noteworthy in these final moments is the use of organ speech (stomachs growling) as an aftermath of the *nodal moment*. It emphasizes the somatosensory connection between analyst and patient.

Commentary on the nodal moment

There are at least two readings of this *nodal moment*. First, it could be a direct representation of a classical Oedipal situation, and unlike that of session 245, a positive Oedipal triangulation. The libidinal wish towards the male professor is relived in memory, while the aggressive thoughts are implicitly reserved for the female analyst. Evoked is the image of the desired, "quirky", attractive psychology professor pitted against the listening, perhaps critical or jealous analyst. (Note that the analyst is a psychologist as well.) These images suggest a clash of antagonistic object relational wishes in the transference. Yet this appears to be an incomplete view of what transpired. The very form in which this *nodal moment* was rendered suggests other processes at work.

With the evocation of memory and the imaginary, this *nodal moment* can be viewed from a fresh perspective. A more profound form of symbolization seems to have occurred. Ms Y tells a story of sensuality, nostalgia, excitement, and humiliation, bringing fantasy to life. Through the use of her imagination, told in the presence of her analyst (the witness), Ms Y created a new kind of triangular space. Note, in this line of thought, we are guided by one overriding assumption, namely, that in this episode, the analyst is experienced by the patient as the observer and witness of the events told. This type of triangular space, as outlined by Britton, portrays the tension of positions between subjective and objective self-awareness, expressed here in the form of being in touch with one's inner self while experiencing being monitored by an evaluating, perhaps persecutory witness.

The use of two memories adds to an understanding of the integrating functions of this *nodal moment*. The first memory, that of the analyst's intervention from the preceding hour, arose amidst confusion and despair seemingly split off in the whirlwind of regression. This memory acted as a precursor to the memory of the sensuous psychology professor; an instance of the power of the *après-coup* in the transference, where the recall of the memory from the preceding session prepares the way for the memory from the past, bringing the transference to life (Green, 2000).

Now, in this use of memory and the imaginary, we find a distinctly different version of triangulation, one that has the attributes of a *third dynamic force* and binds analyst and patient closely together. In the reporting of the memory of the psychology professor, we note a shift from sensuality to bursts of shame and mortification. Ms Y was implicitly expressing a plea to be heard. The analyst became the *mother of need* and heard it, as indicated in her scan, when she refers to her well timed "meaty" intervention: "This time I've said it in the right moment and she was able to take it in at the moment I said it." The analyst's ability to metabolize that which was proffered, was also underscored in an unusual bit of mutual affective recognition. This was played out on the somatosensory level and was the instance in which both the patient's and analyst's stomachs were growling. This kind of rhythmic synchrony on the level of organ speech is one form of intersubjectivity described by Benjamin: a rhythmic or harmonic element of oneness (2004). That this was present affirms that Ms Y and her analyst sensed at the level of the body self that each was perceived by and existed for the other.

During this hour, Ms Y travelled a significant but brief psychic road in the direction of an *analytic third*. In the beginning she was deeply immersed in her subjectivity, but with the arrival of the *nodal moment*, she created an intersubjective space, a symbolizing space, attaining a more intimate connection with her analyst. Furthermore, this was registered on the level of the body soma, as both participants experienced that each existed for the other. This can also be thought of as a move towards the creation of "potential space" in Winnicott's sense (1967), and with it the opening of the door for the experience of otherness.

Session 249

Ms Y opens the session chatting about two women she had seen at various points during the previous day, feeling she had made "neat connections". She described in detail (and twice she wonders why she is spending so much time on the details) running into her neighbour at the launderette, first seeing her legs sticking out from a car, then her heavily made-up face and coiffed hair. There are hints of envy not articulated and some embarrassment for not having a washing machine at home. They have an animated conversation, comparing notes about motherhood and marriage.

Then came an evolving storm, enshrined in depressive reverie. Ms Y spoke of immediately needing to eat after the encounter with her neighbour. Her "storm" that day was her "mission". "I feel like giving up." "I feel like now I stopped pedalling and I'm just kind of cruising backwards and, I feel bummed out."

She then tells of a recent incident where her husband delivered a penetrating insult, telling her she looked like a "dishevelled boat person. ... I cried and I cried and I cried because that comment really bothered me. ... I look like a dishevelled boat person." She reiterated that insult many times and then attacked further her appearance, her hair and clothes. Next she wonders if the analyst feels the same when she criticizes her body and outfits. "I was mad, kind of, that he said that … and then I thought of you and my insults or comments, criticisms toward you and I wondered, I wondered if that's how you reacted to me and I feel like you'll take it in because you're sitting here, you're my doctor, you listen to me in a certain way."

She continues with a joint fantasy of hers and her husband's as to the analyst's wish for revenge. The day before they were imagining what the analyst would write on her notepad after learning about the husband's insult. "I'll tell you what she'll write." "Oh yeah, what?" " 'What goes around comes around.' … Bingo." "A part of me I think felt like you would be glad that I was hurt and angered by a criticism."

* * *

Listeners' Observations: This opening is lengthier and more complex as compared to those of sessions 245 and 247, with Ms Y assuming a more interactive stance. Certainly there was a measure of desymbolization: event reporting, uncontrolled negative affect, and part-object representations; nonetheless, the recalled insult by the husband stirred up Ms Y's brewing inner "storm", leading to successive volleys. First, she internalized her husband's attack and proceeded to vehemently attack herself. She then followed through in imagining with the husband an anticipated counter-attack from the analyst. Sadistic pleasure was also palpable as they laughed at the analyst's probable need for revenge. This prepared Ms Y for the *nodal moment*.

* * *

Nodal Moment: "I just started shaking like I'm nervous [8 second silence] you know, God forbid you might wake up and feel like putting on a sweatshirt and just coming over here and, you know, and you'd get the same type of thing from me—oh I just, which reminds me I don't like your outfit and I think it was the same, I think it was the same outfit that you were wearing a couple days ago or last week or whenever when I didn't like it: I don't like the pants … [sighs] … maybe it's looking down on you sitting but you look heavy [29 second silence] and now I'm kind of stuck, I mean not stuck but sort of, that sort of stumped me, ah, … , because I had a lot of reactions to what just happened, because now I'm nervous."

* * *

Listeners' Observations: An ordinary hostile transference fantasy was rendered explicit through a verbal enactment, giving expression to the triumph of sadistic desire. First, there was registration on the level of the body ego, then there was the direct expression, "I don't like your outfit", representing a simple Oedipal wish to humiliate the analyst. But when she added in a burst, "maybe it's looking down on you" (in fact, she was lying on the couch), the attack had the quality of an enacted symbol, a provocative act demanding further response. As will be described, this *enacted symbol*, delivered in a vivid, presentational mode of thought, led to the unfolding of further reminiscences, the retrieving of earlier events and the telling of a dream, all within the unfolding timeline of *Progressive Symbolization*.

* * *

Returning to the session, the analyst encourages Ms Y to elaborate on her "reactions" to her outburst, and this enables the patient to ultimately interpret for herself the meaning of her "storms" as a form of self-punishment for her anger. Then after a 66 second silence, Ms Y states that during the silence she was reliving the memory from the day before with her husband, when they were imagining what the analyst might write on her notepad. Reflecting upon what had just happened in the session, Ms Y has a fantasy of going home and having the following conversation with her husband: "'Did you tell her?' and I would say 'Yes, actually I did.' 'What did she say?' 'Actually she laughed.' 'She laughed? Oh wow.' 'I got a rise out of her.'"

The session then continues with the telling of a dream, involving Ms Y and her two male employers, where feelings of affection were expressed, as well as the hope of connection, and the linking of a house for sale with a vacation spot. But then Ms Y's ability to contain her affective burst, and to follow through with symbolized reflection, collapsed: "Ah, fuck it, what's the difference, well [17 second silence] I heard that, I've heard the pattern over and over and over and over and over and over and over and over and over and over [13 second silence] it's so unhealthy [13 second silence] and I don't know what to do with it any more, I feel like I've honestly, I've honestly tried approaching it from different angles and that nothing, nothing has worked."

* * *

Listeners' Observations: The sequelae to this *nodal moment*, with its evocative force, were more pronounced than those of the two previous criterion sessions. Here we witness the introduction of a more complex quality of mind—the intertwining of memory and fantasy. The memory anticipates the fantasy and the fantasy gives flesh to the memory as Ms Y allows herself to laugh at her own sadistic wishes. It appears that the enacted symbol created a new context for working through. It was, however, an apparent gain that proved to be short-lived.

Commentary on the nodal moment

This *nodal moment* can be viewed within the timeline of the evolving sadistic fantasy. It was organized around the *enacted symbol*, was preceded by the evolving storm, reached its peak through the confrontative verbal enactment towards the analyst, and culminated in the reliving of a memory, which enabled Ms Y to connect with her sadistic desires. The *nodal moment* in session 245 was an instance of symbolization, involving the direct engagement of the analyst as psychic organizer. In session 247, it was marked by an internal dialogue between subjectivity and objectivity, and in this session, the *nodal moment* involved both the direct engagement of the analyst and a rich internal dialogue. But there was one additional feature, the *enacted symbol*, a forceful image, both concrete and metaphoric, was designed to impact the analyst's subjectivity. It was an enactment of Ms Y's wish to torture the analyst and served as a further breeding ground for *Progressive Symbolization*.

Reflections on nodal moments *during the desymbolizing phase*

To summarize, we have described the phenomenon of a *nodal moment*, which is a reversal in mental organization and the beginning of the upward slope, appearing late in predominantly desymbolizing sessions. In each of the three criterion sessions, *nodal moments* appeared in triangular space, giving rise to symbolized thought. This phenomenon was confirmed empirically when the symbolizing process during each session was evaluated by the measures of the referential process, and corroborated by a qualitative and interpretive reading of the clinical material.

For each of these moments, we were able to discern a definable shift in the patient's position towards the analyst. Moreover, each *nodal moment* depicted a particular way of resolving impasse: naming and confronting the triangular conflict (Kernberg); evoking an imaginary dialogue, buttressed by memories of the past (Britton); and creating an enacted symbol to draw the analyst more closely into the web of the analytic interchange (Steingart). Such juncture points were first discovered in this desymbolizing phase, but as we shall see, others of their kind emerge in the material to come. These events and the manner in which they unfold over time tell much about the essence of *Progressive Symbolization*—the theme of our concluding chapter (Chapter Eighteen).

We are tempted to end in a speculative vein. The clinical markers that depict these unfolding *nodal moments* from naming to imagining and remembering suggest a developmental progression crucial to the expansion of symbolizing space and to working through. Yet the expectation of such apparent linear progression can be deceptive, for even as we examine the sequelae to these current *nodal moments*, we see a return to desymbolization and regression. This observation reminds us of the fragility of this initial toss in the direction of an upward slope, and also of the psychical alternations, the ups and downs that are characteristic of all psychoanalytic work. We shall further discover in the next chapter how such nonlinear forces contribute to psychoanalytic change. To cite T. S. Eliot (1944):

> Time present and time past
> Are both perhaps present in time future,
> And time future is contained in time past.

Endnotes

i. For session 245: $A = 1.5$, $Z = 9.5$ and $A\text{-}Z = -8$; for session 247: $A = 2.5$, $Z = 10$ and $A\text{-}Z = -7.5$; and for session 249: $A = 3.5$, $Z = 9$ and $A\text{-}Z = -5.5$.

ii. Mean WRAD scores: for session $245 = 0.4309$; for session $247 = 0.4346$; and for session $249 = 0.4916$.

CHAPTER SIXTEEN

The enactive phase: sessions 252 to 255

Norbert Freedman and Rhonda Ward

Almost immediately following the *nodal moments* of the desymbolizing phase, there appeared a sequence of sessions which we could not classify as either *A* or *Z*, and were, thus, neither predominately symbolizing nor desymbolizing sessions. Even more striking was another "objective fact", alerting us to a potentially informative event: during these sessions, the analyst's scans increased in length. This could mean that the patient had more to say and/or that the analyst was more engaged, but whatever the interpretation, there was a veritable surge of analyst's comments at this point. During the desymbolizing phase, the length of the analyst's scan (expressed in words spoken) was for session 245, 247, and 249, 555, 719, and 452 words, respectively. For sessions 252, 253, 254, and 255, the word output was 823, 1010, 1003, and 709, respectively. Noteworthy is that the scan for session 257, an unambiguous *A* session and the last of this specimen, had a word count of 1475. From the vantage point of referential activity, there also appeared to be an upward trend: the RA score for session 252 was 0.449 and for session 255, 0.467. It seemed we had entered a new phase in the analytic process, be it patient activity or analyst engagement. Perhaps we were, to use Palombo's memorable metaphor, "[At] the edge of chaos when a small change in input from the environment can lead to a reorganization of the system's structure at a level of increased complexity" (1999, p. 175). Perhaps the upward slope involves a process of differentiation occurring only "at the phase transition between frozen ice and chaotic fluid states" (ibid., p. 176).

This sequence of sessions was also marked by a series of definable actions: they were kinesic (nonverbal) as well as verbal, disruptive of the ongoing dialogue, tended to be patient- or analyst-induced, and seemed to have a major impact on the subsequent engagement of the two participants. Towards the end of the sequence another *nodal moment* emerged, and with it another instance of *Progressive Symbolization*. This overall event sequence we are calling the "enactive phase".

In order to appreciate this turn of events, we need to situate these observations within the fabric of current psychoanalytic thought. The concept of enactment has become a recent icon in our psychoanalytic vocabulary, and once more, at the risk of oversimplification, we shall single out selected voices—those of Boesky, S. J. Ellman, Smith, and Katz—asking how their formulations might shed light on this particular phase of working through.

Enactments as the nonverbal expression of intolerable thought: Boesky and beyond

Ever since Boesky (1982) revised the concept of "acting out" as that of actions reflecting an attempt at actualization and expressing the psychic reality of the transference, the term "enactment", has come into use, freeing us from the pejorative meaning associated with that earlier Freudian concept. While enactment involves the interactive, the imagistic, and is a continuous aspect of the analytic interchange, it is also a discrete event, having a definable impact on the analytic dialogue. It is an observable expression of a surge of unthinkable thought. In a recent review article, Boesky (2000) notes that the term has become the *"lingua franca* for the communication of dangerous and repudiated affects" (p. 257, italics in original). Enactment closes the gap between what is expressible and inexpressible, or what is forgotten and pressing for revival, and offers a bridge between a

THE ENACTIVE PHASE 269

one-person and a two-person psychology (Boesky, 2000). Thus, it would not be surprising that following the sadistic burst in session 249, "I don't like your outfit" (a verbally enacted symbol), Ms Y would be overcome by further moments of unthinkable promptings, which then might become transformed and surface further in the motor realm of communicated thought. When such discrete events arise, as we shall describe below, the further question must be confronted: what do such acts, which emerge with considerable force, suggest about the underlying psychic process that impels transformation to take place?

Let us situate the evolution of the concept of enactment within the spectrum of psychoanalytic ideas over the past two decades. Sandler's (1976) introduction of the phenomenon of "role responsiveness" led to the discovery of new meanings of action. But it was Jacobs (1986) who introduced the term enactment into our arsenal of concepts, doing so with a dramatic clinical vignette in which an analyst, small in stature, meeting for the first time a Paul Bunyon-like figure, said with hesitation and a shrug of the shoulder: "Come on in, anyway" (p. 289). This quick gesture with its multiple meanings had a plethora of consequences for the ensuing analysis.

Also of historical significance is McLaughlin's (1987) emphasis on nonverbal communications such as those revealed in the fingering motions by Dora in her secret struggle with Freud, a situation in which both members of the analytic couple perceive the impossibility of being heard by the other (a phenomenon also emphasized by Jacobs). This phenomenon has been further developed by Chused (1991), who states that "[E]nactments in analysis are inevitable.... Enactments are symbolic interactions between analyst and patient which have unconscious meaning to *both*" (p. 615, italics in original). Here Chused's vision is continuous with Steingart's notion of the enacted symbol, which as we have seen, is a mode of communication having a specific impact on the analytic dialogue.

S. J. Ellman and Moskowitz (1998), in their comprehensive review of the concept of enactment, make a valuable contribution in their distinction (already anticipated in McLaughlin's notion of mutual enactment) between patient-induced and analyst-induced enactment. Enactments may occur in sequence, where one member of the dyad follows the other with an enactment. The net result of such a sequence is the failure to recognize the affective experiences of the other. For us, it is in the diverse directions which enactments may take, that the "nonlinear" motion, envisaged by Palombo (1999) in his phrase, "at the edge of chaos", can be pinpointed. It is in the ups and downs of the phase of transition that these enactive qualities are of particular relevance. It may well be that in this play of nonlinear dynamics, where minimal events are of great consequence, that the analytic process can ultimately be efficacious. This is a conclusion we shall reach concerning the trajectory of this transformation cycle, for following the enactive phase, we find a phase of resymbolization containing an unambiguous symbolizing session (session 257).

Enactments as the loss of narcissistic equilibrium: Ellman

With the introduction of the notion of a patient-induced and an analyst-induced enactment, S. J. Ellman (2007) squarely directs us towards the bi-directional aspects of transference communication. He also singles out salient moments during enactments, when either patient or analyst may have a loss of reflectivity, that is, a loss of connection to an inner psychic reality. At such moments, there arises a breakdown in the affective interpenetration between analyst and patient, which Ellman terms "the loss of analytic trust", and which is a phenomenon recognized by other authors, but with different designations (e.g., Grunes, 1984). These are moments when the patient is overcome by intolerable affects or thoughts, ceases to reflect, and experiences a profound disillusionment, that is, a loss of transference expectancies (McLaughlin, 1991). In this situation, the patient experiences the analyst as having lost the capacity to sense his or her psychic pain, and hence feels no longer included in the mental life of the other. The patient feels unable to trust the analytic situation. This is a traumatic moment and the origin of the recourse to action. This formative moment, which Ellman (2007) terms, "the loss of narcissistic equilibrium", forces the patient to resort to other, that is, enactive, forms of communication.

Of special interest is Ellman's (2009) observation that an enactment tends to arise at points of transition. Applied to the study of transformation cycles, it may well be that enactments play a special role in the transition from a state of desymbolization to that of symbolization. Thus, in session 249, when the patient blurts out, "I don't like your outfit", the analyst might have then lost her narcissistic equilibrium and perhaps the enactive phase was the result.

The enactive dialogue as a deepening engagement in intra-psychic conflict: Smith and Katz

Enactments, when observed or reported, appear to be merely discrete events. To be sure, a quality of distinctness is implied in Boesky's emphasis on nonverbal actions as expressions, even bursts, of intolerable thought. Historically, this view has its origin in Freud's notion of "acting out". But for Smith (2000), enactments must be viewed within the context of an ongoing dialogic process. When enactments are apprehended by both participants, they offer an opportunity for a deepening engagement in the analytic process. We, too, have observed that nonverbal acts may appear as discrete events—a pause, a change in tone, or even a sudden disruption, often carrying signals of surprise—but when they arise—and they inevitably do—they can be heard as a statement of inner conflict, evoked through the interchange of the analytic couple.

Smith (2000) stresses that enactments offer an opportunity to the analyst for conflictual listening. For the patient, in their vividness, they pave the path to more convincing self-observations through new perceptions. For the dyad, they sharpen for both participants the awareness of the core conflict. In the material to follow, we hope to describe such a deepening of engagement as it surfaces towards the end of the enactive phase.

Katz (2002) advanced the view that "a patient's enacted transference ... can create an analytic version of the patient's conflicted object relationship" (p. 407). Like Ellman, he appreciates the reciprocal nature of the transference–countertransference dialogue, and like Smith, he embraces the crucial role of "conflictual listening". But in his extension of these perspectives, Katz shows how the nonverbal dialogue, "the enacted dimension" as he calls it, running alongside the verbal dialogue, can be heard by both participants, bringing into focus encapsulated traumatic moments arising from the patient's forgotten past (ibid., p. 407). Moreover, Katz illustrates that when the enacted transference becomes conscious, it undergoes transformation and emerges in the arena of verbally symbolized thought. From this vantage point, Katz's work speaks to and is of great relevance to the phenomenon of *nodal moments*, the topic of the previous chapter.

In the following highlights from sessions 252 to 255, we hope to show how each of these formulations has its place in an understanding of this enactive phase. The observed discrete, nonverbal, and/or verbal communications can be construed as (with Boesky) expressions of intolerable affects, as (with Ellman) representative moments of breakdown in narcissistic equilibrium, as (with Smith) a progressive heightening of engagement in core conflicts, and as (with Katz) a transformation of a biographically-based traumatic moment into verbal symbolic form. Such manifestations of "enactment" will arise in this sequence of sessions, and at the end point, a *nodal moment* will once more be encountered.

The faces of enactment clinically defined

Session 252

Ms Y begins with a childhood memory in which she is a frightened little girl. She is tearful as she speaks of her current desperate sadness, feeling weighed down, and so disconnected from herself and others. She connects the intense sadness to "how I want to be and how I really am are so discrepant."

She reports a dream that stresses a sense of being fused: "My mom tries on my wedding gown. She looks great in my dress. Why is my mother in my dress? ... Am I identifying with her, or is it more like an intrusion?" Her associations lead to how mean and spiteful she feels when changing her daughter's nappy and her guilt about such feelings.

Then a patient-induced enactment ensues. Ms Y remembers that just before the session she had accepted an invitation for a picnic that conflicts with the next analytic hour. She asks to reschedule. The analyst is drawn into the action, expressing apparent discomfort through the shuffling of papers, interrupting the patient, becoming excessively accommodating, and reassuring Ms Y that she is not rigid. The patient retorts, "I am at the mercy of your response." An interchange follows involving misunderstanding and confusion.

In spite of this enactment, Ms Y continues with a series of associations about her efforts to stay internally connected to others and to the analyst. Having taken as an assignment her analyst's comments from a previous session, she announces that she has been trying to attend to the lustful side of herself—dancing to the music she loves in order to get her juices flowing, having sex, and masturbating.

* * *

Listeners' Observations: This hour was organized around the patient's announced decision to "break the frame". This was followed by the analyst's "counter-enactment", which seemed to end in a state of mutual confusion and surrender on the part of the analyst. Hence, this sequence is best viewed as a dialogue beginning with a patient-induced enactment, followed by one that is analyst-induced. These are non-reflective acts by both participants. The patient took the action before the hour began, voicing it midway through the session and the analyst responded immediately with a counter-enactment, probably having felt the jolt of being excluded. Now it might be that the breaking of the frame by the patient was an "action", expressive of an intolerable sadistic wish, following the events of previous sessions (Boesky); yet we believe it is also important to understand the entire enactive sequence between patient and analyst.

Following Ellman, this sequence marks a loss of narcissistic equilibrium for both participants. Elsewhere (Freedman, Lasky & Webster, 2009), it has been shown that this analyst was quite vulnerable to the threat of being judged as professionally incompetent, and the experience of being suddenly excluded might well have been a psychic onslaught. (Her surrender of the analytic stance speaks in this direction.) This counter-enactment of the analyst induced a subsequent enactment on the part of the patient, where she became excessively compliant (having taken on the "assignment" of the analyst). In both cases, enactment seems to follow the possible dread of not being perceived as the idealized other.

This event sequence is a nonlinear progression of analytic engagement. At first, the patient seemed to stand outside the relationship (the scheduling conflict), that is, standing outside the analytic space. In a counter-enactment the analyst, unable to contain the patient's challenge, also withdrew from her patient through a loss of her analytic stance. But then, perhaps unpredictably so, the patient sought to recover a connection as she evoked a memory from the last session. In doing so, she re-entered the analyst's world.

Session 253

The enactive reverberations between analyst and patient continue in more explicit fashion. Due to an accident on the highway, the analyst was forced to start the session 30 minutes late. She had called the patient, who lives nearby, to alert her about this change. In session, Ms Y has several critical and challenging thoughts evoked by the delay. Reluctant to mention them, she comments, "How many roads can I open up here, how many roadblocks are there to overcome?" Then, quoting her husband about the delay, she adds, "He said I should charge you because you didn't give me 24 hours notice." Significantly, the analyst, in what can be viewed as a concretized denial of the hostile intent, retorts, "Of course he was only teasing." The patient remarks that her husband's joke evokes difficult feelings, in as much as this points to a conflict of loyalty involving herself, her husband, and her analyst. (This crucial conflict, alluded to in session 245, is further elaborated in session 257.)

Later in this session, Ms Y notes how controlled she feels with the analyst: "It's an annoying thought to think that you see other patients for 45 minutes and they may take full advantage of all the space, and I come in here and I feel like I'm laying in a casket on the couch, and can only take this much space." Citing earlier material, the analyst interprets, "It must feel too dangerous. If you're not in a casket, you'll be tossed around by a team of men having them fondle your breasts." The patient reveals another fantasy of being in a whorehouse, bouncing around on the penis of a man she does not know, while women are sucking her nipples.

Then the patient once more addresses the analyst's lateness and the accident. She comments, "Things are not resolved between me and you in here. There is no such thing as an innocent question because I'm not innocent in here. I'm always somehow sneakily looking for a way in." Towards the end of the hour, the patient returns to her default position: "Things are not clear, we are in the muck and the mud. ... I feel discouraged. I have felt like I've wanted to ask you, like, guide me, show me where to go. ... I hear my stomach growling, I hear your stomach growling."

* * *

Listeners' Observations: The analyst's 30 minute lateness was certainly an unintended act, but for the patient it was perceived as a rupture and a jolt to her transference expectancy. In that sense, it was an analyst-induced enactment. The patient's hostile rejoinder, "He said I should charge you", and the analyst's subsequent denial of the aggressive intent, as both Grunes and Ellman would say, suggests that the ordinary, expectable affective interpenetration between analyst and patient had come to a halt.

This enactive dialogue had notable consequences for the remainder of the session. The hostile barbs were followed by the patient feeling controlled, abused, helpless, "laying in a casket on the couch". But as Ms Y heard both their stomachs growling, she conveyed the intimately felt inter-subjectivity that permeated this analytic couple. The aggressive derision activated in these moments of enactment, giving rise at other points in this specimen to torture fantasies, harks back here to a desire for transference regression. This alerts us to Smith's advice to attend to conflictual listening. The moments of non-reflective interchange between patient and analyst appear to crystallize an ongoing conflict that emerges as the hour progresses.

Through the lens of conflictual listening, we can discern a continuous line of thought steeped in fantasies of abuse and surrender, which in turn are the source of desire for sadistic triumph that will re-emerge a few sessions later. The enactive sequence here, viewed retrospectively, is reflective of Ms Y's ongoing core conflictual object relations theme. The enactive sequence is a flag, an alerting signal of ensuing transference events.

Once more we discern in this session the pattern of nonlinear progression. The session opened with a profound state of disconnectedness; then there seemed to be a coming together, as the patient moved towards the analyst and the analyst received her with empathy; but by the end, when Ms Y implored, "guide me", she seemed to feel quite alone.

Session 254

The patient opens this session with an awareness that she looks at a book on the analyst's desk as a way of shutting her out. She had noticed the analyst's tight knitted top and breasts upon entering the office. A great deal of self-preoccupied rambling ensues, with minimal interaction between the two participants. Then the patient resumes her complaining stance, stating that she is still in the same place, with the world spinning around her. She adds, "You are my best friend, although something in me feels you are an enemy."

About two-thirds of the way into the session, the analyst excuses herself, saying she has to go to the bathroom. One hears the door closing, the sound of vomiting, and then the toilet flushing. She returns a few minutes later and resumes the session. Ms Y inquires if she is alright. The analyst answers that she is feeling better, explaining that she had an upset stomach. Despite her illness, the analyst makes an effort to continue the hour, but she sounds depressed.

* * *

Listeners' Observations: In this session we find the crystallization of "mutual enactment", with the analytic dialogue throttled from both sides of the couch. The reference to the analyst's book and the vomiting scene were powerful signals that each was unavailable to the other. The analyst's sudden illness evoked for the patient a flurry, a plethora of unspoken virulent thoughts, which would surface in the beginning of the next session.

Session 255

The opening of this session is so remarkable, we shall quote it verbatim:

> I had two reactions to it, but I was thinking, uh, all day yesterday and last night, uh, well, I don't have like a compassionate reaction, but I felt for you ... and remembered nausea during my pregnancy. I found myself going over it, and over it, and over it in my mind like with a still camera, wondering how many seconds or minutes you were sitting there feeling uncomfortable before you realized you were going to throw up, because

THE ENACTIVE PHASE   277

it's a, that's the worst part. I would think, I just ... a ... and wondering, if you felt, uh, uncomfortable or embarrassed that you, that that happened at all, or if it was no big deal inside of you, um, it made you seem human you know and I, and I just felt for you. And the other, uh, fantasy thing that was coming out last night was that I started having these fantasies of, um, I don't even know if I'd call them fantasies or just like thoughts that, that, uh, came to mind, you know. Instead of pushing them away or just sort of discounting them I would try to feed them to sort of see where they would go. It was real, uh, mean, um, uh, brutal type of, uh, imagery where you're over the [laughs] kneeling down over the toilet bowl and I have, and I'm there too, and I have your hair, like I'm pulling, you know, like I could flip your head back if I pull your hair, or else push your head in the toilet or, um, like, uh, almost like I would say, you know, "Throw up," and if you didn't throw up I'd kick you in the back or something, or on the behind or something like that. Like real mean! And then I also thought of more embarrassing scenarios where, how you'd be, uh, throwing up and then you would fart too because you had no control over anything, you know, any, the mouth or the other part of your body. And you know what's interesting? Before I walked in here, when I was walking to the cabin, I was actually, it came to mind the time that you went into the bathroom during our session. That happened like a year or two ago, um, where you just excused yourself for a minute. And I think that when I thought that, I just thought, "Yes, I remember when that happened and, kind of, wasn't that something?" But I thought, I remembered that yesterday before our session, so that when you went to the bathroom, it was as if something was familiar about it, because I had remembered the other time. I feel uncomfortable right now. I think the reason I feel uncomfortable is because, I wish I could just, um, have that compassionate reaction.

* * *

Listeners' Observations: The passage just cited presents a convincing instance of a transformation, occasioned by a *nodal moment*.[i] In this *nodal moment*, occurring at the beginning of the hour, reflectivity and narrative alternated in the successive timeline of spoken language;

hence the patient was able to offer a vivid, integrated presentation of what she wished to communicate. It is noteworthy that this integration took place at the end of this sequence of enactive sessions. This is most clearly illustrated in the shift from session 254 to session 255—the shift from mutual enactment to symbolization.

This transformation can be further delineated by considering the trend of this enactive phase as a whole. We described how disruptive nonverbal actions reflected the breakdown of narcissistic equilibrium, how they became the occasion for increased analyst engagement, and how a mutual enactment signified an impasse in analytic communication. But then in session 255, the patient's throttled experiences were transformed into a veritable outcry. Katz (2002) has shown how the enactive dimension is a compromise formation, a carrier of unconscious content, and how, at crucial moments of treatment, it becomes transformed into verbal symbolic language. This is what we observe in the transformation from session 254 to session 255.

This *nodal moment* is a pivotal event similar to those described in the earlier desymbolizing phase, though there they appeared towards the end of the hour. Here, with the impact of the mutual enactment, occasioned by the analyst's sudden illness, this *nodal moment* surfaced at the start of the session.

The symbolic conflict expressed in this *nodal moment* was given a sense of immediacy through the magic of two memories: a memory from a year ago, and the other, the recall of the fantasy related to the vomiting scene. It is remarkable how two distinct forms of memory—one specific and perceptual, the other evocative and conceptual (Loewald, 1980), lend force and vitality to the experience of the imaginary in the here and now (a sequence also noted in sessions 247 and 249). Here, the surfacing of these flashes of recall were the immediate precursors to the play of the imaginary in this opening.

Finally, in this scene we witness once more an instance of *Progressive Symbolization*. Considering the events of the enactive phase, we ask: in what way do enactments contribute to working through?

Reflections on enactment

In our earlier study on this upward slope (Freedman, Lasky & Ward, 2009), we concluded that mutual regulation during an enactive phase can be a precursor to the activation of the synthetic function of the ego. Here we would like to be more specific. Our general view is that at the moment an enactment arises, the patient and analyst find themselves "at the edge of chaos". We surmise that Ms Y experienced a brief loss of narcissistic equilibrium, and this loss had its impact in the form of alternating analyst-induced and patient-induced acts. The ensuing result was that in a spiralling fashion, new forms, images, memories, and fantasies became integrated, giving a more differentiated voice to desire.

The enactive sequence evoked an increase in the analyst's engagement in Ms Y's psychic life. Our quantitative findings, the increase in words uttered by the analyst during her scans, were one source of evidence for this spiralling process. But we also wondered about the analyst's activity inside the hour. In tackling this issue we undertook one additional piece of empirical inquiry. We considered two extreme moments, session 245, an unambiguous desymbolized session, and session 255, the end of the enactive phase. We enquired whether the analyst's contribution to the session differed during the desymbolizing phase as compared to that of the enactive. Not only was the latter marked by greater analyst participation in the scan, but within the actual session the analyst's contribution to the dialogue was also markedly higher (3% within session 245 as compared to 8% in session 255). Thus, by the end of the enactive phase and probably throughout this phase, the analyst made her presence felt more forcefully. We infer that the enactments created a need in the analyst to express herself and give voice to what she sensed had happened. The patient seemed to have reached her and the analyst responded. The result was a greater interpenetration of affective experiences, not only in the analyst's consciousness but also within the analytic couple.

The enactive phase also appeared to have heightened within the patient a shift from a subliminal to a focal awareness of inner conflicts—another sign of affective interpenetration. The combination of memory flashes, first specific and then evocative, observed in different sessions in this specimen, as they evolved into more composite stories told, were then articulated in the form of verbalized fantasies expressing desire. Such a sequence seemed to have alerted the analyst to conflictual listening (Smith, 2000). Through the occurrence of the enactments, the frightening images, throttled during earlier sessions, rose closer to the analytic surface, giving life to fantasies of long standing.

Significantly, by the end of this enactive phase, the patient felt a more intimate connection to the analyst. She concludes session 255 with the following: "I was thinking about what happened yesterday when you went into the bathroom and for some reason that whole incident made me feel closer to you or made me feel more connected to you."

We have asserted that the enactive phase is a further step in the direction of *Progressive Symbolization*. A final look at the constituents of session 255, the culmination of this phase, will clarify this point. Not only do we find in the *nodal moment* in this session a greater vividness (as compared to that containing the enacted symbol in session 249), in that it is more evocative, specific, imagistic, and expressive of sadistic desire through yet another enacted symbol (kicking the analyst in the behind), not only is there greater implicit and explicit engagement on the part of the analyst, but concurrent with the experience of the depths of the regressive moment, there occurs at the end of the hour, the feeling of closeness and intimacy, when the patient states, "That whole incident made me feel closer to you." Achieved in this moment of *Progressive Symbolization* is the activation of the synthetic function of the ego, where the experience of the depths of sadism is integrated with feelings of love in the transference.

In concluding, we are tempted to muse about the early biographical roots of desire and memory, which can be crystallized through action. Katz (2002), more than any of the other "enactment" theorists, asserts that it is the "enacted dimension" which is the vehicle for the expression of earliest unconscious phantasy. The enacted dimension involves the unmetabolized, unverbalized representation of rage and terror, including somatosensory experiences that may become verbalized in the transference–countertransference matrix. This transformation is demonstrated in the phenomenon of transgenerational transmission, and Talby-Abarbanel (in press) and Katz (in press) illustrate this shift with a high degree of specificity. In their case example, signals of traumatic episodes were recapitulated not only in the life of the patient, but also in the life of the parent and even in the lives of the ancestors. Derivatives of these themes reappeared in the analysis, and the authors describe a powerful shift where in only one week of treatment, unnamed signals of despair were followed by verbalized emotional bursts. (Here we are reminded of Ms Y's rapid shift from session 254 to session 255.) For Katz, this marks the reactivation of life-long trauma in the transference, where the enactment, the carrier of unconscious phantasy, had become symbolized in verbal form. While we also observed rapid fire transformations in Ms Y's mode of mental organization, her biographical roots are beyond our knowledge, and cannot be explored within the limits of a specimen study.

Endnote

i. At the peak of this enactive phase, we once more encounter a nodal moment. We inquired whether what was communicated in this passage has its objective counterparts, and we applied our method of segmentation analysis. Inspection of the data suggested that this time, reflectivity appeared to be the most discriminating variable (the covariation between reflectivity and referential activity was −0.83). This finding was not surprising, since this passage contains both fantasies and memories reflected upon.

CHAPTER SEVENTEEN

The cycle and the spiral during the re-symbolizing phase: the erotic transference, the extraordinary countertransference, and the preservation of the analytic process: session 257

Norbert Freedman and Rhonda Ward

Session 257 represents a stellar moment in this specimen of *working through*. It is an unambiguous symbolizing hour, marking a return to symbolization and the completion of the transformation cycle. But it is more than this, for it not only contains the highest level of symbolization in this cycle (as reflected in the peaking of referential activity measures), but it also contains the highest levels of non-integration (as reflected in low measures of interactional synchrony). Thus, this session not only completes the cycle but in its peaks and troughs has the properties of a spiral.

Furthermore, this session contains within its structure all the phases of this transformation cycle, that is, a phase of symbolization, desymbolization, and re-symbolization. In the broadest sense, this replication allows us to translate and revisit the specific way-stations encountered in this specimen. The symbolizing phase of this session reveals paradoxically a *downward slope* and with it the induction of regression reverberating in the transference (Chapter Fourteen); patient-induced and analyst-induced enactments, resulting in a moment of mutual enactment, reflect a peak of desymbolization and paradoxically initiate the upward slope (Chapter Sixteen); and finally, a *nodal moment* at the end of the session results in a reversal and a return to symbolization (Chapter Fifteen).

The phases of this session also lead to a particular event sequence. During the initial symbolizing phase, the patient tells of vivid experiences in imaginary form while also employing increased somatosensory speech, paradoxically moving towards regressive desires. A particular kind of somatosensory imagery emerges this time: the patient focuses on the analyst's body, specifically her genitals, marking an explicit erotic transference. Such an unambiguous communication can offer a special challenge, even threat, to the engaged analyst, and as will be seen, this erotic transference evoked a particular kind of countertransference enactment—the *extraordinary countertransference*. Not only did the analyst reveal a loss of identification with her patient, but she did so with destructive overtones. This is followed in the final phase by the *nodal moment* and with it the re-activation of symbolic synthesis. This event sequence—the erotic transference, the extraordinary countertransference, and the return to symbolic synthesis—will be the subject matter for the remainder of this chapter.

Each of these events carries its own set of unique dynamic controversies, the implications having been voiced in the annals of analytic writings. Once more we have selected particular voices as guides: Gabbard on the Erotic Transference, Lasky in his understanding of countertransference, and Loewald as well as Nunberg in their visions of symbolic synthesis.

The erotic transference and the aftermath

With the introduction of frankly erotic themes into the play of transference, a patient offers some of the most intimate private thoughts to the analyst, often in the form of raw affect, given with excitement, and signalling an intense transference engagement. The expression of erotic love is a component of transference love, having its own particular complexities. The erotic dimension contains ingredients of often dissociated, deeply conflictual relationship themes. Although Freud considered erotic longings an aspect of the positive transference, this has been challenged through an extensive literature over the decades. Blum (1973) introduced the term, the "erotized transference", stressing latent sadistic aspects: the expression of a wish to shame, humiliate, haunt, destroy, even torture the analyst. He regards the erotized transference as defensive: the patient plays out a personal drama in highly condensed form, signalling the desire to attain mastery over early childhood trauma. It is Janus-faced: in its libidinal layering, the sexual messages offer vitality to the treatment process, but in its dissociative substrate, conditions are created for impasse.

While the erotized transference may be communicated within the frame of a positive and even idealized transference, its implied dual message to the analyst often discombobulates even the most receptive clinician. Its emergence is a form of enactment and often results in feelings of confusion in the countertransference. In our specimen, it is not surprising that after the string of enactive sessions culminating in the *torture fantasy* of session 255, the patient might wish to express her desire to torture through other means. Once more, whereas the erotic transference may at first become the psychic soil for the expression of evocative, imagistic, and symbolized thought, it can also become the precursor to those countertransference enactments which result in a transference crisis.

The path to disentangling the destructive from the positive, idealizing erotic transference has been creatively suggested in Gabbard's essay "On Lust and Love in Erotic Transference" (1994). Some eroticized love may signal transference love gone awry. There is a voluminous literature of love affairs among our psychoanalytic founders, and Gabbard cites the romantic entanglements of Jung with Spielrein, Fromm Reichman with Erich Fromm, Margaret Mahler with August Aichorn, and Karen Horney with one of her patients. These episodes, the concretization of transference love, led to ended analyses.

Since in the erotized transference the sadistic components, implicit in the sexual experience, are dissociated and inaccessible to consciousness, Gabbard believes that the analyst must be able to maintain a stance of being both witness and participant in order to remain in touch. The ability to sustain such a stance is of course precisely what we aim at in any analytic treatment, but this becomes an especially challenging task when love and lust are dissociated in the patient, possibly dissociated in the analyst as well. The analyst might be quite conscious of the erotic themes but disregard the very personal libidinal tie, or hear the plea for love while not attending to the sadistic overtones. To us, the second eventuality can have more serious consequences in the countertransference. The analyst may attend to the content of the quest for love, yet be unable to hear the themes of personal attack. Such an event sequence may render the analyst helpless and evoke counter-sadistic wishes. An unconscious identification with the patient's sadism may arise leading to a destructive countertransference and then to transference regression, a return to equivalence, and the downward slope. Let us now turn to our clinical material.

Session 257: the opening phase and the peak of the symbolized transference

Ms Y began the hour with a reference to having cancelled the previous session due to severe back pain. Then she told a dream that felt to her like a nightmare. The day residue involved her husband having discovered a wild animal in their garden as he was attempting to bring their children from the car into the house. "I dreamt that I was in this cabin and there was a threat of a dangerous wild animal outside. Both the kids were on infant seats, and I had to get them before this animal got them."

Ms Y then turned to a playful image, a game she had played with her five-year-old son while lying on the couch nursing her back. He was sitting on his Lego bucket, pretending to poop in the potty, then spreading it everywhere. Her pleasure was palpable as she quoted her son, "I made mommy laugh." But the poop game evoked the ire of her husband, who with his foul mood, became withdrawn and an "oppressive presence" in the house.

The atmosphere in the session shifted dramatically as Ms Y then turned her attention to the analyst. After expressions of confusion, guilt, and remorse for not making her husband a priority, she revealed an elaborate rendition of her conflict-ridden erotic thoughts about her: "I feel like I've done something with you and with this process that's beyond just me coming here for help. I feel like I've intentionally made this a priority, as if I were having an affair. … It's odd, I started to have this fantasy of us making love, and our groin areas were pressed against each other, but what struck me, and what was different from other fantasies, is that it didn't feel satisfying to me and you didn't have a penis. And, even though you can put your finger inside of me you didn't, you weren't able to put, your penis, your, like, body inside of me." After some silence Ms Y states, "Jack's kind of the safety, secure person, but you're the exciting, uh, you know, you're the one I want to be even closer to ... and I thought maybe that's why, in the past I've gotten so angry that you haven't, given back, in my fantasy. Maybe in part it's why I criticize you, although I don't know."

* * *

Listeners' Observations: The session opened in the spirit of a symbolizing hour (the dream, the play with the son). In fact, the dream, told in vivid language represented a peak of referential activity. But darker themes emerged with the expression of contempt towards the husband. The explicit erotic transference was stated with passion and guilt, and what began as an imagistic, evocative, symbolized hour, now turned towards transference regression.

Following Gabbard, this erotic surge could be seen as an expression of a state of lust, appearing as *a thing apart*, removed from the earlier "poop game", a scene of warm, playful, mother-child love. Lust was initially dissociated from love, but towards lust she then fled. In a state of imagined mutual arousal, Ms Y permitted herself to voice feelings of anger, manifestly aimed at the husband but implicitly directed towards the analyst. The analyst had not given her what she wanted, for she lacked a penis.

The shadow from earlier sessions of familiar outbreaks of wishes to inflict torture or humiliation, or to see the analyst in a state of psychic impotence, can also be discerned here. This surfacing of frank sexual desire (within the context of contempt for the husband) renders reasonable the hypothesis that this newly found expression was also a vehicle for attack by other means. The direct expression of lust ultimately left the patient confused, also sending a shock wave towards the listening analyst. Just how the analyst absorbed this shock is an unfolding story, but first, some theoretical reflections.

The extraordinary countertransference and the aftermath

The transference–countertransference dialogue has become the lore of contemporary mainstream psychoanalysis, though this very general notion can obscure crucial distinctions. Broadly speaking, everything we previously attributed to the *enactive phase* (Chapter Sixteen) has ingredients of what is often termed *countertransference enactment*. But in further defining this, a distinction needs to be made between what we call the *ordinary countertransference*—feelings towards the patient that remain within the analyst's conscious awareness and lead to a transitory disruption, and the *extraordinary countertransference*—feelings so intolerable to the analyst that they remain outside awareness and lead to impasse.

Historically, what we call the ordinary countertransference has its beginnings with Paula Heimann (1950), who emphasized the broad construction of countertransference: "all the feelings that the analyst experiences toward the patient" (p. 81). More formally speaking, it is in the area of the analyst's identification with the patient that the type of countertransference being encountered can be delineated. Following Racker (1957), both concordant and complementary identifications indicate that the patient is very much alive in the analyst's mind, but when this identification breaks down, we would say, the extraordinary countertransference has set in.

In a recent study (Freedman, Lasky & Webster, 2009), the extraordinary countertransference was specified as a breakdown in triangulation. Following Britton (1989), the analyst is in the dual position of subjectively experiencing herself as both participant and witness in relation to the patient. When the analyst combines these two perspectives, symbolizing space is created and analytic work can move forward; but when there has been an extraordinary disruption in the analytic process, symbolization breaks down. Moreover, when the analyst is confronted with the erotic transference, specific challenges to the countertransference may arise.

Lasky (2002) sharpened the concept of countertransference with a distinction that has a special relevance to our understanding of the analyst's experience of the erotic transference. In his essay, Lasky offers a case example with a vivid portrayal of the analyst's thoughts, desires, and fantasies, evoked by and as a counter to the patient's seduction. Lasky refers to his notion of the "analytic instrument" (similar to but significantly different from Isakower's analysing instrument (1992)), as the utilization of the analyst's internal world as a means of enabling a close attunement to the patient's inner life, thus facilitating the analytic process. This notion is similar to what we call the ordinary countertransference. Lasky crucially distinguishes the analytic instrument from "countertransference proper".

He reconnects to Freud's original meaning of countertransference, which emphasizes the process by which the analyst's neurotic unconscious unwittingly enacts in a way that counters the patient's transference. More specifically, Lasky believes that this countertransference proper becomes complementary to the patient's transference, that is, the analyst's unconscious fantasies become partners to the patient's fantasies. In Lasky's rendition of countertransference proper, he offers, through a case example, a vivid portrayal of the analyst's discovery of his own fantasies as they match, but also counter, similar unconscious thoughts inherent in the patient's provocations (e.g., fleeting scenes of torture and punishment). Such parallel experiences can drag the analyst down unconsciously and, if not contained, have the effect of dragging the patient and the analysis down as well. Following our earlier formulation that the erotic transference can evoke a continuation of sadistic attack, we would have to say that in this countertransference configuration, a dialogue of reciprocal sadistic fantasies can result—two unconscious fantasies interacting with one another.

Any confirmation of this line of thought—namely, the patient's unconscious wish to attack and the analyst's unconscious counter-attack—poses difficult methodological issues for the study of recorded psychoanalysis. We can document the patient's erotic transference, for it is expressed in spoken words. Similarly, we can discern the analyst's sudden, unexpected counter-attack, where she functions not at her usual level. Concurrently, we can also show that the patient then gets dragged down in the regressive process. But what cannot be documented are the crucial intervening events, namely, the possible unconscious sadistic fantasies that get stirred up in both participants. For this, we now turn to our research procedure, outlined in Chapter Thirteen, a method that might bring clarification to the ambiguity inherent in the presumed dialogue of sadistic fantasies. This will be followed by the clinical material.

Session 257: the middle phase and desymbolization in the face of the extraordinary countertransference

To elucidate the presence of countertransference fantasies in this phase, we resorted to our method of comparing the scan to the session. We looked for evidence of distortions in the analyst's memory of the session manifest in deletions and alterations in event sequences. This allowed us to trace difficulties in identification with the patient and/or the patient's inner objects. As a baseline, we used for comparison another A session and its scan, session 232, the first session of this transformation cycle.

In this scan, we found a near exact chronological rendition of the content of the session and a good match in the recounting of the patient's major concerns. Throughout the scan, the analyst interjected her reactions to and theoretical understanding of the patient's material. But the scan for session 257 diverged markedly from this pattern.

First, it was twice as long as that of 232. The analyst was clearly stirred and involved. Rather than interjecting her reactions and dynamic understanding of the material throughout the scan, she left this to the very end. Secondly, the events of the session were reported out of order: the opening dream was omitted and the "poop game" was remembered as having occurred later in the session. Instead the analyst began the scan with the tremendous anger of the weekend between the patient and her husband. Furthermore, the analyst may have been defending against possible discomfort stirred up by the patient's frank erotic fantasy, for she seemed strikingly "cool" in the scan in relation to the erotic transference—a transference that might have been discombobulating. Another notable discrepancy between scan and session was around an important moment about to be described, in which the analyst shifted her identification, voicing support for the husband while the patient was expressing profound dissatisfaction with him. This shift and the patient's subsequent regression were omitted in the scan. Let us now turn to this important moment in the session.

After voicing her erotic fantasy, Ms Y gave a very detailed account of the fighting with her husband during the weekend. Although they made efforts to stay connected, she was clearly furious with him and guilt ridden about her aggression. She returned to her erotic desire for the analyst, stating again, "I am afraid that I am playing something out in here." The analyst inquired: "What do you think you are playing out? ... From the beginning you told me, I remember you telling me once that you will wear me down, that ultimately you would get what you wanted from me ... and that if it wasn't me ... it could have been anyone." Ms Y conceded to the suggestion, adding: "Yeah, I think so, um, I think it's trying to connect with someone in a way that I can't connect with Jack, so I'm left feeling unfulfilled." The analyst questioned this, saying: "What is this way of connection? 'Cause Jack certainly sounds like he's very interested in being connected with you."

* * *

Listeners' Observations: In the last intervention, the analyst appears to have lost her identification with her patient's inner feelings. This "attack" seemed to have brought home to Ms Y a feeling of overwhelming badness, leaving her bereft.

* * *

After a silence, Ms Y continues: "I'm getting a headache. [11 second silence] ... I kind of have glimpses but [10 second silence, crying] but I don't get it [56 second silence]." She tries to associate further, falls into a 34 second silence and then states: "I'm not thinking very well right now. It's just because, I'm, [crying] it's not very clear [19 second silence] ...."

* * *

Listeners' Observations: A moment of extraordinary countertransference had taken its toll. But happily the destructive dialogue that seems to stem from the analyst's difficulty tolerating Ms Y's erotic fantasies, a derivative of the torture fantasy that pervades this transformation cycle, is not the end of this session. Once more we will encounter a reversal in the form of another *nodal moment*, and rather fascinatingly, a return to symbolic synthesis.

The preservation of the analytic process

Now we reach a central problematic in relation to *working through*, as it appears within the course of this specimen. Thus far, at the end of each phase of the cycle, we have seen signs of reversal and re-symbolization in the direction of the upward slope. Though there were instances of increased metabolization on the part of the analyst, there were also signs of withdrawal and/or attack, leading nonetheless to unexpected attainment within the patient of new symbolic forms. Such an achievement reached its most explicit manifestation in the session under discussion. How was Ms Y able to attain this? In her regressive reaction to the analyst's assault, Ms Y seemed to suffer not only a moment of inner despair, but also a sudden confrontation with apparent object loss. How can a patient, preoccupied with external attack, move towards the refinding of an inner object? How can the path of overcoming the impact of a moment of extraordinary countertransference be formulated? The issue is a broad one. Abend (1989), in a review article, confirms this quandary in his statement that a process of ego synthesis can sometimes be created in the face of the analyst's narcissistic preoccupation and breakdown of objective self-awareness. This is a line of thought implicit in the writings of Nunberg and Loewald, which will be elaborated below, but let us return to the clinical material.

Session 257: the final phase and the return to the symbolized transference

After a long pause, Ms Y attempted to consolidate her thoughts. Referring to the husband, Ms Y noted: "We hugged each other this morning and told each other that we love each other. We just both felt sad. Jack said he felt sad, and I feel bad too. But I feel more complicated than just sad."

After a 37 second silence, Ms Y associated to her chiropractor, who had encouraged her to call him at home over the weekend if her back pain worsened. She spoke of how making the call had become conflictual because of her crush on him and of fantasies of making love to him on the chiropractic table. "My fantasies get in the way so much that I feel so uncomfortable calling, because I feel like, oh no I know who his wife is and she's so nice, I really like her but, you know I'm like, in my head I'm after her husband."

Reflecting upon the phone message that she finally did leave, Ms Y spoke of having felt so upset to the point of tears: "I wish that I had said hi to his wife or I wish I had, you know, just, given more of myself. ... I really wanted to give of myself and I just couldn't, I just, absolutely withdrew and just left just the minimum ... information ... and how upset and pained it made me afterwards because I wasn't giving what was inside of me, that I wanted to give just naturally, because my fantasies get so full-blown."

* * *

Listeners' Observations: The regressive episode was reversed through a *nodal moment* (the chiropractor scene), where the articulation of

Oedipal conflict led Ms Y to poignantly reflect upon her pain of not having lived up to her ego ideal.

* * *

This is the end of the hour and the occasion for the final scan of this transformation cycle. The analyst concludes her remarks with the following: "I am impressed with how far she's come in being able throughout the session to have intense feelings and observe them at the same time. This is really quite a growth for her I think. She's able to reflect on these things, and I mean there really is evidence of some symbolization here. I think that that's what you would call it—the ability to symbolize and to think about her own fantasies and to use them, which is quite different than even a year ago. Certainly different than two years ago."

It is clear that the analyst took pride in her patient, pleasure in their work together, and resonated with what her patient had experienced. It had been a difficult session, and the end seemed to be a toss in the direction of closure to a difficult transference–countertransference crisis.

Reflections on the cycle and the spiral

This hour offers an unusual exemplar of a process that stretches from *rupture to repair*. In it we find a particular nonlinear progression involving the re-finding of a *good object*, a gradient of internalization with increased reflectivity, and the overcoming of paradox through the *state of play*. These processes enable Ms Y to move beyond cyclic repetition in the direction of a *spiralling* process. In Chapter Thirteen, we presented statistical evidence in support of our hypothesis that this cycle leads to a spiral transformation, but now we can supplement this assertion with a qualitative interpretation of this final hour.

The analytic process can be preserved through the implementation of the synthetic function of the ego, occurring even at moments of countertransference crisis, when the patient's state of consciousness may be blurred and confused. At such moments, there may ensue a surge towards repair, towards the recapturing of the lost object, and towards the sorting out of conflictual promptings—all within the frame of time unfolding. Through the mobilization of latent synthetic resources, symbolizing can be activated and a spiralling process perhaps initiated. The denouement just described, occurring after apparent impasse, can best be accounted for in terms of the patient's yearning for a *good object*. This phenomenon affirms Nunberg's basic view (1931), alluded to above (and elaborated below in Chapter Eighteen), that the synthetic function of the ego is guided by the force of libido.

This motivational source has been affirmed throughout many quarters: as a surge of positive affect activating the "alpha function" (Steiner, 1993), a crisis leading to the creation of a state of unification with the object (Beland, 1994), and perhaps most crucially, as an experience of impasse stirring belief in the "good" object (Bion). When, in session 257, Ms Y returned to a symbolizing mode of thought, she might well have done so aided by the hope and belief that the crisis had passed. Hope is a powerful motivator of repair; not simply hope expected, but hope confirmed.

Another aspect of the spiralling process can be described in the language of object relations and internalization. Loewald's notion of a gradient of internalization unfolding over time is suggested here. He introduces this at the end of his essay, "Internalization, Separation, Mourning, and the Superego" (1962). Internalization, in part, involves the capacity to mourn one's inability to live up to one's ego ideal. In the last few minutes of this session, with the revelation of the erotic fantasy involving the chiropractor, Ms Y reflects upon her guilt towards the wife and expresses pain at how her fantasies "get so full blown". With this recognition, Ms Y achieved a gradient of internalization. For Loewald, the process of internalization takes place over many years of analysis, but here, an aspect was revealed in analogue form, taking but a few minutes for the ego to achieve a measure of synthesis.

Perhaps the most persuasive aspect of the spiralling nature of *working through* is its nonlinearity, as reflected in the very structure of this hour. The three phases of this session depict a mini-transformation cycle and contain paradoxical elements within each: the symbolizing phase was highlighted by the paradox of erotic longings, the yearning for love, and perhaps the desire to humiliate; the regressive phase contained psychic blankness and perhaps also a plea for love; and the re-symbolizing phase might have contained a yearning for remorse and even the undoing of guilt.

The contradictory, even paradoxical, aspects inherent in the peaks and troughs of this session reverberated in the analyst's process of listening. In her scan, the analyst heard the erotic longings of the symbolizing phase, was unable to take in the plea for help during the extraordinary countertransference of the regressive phase, yet was ultimately able to resonate with her patient and rejoice in her symbolizing work. The nonlinear motion of *working through* had found its mirror in the course of the countertransference.

With this third aspect of the spiralling process, some reflections are called for regarding the word *paradox*. Throughout this study, we have emphasized the phenomenon of paradox, and in Chapter Fourteen, with the introduction of the *nodal moment*, we held that symbolization is preceded, indeed created by paradox. Why paradox, not conflict?

Paradox refers to the simultaneous impact of contradictory, incompatible, and irreconcilable conflictual experiences, defying resolution at the very moment they occur. Paradoxes appear to be irresolvable. As Ghent (1992) notes, "A paradox must be accepted on its own terms, without resolution, and at the same time, valued as a pointer to a new level of comprehension" (p. 135). But underlying every moment of paradox is a potential process through which the paradox can be reconciled and apprehended. The transformation from paradox to process is the task of analytic work—that of creating symbolizing space.

Frankel (in press), in his work on the "foundational transference", has suggested the intriguing hypothesis that in analysis, such transformative space is created through what he terms a "state of play". This state is not merely equivalent to symbolization, but is that state that in analysis is the genesis of symbolization. It is a state which in its peaks and troughs can facilitate the process of meaning making. We believe that such a state of consciousness was present in each phase of session 257: in the first phase with the "poop game", we noted a pretend mode of thought—as in play; with the emergence of erotic longings, the patient perhaps felt "naughty" and provocative—as in play; in the middle phase during the extraordinary countertransference, action and counteraction was evoked—as in play; and in the final phase, the chiropractor fantasy resulted in mutual admiration—as in play. Each instance of play facilitated a process of meaning making, each instance of paradox resolved into symbolic form.

In this unusual session, with its peaks and troughs of mental functioning, we do observe a spiral, affirming the view of change that transcends psychic repetition. It revealed itself in the overcoming of the extraordinary countertransference, where both analyst and patient were ultimately able to affirm an intensely felt libidinal tie; in the gradient of internalization, where the patient was able to mourn with greater affect how she had fallen short of her ego ideal; and finally, in how the state of play reached a range of metaphor from new depths to new heights. Here we find the essential ingredients of *Progressive Symbolization*, which will be elaborated in our next and concluding chapter.

CHAPTER EIGHTEEN

Nodal moments and the essence of Progressive Symbolization

Norbert Freedman and Rhonda Ward

The question is: "What have we learned about *working through*?" For some authors, this concept, given to us by Freud in 1914, is too vague, too all-encompassing, refers simply to a higher level of compromise formation, and hence should be discarded. Notwithstanding this pessimistic assessment, we undertook a specimen study, using the *Propositional Method* to illuminate the specific components of *working through*. We examined a transformation cycle, delineated its four phases, and distilled the specifics of each.

To review, within every phase we noted a paradoxical move: the initial symbolizing phase was marked by the appearance of induced transference regression and with it the onset of the *downward slope* (Chapter Fourteen); the desymbolizing phase, one of unambiguous regression, contained at critical junctures *nodal moments*, signs of reversal and signifiers of the *upward slope* (Chapter Fifteen); the enactive phase, marked by both patient and analyst centered enactments, culminated in higher symbolic forms (Chapter Sixteen); and the re-symbolizing phase, with the appearance of a frankly erotic transference, contained a mini-cycle, a recapitulation of the previous phases, leading to both higher as well as lower levels of symbolic functioning (Chapter Seventeen).

Then through a closer look at these initial findings, we formulated an overriding multi-dimensional concept descriptive of *working through*, which we termed *Progressive Symbolization* with four definable components. Incrementally within the specimen, Ms Y assimilated a symbolizing mode of mental organization (component 1); found herself pulled into a more intense intersubjective engagement with her analyst (component 2); was able to survive the inroads of disruptive countertransference enactments (component 3); and arrived at a new level of ego synthesis (component 4). This is a portrait of analytic process deserving the name *working through*, or in our language, *Progressive Symbolization*.

Having reviewed our overall findings, we would now like to single out for discussion one particular phenomenon, that of the *nodal moment*, for it contains in its structure and dynamics essential aspects of *Progressive Symbolization*. The *nodal moment*, for us at first a discovery, was ultimately found in all phases of the cycle, appearing as a reversal at points of regression and creating symbolizing space. Now it may well be that one *nodal moment* begets the next, that when strung together they depict the trajectory of *Progressive Symbolization*, and furthermore, that each *nodal moment*, no matter when it arises, may have its invariant core (reminding us of Freud and the compulsion to repeat).

Thus, *nodal moments* and their varied role in the analytic process will be the subject for the remainder of this concluding chapter. We will first explore *nodal moments* as instances of symbolic transformation; then how *nodal moments* in sequence define the trajectory of *Progressive Symbolization*; and finally, how their invariant core can be the site of therapeutic action.

Nodal moments as pathways to symbolic knowing

Every *nodal moment* is an act of transformation. We advanced the thesis that the transformations inherent in the *nodal moment* involve the invocation of a highly conflictual, traumatic, unconscious fantasy, which at that very point finds representation. It highlights a process of movement from a state of non-representation to one of representation, a shift from disorganization to reorganization. Strictly speaking, the *nodal moment* is not simply a *moment*, but a process encapsulated within a short time space: it marks a process that separates out throttled desire of a conflictual nature and prepares the way for the articulation of that desire. More specifically, it marks a process where latent triangular conflicts and wishes can be represented so that integrative functioning can be restored.

As seen in the descriptions of *nodal moments* in Chapter Fifteen, they have distinct constituents. There first occurs a period of apparent non-representation, or "messiness", as Harrison and Tronick (2007) would call it, which is redundant, concretized, replete with conflictual albeit throttled desire, reliant upon primary process thought, and driven by an unsymbolized triangular force. This quality of "messiness" or "stuckness" is the impetus for an implicit or explicit turn towards the object. Only then is translation realized through the *nodal moment* proper, where first there is a nonverbal impasse of blocking, hesitation, then a burst of affect, followed by the owning of affect carried by transference utterances in which the triangular conflict is sorted out and communicated. Desire then receives symbolic form in the language of secondary process.

Every *nodal moment* is also activated by a shift in position towards the object. Thus, it is simultaneously an act of conflict resolution as well as an intensification of the transference. This leads us to the notion of intersubjectivity, the second component of *Progressive Symbolization*, and it is in this context that the *nodal moment* invites comparison to a related yet distinctly different notion, the *now moment*.

The *now moment*, like our *nodal moment*, signifies a crucial organizer of change in the course of a given session. Advanced by the Boston Change Process Study Group (1998), this concept describes a shared communicative event between patient and analyst that presages psychic shifts yet to come. It embodies a surge of shared emotional experience arising in the context of mutual regulation, leading to a coming together—a meeting of meaning—and it marks the activation of procedural memories, not conflictual, not conscious (but not unconscious in the dynamic sense).

A critical examination of the assumptions underlying the *now moment*, and more generally, implicit relational knowing, has been set forth in a recent paper by S. J. Ellman and Moskowitz (2008). They argue that it is in the pivotal role of symbol formation in the development of psychic representations that we find the fault line between a Freudian and a Relational perspective. Conflict must be symbolized in order for change to take place. Symbol formation in Melanie

Klein's historic 1923 paper is born of the conflicts arising in the earliest phases of human life, appearing first as symbolic equations and then as true symbols. Ellman and Moskowitz (2008) affirm that different Freudian theories place symbol formation at different points of development; however, in each model there is the recognition of the progressive integration of something felt, symbolized, and synthesized. In each we find the transplantation and translation of *raw* emotional experiences into symbolic form.

We agree that the line of demarcation between a Freudian and a Relational vision of change lies in the symbolization of conflict, and we conclude that in the *nodal moment* we observe symbolization through transplantation and translation. We now turn to Freud, who recognized in his earliest work the dual role of conflict emerging within the state of intimate relatedness.

Freud's "nodal moments"

During the mid-1890s and the early 20th century, from *Studies in Hysteria* to *Dora* and the *Rat Man*, Freud's clinical thinking was permeated by the notion of a *nodal point*—a singular, evocative percept that functioned as a dynamic signifier, stringing together the historical roots of a core conflict and casting its shadow on the awareness of transference. In his psychotherapy of hysteria, Freud (1895) describes successive events emanating from a nodal biographical thread, extending along irregular and twisting paths from the surface to the deepest layer and back to the present. The threads form divergent and convergent lines, and contain nodal points, often uniting to move forward as one. The detail of this zigzagging of lines surrounding a nodal organizing point is impressive and reached the peak of specificity in Freud's 1909 account of the *Rat Man*.

The *rat story* is a gruesome tale of rats invading the anus of their victim, told to Freud's patient by a cruel army captain. It is a tale told and retold to Freud by the Rat Man, an obsessive-compulsive patient, and, as told, it spells out the kernel of the conflicts inherent in the pathological syndrome. The rat image strings together signifiers which contain the historical roots important to the Rat Man and which come alive in the transference. The *rat world* functions as a *nodal point*, a term used by Freud and elaborated in an interpretive reading of the text by Schneiderman (1986). "Rat" is a word that denotes an image of cruelty, of aversion and disgust ("the big fat rat"). It contains the patient's fear of sexuality and of his desire (rats carry diseases like penises). It carries fantasies of being swallowed up and overwhelmed ("the number of invading rats"), and is connected to the memory of his dead sister, whom he bit at a young age. Linguistically, it is also an image of indebtedness (the word *raten* in German refers to debt), of the conflict of money and love between his father and mother (*heiraten* is to marry in German), and of his father's criminal history of not paying his debt, miserliness in general (*ratten* means instalments in German). This nodal point functioned as a condensed symbolic structure.

The successive scenes that branch out from the telling of the rat torture to Freud allow us to observe how the translation comes about. The tale of the rat torture is addressed to a suffering victim dear to his heart, to his father, his lady, and many others, spiralling towards Freud, in the explicit transference. Having appeared, the image of the rat is contained in all the crucial scenes in the analysis, and expresses the Rat Man's deep conflict between love and hate. It serves as a way to preserve the affection he hopes to receive from his analyst as well as to establish the differentiation between Freud the analyst and Freud the imagined torturer.

Let us turn to the session where the Rat Man tells the rat story to Freud. In that session the Rat Man became very confused and incoherent, could not fill in the story, paced around the room, begged Freud not to *torture* him by making him say what he was thinking, and finally in a slip, called Freud "Captain" (Freud, 1909, p. 69). When the Rat Man finally explained the rat torture scene, Freud noted the look of disgust and excitement on his face, revealing both his fear and pleasure in the anal-sadistic wish.

This *nodal moment* marked an intensification of the transference. At that point, it was Freud and it was not Freud whom he addressed. Freud was both the "cruel captain" and not the cruel captain, for as the Rat Man noted, Freud was also the friend (German: *Freund*). Having articulated this nodal point, this traumatic moment was now transplanted through displacement into the scene of the transference. It was not simply a slip of the tongue or a terrible tale, but it marked a shift in position towards the object. For us, this is a *nodal moment*, that is, the symbolization of the core dynamic conflict.

Nodal moments *and their role in* Progressive Symbolization

Having affirmed the crucial role of the *nodal moment* as an act of transformation, we would now like to describe how this psychic event contributes to the deepening of the analytic process. In viewing the *nodal moments* successively, it appears that one moment begets the next. We will revisit the four components of *Progressive Symbolization* and discuss how the *nodal moments* strung together reveal a gradient of change, the understanding of which enhances our portrait of *Progressive Symbolization*.

The first salient component of *Progressive Symbolization* is the increased mobilization of more complex aspects of mental functioning. We have previously described such events as a move from the desymbolized to the symbolized, or a shift from the sub-symbolic towards the symbolic, as marked by the unfolding of the referential process. But replaying the *nodal moments* across the specimen, we also found an important gradient: symbolization was first implied, then made explicit in the transference, then elaborated into verbalized fantasies and memories reflected upon, peaking with the expression of the imaginary not previously articulated. The unsymbolized became part of a felt actuality.

To illustrate, out of desymbolized despair, the *church scene* of session 243 represented an implicit move from psychic equivalence to the use of triangular space (God as the idealized source of unification); the *nodal moment* in session 245 reflected an explicit move towards the naming of triangular conflict; in session 247, in the *college professor scene*, both recent memories as well as memories of early vintage became intertwined with the imaginary, leading to self-reflection; in session 249, the further interweaving of memory and fantasy led to the outburst in the form of an enacted symbol; and most strikingly in session 255, out of the unusual interplay between a remote memory from a year earlier and the uncanny feeling of familiarity when the analyst left the room to vomit, came the verbalization of an elaborate torture fantasy of the analyst in a humiliating state of absolute helplessness. This all culminated with the superego reprimand, "I wish I just had that compassionate reaction."

The second component, or major organizer of *Progressive Symbolization*, is the intensification of intersubjectivity. The expression of desire, no matter how fragmented or desymbolized, contains intersubjective aspects. Through the enhancement of intersubjectivity, a kind of interpenetration between analyst and patient, psychoanalytic treatment comes to life. In Chapter Fifteen we asked: "Why should a patient moored in the morass of concreteness engage in the direction of symbolized representation?" Our answer, guided by the work of Klein and more recently Friedman, is that it always implies a shift in position towards the object. Indeed, there are distinct ways in which such alterations come about and different types of intersubjective engagement, and in surveying our *nodal moments* this kind of gradient becomes evident.

The *church scene* of session 243 reflected an implicit turn towards the object, while in session 245 the analyst became the explicitly named addressee. Following the college memory of drunkenness in session 247, there occurred a moment of mutual recognition on the body level when both their stomachs growled, an instance of an analytic third. Finally, in session 249, the enacted symbol ("looking down on you sitting") and the explosion, "I don't like your outfit", were provocative and virulent expressions designed to further impact the analyst.

This incremental movement towards shared intimacy is a sine qua non of intersubjectivity. Here we see how each member of the dyad becomes alive in the other's consciousness (Bach, 2006), how each member can impact the other through affective interpenetration (S. J. Ellman, 2007; Grunes, 1984), and how shared intimacy is revealed through what Benjamin (2004) refers to as the psychosomatic rhythmic analytic third, a synthesis of three images: the patient, the analyst, and dyad—all coming together at a crucial moment. Here *Progressive Symbolization*, rooted in intrapsychic conflict, culminates in a moment of coming together.

The third component of *Progressive Symbolization*, challenging to be sure, rests on the paradoxical aspects of its nonlinearity. The fact that *Progressive Symbolization* involves phasic oscillations, paradoxical movements, and moments of reversal has been documented. However, when the analyst loses her identification with her patient, when there is a breakdown of the boundaries between her role as observer and participant, and yet the patient continues to respond to the presence of the analyst in her path to symbolization, then we are challenged in our understanding of the analytic process. This juxtaposition of forces reflects the patient's ability to survive countertransference enactment. The tension inherent in this dialogue must be overcome in order for working through to take place. Such moments of nonlinearity represent a *thing apart* in our quest to understand *Progressive Symbolization*, and such discontinuities were noted in our specimen.

In session 245, the patient, after a prolonged period of desymbolization, with the analyst silent and seemingly remote, suddenly recouped, was able to choose, and affirmed her commitment to the analyst: "That's a very strong tie." Despite apparent disengagement on the part of the analyst, a *nodal moment* ensued. A similar instance of reversal was noted in the shift from session 254, a session of paralysis born of mutual enactment, to session 255, where imagination evoked the telling of a torture scene. Equally striking was the extraordinary countertransference sequence in session 257: following the patient's elaboration of the erotic transference, the analyst shifted identification in support of the husband. This led the patient in the direction of a brief regressive episode, then to a recovery with a nodal moment and a measure of self-reflection.

These are analyst-induced instances of what Tronick and Cohn (1989) would call mismatch and repair. Such nonlinearity has also been articulated in studies of infancy observations (Beebe & Lachmann, 1994). When a child is confronted with the mother's misattunement, the ensuing response is a heightened affective engagement by the child as an attempt to recapture the lost caretaker.

The fourth component of *Progressive Symbolization*, one that is overriding and metapsychologically driven, is that of the synthetic function of the ego. Our clinical observations were compelling. When we wished to account for increased complexity of mind, intensification of intersubjectivity, the resolution of countertransference tension, culminating in a spiralling effect, we could not escape the gnawing question regarding the underlying driving force. To answer this question, we will take a brief historical detour, concerning the basic assumption, first formulated by Freud, then articulated by Nunberg, of the organizing impact of ego synthesis.

In 1919 Freud took note that a form of psychosynthesis could be achieved, apart from any interventions "automatically and inevitably" (p. 161). In a later paper, he noted that this was a process of unification, in which "this necessity to synthesize grows stronger in proportion as the strength of the ego increases" (1926a, p. 98). Nunberg (1931) elaborated this view, equating this synthetic function with the force of Eros and libido. For Nunberg, synthesis had the quality of an impulse.

Elaborating his 1931 paper, Nunberg (1955) maintained that "the synthetic function ... manifests itself in the assimilation of external and internal elements, in reconciling conflicting ideas, in uniting contrasts, and in activating mental creativity" (p. 151). This vision of unification was challenged by Hartmann (1951), who emphasized the distinction between integration and synthesis, where integration depends on "the neutralization of aggression" whereas synthesis indeed is guided by libido. Hartmann thus maintained that the concept of synthesis should be widened "to comprise not only libidinal, but also non-libidinal tendencies" (p. 386). Indeed, every *nodal moment* in our specimen was preceded by the onslaught of acute conflict, resulting in fragmentation and destructiveness needing *integration* before the possibility of synthesis. Integration of aggression is as important as unification.

But to us, this issue was laid to rest some 30 years later in Loewald's (1960) paper, "On the Therapeutic Action of Psycho-Analysis". There he saw the task of unification as mediated by the synthesizing power of object relations. He states:

> The transference neurosis takes place in the influential presence of the analyst and, as the analysis progresses, more and more "in the presence" and under the eyes of the patient's observing ego. The scrutiny, carried out by the analyst and by the patient, is an organizing, "synthetic" ego-activity. The development of an ego function is dependent on interaction. One could say that in the analytic process this environmental element, as happens in the original development, becomes increasingly internalized as what we call the observing ego of the patient (p. 19).

Reviewing the *nodal moments* in our specimen, we note of course that each by definition could be viewed as a shift from an *un-neutralized*, sadistically driven, fragmented event into a unified form. Hartmann might ask if these are acts of defensive integration or of libidinally motivated synthesis. When a quality marking the creation of an "analytic third" emerges with the progression of our *nodal moments*, we cannot help but be impressed with the unifying drive towards synthesis. And when in the face of the analyst's countertransference enactment in session 257, the crisis was resolved by calling upon an inner sense of morality (vis-à-vis the chiropractor's wife), creating a new kind of moral reality, we could conclude that the synthetic function was motivated by an effort to placate a sadistic superego. But in reviewing the clinical scan for this last session of the cycle, where the analyst voiced appreciation of how far the patient had come in her ability to symbolize her conflicts, then we must affirm the libidinal, object seeking role of ego synthesis.

Nodal moments and therapeutic action

We wish to refocus our inquiry and ask: what are the special properties inherent in *nodal moments*, no matter when they arise? Clearly, these events are inherently evocative and unforgettable for both patient and analyst. They represent selective replays of traumatic moments traceable to latent roots, and are shaped and re-interpreted within the context of the analytic dialogue.

But there is one further common denominator: every *nodal moment* contains the seed of an essential invariance, and hence is the staging ground for transformation. This notion of invariance is a key idea advanced by Bion (1965) in his treatise on *Transformations*:

> Suppose a painter sees a path through a field sown with poppies and paints it: at one end of the chain of events is the field of poppies, at the other a canvas with pigment disposed on its surface. We can recognize that the latter represents the former, so I shall suppose that despite the differences between a field of poppies and a piece of canvas, despite the transformation that the artist has effected in what he saw to make it take the form of a picture, *something* has remained unaltered and on this *something* recognition depends. The elements that go to make up the unaltered aspect of the transformation I shall call invariants (p. 1, italics in original).

We propose that the greater the distance from the invariant core to the scene in which it reappears, the more profound the transformation. The new context may even be antithetical, following Ricoeur (1970), who held that transformation is an issue of thesis, antithesis, and synthesis. The painting in Bion's example may well be a very modernistic version—one at great distance from the field of poppies; yet the essential invariance that alludes to the bed of flowers can still be discerned. When Mohamed *tortured* his analyst by likening his plight to an imaginary drowning scene, it was at a distance from his suffering during incarceration. Through transference he had travelled a long way, psychically speaking (Chapter Eight). For Ms K, the image of the dead kitten was transformed over many years of treatment into an image of a rescued, nourished, loved cat, though the invariant—the threat of death—remained a constant (Chapter Ten). And for Ms Y, the invariant—the torture image—was at first disavowed (session 232), but then became progressively embedded in symbolizing space by session 257.

Every *nodal moment* is an invitation to confront the invariant core, and with each juncture there is the challenge to transform these instances into new contexts through the use of the imaginary. Here we revisit an essential aspect of Winnicott's work, namely, that symbolization is formed at points of transition—*nodal moments*, as developmental moments—resolving invariance within transitional space. Herein lies the therapeutic action of *nodal moments*.

Recapitulation and perspective

Through the study of *nodal moments*, as they emerged in successive sessions of our specimen, we have sketched out our version of the *working through* concept, *Progressive Symbolization*. This is a multidimensional notion highlighted by four components, advanced at first as four propositions to be confirmed, and then elaborated upon through detailed clinical observations.

The first component, the move towards a more symbolizing state of consciousness, revealed a gradient from experiences reported, then elaborated through fantasy, and then reflected upon. The second component defined the heightening of intersubjective engagement, where desire was at first sensed in one and then both participants, leading to a felt interpenetration of affect. The third component dealt with the survival of the symbolizing process in the face of countertransference enactments. Finally, the fourth component, strengthened by a metapsychological assumption, stressed that the moves implied in the first three components can not occur without recourse to the libidinal drive towards ego synthesis.

It was our understanding of the structure and dynamics contained within the *nodal moment*, no matter when it occurs, that enabled us to discern its therapeutic action. Each *nodal moment* is an act of transformation in which the patient seeks to overcome a fundamental invariance—the task of transformation. This leads to the final question: what is the nature and scope of the transformation encompassed by our formulations of *Progressive Symbolization*?

Surely, the transformation of which we are speaking is not the lengthy modification of stable psychic structures (Rapaport & Gill, 1959); nor is it the transitory modification of dominant moods described by Jacobson (1957); but rather, the modification of mind that may traverse both, namely the creation through the analytic process of the metaphoric mind. It is in relation to this state of consciousness that our four components find participation. The imaginary inherent in metaphoric thought is the icon for psychoanalytic thought. As poignantly described by Modell (1988), metaphor implies a self that is engaged in the life of others, a shift from involuntary to voluntary repetition. When experiences are all in the present, they can be crazy making, but with metaphor they are given space. Through the use of open and fluid metaphor, the self becomes the transformer, promoting a shift from a passive to an active, generative mode of thought. It implies a shift towards a higher state of consciousness where frozen images can be transformed. It frees us from the onslaught of overwhelming internal or external input. It implies a very fundamental shift from language to mind to brain. This is the mode of overcoming the dependence on invariance.

It is the transformation of invariance towards metaphoric thought that defines our vision of the *symbolization of the analytic process*.

POSTSCRIPT

Towards a psychoanalytic definition of symbolization and desymbolization

Norbert Freedman, Rhonda Ward, and Jamieson Webster

Much attention in this volume has been given to the concepts of symbolization and desymbolization. We have defined them empirically through the *referential process*, and our understanding of these notions, derived in large measure from several decades of psychoanalytic literature, has informed our interpretation of the clinical material (Freedman, 1997; Freedman & Berzofsky, 1995; Freedman & Russell, 2003). In this Postscript, we will attempt to spell out these concepts in the language of psychoanalysis.

On symbolization

Symbolization, as it has evolved over a century of psychoanalytic writing, has a unique meaning that transcends its cognitive linguistic counterpart. Both versions, linguistic and psychoanalytic, can be revealed in clinical observations.

Symbolization is meaning making. At its core, symbolization involves the process of linking and triangulation. Linguistically, all symbolization involves three components: the symbol or abstract signifier, the thing being signified, and the integration of such in the mind of the interpreting subject. By giving the signifier and that which is signified a shared meaning, a unity is created within a system that recognizes difference. Green (2004) translates this position into psychoanalytic parlance: "In symbolization, two parts of a broken unity are reunited; and the overall result can be considered not only as the rebuilding of a lost unity, but also as the creation of a third element that is distinct from the other two split-off parts" (p. 107). Indeed, symbolization is the act of integration. There are different visions that highlight just how symbolization takes place, richly contributing to our understanding of what makes for psychic integration. We will now translate these visions into six psychoanalytic dimensions, stating them in the form of clinical propositions.

Dimension 1: Symbolization is the integration of unformulated affective arousal with formulated spoken language. This is the essence of what Bucci (1985) calls the "referential" process, where symbolizing is the incorporation of the emotion schema of the subsymbolic into referential speech. The role of transformed arousal finds vivid illustration in Helen Keller's discovery of the symbol, "w-a-t-e-r". Keller rejoiced: "That living word awakened my soul, gave it light, hope, joy, and set it free" (1990, p. 15). This process was also documented in sessions 232 and 257 in the case of Ms Y (Chapters Thirteen, Fourteen, and Seventeen).

The notion of arousal as a substrate of symbolization dates back to the beginnings of psychoanalysis. It evokes Jones's understanding of symbolism and its relation to repression. Thus, the formula, "penis" (arousal) equals "snake" (symbol), implies a sequence: the signifier of arousal is a precondition for repression, which leads to its transformation into symbolic form. As Jones (1916) states, "Only what is repressed is symbolized; only what is repressed needs to be symbolized" (p. 116). This repression hypothesis as a necessary source of symbol formation has been criticized from many quarters (e.g., Loewald, 1988b). Bucci's (2007a, 2007b) dissociation hypothesis is yet another example of this current trend. For her, a strong affective burst, first registered in the sub-symbolic sphere, is transformed at the peak of referential activity. But more generally, it is still considered true that strong affective erotic or sadistic wishes, with their psychic roots inaccessible to consciousness, play a major role in the shaping of symbolic forms.

Dimension 2: Symbolization is a process of integration through the subject's shift in position towards the object. Here we refer to the shift from a persecutory disorganized state of consciousness (the paranoid-schizoid position) to one that is organized and integrated (the depressive position). This is the essence of Klein's (1930) vision in "The importance of Symbol-Formation in the Development of the Ego", elaborated by Segal (1957), in which they rejected Jones's "repression hypothesis" and advanced their own vision of symbol formation. Klein considered this one of her most lasting contributions to psychoanalysis.

In this vision of a shift towards the depressive position, the patient not only expresses intense affects, but gives shape to an integrated "symbolic form" by finding connection to a "good object". The transference becomes elaborated with affect both evocative and provocative, yet the search for the good object prevails. Ms Y exclaims during a peak symbolizing hour (session 232): "I don't want to torture you; but on the other hand, I think. ... I don't want to let you off the hook too easy either until I understand" (Chapter Fourteen).

This vision of symbolic attainment has far-reaching implications for analytic work. To begin with, what is yearned for in the depressive position is not simply the actual object, but its ideal form; encountered is not merely the object of presence, but an internal object representation as well. Symbolic representations are generative as the symbol attained becomes available for new symbolic representations. The internal and the external, the past and the present are all brought together through symbolization, resulting in greater access to unconscious fantasy.

Dimension 3: Symbolization is an integration arising in transitional space. A moment arises in a particular state of consciousness—what Winnicott (1971) calls "transitional space"—a state in which self and object are not as yet differentiated, where there exists the potential for symbolization through allusion, illusion, and the use of the imaginary. While transitional space is rooted in early developmental events, such a state can be reactivated throughout life and can be translated into clinical observations. In the case of Ms Y (Chapter Fifteen), *nodal moments*, crucial signs of reversal towards symbolizing activity, were preceded by regressive, desymbolizing states. It can be said that they were born in "transitional space", wherein the "other" was felt to be absent, yet potentially present. Following Bion (1965), the creation of the imaginary other is rooted in a sense of hope for the finding or re-finding of a lost object. And yet while its source is potential, by creating a symbol that can be shared, the patient retains objectivity.

For Winnicott, illusions can be transformed into play—his metaphoric vision of transference, where projections can co-exist with the making of new forms. The familiar can be found in the unfamiliar. Magic evokes the imaginary, and with this, one reconnects to one's cultural base (the case of Mohamed, Chapter Eight).

Dimension 4: Symbolic integration is created through triangulation. Here the term *triangulation* is used not only in its linguistic sense, but also as a broadened psychoanalytic construction. The triangulation hypothesis is a crucial component of Green (1975), who summarizes his position with the aphorism, "[T]here is no such thing as a baby [quoting Winnicott] … there is no such couple formed by mother and baby, without the father" (p. 13). Here, Green's position coincides with Lacan's concept of "the symbolic", inherited through the Oedipus complex, as "the-name-of-the-father" (1979, p. 423). This *third* acts as a differentiating force and is a crucial ingredient of symbolization, namely, breaking up the closed unity of the dyadic. Hence, a third antagonistic voice, that which is not desired, is crucial for the emergence of creative thought.

We observed such a process in the case of Ms Y In our reading of *nodal moments*, the presence of the antagonistic third other precedes unification and the attainment of symbolic forms. Each *nodal moment* is followed by much reflective thought. Such observations underscore the dialectical nature of symbolization, and for Green, this nonlinear nature is a crucial component in forming the matrix of the mind.

Dimension 5: Symbolization is a process of integration dependent upon boundary definition, that is, the boundary between the signifier and the thing being signified. Loewald (1983) introduces this structural consideration when he notes that symbolization is a process of linking specific items of experience derived from different and distinct spheres of the mind, where one sphere represents the other. In his use of the words *distinct spheres*, boundary definition and the importance of psychic structure are stressed; in adding that one represents the other, Loewald describes a process of integration that in turn opens up new vistas. This structural view cuts across the four previous dimensions, for while the patient is faced with intense affect, is positioned towards the object, is evoking the imaginary, and is engaged in a triangular conflict, the presence of psychic structure remains a transcendent requirement.

Through boundary definition, meaning can be created. When two items inhabit the same space, as we shall see in our discussion of desymbolization below, confusion reigns. When boundaries are blurred, we are dealing with protosymbols at best, or in more extreme instances, with psychosis. Boundedness is created through symbolization. As Loewald (1988), contrasting his view with that of Jones, contends, in analysis what is recovered is not the repressed memory but that kind of connection that was once lost but which is now re-found in a new object relationship.

Dimension 6: The essence of symbolization is spatialization. This is a conclusion derived from Loewald's emphasis on boundary definition as crucial to symbolization. Psychoanalytic process depends upon the creation of symbolizing space; in turn, symbolization is a process of spatialization. Spatialization is the ability to create distance between that which is perceived and what is represented. Through this distance, psychic reality is expanded. As Loewald (1988) writes: "It is the capacity for symbolization that clinical psychoanalysis promotes, usually by progressively leading the patient from repressed symbolism to actualizing and verifying live symbolic connections between hitherto disparate items of experience and thought" (p. 57). For us, spatialization can be found in any of the five previous dimensions, which come to life cumulatively, even within a single psychoanalytic hour. Here, we will emphasize three components of spatialization: object relational space, fantasy space, and temporal space.

Object relational space is a vehicle for the creation of psychic space through the relationship to the other. There is an intrinsic validity to Klein's and Segal's notion that through symbolization, the position vis-à-vis the object is defined. Symbolization is a statement of a libidinal object choice, and even when the manifest content is negative, the mere fact that the image is offered is a gesture towards object choice. Object relational space implies alterity: the *other* is given physical, as well as mental attributes, and is experienced as having a separate mind. Thus, object relational space is mentalizing space.

Fantasy space is a vehicle for the creation of psychic space through the apprehension of the imaginary. Through the evocation of the imaginary, the potential presence of the other is affirmed and becomes a means towards titrating the dread of object loss. Here, we are affirming a crucial insight offered by Winnicott whereby the imaginary exists as a potential for reflection in both analyst and patient, rendering symbolization an intersubjective event.

Temporal space, and as we shall suggest triangular space, is a vehicle for the creation of psychic space through the awareness of time. Time is a crucial signifier of inner space. Does the patient tell the "story" shifting focus from the present, to the past, and into the future? Shifts in time-perspective imply an alteration in the state of consciousness, emphasizing what is, what was, and what might be. Temporal space invites triangular space, as that which breaks up the power of immediacy—what is to be and what not to be, what is included and what is excluded. Reflection arises through the opportunity to confront alternatives. This is the deeper meaning of the Oedipal situation and a view explicit in Green's vision of the symbolizing process as a rebinding after separation and reunion.

Concluding remarks on symbolization

We cannot leave the notion of spatialization without appreciating Fonagy and Target's crucial contribution to the concept of mentalization and its clinical manifestation, reflective functioning. Their ideas have been confirmed over the past 20 years through a body of developmental and clinical research (Fonagy & Target, 1995, 1996, 1998). Through the deployment of reflective functioning, one can sense one's own mind, as well as the existence of a mind external to oneself, as in object relational space. In reflective functioning, one can entertain illusion and allusion within a frame of play, as long as the "as if" stance is sustained, as in fantasy space. Finally, in reflective functioning, one can scan and connect to different phases of life, as in temporal space. Here we would like to suggest that reflective functioning is a symbolizing function which facilitates spatialization.

In the evaluation of clinical process, this apparent overlap between our notion of spatialization and that of reflective functioning must not cloud over the specificity inherent in each of the above dimensions of symbolization. In the clinical accounts throughout this volume, the particularities of the five dimensions have been documented, yielding valuable insights into the unique pathways to the shaping of new symbolic forms.

On desymbolization

Whereas the core of the concept of symbolization is that of linking, and with it the process of triangulation leading to integration, in desymbolization we find the obverse: an event sequence that moves towards the cessation of linking and the destruction of the triangular. Desymbolization implies not simply the absence of the symbolic, but the destruction of the meaning-making process. In symbolization there is differentiation, in desymbolization equivalence. The origin of this term, to the best of our knowledge, can be traced to Rycroft, who in 1956 designated "desymbolization" as preferable to the term "regression".

Desymbolization is a challenging concept for it confronts us with the difficult task of defining the presence of absence; nonetheless, desymbolization for us is a signifier of a definable psychic presence. We speak not of the unsymbolized, or the unmentalized, as is currently in vogue, nor simply of the absence of the symbolic, but, instead, of a motivated act, the wish to eject knowing, to evacuate meaning, to disavow significance. Such mental events have been represented in a host of analytic ideas, to wit, Green's work of the negative, Bion's attacks on linking, and of course, Freud's pull towards the inorganic. These represent psychic organizers, which underlie primitive defence.

Desymbolization in clinical discourse, for us, can be encountered in three ways: psychic blankness, symbolic equation, and the frozen constellation. Further, these three dimensions leave their mark on the manner in which emotions can be processed, all resulting in trends towards disrupted affect and affect foreclosure.

Equivalence: the psychic organizer of desymbolization

Equivalence is the signifier of those traumatic experiences one does not wish to know. It underlies all manifestations of desymbolization. When all is equal, blankness, confusion, and globality of affect prevail, undermining perception. Indeed equivalence is a mental state which is the substrate of what in the analytic literature has been called "concrete" (Bass, 1997). Bass correctly holds that the emphasis on sameness, on non-difference, is an unconscious defence against differentiation, which is intrinsically traumatic. Our three dimensions of desymbolization elaborated below fulfil this notion of psychic equivalence.

There is, however, a gradient in psychic equivalence, which moves progressively towards the symbolic. The distinctions by the philosopher Peirce of *index*, *icon*, and *symbol* (applied to psychoanalysis by Ricardo Steiner) are useful here, for psychic equivalence may function in these three ways as precursors to symbolization. Index is a relationship where one signifier completely eclipses another, whereas icon approaches differentiation as one signifier can be equated with another without the two being completely collapsed. The symbol is further afield in the realm of differentiation, though the symbol freezes a constellation of meanings. The symbol represents a sign that meaning can perhaps be unpacked with analytic work. With this in mind, we will now spell out our three dimensions of desymbolization.

Dimension 1: Desymbolization can reveal itself in a state of psychic blankness. For this form of equivalence we borrow a term from André Green: "blank psychosis" (1975). We speak here of instances of the emptying out or the deletion of thoughts, of an experience of a blank hole or inner void, and of the destruction of all efforts to symbolize. This is the most explicit form of desymbolization. For Green, it exemplifies a thought without a thinker, and for Lacan, an instance of profound foreclosure. A single word can unleash a state of blankness, the word functioning as an index, where all metaphorical thought is throttled and with it, the "as if" attitude. Here there is no room for the imaginary or reflection, and the indexed word can only portray a state of helplessness, inundation, or emptiness.

Psychic blankness can show its presence in patients suffering from severe psychopathology, in panic states, and also in moments of transference crisis as our material has shown. In session 42 of the case of Mohamed, the mere utterance by the therapist of the words "fire alarm" unleashed a panic attack where Mohamed was almost instantly unable to breathe. For him the word "fire" was identical to suffocation, serving as an index for the ensuing panic attack. Mohamed began to feel pain all over his body, indeed seemed to suffocate, and induced the therapist to give him a cup of coffee. By the end of the session, Mohamed briefly recovered and recalled a memory of another alarm that had shocked his wife. An episode of the past had been reclaimed (Chapter Nine).

With Mohamed, a single signifier, one uttered by the analyst, concretized conflictual feelings through a focus on the body self, extirpating for a moment all thoughts, images, and memories. In such a scenario, it may well be that implicitly the patient feels throttled by unconscious persecutory ideas (as would be suggested by a Kleinian view), though such fantasies cannot at that point be formulated.

Dimension 2: Desymbolization can reveal itself in symbolic equation. The very use of the two words "symbolic" and "equation" is an example of an "icon", in that two words can be associated with one another without each word losing specific meaning. Symbolic equation, a concept first introduced by Klein (1923) and elaborated by Segal (1957), speaks to the manner in which regressive experiences can be catapulted in the analytic process, yet sow the seeds for important reversals. In the word *equation* we find the roots of the destructive aspects of meaning making, and in the word *symbolic* the communicative, even constructive pockets that can facilitate a therapeutic object relationship. Let us elaborate.

Once more the word *equation* affirms the fusion, confusion, and conflation of two distinct spheres of mind and hence the breakdown of the representational process. In the symbolic equation, two images of a perceived actuality are conflated: the objective with the subjective, the signifier with the thing being signified. Segal's (1957) famous example concerns the equation of "a violin with masturbation", and in the excerpt below, the "hardened testicles" are equated with the suffering of torture. In such instances, the focus is on the repetitive use of part-object images, the affirmation of the perceived reality, and the disavowal of alternative meanings.

Additional specificity to the concept of symbolic equation is assumed: strongly charged affect, some level of differentiation, and part-object representations. These mental events lead to projective-introjective identification, a defining aspect of symbolic equation. In view of the virulent motivational force imposed on the person of presence, the analyst, symbolic equation reveals the patient's core conflict and becomes a crucial component of the analytic interchange.

In session 3, Mohamed exclaimed: "The testicle, it is very hard, and this thing is very hard, and it's very big, and I am feeling pain on the artery ... sometimes it's so difficult and painful. I now feel pain on the artery, and it feels as if there is pus in it ... it gets very tight, tensioned in the blood vessel, and then it could empty the blood and so it feels normal and then it could expand and yes, and it is very hard." He spoke repetitively, giving a vivid rendition of a valued part of his body. It was a concrete representation of the consequences and memories of the torture. The hardened testicles were an objective medical fact, yet this was stubbornly conflated with the rage he felt at his torturers and his present caretakers (including the therapist)—rage, which was disavowed and transformed into repetitive utterances of bodily tensions. The testicle might have been an inner symbol, but in the following session (session 4) it took on an aspect of symbolic equation. It is of interest that in that session following repeated references to hardened testicles, Mohamed expressed some truly symbolized thoughts in the form of an imaginary drowning scene, but then assumed a challenging stance towards his therapist, demanding rescue (Chapter Eight).

Symbolic equation as an instance of desymbolization is the affirmation and concretization of an objective perception, the fusion and disavowal of an inner subjective experience, draining further the symbolizing function. This sequence was also present in session 245 of the case of Ms Y, although the dissociation of affect was less marked. She says to her analyst: "I love your legs. I wish I had your legs." This was intertwined with, "I hate my legs." The idealized perception of the analyst's body was fused with hatred towards her own. The perception was a concretized fusion of idealization, love, hate, even envy in the transference. As with Mohamed, there was a reversal this time at the end of the session where Ms Y connected to and verbalized her feelings. Referring to her commitment to the analysis she states: "That's a pretty strong tie." Notably, the word "tie" contains the previous mixing of love and hate, dependence and envy, but in the form of a new symbolization (Chapter Fifteen).

Dimension 3: Desymbolization can reveal itself as an affectively frozen constellation. Here, in spite of perceived differences, affect is concretized. In symbolic equation, facts are equated, but in the frozen constellation, emotions remain undifferentiated. The affective force homogenizes perception. Traceable to an unconscious hallucinatory fantasy, the affect, manifest in shame, guilt, rage, makes all events feel alike, even though on another level the patient knows it is not so. Things simply feel real, governed by a sense of immediacy.

The patient is midway between hallucination and fantasy as the inner and the outer world are felt to be one. Fonagy and Target (1996) have termed this phenomenon *psychic equivalence*, an unfortunate nomenclature, for it equates equivalence, an underlying aspect of all desymbolization, with this particular phenomenon; nonetheless, they agree that affect is the guiding theme. Frosch (1995) is also in agreement and uses the term *pre-conceptual emotional organization* to refer to the overwhelming impact of the experience of affect. Citing Steingart, Frosch notes that a powerful affective image pales in the face of natural perception. For Bass (1997), such a process of affectively guided concretization would be considered as a defensive use of hallucinatory wish fulfilment fantasy.

The phenomenon of the affectively frozen constellation was manifested in a scene from session 238 in the case of Ms Y. The onset occurred when the patient had the thought that she might be prejudiced against her analyst. This led to the horrifying idea that she was prejudiced against her adopted daughter, who had dark skin. This evoked overwhelming shame, leading to a feeling of confusion and a state where everything seemed equivalent. She became overwhelmed, unable to think, to choose, and worried that her hatred would go on and on (Chapter Fourteen).

Affect disregulation and desymbolization

Our three dimensions of desymbolization find many scorable manifestations in various forms of the throttling of emotions. We have grouped these manifestations under the term *affect disregulation*, which corresponds in many ways with what in the literature has been called *alexithymia* (Taylor, Doddy & Newman, 1981). This hypothetical construct is characterized by "(1) a difficulty in identifying and communicating feelings, (2) a difficulty in distinguishing between feelings and bodily sensations, and (3) a preference for focusing on external events rather than inner experiences (Taylor & Bagby, 1988, p. 352)". Our categories of affect disregulation find their mirror in this description.

Our first category, difficulty in the naming of affect, subsumes the following attributes: disfluency of speech, perseveration and mechanical repetition, globality of affect, and psychophysiological manifestations of unnamed affect. Here are some scoring examples for each attribute, all taken from the case of Mohamed.

Disfluency of speech: "Sometimes they were telling me about what they was thinking, and, and then I was really getting sick. [sniffling] [crying silently] [sniffling] I really cannot tell. [sniffling] I cannot tell sometimes I don't know, I don't know what's happening."

Perseveration and mechanical repetition: "Because I have no one, eh, who can help me at home. And then it's, eh, it's too much pressure for me, I cannot resist, and I am ... if have I would have get [sic] someone who can help me on the things in the house, some of the relatives who have been with me, it would have been less tension for me."

Globality of affect: "Yes it's, everything is making me very tired ... it gets me tired and when I get tensioned and nervous and I, I am more tired."

Psychophysiological manifestations of unnamed affect: "oh [the patient is breathing heavily] ... [the patient is still breathing heavily] I cannot breathe."

Our second category is fragmentation of the body schema. To illustrate, "You know my testicle is very strange. Sometimes it's completely normal, and sometimes when I am not tensioned, I am not feeling any sort of illness, and I'm very relaxed and my body is completely normal, and the testicle is very normal, and all the arteries are also normal."

Event reporting is our third category, illustrated by the following: "It was ... it was Tuesday or Wednesday when I have been with you ... last time? It was last Wednesday when I came, I came from ... it was on the 7th. Did I came to you on the 7th? No, I came to you on the 6th. On the 6th, yes. On the 7th, I had the physiotherapy, and then I had an appointment in the central hospital, they told me to come, and then I had appointment for the testicle."

Affect disregulation as applied to the three dimensions of desymbolization

It is probable that each dimension of desymbolization (psychic blankness, symbolic equation, and the frozen constellation) have salient markers in the sphere of affect disregulation. Below we will chart out some tentative formulations as to how the failure to achieve symbolic representation may be registered in the realm of affect.

Psychic Blankness: We have already noted that psychic blankness begins with the utterance of a paralyzing word, followed by long pausing and a sequella in which signs of affect disregulation in the form of globality of affect appear. This sequence was exemplified in session 42 of the case of Mohamed. Clearly, the naming of strong emotions was throttled by the surge of uncontained affects. Concurrent physiological arousal (e.g., heavy breathing, and headache) attests to the inner evacuation of affect into the soma.

Symbolic Equation: In symbolic equation, we look for affect disruptions associated with the fusion, confusion, and conflation of self and object representations. Here our attention centered around the perception of the "body objectified".

The Frozen Constellation: In the frozen constellation, sameness of affect is a leading characteristic, indeed by definition, affect governs perception.

* * *

In concluding, despite the overlap, a perusal of the clinical data contained in this volume suggests that each of the three dimensions of desymbolization has its specific link to different forms of affect disregulation. It also appears that different dimensions are likely to elicit distinct emotional expressions. If, in future work, we can make this linkage more explicit, such a finding would enhance the validity of our dimensions of desymbolization.

REFERENCES

Abelin, E. L. (1975). Some further observations and comments on the earliest role of the father. *International Journal of Psychoanalysis, 56*: 293–302.

Abend, S. M. (1989). Countertransference and psychoanalytic technique. *Psychoanalytic Quarterly, 58*: 374–395.

American Psychiatric Association (1994). *Diagnostic and Statistical Manual of Mental Disorders* (4th ed.). Washington, DC: American Psychiatric Association.

Arnold, E. G., Farber, B. A. & Geller, J. D. (2004). Termination, post-termination, and internalization of therapy and the therapist: internal representation and psychotherapy outcome. In: Chapman, D. (Ed.), *Core Processes in Brief Psychodynamic Psychotherapy* (pp. 289–308). Hillsdale, NJ: Erlbaum.

Atwood, G. E. & Stolorow, R. D. (1980). Psychoanalytic concepts and the representational world. *Psychoanalysis and Contemporary Thought, 3*: 267–290.

Bach, S. (2006). *Getting From Here to There: Analytic Love, Analytic Process*. Hillsdale, NJ: The Analytic Press.

Bachrach, H. M., Galatzer-Levy, R., Skolnikoff, A. & Waldron, S. (1991). On the efficacy of psychoanalysis. *Journal of the American Psychoanalytic Association, 39*: 871–916.

Bak, R. C. (1943). Dissolution of the ego, mannerism and delusion of grandeur. *Journal of Nervous and Mental Disease, 98*: 457–464.
Bakhtin, M. M. (1981). *The Dialogic Imagination*. Austin, TX: University of Texas Press.
Bakhtin, M. M. (1986). *Speech Genres and Other Late Essays*. Austin, TX: University of Texas Press.
Bandura, A. (1977). *Social Learning Theory*. New York: General Learning Press.
Barchat, D. G. (1989). Representations and separations in therapy: The August Phenomenon. Paper presented at the annual meeting, Society for Psychotherapy Research, Toronto (June).
Bass, A. (1997). The problem of concreteness. *Psychoanalytic Quarterly, 66*: 642–682.
Beebe, B. & Lachmann, F. M. (1994). Representation and internalization in infancy: three principles of salience. *Psychoanalytic Psychology, 11*: 127–165.
Beenen, F. (2004). Psychoanalysis and science: some remarks on demarcation and legitimation. In: Leuzinger-Bohleber, M., Drerer, A. U. & Canestri, J. (Eds.), *Pluralism and Unity: Methods of Research in Psychoanalysis* (pp. 222–230). London: International Psychoanalytic Association.
Beland, H. (1994). Validation in the clinical process: four settings for objectification of the subjectivity of understanding. *International Journal of Psychoanalysis, 75*: 1141–1158.
Bellak, L., Hurvich, M. & Gediman, H. K. (1973). *Ego Functions in Schizophrenics, Neurotics, and Normals: A Systematic Study of Conceptual, Diagnostic, and Therapeutic Aspects*. New York: John Wiley & Sons.
Bender, D. S., Farber, B. A. & Geller, J. D. (1997). Patients' representations of therapist, parents, and self in the early phase of psychotherapy. *Journal of the American Academy of Psychoanalysis and Dynamic Psychiatry, 25*: 571–586.
Bender, D. S., Farber, B. A., Sanislow, C. A., Dyck, I. R., Geller, J. D. & Skodol, A. E. (2003). Representations of therapists by patients with personality disorders. *American Journal of Psychotherapy, 57*: 219–236.
Benjamin, J. (2004). Beyond doer and done to: an intersubjective view of thirdness. *Psychoanalytic Quarterly, 73*: 5–46.
Benjamin, L. S. (1974). Structural analysis of social behavior. *Psychology Review, 81*: 392–425.
Benveniste, E. (1970). L'appareil formel de l'énonciation. In: *Problèmes de Linguistique Générale, II* (pp. 79–88). Paris: Gallimard.

Benveniste, P. S., Papouchis, N., Allen, R. & Hurvich, M. (1998). Rorschach assessment of annihilation anxiety and ego functioning. *Psychoanalytic Psychology*, 15: 536–566.
Bergmann, M. S. & Hartman, F. R. (Eds.) (1976). *The Evolution of Psychoanalytic Technique*. New York: Basic.
Berzofsky, M., Wilke, S. & Freedman, N. (2000). The clinical scan method. New York: Psychotherapy Research Unit, Downstate Medical Center [unpublished manuscript].
Bick, E. (1968). The experience of the skin in early object-relations. *International Journal of Psychoanalysis*, 49: 484–486.
Bion, W. R. (1962). *Learning from Experience*. London: Tavistock.
Bion, W. R. (1965). *Transformations*. New York: Basic.
Bion, W. R. (1967). *Second Thoughts*. New York: Jason Aronson.
Blatt, S. J. (1998). Contributions of psychoanalysis to the understanding and treatment of depression. *Journal of the American Psychoanalytic Association*, 46: 723–752.
Blatt, S. J., Auerbach, J. S. & Levy, K. N. (1997). Mental representations in personality development, psychopathology, and the therapeutic process. *Review of General Psychology*, 1: 351–374.
Blum, H. P. (1973). The concept of erotized transference. *Journal of the American Psychoanalytic Association*, 21: 61–76.
Boesky, D. (1982). Acting out: a reconsideration of the concept. *International Journal of Psychoanalysis*, 63: 39–55.
Boesky, D. (2000). Affect, language and communication: 41st IPA congress plenary session. *International Journal of Psychoanalysis*, 81: 257–262.
Bowlby, J. (1980). *Attachment and Loss, Vol. 3*. New York: Basic.
Brenner, C. (1987). Working through: 1914–1984. *Psychoanalytic Quarterly*, 56: 88–108.
Britton, R. (1989). The missing link: parental sexuality in the Oedipus complex. In: Steiner, J. *The Oedipus Complex Today: Clinical Implications* (pp. 11–82). London: Karnac.
Britton, R. (1998). *Belief and Imagination: Explorations in Psychoanalysis*. New York: Routledge.
Britton, R. & Steiner, J. (1994). Interpretation: selected fact or overvalued idea? *International Journal of Psychoanalysis*, 75: 1069–1078.
Bromberg, P. M. (1979). Interpersonal psychoanalysis and regression. *Contemporary Psychoanalysis*, 15: 647–655.
Bruner, J. S. (1964). The course of cognitive growth. *American Psychologist*, 19: 1–15.
Bruner, J. S. (1968). *Processes of Cognitive Growth: Infancy*. Worcester, MA: Clark University Press.

Bucci, W. (1985). Dual coding: a cognitive model for psychoanalytic research. *Journal of the American Psychoanalytic Association, 33*: 571–607.

Bucci, W. (1997). Patterns of discourse in "good" and troubled hours: a multiple code interpretation. *Journal of the American Psychoanalytic Association, 45*: 155–187.

Bucci, W. (2005). Basic concepts and methods of psychoanalytic process research. In: Person, E., Cooper, A. & Gabbard, G. (Eds.), *Textbook of Psychoanalysis* (pp. 339–355). Washington, DC: American Psychiatric Press.

Bucci, W. (2007a). Dissociation from the perspective of Multiple Code Theory, part I: psychological roots and implications for psychoanalytic treatment. *Contemporary psychoanalysis, 43*: 165–184.

Bucci, W. (2007b). Dissociation from the perspective of Multiple Code Therapy, part II: spectrum of dissociative process in the psychoanalytic relationship. *Contemporary Psychoanalysis, 43*: 305–326.

Bucci, W. & Maskit, B. (2007). Beneath the surface of the therapeutic interaction: The psychoanalytic method in modern dress. *Journal of the American Psychoanalytic Association, 55*: 1355–1397.

Buckley, P., Karasu, T. B. & Charles, E. (1981). Psychotherapists view their personal therapy. *Psychotherapy: Theory, Research and Practice, 18*: 299–305.

Burnham, D. L., Gladstone, A. I. & Gibson, R. W. (1969). *Schizophrenia and the Need-Fear Dilemma*. New York: International Universities Press.

Cassirer, E. (1955). *The Philosophy of Symbolic Forms*. New Haven, CT: Yale University Press.

Chiozza, L. (1999). Body, affect, and language. *Neuropsychoanalysis, 1*: 111–123.

Chused, J. F. (1991). The evocative power of enactments. *Journal of the American Psychoanalytic Association, 39*: 615–639.

Consumer Reports. (1995). Mental health: does therapy help? (pp. 734–739) (November).

Craige, H. (2002). Mourning analysis: the post-termination phase. *Journal of the American Psychoanalytic Association, 50*: 502–550.

Cramer, P. (1998). Coping and defense mechanisms: what's the difference? *Journal of Personality, Special Issue: Defense mechanisms in contemporary personality research, 66*: 919–946.

Dahl, H. & Teller, V. (1994). The characteristics, identification, and applications of frames. *Psychotherapy Research, 4*: 253–276.

Damasio, A. (2000). *The Feeling of What Happens: Body and Emotion in the Making of Consciousness*. London: Vintage.

De Mijolla, A. (Ed.) (2005). *International Dictionary of Psychoanalysis (3 vols.)* (pp. 1049–1050). Detroit: Thomson/Gale.
Dewald, P. A. (1990). Conceptualizations of the psychoanalytic process. *Psychoanalytic Quarterly, 59*: 693–711.
Dorpat, T. L. (1974). Internalization of the patient-analyst relationship in patients with narcissistic disorders. *International Journal of Psychoanalysis, 55*: 183–188.
Edelson, M. (1963). *The Termination of Intensive Psychotherapy.* Springfield, IL: Charles C. Thomas.
Eliot, T. S. (1944). *Four Quartets.* London: Faber & Faber.
Ellman, S. J. (2007). Analytic trust and transference: love, healing ruptures and facilitating repairs. *Psychoanalytic Inquiry, 27*: 246–263.
Ellman, S. J. & Moskowitz, M. (1998). *Enactment: Towards a New Approach in the Therapeutic Relationship.* Northvale, NJ: Jason Aronson.
Ellman, S. J. & Moskowitz, M. (2008). A study of the Boston Change Process Study Group. *Psychoanalytic Dialogues, 18*: 812–837.
Erikson, E. H. (1954). The dream specimen of psychoanalysis. *Journal of the American Psychoanalytic Association, 2*: 5–56.
Farber, B. A. (2003). Patient self-disclosure in psychotherapy practice and supervision: an introduction. *Journal of Clinical Psychology, Special Issue: In Session: Self-Disclosure, 59*: 525–528.
Farber, B. A. & Geller, J. D. (1994). Gender and representation in psychotherapy. *Psychotherapy, 31*: 318–326.
Fenichel, O. (1930). Statistischer Bericht über die therapeutische Tätigkeit 1920–1930. In: Deutsche Psychoanalytische Gessellschaft (Hrsg.), *Zehn Jahre Berliner Psychoanalytisches Institut* (pp. 13–19).
Ferenczi, S. (1950). The ontogenesis of the interest in money. In: *Contributions to Psychoanalysis* (Vol. 2) (pp. 319–331). New York: Basic.
Festinger, L. (1957). *A Theory of Cognitive Dissonance.* Stanford, CA: Stanford University Press.
Fonagy, P. (1995). Playing with reality: the development of psychic reality and its malfunction in borderline personalities. *International Journal of Psychoanalysis, 76*: 39–44.
Fonagy, P. & Target, M. (1995). Understanding the violent patient: the use of the body and the role of the father. *International Journal of Psychoanalysis, 76*: 487–501.
Fonagy, P. & Target, M. (1996). Playing with reality: I. theory of mind and the normal development of psychic reality. *International Journal of Psychoanalysis, 77*: 217–233.
Fonagy, P. & Target, M. (1998). Mentalization and the changing aims of child psychoanalysis. *Psychoanalytic Dialogues, 8*: 87–114.

Frankel, J. (in press). The analytic state of consciousness as a form of play and a foundational transference, and implications for the concept of abstinence and for a restrained analytic stance.

Freedman, N. (1985). The concept of transformation in psychoanalysis. *Psychoanalytic Psychology*, 2: 317–339.

Freedman, N. (1997). On receiving the patient's transference: the symbolizing and desymbolizing countertransference. *Journal of the American Psychoanalytic Association*, 45: 79–103.

Freedman, N. (1998). Psychoanalysis and symbolization: legacy or heresy? In: Ellman, C., Grand, S., Silvan, M. & Ellman, S. J. (Eds.), *The Modern Freudians: Contemporary Psychoanalytic Technique* (pp. 79–97). Northvale, NJ: Jason Aronson.

Freedman, N. & Berzofsky, M. (1995). Shape of the communicated transference in difficult and not-so-difficult patients: symbolized and desymbolized transference. *Psychoanalytic Psychology*, 12: 363–374.

Freedman, N., Hoffenberg, J. D., Vorus, N. & Frosch, A. (1999). The effectiveness of psychoanalytic psychotherapy: the role of treatment duration, frequency of sessions, and the therapeutic relationship. *Journal of the American Psychoanalytic Association*, 47: 741–772.

Freedman, N., Lasky, R. & Hurvich, M. (2003). Two pathways towards knowing psychoanalytic process. In: Leuzinger-Bohleber, M., Drerer, A. U. & Canestri, J. (Eds.), *Pluralism and Unity: Methods of Research in Psychoanalysis* (pp. 207–221). London: International Psychoanalytic Association.

Freedman, N., Lasky, R. & Ward, R. (2009). The upward slope: a study of psychoanalytic transformations. *Psychoanalytic Quarterly*, 78: 201–231.

Freedman, N., Lasky, R. & Webster, J. (2008). A specimen of working through. Paper presented at the Winter Meeting of the American Psychoanalytic Association, New York (January).

Freedman, N., Lasky, R. & Webster, J. (2009). The ordinary and the extraordinary countertransference. *Journal of the American Psychoanalytic Association*, 57: 303–331.

Freedman, N. & Russell, J. (2003). Symbolization of the analytic discourse. *Psychoanalysis and Contemporary Thought*, 26: 39–87.

Freud, A. (1936). *The Ego and the Mechanisms of Defense: The Writings of Anna Freud, Vol. II*. New York: International Universities Press.

Freud, S. (1895). Project for a scientific psychology. *S. E., 1*. London: Hogarth.

Freud, S. (1896). Further remarks on the neuro-psychoses of defense. *S. E., 3*. London: Hogarth.

Freud, S. (1900). *The interpretation of dreams. S. E., 4*. London: Hogarth.
Freud, S. (1905). Fragment of an analysis of a case of hysteria. *S. E., 7*. London: Hogarth.
Freud, S. (1909). Notes upon a case of obsessional neurosis. *S. E., 10*. London: Hogarth.
Freud, S. (1914). Remembering, repeating and working-through. *S. E., 12*. London: Hogarth.
Freud, S. (1916). Introductory lectures on psycho-analysis: Lecture XVI, Anxiety. *S. E., 16*. London: Hogarth.
Freud, S. (1917a). *Mourning and melancholia. S. E., 14*. London: Hogarth.
Freud, S. (1917b). On transformations of instinct as exemplified in anal erotism. *S. E., 17*. London: Hogarth.
Freud, S. (1918). From the history of an infantile neurosis. *S. E., 17*. London: Hogarth.
Freud, S. (1919). Lines of advance in psycho-analytic therapy. *S. E., 17*. London: Hogarth.
Freud, S. (1920). *Beyond the pleasure principle. S. E., 18*. London: Hogarth.
Freud, S. (1921). Group psychology and the analysis of the ego. *S. E., 18*. London: Hogarth.
Freud, S. (1926a). Inhibitions, symptoms and anxiety. *S. E., 20*. London: Hogarth.
Freud, S. (1926b). The question of lay analysis. *S. E., 20*. London: Hogarth.
Freud, S. (1937). Analysis terminable and interminable. *International Journal of Psychoanalysis, 18*: 373–405.
Freud, S. & Breuer, J. (1895). Studies on hysteria. *S. E., 2*. London: Hogarth.
Friedman, L. (2003). Symbolizing as abstraction: Its role in psychoanalytic treatment. In Lasky, R. (Ed.), *Symbolization and desymbolization: essays in honor of Norbert Freedman* (pp. 204–230). New York: Other Press.
Frosch, A. (1995). The preconceptual organization of emotion. *Journal of the American Psychoanalytic Association, 43*: 423–447.
Gabbard, G. O. (1994). On love and lust in erotic transference. *Journal of the American Psychoanalytic Association, 42*: 385–403.
Gallese, V., Eagle, M. N. & Migone, P. (1988). Intentional attunement: mirror neurons and the neural underpinnings of interpersonal relations. *Journal of the American Psychoanalytic Association, 55*: 131–176.
Gedo, J. E. (2001). The enduring scientific contributions of Sigmund Freud. *Annual of Psychoanalysis, 29*: 105–115.

Geller, J. D. (1984). Moods, feelings and the process of affect formation. In: Zegans, L. S., Temoshok, L. & van Dyke, C. (Eds.), *Emotions in Health and Illness: Applications to Clinical Practice* (pp. 171–186). New York: Grune & Stratton.

Geller, J. D. (1987). The process of psychotherapy: separation and the complex interplay among empathy, insight, and internalization. In: Bloom-Feshbach, J. & Bloom-Feshbach, S. (Eds.), *The Psychology of Separation through the Life Span* (pp. 459–514). San Francisco: Jossey-Bass.

Geller, J. D. (1998). What does it mean to practice psychotherapy scientifically? *Psychoanalysis and Psychotherapy*, 15: 187–214.

Geller, J. D. (2005). Style and its contribution to a patient-specific model of therapeutic technique. *Psychotherapy: Theory, Research, Practice, Training, Special Issue: The Interplay of Techniques and the Therapeutic Relationship in Psychotherapy*, 42: 469–482.

Geller, J. D., Behrends, R., Hartley, D., Farber, B. A. & Rohde, A. (1989). *Therapist Representation Inventory—II*. [unpublished manuscript].

Geller, J. D. & Farber, B. A. (1993). Factors influencing the process of internalization in psychotherapy. *Psychotherapy Research*, 3: 166–180.

Geller, J. D., Farber, B. A. & Schaffer, C. E. (2010). Representations of the supervisory dialogue and the development of psychotherapists. *Psychotherapy: Theory, Research, Practice, Training*, 47: 211–220.

Geller, J. D., Lehman, A. K. & Farber, B. A. (2002). Psychotherapists' representations of their patients. *Journal of Clinical Psychology*, 58: 733–745.

Geller, J. D., Smith Cooley, R. & Hartley, D. (1981). Images of the psychotherapist: a theoretical and methodological perspective. *Imagination, Cognition, and Personality*, 1: 123–146.

George, C. & West, M. (2001). The development and preliminary validation of a new measure of adult attachment: the adult attachment projective. *Attachment and Human Development*, 3: 30–61.

Ghent, E. (1992). Paradox and process. *Psychoanalytic Dialogues*, 2: 135–159.

Gilani, Z. H., Bucci, W. & Freedman, N. (1998). The structure and language of a silence. *Semiotica*, 56: 99–114.

Giovacchini, P. L. (1975). Self-protections in the narcissistic transference. *International Journal of Psychoanalytic Psychotherapy*, 4: 142–166.

Gottschalk, L. A. & Gleser, G. C. (1969). *The Measurement of Psychological States through the Content Analysis of Verbal Behavior*. Berkeley, CA: University of California Press.

Green, A. (1975). The analyst, symbolization and absence in the analytic setting (on changes in analytic practice and analytic experience)—in memory of D. W. Winnicott. *International Journal of Psychoanalysis*, 56: 1–22.

Green, A. (2000). The intrapsychic and intersubjective in psychoanalysis. *Psychoanalytic Quarterly*, 69: 1–39.

Green, A. (2004). Thirdness and psychoanalytic concepts. *The Psychoanalytic Quarterly*, 73: 99–135.

Green, D. J. (2007). The schedule of therapy remembered: aspects of patients' internalization of the therapeutic experience in relation to evoked interviewer interventions [doctoral dissertation, Union Institute and University, 2007]. *Dissertations Abstracts International*, 68, AAT 3278514.

Grubrich-Simitis, I. (1981). Extreme traumatization as cumulative trauma—psychoanalytic investigations of the effects of concentration camp experiences on survivors and their children. *Psychoanalytic Study of the Child*, 36: 415–450.

Grubrich-Simitis, I. (1984). From concretism to metaphor—thoughts on some theoretical and technical aspects of the psychoanalytic work with children of Holocaust survivors. *Psychoanalytic Study of the Child*, 39: 301–319.

Grunes, M. (1984). The therapeutic object relationship. *Psychoanalytic Review*, 71: 124–144.

Harrison, A. M. & Tronick, E. Z. (2007). Contributions to understanding therapeutic change: now we have a playground. *Journal of the American Psychoanalytic Association*, 55: 853–874.

Hartmann, H. (1939). Psycho-analysis and the concept of health. *International Journal of Psychoanalysis*, 20: 308–321.

Hartmann, H. (1951). Technical implications of ego psychology. *Psychoanalytic Quarterly*, 20: 31–43.

Hartmann, H. (1956). Notes on the reality principle. *Psychoanalytic Study of the Child*, 11: 31–53.

Heimann, P. (1950). On countertransference. *International Journal of Psychoanalysis*, 31: 81–84.

Holt, R. R. (1985). The current status of psychoanalytic theory. *Psychoanalytic Psychology*, 2: 289–315.

Hoppe, K. D. (1971). Chronic reactive aggression in survivors of severe persecution. *Comprehensive Psychiatry*, 12: 230–237.

Horwitz, L. (1974). *Clinical Prediction in Psychotherapy*. Northvale, NJ: Jason Aronson.

Hurvich, M. (1989). Traumatic moment, basic dangers and annihilation anxiety. *Psychoanalytic Psychology*, 6: 309–323.

Hurvich, M. (2000). Fears of being overwhelmed and psychoanalytic theories of anxiety. *Psychoanalytic Review, 87*: 615–649.

Hurvich, M. (2002). Symbolization, desymbolization, and annihilation anxieties. In: Lasky, R. (Ed.), *Symbolization and desymbolization: essays in honor of Norbert Freedman* (pp. 347–365). New York: Other Press.

Hurvich, M. (2003). The place of annihilation anxieties in psychoanalytic theory. *Journal of the American Psychoanalytic Association, 51*: 579–616.

Hurvich, M. (2011). New developments in the theory and clinical application of the Annihilation Anxiety concept. In: Druck, A. B., Ellman, C., Freedman, N. & Thaler, A. (Eds.), *A New Freudian Synthesis*. London: Karnac.

Inderbitzin, L. B. & Levy, S. T. (2000). Regression and psychoanalytic technique: the concretization of a concept. *Psychoanalytic Quarterly, 69*: 195–223.

Isakower, O. (1992). The analyzing instrument in the conduct of the analytic process. *Journal of Clinical Psychoanalysis, 1*: 181–194.

Jacobs, T. J. (1986). On countertransference enactments. *Journal of the American Psychoanalytic Association, 34*: 289–307.

Jacobson, E. (1957). Normal and pathological moods: their nature and functions. *Psychoanalytic Study of the Child, 12*: 73–113.

Jones, E. (1948). The theory of Symbolism. In: *Papers on Psycho-Analysis* (5th ed.) (pp. 87–144). London: Maresfield Reprints.

Kantrowitz, J. L. (1986). The role of the patient-analyst "match" in the outcome of psychoanalysis. *Annual of Psychoanalysis, 14*: 273–297.

Kantrowitz, J. L., Katz, A. L. & Paolitto, F. (1990). Follow-up of psychoanalysis five to ten years after termination: III. The relation between the resolution of the transference and the patient-analyst match. *Journal of the American Psychoanalytic Association, 38*: 655–678.

Katz, G. A. (2002). Missing in action: the enacted dimension of analytic process in a patient with traumatic object loss. In: Lasky, R. (Ed.), *Symbolization and desymbolization: essays in honor of Norbert Freedman* (pp. 407–430). New York: Other Press.

Katz, G. A. (in press). Trauma in action: the enacted dimension of an analytic process in a third generation Holocaust survivor. In: Druck, A. B., Ellman, C., Freedman, N. & Thaler, A. (Eds.), *A New Freudian Synthesis*. London: Karnac.

Kazdin, A. E. (1998). *Research Design in Clinical Psychology* (3rd ed.). Boston: Allyn & Bacon.

Keller, H. (1990). *The Story of my Life*. New York: Bantam.

Kernberg, O. F. (1975). *Borderline Conditions and Pathological Narcissism*. Northvale, NJ: Jason Aronson.

Kernberg, O. F. (2001). Object relations, affects, and drives: toward a new synthesis. *Psychoanalytic Inquiry, 21*: 604–619.
Khan, M. R. (1960). Regression and integration in the analytic setting—A clinical essay on the transference and countertransference aspects of these phenomena. *International Journal of Psychoanalysis, 41*: 130–146.
Killingmo, B. (1995). Affirmation in psychoanalysis. *International Journal of Psycho-Analysis, 76*: 503–518.
Klein, G. S. (1956). *Psychoanalytic Theory: An Exploration of Essentials.* New York: International Universities Press.
Klein, M. (1923). The development of a child. *International Journal of Psychoanalysis, 4*: 419–474.
Klein, M. (1930). The importance of symbol-formation in the development of the ego. *International Journal of Psychoanalysis, 11*: 24–39.
Klein, M. (1975). *Envy and Gratitude and Other Works 1946–1963.* London: Hogarth.
Kohut, H. (1971). *The Analysis of the Self.* New York: International Universities Press.
Kris, E. (1956). On some vicissitudes of insight in psycho-analysis. *International Journal of Psychoanalysis, 37*: 445–455.
Krystal, H. (1971). Trauma: considerations of its intensity and chronicity. In: Krystal, H. & Niederland, W. (Eds.), Psychic Traumatization (Vol. 8 of *International Psychiatry Clinics*) (pp. 11–28). Boston: Little, Brown.
Krystal, H. (1978). Trauma and affects. *Psychoanalytic Study of the Child, 33*: 81–116.
Krystal, H. (1988). *Integration and Self-Healing: Affect, Trauma, Alexithymia.* Hillsdale, NJ: Analytic Press.
Küchenhoff, J. (1998). Trauma, Konflikt, Repräsentation. In: Schlösser, A. & Höhfeld, K. (Eds.), *Trauma und Konflikt* (pp. 13–33). Giessen, Germany: Psychosozial Verlag.
Lacan, J. (1979). The neurotic's individual myth. *Psychoanalytic Quarterly, 48*: 405–425.
Laing, R. D. (1959). *The Divided Self: An Existential Study in Sanity and Madness.* London: Tavistock.
Lambert, M. J. & Ogles, B. M. (2004). The efficacy and effectiveness of psychotherapy. In: Lambert, M. J. (Ed.), *Bergin and Garfield's Handbook of Psychotherapy and Behavior Change* (5th ed.) (pp. 139–193). New York: Wiley.
Langer, S. K. (1942). *Philosophy in a New Key: A Study in the Symbolism of Reason, Rite, and Art.* Cambridge, MA: Harvard University Press.
Laplanche, J. (1997). The theory of seduction and the problem of the other. *International Journal of Psychoanalysis, 78*: 653–666.

Laplanche, J. (1999). *Essays on Otherness*. New York: Routledge.
Lasky, R. (2002). Countertransference and the analytic instrument. *Psychoanalytic Psychology, 19*: 65–94.
Laub, D. (1998). The empty circle: children of survivors and the limits of reconstruction. *Journal of the American Psychoanalytic Association, 46*: 507–529.
Lecours, S. & Bouchard, M. A. (1997). Dimensions of mentalization: outlining levels of psychic transformation. *International Journal of Psychoanalysis, 78*: 855–875.
Leiman, M. (1992). The concept of sign in the work of Vygotsky, Winnicott, and Bakhtin. *British Journal of Medical Psychology, 65*: 209–221.
Leiman, M. (1998). Words as intersubjective mediators in psychotherapeutic discourse: the presence of hidden voices in patient utterances. In: Lähteenmäki, M. & Dufva, H. (Eds.), *Dialogues on Bakhtin: Interdisciplinary Readings* (pp. 105–116). Jyväskylä, Finland: Centre for Applied Language Studies.
Lepper, G. (2009). The pragmatics of therapeutic interaction: an empirical study. *International Journal of Psychoanalysis, 90*: 1075–1094.
Leuzinger-Bohleber, M., Stuhrast, U., Rüger, B. & Beutel, M. (2003). How to study the well-being: a representative, multi-perspective, follow-up study. *International Journal of Psychoanalysis, 84*: 263–290.
Lewy, E. & Rapaport, D. (1944). The psychoanalytic concept of memory and its relation to recent memory. *Psychoanalytic Quarterly, 13*: 16–42.
Lifton, R. J. (1976). Advocacy and corruption in the healing professions. *International Review of Psycho-Analysis, 3*: 385–398.
Little, M. (1958). On delusional transference (transference psychosis). In: M. Little, *Transference Neurosis and Transference Psychosis: Toward Basic Unity* (pp. 88–91). New York: Jason Aronson, 1981.
Loewald, H. W. (1960). On the therapeutic action of psycho-analysis. *International Journal of Psychoanalysis, 41*: 16–33.
Loewald, H. W. (1962). Internalization, separation, mourning, and the superego. *Psychoanalytic Quarterly, 31*: 483–504.
Loewald, H. W. (1980). *Papers on Psychoanalysis*. New Haven, CT: Yale University Press.
Loewald, H. W. (1983). Comments on the psychoanalytic concept of symbolism. Hartmann award lecture at the New York Psychoanalytic Institute and Society (March).
Loewald, H. W. (1988a). Termination analyzable and unanalyzable. *Psychoanalytic Study of the Child, 43*: 155–166.
Loewald, H. W. (1988b). *Sublimation*. New Haven, CT: Yale University Press.

Loewald, H. W. & Meissner, W. W. (1976). New horizons in metapsychology: view and review. *Journal of the American Psychoanalytic Association, 24*: 161–180.

Lord, R., Ritvo, S. & Solnit, A. J. (1978). Patients' reactions to the death of the psychoanalyst. *International Journal of Psychoanalysis, 59*: 189–197.

Luborsky, L. & Crits-Christoph, P. (1990). *Understanding Transference: The Core Conflictual Relationship Theme Method.* New York: Basic.

Luborsky, L., Popp, C., Luborsky, E. & Mark, D. (1994). The core conflictual relationship theme. In: Luborsky, L., Barber, J. P., Popp, C. & Shapiro, D. (Eds.), Seven transference-related measures: each applied in an interview with Ms. Smithfield [monograph]. *Psychotherapy Research, 4*: 172–183.

Macalpine, I. (1950). The development of the transference. *Psychoanalytic Quarterly, 19*: 501–539.

Main, M. & Goldwyn, R. (1990). Adult attachment rating and classification systems. In: Main, M. (Ed.), *A Typology of Human Attachment Organization Assessed in Discourse, Drawing and Interviews.* New York: Cambridge University Press.

Main, M. & Goldwyn, R. (1998). *Adult Attachment Scoring and Classification Systems.* Department of Psychology, University of California [unpublished manuscript].

Martinez, D. & Hoppe, S. K. (1998). The analyst's own analyst: other aspects of internalization. Paper presented at the annual meeting of the Society for Psychotherapy Research, Snowbird, UT (June).

Mayman, M. (1968). Early memories and character structure. *Journal of Projective Techniques & Personality Assessment, 32*: 303–316.

McDougall, J. (1974). The psychosoma and the psychoanalytic process. *International Review of Psycho-Analysis, 1*: 437–459.

McDougall, J. (1980). *Plea for a Measure of Abnormality.* New York: International Universities Press.

McLaughlin, J. T. (1987). The play of transference: some reflections on enactment in the psychoanalytic situation. *Journal of the American Psychoanalytic Association, 35*: 557–582.

Modell, A. H. (1988). Changing psychic structure through treatment: preconditions for the resolution of the transference. *Journal of the American Psychoanalytic Association, 36S*: 225–239.

Norcross, J. C. (2004). Tailoring the therapy relationship to the individual patient: evidence-based practices. [Invited distinguished contribution.] *Clinician's Research Digest, Supplemental Bulletin, 30*: 1–2.

Norcross, J. C. & Goldfield, M. K. (2005). *Handbook of Psychotherapy Integration.* New York: Oxford University Press.

Nunberg, H. (1931). The synthetic function of the ego. *International Journal of Psychoanalysis, 12*: 13–140.
Nunberg, H. (1955). *Principles of Psychoanalysis*. New York: International Universities Press.
Ogden, T. H. (2004). The analytic third: implications for psychoanalytic theory and technique. *Psychoanalytic Quarterly, 73*: 167–195.
Olds, D. D. (2006). Identification: psychoanalytic and biological perspectives. *Journal of the American Psychoanalytic Association, 54*: 17–46.
Oremland, J. D., Blacker, K. H. & Norman, H. F. (1975). Incompleteness in "successful" psychoanalyses: a follow-up study. *Journal of the American Psychoanalytic Association, 23*: 819–844.
Orlinsky, D. E. & Geller, J. D. (1993). Patients' representations of their therapists and therapy: new measures. In: Miller, N. E., Luborsky, L., Barber, J. P. & Docherty, J. P. (Eds.), *Psychodynamic Treatment Research* (pp. 423–466). New York: Basic.
Orlinsky, D. E. & Howard, K. I. (1967). The good therapy hour: experiential correlates of patients, and therapists' evaluations of therapy sessions. *Archives of General Psychiatry, 16*: 621–632.
Palombo, S. R. (1999). *The Emergent Ego: Complexity and Coevolution in the Psychoanalytic Process*. Madison, CT: International Universities Press.
Peirce, C. S. (1955). *Philosophical Writings of Peirce*, Buchler, J. (Ed.). New York: Dover Publications.
Pfeffer, A. Z. (1959). A procedure for evaluating the results of psychoanalysis—a preliminary report. *Journal of the American Psychoanalytic Association, 7*: 418–444.
Pfeffer, A. Z. (1963). The meaning of the analyst after analysis—A contribution to the theory of therapeutic results. *Journal of the American Psychoanalytic Association, 11*: 229–244.
Pfeffer, A. Z. (1993). After the analysis: analyst as both old and new object. *Journal of the American Psychoanalytic Association, 41*: 323–337.
Piaget, J. (1954). *The Construction of Reality in the Child*. New York: Basic.
Pine, F. (2007). The four psychologies of psychoanalysis and their place in clinical work. *Journal of the American Psychoanalytic Association, 36*: 571–596.
Plato. *Theaetetus*, Robin Waterfield (Trans.). New York: Penguin, 1987.
Plato. *Meno and Other Dialogues*, Robin Waterfield (Trans.). New York: Oxford University Press, 2005.
Priel, B. (1999). Bakhtin and Winnicott: on dialogue, self, and cure. *Psychoanalytic Dialogues, 9*: 487–503.

Quintana, S. M. & Meara, N. M. (1990). Internalization of therapeutic relationships in short term-therapy. *Journal of Counseling Psychology*, 37: 123:130.
Racker, H. (1957). The meanings and uses of countertransference. *Psychoanalytic Quarterly*, 26: 303–357.
Rangell, L. (1966). An overview of the ending of an analysis. In: Litman, R. E. (Ed.), *Psychoanalysis in the Americas* (pp. 141–165). New York: International Universities Press.
Rapaport, D. & Gill, M. M. (1959). The points of view and assumptions of metapsychology. *International Journal of Psychoanalysis*, 40: 153–162.
Ricoeur, P. (1970). *Freud and Philosophy: An Essay on Interpretation*, D. Savage (Trans.). New Haven, CT: Yale University Press.
Rogers, C. R. & Dymond, R. F. (1954). *Psychotherapy and Personality Change*. Chicago: University of Chicago Press.
Rohde, A. B., Geller, J. D. & Farber, B. A. (1992). Dreams about the therapist: mood, interactions, and themes. *Psychotherapy: Theory, Research, Practice, Training*, 29: 536–544.
Rose, J. (2000). Symbols and their function in managing the anxiety of change: an intersubjective approach. *International Journal of Psychoanalysis*, 81: 453–470.
Rosenbaum, B. (2000). Schizophrenia and enunciation. In: Rosenbaum, B. *Tankeformer og talemåder: en undersøgelse af skizofrenes udsigelse, tankeforstyrrelse og kommunikation* (Forms of thoughts and modes of speech: an investigation of enunciation, thought disorders and communication in schizophrenia) (pp. 299–314). Copenhagen: Multivers.
Rosenzweig, D. L., Farber, B. A. & Geller, J. D. (1996). Clients' representations of their therapists over the course of psychotherapy. *Journal of Clinical Psychology*, 52: 197–207.
Roy, M. (2007). Patients' post-termination, self-reported effectiveness of treatment and the representation of the therapeutic dialogue [doctoral dissertation, Adelphi University, 2007). *Dissertation Abstracts International*, 68, AAT 3281747.
Rycroft, C. (1956). Symbolism and its relationship to the primary and secondary processes. *International Journal of Psychoanalysis*, 37: 137–146.
Sandell, R., Blomberg, J., Lazar, A., Carlsson, J., Broberg, J. & Schubert, J. (2002). Psyche. Zeitschrift für Psychoanalyse und ihre Anwendungen. LV, 3, 2001: Differences in long-term effects of psychoanalysis and extended psychotherapy: findings from the Stockholm Psychoanalysis and Psychotherapy Project. *Psychoanalytic Quarterly*, 71: 170.

Sandler, J. (1976). Countertransference and role-responsiveness. *International Review of Psycho-Analysis, 3*: 43–47.

Sandler, J. (1983). Reflections on some relations between psychoanalytic concepts and psychoanalytic practice. *International Journal of Psychoanalysis, 64*: 34–45.

Sandler, J. & Rosenblatt, B. (1962). The concept of the representational world. *Psychoanalytic Study of the Child, 17*: 128–145.

Schafer, R. (1968). *Aspects of Internalization*. New York: International Universities Press.

Schlessinger, N. & Robbins, F. (1974). Assessment and follow-up in psychoanalysis. *Journal of the American Psychoanalytic Association, 22*: 542–567.

Schneiderman, S. (1986). *Rat Man*. New Haven, CT: Yale University Press.

Segal, H. (1957). Notes on symbol formation. *The International Journal of Psychoanalysis, 38*: 391–397.

Seligman, M. E. P. (1995). The effectiveness of psychotherapy: the Consumer Reports study. *American Psychologist, 50*: 965–974.

Seligman, M. E. P. (1996). A creditable beginning. *American Psychologist, 51*: 1086–1087.

Shedler, J. (2010). The efficacy of psychodynamic psychotherapy. *American Psychologist, 65*: 98–109.

Smith, H. F. (2000). Countertransference, conflictual listening, and the analytic object relationship. *Journal of the American Psychoanalytic Association, 48*: 95–128.

Steiner, J. (1993). *Psychic Retreats*. London: Routledge.

Steiner, R. (2007). Does the Peirce's semiotic model based on index, icon, symbol have anything to do with psychoanalysis? In: Ambrosio, G., Argentieri, S. & Canestri, J. *Language, Symbolization, and Psychosis* (pp. 219–272). London: Karnac.

Steingart, I. (1995). *A Thing Apart. Love and Reality in the Therapeutic Relationship*. Northvale, NJ: Jason Aronson.

Stern, D. N., Sander, L. W., Nahum, P. J., Harrison, A. M., Lyons-Ruth, K., Morgan, A. C., Bruschweilerstern, N. & Tronick, E. Z. (1998). Non-interpretive mechanisms in psychoanalytic therapy: the "something more" than interpretation. *International Journal of Psychoanalysis, 79*: 903–921.

Stinson, C. H., Milbrath, C., Reidbord, S. P. & Bucci, W. (1994). Thematic segmentation of psychotherapy transcripts for convergent analyses. *Psychotherapy, 31*: 36–48.

Strupp, H. H., Hadley, S. W. & Gomes-Schwartz, B. (1977). *Psychotherapy for Better or Worse: An Analysis of the Problem of Negative Effects*. New York: Jason Aronson.

Stuhr, U. (2002). Combining qualitative and quantitative methods in psychoanalytic follow-up research. In: Leuzinger-Bohleber, M. & Target, M. (Eds.), *Outcomes of Psychoanalytic Treatment. Perspectives for Therapists and Researchers* (pp. 110–121). London: Whurr.

Talby-Abarbanel, M. (in press). "Secretly attached, secretly separate": Art, dreams, and transference-countertransference in the analysis of a third generation Holocaust survivor. In: Druck, A. B., Ellman, C., Freedman, N. & Thaler, A. (Eds.), *A New Freudian Synthesis*. London: Karnac.

Taylor, G. J. & Bagby, R. M. (1988). Measurement of alexithymia: recommendations for clinical practice and future research. *Psychiatric Clinics of North America, 11*: 351–366.

Taylor, G. J., Doddy, K. & Newman, A. (1981). Alexithymic characteristics in patients with inflammatory bowel disease. *Canadian Journal of Psychiatry, 45*: 134–142.

Tessman, L. H. (2003). *The Analyst's analyst within*. Hillsdale, NJ: The Analytic Press.

Tronick, E. Z. & Cohn, J. F. (1989). Infant-mother face-to-face interaction: age and gender differences in coordination and the occurrence of miscoordination. *Child Development, 60*: 85–92.

Tulving, E. (2002). Episodic memory: from mind to brain. *Annual Review of Psychology, 53*: 1–25.

van der Kolk, B., McFarlane, A. & Weisæth, L. (1996a). *Traumatic Stress: The Effects of Overwhelming Experience on Body, Mind, and Society*. New York: Guilford Press.

Varvin, S. (2002). Body, mind, and the other. Symbolisation and mentalisation of extreme trauma. In: Varvin, S. & Stajner-Popovic, T. (Eds.), *Upheaval: Psychoanalytic Perspectives on Trauma* (pp. 163–192). Belgrade: International Aid Network.

Varvin, S. (2003). *Mental survival strategies after extreme traumatisation*. Copenhagen: Multipress.

Varvin, S. & Rosenbaum, B. (2003). Extreme traumatization: strategies for mental survival. *International Forum of Psychoanalysis, 12*: 5–16.

Volosinov, V. N. (1973). *Marxism and the Philosophy of Language*, Matejka, L. & Titunik, I. R. (Eds.). Cambridge, MA: Harvard University Press.

Waelder, R. (1960). *Basic Theory of Psychoanalysis*. New York: International Universities Press.

Waelder, R. (1962). Psychoanalysis, scientific method, and philosophy. *Journal of the American Psychoanalytic Association, 10*: 617–637.

Wallerstein, R. S. (1986). *Forty-Two Lives in Treatment: A Study of Psychoanalysis and Psychotherapy*. New York: Guilford Press.

White, R. (1952). *Lives in Progress*. New York: Dryden.
Williams, P. (2004). Incorporation of an invasive object. *International Journal of Psychoanalysis, 85*: 1333–1348.
Winnicott, D. W. (1949). Birth trauma, birth memories and anxiety. In: *Collected Papers* (pp. 174–193). New York: Basic.
Winnicott, D. W. (1955). Metapsychological and clinical aspects of regression within the psycho-analytic set-up. *International Journal of Psychoanalysis, 36*: 16–26.
Winnicott, D. W. (1956). On transference. *International Journal of Psychoanalysis, 37*: 386–388.
Winnicott, D. W. (1960). The theory of the parent-infant relationship. *International Journal of Psychoanalysis, 41*: 585–595.
Winnicott, D. W. (1962). Ego integration in child development. In: *The Maturational Processes and the Facilitating Environment* (pp. 56–63). New York: International Universities Press.
Winnicott, D. W. (1967). The location of cultural experience. *International Journal of Psychoanalysis, 48*: 368–372.
Winnicott, D. W. (1971). *Playing and Reality*. London: Tavistock.
Winnicott, D. W. (1974). Fear of breakdown. *International Review of Psycho-Analysis, 1*: 103–107.
Wzontek, N., Geller, J. D. & Farber, B. A. (1995). Patients' post-termination representations of their psychotherapists. *Journal of the American Academy of Psychoanalysis, 23*: 395–410.

INDEX

acting out 268
adaptation-enhancing self-analytic
    activities 58
adaptive life gains 14–15
adhesive identification 109
adjectives 26
adult-onset trauma 93
affective interpenetration 279
affirmative interventions 181
agent provocateur 76
aggression, integration of 305
alexithymia 113
allusions 62
American Psychiatric Association
    106
Amy's therapy 48
    conversational "style" 51
    criticisms 50
    EQ score 48
analyst introject fantasies 57
analyst-patient relationship 216

analytic engagement, nonlinear
    progression of 273
analytic process
    preservation of 291–292
    symbolization of 308
analyzing functions 57
Annihilation Anxiety (AA) 67, 90,
    99, 104, 107–108, 113, 115–117,
    136–137, 154–155, 157, 160–161
    accentuation of 159
    activity 114, 126, 134–135, 154
    activity cluster 131
    application 116–117
    cluster 125, 133, 146
    concept 134, 137
    core and dimensions 107–110
    cumulative 156
    defining 107
    desymbolization and
        symbolization of 186
    desymbolized 184

342   INDEX

dimensions 109, 160–161
dissociative defences in 185
empirical observations and
   clinical validity 147–148
experience 158
Hurvich's 99, 101
modification of 87, 117,
   123–125, 158, 183
prevalence 147
pervasiveness of 123, 131
process 125, 184
projected-introjected 162, 164
quantitative empirical
   documentation and clinical
   validity 126–127
quantitative empirical
   observations concerning 123,
   143–144, 151–153
recurrence of 139
relationship 102
scoring of 113–114
symbolization of 135, 147, 184,
   186
symbolizing transformation
   of 164
targeted 125, 133, 146, 153
targeted cluster analysis
   through the method of visual
   analysis 131, 146, 153
transformation 119, 159, 161
visual analysis 127
anti-symbolic processes 224, 231
anxiety 89
anxious depression 13–15
arousal-symbolization-
   reorganization 135
averaged typical instance 34

Bakhtin's idea 173
Bender, Donna, S. 17
Bion 99
   notion of selected fact 99

Transformations 98, 115
blank psychosis 316
borderline personality 8
Boston change process study group
   215, 299
Britton 247
   line of thought 249
   patient 248
Bromberg 224
Bucci's notion of referential process
   111

Calgary attachment questionnaire
   34, 63
calm demeanour 42, 59
case of Ms K 160–164
case of Ms Y
   method and findings 203
cat dream #1 161
cat dream #2 161–162
cat dream #3 162
cat dream #4 163–164
chronicity 13
clinical syndrome 12–13
cognitive dissonance 11–12
   hypothesis 12
cognitive linguistic regulation 98
cognitive psychology 59
cognitive styles 40
communicating modes 32–33
conflictual listening 271, 279
consciousness 311
   beneath the surface of 212
   ongoing stream of 23
consumer reports 7
controlled regression 227
counter-sadistic wishes 286
countertransference
   configuration 289
   desymbolization 289–291
   enactments 100, 198–199, 285,
      306

extraordinary 201, 283, 287–289, 292, 295
  Lasky's rendition of 289
  ordinary 288
  proper 288
  resolution of 304
  tension 304
countertransference reactions, extraordinary 197, 284
countertransference-intensive 156
countertransferential empathic communication 176
cumulative facilitating treatment condition 11

daydreams 42
depression 13
destructive countertransference 286
destructiveness 137
desymbolization 69, 75, 80, 86, 96, 103, 105, 107, 113–117, 125–127, 130, 133–134, 137, 144, 146, 148, 154–155, 157–158, 172, 186, 213–214, 246, 270, 283, 289, 297, 315, 317–319, 321
  disregulation 319–320
  in clinical discourse 315
  in extraordinary countertransference 289–291
  intensity of 126
  manifestations of 161
  modification 184
  process of 220
  psychic organizer of 315–319
  psychoanalytic definition of 309–321
  scale 69–70
  sequence 144
  signifier of 231
  units 70
desymbolizer 81

desymbolizing, regressive phase 199–200, 203, 217–218, 245–246, 267
dialogic partner 23
differential responsiveness 12
differentiated transference 196
Discourse Attribute Analytic Procedure (DAAP) 211
discursive symbolization 69
doomsday orientation 109
dreams during treatment 26
dual code theory
  of psycholinguistics 99, 212
dynamic psychotherapy 16, 18

eating disorders 13
effectiveness 5, 12–13, 15
  model 6
  of dynamic psychotherapy 16
  of therapy 39
  psychoanalytic 16
effectiveness questionnaire 7–8, 11, 14–15, 19, 27, 53, 67
  post-termination interview 67–71
effectiveness quotient (EQ) 8–11, 15
  patients 70
  ratio of 41
  scores 40–41
efficacy vs. effectiveness 18–19
ego
  executive system 57
  fragmentation 194
  functioning 59, 122
  propensity 70
  psychology 74
  synthesis 245, 292, 304
  synthetic function of 280, 304
  transformation 57
ego-supportive analyst-mother function 174
Ellman, S. J. 200, 268, 270, 299–300

emotional communication 250
emotional subject
emotionality scoring 34
empirical psychoanalytic
    literature 19
enacted annihilation anxiety 154
enacted symbol 249, 263–264
enactive dialogue 271
enactive phase 199, 203, 267
enactive reverberations 274
enactments 268–270
    as loss of narcissistic
        equilibrium 270–271
    patient-induced 277
    reflections on 278–281
    theorists 280
Enunciation Analysis (EA)
    172–173
    functionality/dysfunctionality
        176
erotic transference 283–286, 288
erotized transference 284–285
extraordinary countertransference
    194
extra-therapeutic
    relationship 23
    situations 25

family disorganization and stress
    factor 13
fantasies 23–24
fantasy space 313
firstness 173
focal symptomatic gains 14
Fonagy's notion of mentalization
    74
foundational transference 295
Freedman, Norbert 5, 17, 29, 55,
    67, 83, 89, 91, 105, 119, 139, 159,
    191, 203, 223, 245, 267, 283, 297,
    309
    advanced the proposition 116

Freud 17, 21, 57, 61, 69, 73–74, 81,
    84, 108, 193, 289, 297, 300–301,
    304
    captain 301
    classic work 115
    clinical thinking 300
    cruel captain 301
    delineation 95
    discoveries 92
    discovery of the unconscious
        73
    dream specimen 193
    erotic longings 284
    hallucinatory wish fulfilment
        69
    nodal moments 300–302
    notion of "acting out" 271
    philosophical pre-suppositions
        95
    psychotherapy of hysteria 300
    recognition of a theoretical
        inconsistency 93
    *The Ego and the Mechanisms
        of Defense* 99
    theoretical inconsistency 93
    transformative psychic actions
        198
    trauma theory and the
        traumatic moment 99
Freudian
    concept 268
    theories 300
Frosch, Allan 5
    pre-conceptual emotional
        organization 112
    frozen constellation 320–321

Geller, Jesse, D. 17, 29, 55
generalizations 94
German psychoanalytic society 20
good/difficult moments and
    perceived outcome 26

Green, Andre,
  blank psychosis 112
  grief depression 13–15, 84

Heimann, Paula 288
  History of Psychoanalytic Technique 92
helplessness 227
Hoffenberg, Joan 5, 17, 29, 83
homogenization 234
homosexual feelings 43
homosexuality 69
horrifying aggressive thoughts 256
Hurvich, Marvin 89, 91, 105, 119, 139, 159, 183
  concept of annihilation anxiety 99, 101

idealizing allusions 233
implicit relational knowing (IRK) 215
incompleteness
  sources of 46–48
incremental treatment effect 9
induction hypothesis 224
Institute for Psychoanalytic Training and Research (IPTAR)
  clinical center (ICC) 27, 83
  clinic setting and population 7
  measurement of effectiveness at 7–9
intense transference engagement 284
interactional synchrony 283
internalization 51, 71, 85, 294
  Amy's style 85
  concept 84
  process of 294
intersubjective matrix 169
intra-psychic
  conflict 271
  equivalents 17
intrapsychic concomitant 25
introjective-projective identifications 229
introjects identification 41
Isakower's analyzing instrument 288

Janus-faced challenge 229
Jim's
  conflicts 46
  EQ score 44
  incompleteness therapy 46
  STR 43
  therapy 43–44, 47
Jones's "repression hypothesis" 311

Kagan, Denise 17, 29
Keller, Helen, discovery 310
Kernberg 247
Kernel of Truth 75
Klang association 241
Klein's
  assertion 246
  historic 1923 paper 300
  symbol formation 111
Kleinian
  distinction 184
  position 93
Kris's "good hour" 234
Kris's notion, difficult psychoanalytic hour 97

Lacan's concept of "the symbolic" 312
Langer, Suzanne 156, 229
Laplanche 221
  Essays on Otherness 74
  notion of alterity 226
Lasky, Richard 203
Loewald 313

Macalpine 228
masochistic technical analysis 206
McDougall
   A Plea for a Measure of Abnormality 229
   language 239
   notion of mutual enactment 269
mean effectiveness quotient (EQ) 10
meaning-making process 315
meet Mohamed, method implemented 105
memory, structure, and process 71–75
Menninger psychotherapy research program 96
Meno's paradox 73
mental
   functioning 193
   organization 223, 281
   processes 246
   transformation 160
mentalization 112
messiness 299
meta-psychological formulations 9, 95–96
mirror neurons 197
mirroring 196
mobilization of defence 185
Mohamed 90, 101, 105–106, 110, 113, 120–122, 126–131, 134–137, 139–142, 144, 147–151, 155–160, 164–165, 168–171, 307, 316–319, 321
   case 160
   consciousness 136
   panic attack 185
   participation in war 119
   psychoanalytic therapy of 105, 117, 119
   therapy 171
   therapy in light of imaginary 176

Moskowitz 299–300
mourning 294

narcissistic
   character disorders 8
   equilibrium 271, 273, 278–279
negative relationship index 11
negative therapeutic reaction 92
negativistic desymbolizing 79
neurotic character disorders 8
neutralization of aggression 305
nodal moment 78, 80, 86, 191, 194, 198–199, 201, 218–219, 241, 243, 245–247, 249–250, 252–255, 257–259, 262, 264, 267, 277–278, 280–281, 291–292, 295, 297, 301, 308, 311–312
   as pathways to symbolic knowing 298–300
   clinically defined 253–254
   commentary on 256, 259–261, 264
   during the desymbolizing phase 264–265
   emergence of 245
   empirically defined 251–252
   essence of progressive symbolization 297
   Freud's 300
   poignant memory 258
   recapitulation and perspective 307
   role in progressive symbolization 302–306
   segmentation analysis 252–253
   successive 199
   therapeutic action 306–307
   unfolding 265
nonverbal vocalized responses (NVR) 221

object relatedness 255
object-representation 175

Oedipal
   conflict 293
   struggles 248
   triangle 246
   triangulation 256, 259
   wish 263
Oedipal situation 247, 259, 314
   prototypical negative 256
Oedipus complex 92, 312
open-ended narrative 26
operational thinking 229
optimal responsiveness index 11
Oslo asylum camp 121
over-generalization 92

Palombo's memorable metaphor 268
panic attack 139
   proper 148–151
paradoxical attitude 241
paranoid-schizoid position 75, 200, 311
pathogenesis 89
patient's
   psychic equilibrium 156
   representations of therapeutic dialogue 17
   subjective experiences 168
   subjectivity 83
patient-analyst relationship 57
patient-therapist relationship 64
persecutory anxiety 122
Petrou, Alexandra 119, 139
Piaget 28
Plato's dialogues 72
   Theaetetus 72
Platonic sense 73
poop game 290
positive covariation results 251
positive relationship index 11
post-depressive position 248
post-termination phase of psychotherapy 55, 84–85

post-traumatic stress disorder 106, 171
pre-conceptual emotional organization 319
predepressive paranoid-schizoid position 248
prevalence 113
progressive desymbolization 224
progressive symbolization 86, 164, 192, 194–196, 199–201, 207, 214, 217, 229, 238, 249, 263–265, 268, 278, 280, 296, 298, 304
   direction of 218
   formulations of 308
   hallmark of 195
   interpretive account of 238
   major organizer of 303
   nodal moments and essence of 297–308
   nodal moments and their role in 302–306
   phasic oscillations 303
   proposition of 198, 210–212
   salient component of 302
   symbolization or desymbolization 210
   trajectory of 298
   working through concept 307
propositional method 9, 94–96, 103–105, 297
   current theory of narcissism 100
   delineated 98
   earlier and current versions of 96–98
   modifiers and probabilistic nature of 102–103
   probabilistic nature of 186
   return to 114–115
psychic
   blankness 112, 117, 159, 316, 320–321
   equivalence 70, 234, 319

functioning 107
integration 110
pain 122
symbolization 103
psychoanalysis 5, 17, 61, 72–74, 81, 91, 94–96, 98, 115, 136–137, 147, 167, 191, 193, 310–311
  clinical 313
  comparative 81, 94
  contemporary mainstream 287
  context of recorded 203
  course 207
  French 225
  history of 93, 246
  introject in 35, 60
  language of 217–218, 309
  Plato's dialogues 72
  recorded 203, 289
psychoanalytic
  communication 192
  community 5
  construction 312
  evaluations 20
  experience, internalization 85
  formulateons 91–94
  inquiry 193
  knowledge 92
  loyalties, excessive adherence to 92
  process 91, 223, 313
  situation 226
  theorizing 55, 65
  theory 193
  therapy 5, 9–10, 16–19, 43, 63, 105, 160
psychoanalytic change 99
  organizer of 230
psychoanalytic concepts 91–92, 226
  of mental functioning 95
  propositional method for 91
psychoanalytic ideas 269
  chronicles of 231

psychoanalytic psychotherapy 5–7, 10, 20, 27, 105, 159–160
  effectiveness of 5, 10
  long-term 159–160
  of trauma victim 106–107
  segmentation analysis 106–107
psychoanalytic research, history of 6–7
  Core Conflictual Relationship Theme (CCRT) 6
  Luborsky's measure 6
  Menninger foundation 6
psychoanalytic treatment 89, 104
  course of 89
psychodynamic
  therapy 6
  treatment 6, 84
psychological
  change tools 60
  disturbance 65
  narrations, culture-bound 175
psychometric appraisals 20
psychopathology 230
psychotherapeutic space, symbolizing processes of 172
psychotherapy
  evaluation of 204
  process and outcome 17
  reorganizing their relations to others in 167

quasi-experimental evaluations 18

re-activate cognitive-affective representations 25
reconstruction of therapy 69
  after termination 75
Referential Activity (RA) 211, 252
  process 309
referential process 98, 211
  Bucci's conceptualization 212

Discourse Attribute Analytic Procedure (DAAP) 211
scoring category of 231
referral issues 26
reflective functioning 67
reflectivity, moment of 234
regression
  induced 225–230
  reverberating 225–230
regressive body-ego 229
remembering 30
  forms of 30–32
  patients 71
remembrances of interactions 42
reminiscing 69
  patients 69
reminiscing and recollecting 67
representational process, empirical studies of 22–25
representations 17
  current and former patients 23
  of a supplementary ego 228
  of human interactions 22
  of self in relation 22
  of therapeutic dialogue 56–58, 60
  of therapeutic relationship 66
  of therapist's qualities 60
  of therapy-with-the-therapist 65
  psychoanalytic and cognitive perspectives 20–22
  reactivate 65
  re-experience 65
  studying patients of therapeutic dialogue 29
  therapeutic dialogue coding system 25
Representations of Therapeutic Dialogue (RTD)
  as sources of self-soothing 59
  case by case investigations of 42–43
  clinical application of 29, 42–43
  coding system (RTDCS) 20, 27, 29–30, 33, 36, 42, 53, 56, 64
  components of 30
  composite 49
  configurations 45
  constituent elements of 41
  data 36–37
  emotionally salient 63
  identifying 35
  imagined 32, 51
  in Amy's profile 52
  in Amy's protocol 50
  in STRI transcripts 38
  inhibited 32, 39
  Jim's profile 58
  Jim's protocol 47
  Jim's therapy 43, 46
  Jim's uses of 58
  location of 33
  longed 32, 39, 63
  mediated 39
  negative 41
  of therapeutic dialogue and the post-termination phase of psychotherapy 55
  participant's protocol 41
  patterns of patients 36
  percentage of 38–39
  phenomenological and functional properties 35
  portrayed interactions 40
  positive or negative 34
  positively charged sequence of 49
  possibilities 43
  prevalence of its components 36–41
  recalled 30–31, 39
  sample 36–38
  scoring criteria 31
  scoring examples of 37
  scoring profiles 36

sequence of 51
specific or composite 33–34, 40
STR methodology 56, 64
verbal/nonverbal 32–33, 40
representations-of-therapy-with-histherapist 64
re-symbolization 75, 80–81, 283, 291
cycle and spiral during 283
phase 199–200, 203, 294, 297
reverberation hypothesis 223–225
role responsiveness 269
Rosenbaum, Bent 167
Rosenfeld's thin-skinned and thick-skinned narcissists 248
Rycroft desymbolization 99

saliency 113
Sandler 93, 269
Schaffer, Carrie 17, 29
Schedule of Therapy Remembered (STR) 15, 20, 25–27, 29–30, 34, 38, 42–44, 47–50, 62–64, 69, 78–81, 84–85
Amy's interview 86
demand conditions of 26
Jim's interview 62
RTDCS methodology 56
score 29
transcript 48
scheduling conflict 273
secondness 173
segmentation analysis 219
self-accusatory thoughts 237
self-analytic mental activities 57
self-determination 24
self-disclosing 50
self-integration variables 102
self-reflective capacities 67
Seligman 6, 18
effectiveness questionnaire 19
separation 294
sexual energy 92

sexual inhibitions 92
Shedler 5, 83
research 6
social psychology 21
somatization 122
somato-sensory
bodily experiences 23
communication 241
functions 253
level 260
speech 231
thought 231
somatosensory experience 242
vehicle of 237
spatialization 313
spiked roadblocks 239
spiralling process 279
Steiner, Ricardo 316
Steingart 247
Stockholm psychoanalytic society 19
stuckness 299
subjective/intersubjective matrix 7
subjectivity 250
sub-symbolic
emotional 211
process 212–213
superego 294, 302
theoretical concept 92
symbol formation 300
symbolic
equation 317–318, 320–321
functioning 229
integration 312
synthesis 284
symbolization process 69, 74–75, 86, 103, 105, 107, 114, 117, 123, 126, 130, 133–135, 144, 146, 155, 157–159, 163, 167, 172, 210, 246, 270, 313
crucial relationship to 72
defining 107

dialectical nature of 312
discursive 70
enactment to 278
Jones's understanding of 310
moment of dynamic 81
precursors to 316
progressive 86, 164
psychoanalytic definition
    of 309–321
scales 78
scoring of 113–114
signs of 197
transformation 101
symbolized transference
    224, 292
symbolizer 81
symbolizing
    capacity 178
    process 131, 197
symbolizing countertransference
    238, 241
symbolizing/desymbolizing
    processes 123
symbolizing space 249
symbolizing, working phase
    199–200, 203, 225
    induction of transference
        regression during 223
synthetic/integrative functioning
    186

targeted clusters 114
"terminated" therapy 56
termination crisis 139
*The Dream Specimen in
    Psychoanalysis* 193
therapeutic
    dialogue 17
    dialogue coding system 25
    intensity 5
    relationship 65
therapist involvement subscale 23

Therapist Representation Inventory
    (TRI) 22–23, 63
therapy lives on 83
therapy-with-his-therapist 62
thing-representation 175
thirdness 173
throttling reflectivity 232
transference
    engagement 119
    fantasy 77
    foundational 295
    reactions 56
    repetition 19
    utterances 299
transference–countertransference
    71
    dialogue 249–250, 271, 287
    dynamics 173
    matrix 280
    psychoanalytic ideas of 173
    symbolic 175
    transference 156
transference regression 199, 218,
    223, 237, 241–242
    gradient of 232–234
    induction of 223
    intensification of 241
transferential situation 79
transformations 115, 306
    cycle 199
    in long-term psychoanalytic
        psychotherapy 159
    Kleinian idea of 75
    spiral 220
traumatization 178
traumatized patients 178
    severely 167
treatment relationship 5
triangulation 247–251, 259, 309, 312

unnamed affect 320
unthinkable anxieties 109

Varvin, Sverre 105, 167
victimization 110
Vorus, Neal 5, 17, 29

Ward, Rhonda 159, 191, 203, 223, 245, 267, 283, 297, 309
Webster, Jamieson 67, 309
Wechsler's concept of intelligence 101
Winnicott's sense 261
Wolf Man case report 92

word-representation 175
working memory 85
working phase 199
working through 192
    Brenner's sombre view 192
    nonlinear motion of 295
    progressive symbolization 196
    specific components of 297
    specimen of 189
    spiralling nature of 294
World Trade Center destruction 96